Ethos and Narrative Interpretation

**Frontiers of
Narrative**

SERIES EDITORS

Jesse E. Matz *Kenyon College*

David Herman *Ohio State University*

Ethos and Narrative Interpretation

The Negotiation of Values in Fiction

LIESBETH KORTHALS ALTES

University of Nebraska Press | Lincoln and London

Library of Congress Cataloging-in-Publication Data
Korthals Altes, Liesbeth.
Ethos and narrative interpretation: the negotiation
of values in fiction / Liesbeth Korthals Altes.
pages   cm.—(Frontiers of narrative series)
Summary: "Examines the relevance of the concept
of ethos for analyzing processes of literary inter-
pretation to address the question of what exactly
narratology does, or should want to do."—Provided
by publisher.
Includes bibliographical references and index.
ISBN 978-0-8032-4836-6 (hardback: alk. paper)
ISBN 978-0-8032-5560-9 (ePub)
ISBN 978-0-8032-5561-6 (mobi)
ISBN 978-0-8032-5559-3 (pdf). 1. Fiction—History
and criticism. 2. Values in literature. 3. Narration
(Rhetoric). 4. Rhetoric—Moral and ethical aspects.
5. Literature and morals. I. Title.
PN3491.K67 2014
809.3—dc23   2014004156

Set in Minion Pro by Renni Johnson.
Designed by A. Shahan.

Contents

Preface

What do the shock created by James Frey's *A Million Little Pieces* and debates about the French writer Michel Houellebecq's provocative work have in common? Frey's book, published in 2003, was marketed and hailed as an authentic autobiographical memoir recounting the author's recovery from drug and alcohol addiction. Oprah Winfrey set it on her book club's reading list and invited Frey to her show. Frey's sales, as could have been expected, went soaring sky high. Suspicious, the website the Smoking Gun exposed central autobiographical facts represented in the book as made-up, causing consternation: Oprah was shocked, and so were audiences who had sometimes used Frey's "authentic" work as a kind of self-help book, as attested in heated blog exchanges.

Houellebecq's case is somewhat different. Critics from the start appeared hesitant about how to classify not just his work but also, even very much so, the author's intentions and stance. Should the bleak views on Western society conveyed by his novels be taken as serious analysis, as satire, or more cynically, as just the next commercial cocktail of sex, violence, and stereotypes? Both Frey's and Houellebecq's cases raise questions regarding what I call the author's ethos. In their attempt to determine their own classification of the work, and their own position with respect to it, critics often refer to what they perceive as Houellebecq's deep-down character and intentions. But an author's persona may be just as elusive as his or her work. Besides, interpreters are often sensitive to different clues and frame these in different modes.

In ancient Greek, *ethos* referred to a person's or community's character or characterizing spirit, tone, or attitude. Aristotle famously distinguished ethos as one of the three main means of persuasion, alongside pathos and logos. My use of the notion ties in with this rhetorical coinage, revised in the past decades in institutional art sociology and discourse analysis by scholars such as Pierre Bourdieu, Ruth Amossy, and

Dominique Maingueneau. These approaches, to which I will bring some complements and reorientations, can be profitably articulated to narratology, in its attempts to go beyond textual analysis.

Questions of trust or distrust, of personal or institutional authority and credit, and of ethos management and justification, are evidently not confined to literature. Rather, they are fundamental in all domains of life, from the domestic sphere to the worlds of banking, economics, politics, and media, as the current crises of credit, in both the moral and the financial senses, demonstrate. From childhood on, people develop a workable, but clearly fallible, capacity to detect and estimate in a split second shades of seriousness, irony, or deception in a speaker's utterances, on the basis of all kinds clues, physical, discursive, or other. In many cases, though, we have to navigate uncertainties regarding the extent to which people actually mean their words. What counts as an appropriate ethos also varies according to the social situation and changes over time. Moreover, whatever ethos one may mean to project, interpreters sometimes jump to wholly different conclusions. Many of us know the embarrassment of our ironies falling flat.

Uncertainties about a discursive ethos increase in written speech, as Plato already observed. Fictional narratives augment the risks, as by convention they would uncouple the work, as expression of intentions and beliefs, from its actual author (an idea that will be nuanced in later chapters). Throughout the history of literature, moreover, writers, and whole schools of writing, have cultivated ethos ambiguities, whether for reasons of censorship, out of provocation, or for sheer delight.

This book springs from my long-standing interest in the capacity literary narratives have to make audiences imagine a story world refracting multiple perspectives. Engaging in literary narratives leads readers into taking perspectives on perspective taking, assessing the value of values. My explorations have been nourished by the work of many, and my debts are evident on every page. I wish, however, to explore some aspects of ethos attributions that have remained, to my sense, underaddressed in narratology. More specifically, this book develops the argument that in processes of interpreting and evaluating narrative texts, ideas about characters', narrators', *and* authors' ethos—for instance, about their sincerity, reliability, authority, or irony—are not just the result of interpretive processes. They also play a central framing role even before, and throughout, the reading process. Ethos ascriptions, interwoven with generic classifications, arguably allow readers to frame the kind of game they are engaging in, determining their reading strategies and the value regimes they believe should apply to the work. Some genres, moreover, especially incite readers to construct an author's ethos, though clearly writers can play with such expectations. The explored approach hence also aims to account for the diversity of readers' ethos ascriptions, often overlooked in narratological models but exemplarily evidenced in ideologically or ethically controversial or (possibly) ironic works.

Ethos attributions, I hope to demonstrate, are as crucial in interpretation and evaluation processes as they are impossible to tackle through fail-safe methods of description and analysis, if only because such ascriptions result from interpretations. Hence my interest in hermeneutic, phenomenological, sociological, and cognitive approaches that might help us understand how we understand. Some of these frameworks, however, challenge the formal text-analytic or descriptive stance claimed or suggested by classical narratology, which persists in many so-called postclassical amendments, as well as in the discourse analytic and institutional approaches to which I will refer.

So along the way, this book came to mirror my own reflection on the kinds of intellectual enterprises theories of narrative are, or purport to be. My own perspective, as a narratologist, is hermeneutic, in a double sense: I hope to contribute a heuristic for spotting ethos clues in literary narratives, as other narratologists have done for tracking the unreliability of narrators, for instance, enriching the range of practices of literary interpretation; but my main objective is to propose, in what somewhat redundantly I call a metahermeneutic way, a reconstruction of socially encoded pathways along which interpreters, including myself, assess a discursive ethos. Both perspectives entail a reappraisal of interpretation as either a core activity or a central object of study. While seeking to objectivate interpretive processes, metahermeneutic analysis remains hermeneutic in its procedures and aims. It rests on arguments offered for critical discussion rather than on mere description or on empirical reception research (however, it should be compatible and complementary with respect to the latter).

To give my readers an idea of what to expect, here is a thumbnail outline of the book's argument. The introduction, "Why Ethos?," recalls the main tenets of the notion of ethos in ancient rhetoric and explains the timeliness of a focus on ethos for the theory of narrative and narrative interpretation. Part 1 considers the role of ethos attributions in narrative fiction from a wide-angle view: chapter 1 sets out to establish the relevance of a focus on ethos and on interpretation from a cognitive-anthropological and hermeneutic perspective. Ethos attributions arguably belong to a basic cognitive competence we share with other living beings, allowing us to determine in a split second the intentions of the figures we find in our environment and to react appropriately. Narrative art arguably offers occasions to exercise such a crucial competence. It also allows us to reflect on the pathways through which ethos attributions, and interpretations more generally, are achieved.

So when critics or ordinary readers debate about Frey's honesty or Houellebecq's irony, they not only make explicit what count, for them, as relevant themes and values "in the book," they also strengthen or modify, and even fight over, socially recognized pathways for interpreting and evaluating that reach further than this singular case. These acts of interpretation, and ruminations *about* interpretation, can be considered to be part of what Merlin Donald in his evolutionary theory of culture described as culture's constitutive self-reflection, or metacognition. In this light, the negotiation referred to in the title of this book designates a double process: the individual interpreter's mental negotiation of a variety of potential semantic clues, which is itself inscribed in processes through which cultures articulate and negotiate, or fail to negotiate, competing ways of feeling, thinking, meaning making, and value attribution. The second section of chapter 1 compares hermeneutic models of interpretation and cognitive models of meaning making, pointing out continuities and differences that are not always acknowledged.

Chapter 2 pursues in more detail the ideas that meanings, relevance, and value positions attributed to narratives, as well as the paths along which we attribute them, are socially fabricated and negotiated and that our estimations of the author's ethos play a role in these processes. As narratology does not offer much support here, I will draw, first, on sociological-historical research on authorial postures and conceptions of literature by Bourdieu, Alain Viala, Jérôme Meizoz, Nathalie Heinich, and others; second, on French or Francophone discourse analysis, since Amossy and Maingueneau developed the rhetorical concept of ethos into a rich heuristics for the analysis of ethos in all kinds of discourse genres, including literature; and third, on Luc Boltanski and Laurent Thévenot's research on people's acts of classification, taken to underlie their evaluation practices. These approaches afford valuable insights also for a metahermeneutic understanding of divergences in readers' interpretations and evaluations of literary narratives. To illustrate these perspectives, I discuss the diametrically opposed constructions of Houellebecq's ethos by two critics, as well as some framing difficulties raised by Christine Angot's tricky autofiction.

Part 1 thus forms the context for the discussion of narratology's treatment of issues pertaining to ethos in part 2. In chapter 3, as a prelude to this second part, I comment on the variety of objectives cultivated by narratologists, which lead to quite different kinds of investigation and validation procedures. These various understandings of narratology can be set out on a scale, with on the one side (cognitive) science and ideals of scientific rigor and, on the other, the practice of interpretation. Somewhere in between there is the place for what I call narratology as metahermeneutics.

Chapter 4 zooms in on five key narratological issues that are central for any reflection on how and why one would attribute an ethos to narrative voices or agents: narrative communication, embeddedness, intentionality, fictionality, and reading strategies. The theoretical stances one adopts on these issues determine whether narratology should leave out interpretation or considerations about real authors and readers, including their ethos. Chapter 5 examines, among others, the following questions: Under what conditions would readers attach importance to a character's or narrator's ethos, or rather to an author's? What aspect of authorship would they have in mind? And how would such different ethos attributions affect the interpretation and evaluation of a work? My key examples throughout part 2 include, again, Frey's, Angot's, and Houellebecq's works, as well as Philip Roth's *The Human Stain*, Alain Robbe-Grillet's *Djinn*, and Samuel Beckett's *Not I*.

Part 3 further explores the framework's heuristic potential, concentrating on issues that pop up regularly throughout the book. Chapter 6 investigates the central issue of generic framing. Some (sub-)genres, including novels of ideas and engagé and documentary and autobiographic writing, seem to program particularly strong authorial ethos expectations as part of tacit generic communication contracts. Hybrid or parodic generic framing problematizes such normative ethos expectations, creating, alongside the generic uncertainties, hesitations as to how the works should be interpreted and evaluated, which may turn into critical awareness of such conventions.

François Bon's *Daewoo* will allow me to discuss ethos expectations tied to genres of *writing the social*. In what looks like a nonfiction novel in good engagé tradition, the narrator, who conspicuously recalls Bon himself, sets out to investigate and denounce the consequences for people's lives of the closing down of the Daewoo factories in eastern France. What writerly posture and ethos can be drawn from this work, and, in a loop, how do they feed into readers' interpretation and appreciation of Bon's writing? Christine Angot's *Sujet Angot* similarly offers a good case for analyzing ethos norms attached to *writing the self*, and especially to autofiction as generic hybrid. In this curious autobiography by proxy, often perceived as raw and authentic, the portrayal of "Christine Angot" is delegated to Claude, the name of Angot's ex-husband in real life. How do one's classifications of the text's genre, as autobiography or metafiction, for instance, and of an author's ethos, as sincere, ironic, or authoritative, for instance, affect one's interpretation and evaluation of the book one reads?

Chapter 7 probes into two basic attitudes in terms of ethos: sincerity and irony, often perceived as two sides of the same coin. Though sincerity is frequently considered as the default mode of communication, I argue that more systematic attention to conventional sincerity clues or topoi pays off, as it highlights the intimate connection of such clues to generic framings and the imagined communication situation, as well as to historical and cultural communicational norms. The section on irony considers rhetorical and linguistic theories that may be fruitful for analyzing ethos attributions more generally. I discuss in particular Dan Sperber and Deirdre Wilson's idea that utterances can be framed as mentioned rather than used, with potential effects of ironic distancing, and the idea of ironic interpretation as a form of frame switch. Besides Houellebecq, my key example here are the work and persona of the controversial Russian postmodern writer Aleksandr Prokhanov, as they have been interpreted by scholars and broader audiences. The chapter ends with an analysis of ethos clues, in connection to reading strategies, in Dave Eggers's *A*

Heartbreaking Work of Staggering Genius, appropriately poised between sincerity and irony.

The book's concluding remarks on narrative, ethos, and ethics address, among others, the question of how the analysis of ethos relates to ethical criticism. I expect the proposed conceptual frameworks to have at least some heuristic value for ethical, rhetorical, or ideology criticism. They should sharpen the interpreter's sensitivity to clues that he or she uses to establish the sincerity, reliability, or authority (or lack thereof) of narrative voices and of authors. This assessment, however incomplete and intuitive it may be, affects what stance, what kind of worldviews and values, one takes a text or its author to convey. From a scholarly and analytical perspective, such a metaethical inquiry serves to illuminate the diversity of interpretive and evaluative pathways. It also leads to hypotheses about the grounds on which narratologists, critics, or ordinary readers infer and judge the rhetorical and ethical impact of a text: What kinds of assumptions, about literature, about selves, about ethics, do people's reading habits entail? When and how do they consider fiction to involve an author's or their own responsibility? Metahermeneutic reflection can, however, also become a more personal exercise, as when one reflects on one's own interpretive and evaluative habits and their underlying values and assumptions, in a reading group or a classroom situation, for instance. This perspective has an ethical and (self)reflective potential that could be exploited more actively in educational or professional coaching settings.

For whom is this book intended? It targets an audience of students and scholars interested in perspectives on literature afforded by narrative theory, rhetoric, discourse analysis, literary history and sociology, ethics, and hermeneutics, as well as those curious about cognitive approaches to questions about narrative and interpretation. I also hope to capture the attention of anyone concerned with the role of literature in present-day society: Why do we bother with literary texts and their authors? How do literary texts and their authors ensure their relevance and authority in the world of the Internet, television, and commercialism? Readers who are keen on perspectives that allow them to expand their own understanding of controversial and ethically puzzling literature and art should also find some food for thought here. Those who are afraid of technical detail may want to concentrate on the case studies, located mainly at the end of part 1 and in part 3, though I hope to keep them on board through the thorny theoretical issues by demonstrating the general relevance of such theory for everyday life and by building on examples.

Let me end this preface on a self-critical note. The notion of ethos hardly comes out as a consistently rigorous analytical concept. It functions as an umbrella term, drawing attention to a common denominator in quite heterogeneous aspects of narratives, literary or not, and of their interpretation. Interdisciplinary cocktails, moreover, have their own risks. Specialists may find my use of their theoretical frames or methodologies eclectic and lacking in precision or they may question the function I give them in my work's overall framework. Yet I believe that this particular combination of approaches can be well defended, as each addresses a blind spot in the others. Others, better equipped than myself for empirical research, will hopefully feel inspired to undertake the testing of the proposed hypotheses. The readers I will be speaking about are either the author of this book, with her multiple selves, or the ones I imagine on the basis of my experience with many kinds of readers, though my comments on particular works often also draw on actual reception documents.

Many of my examples involve French literature and theorizing, sometimes not yet translated into English. I trust my readers to extend the arguments to other works, in other languages, alert to the specific cultural backgrounds in which ethos clues would operate. Narrative theories share to some extent with all hermeneutic scholarship the condition of being rooted in national traditions. A collateral aim of this book is the desire to bring together approaches that often happily ignore each other because they operate in different language areas and translations often arrive astonishingly late. If we consider not only the arts but hermeneutic theories and criticism themselves as forms of cultural self-reflection, to make theories travel beyond frontiers of disciplines and languages perhaps contributes to reflexivity about our own cultures and ways of seeing. I hope that this book, in its own ways, thus lives up to the challenges implied in the title of the series in which it appears, Frontiers of Narrative.

I am grateful for the one-year research leave awarded to me in 2009–10 by the Netherlands Organization for Scientific Research (NWO), which allowed me to complete a first draft of this book. During the process of thinking and writing, I felt supported and challenged by many people, only some of whom I can single out here. This book contains my ruminated reply in the ongoing discussion with Barend van Heusden and my other Groningen colleagues, especially from the Department of Arts, Culture and Media, and of course with students in various academic settings, local and international. Henrik Skov Nielsen, Francis Langevin, Kees Meerhoff, and Sjoerd-Jeroen Moenandar generously criticized the manuscript at various stages, holding up to me a humoring mirror of my own discursive ethos. Many colleagues have at some point been inspiring sparring partners or allowed me to present ongoing research, among them: Ruth Amossy, Jan Baetens, Lars Bernaerts, Marina Grishakova, Nathalie Heinich, Elrud Ibsch (my Doktormutter, who, sadly, is not there anymore to share in the pleasure of seeing this book published), Stefan Iversen, Fotis Jannidis, Vincent Jouve, Jakob Lothe, John Hillis Miller, Ansgar and Vera Nünning, Jim Phelan, Gisèle Sapiro, Wolf Schmid and his Hamburg colleagues, Simone Winko.

The insightful and detailed remarks of the two anonymous reviewers for the University of Nebraska Press have been precious for fine-tuning the argument. My thanks also go to Nadja Zadorina, who finalized the bibliography; Thom van Duuren and Bram van Leuveren, my student assistants, as the last-minute close readers; Gorus van Oordt, who took care of the book's formatting; Adam Stier, who polished my English; and [ooo], who compiled the index.

David Herman, editor of the Frontiers of Narrative Series of the University of Nebraska Press until January 2013, has been of invaluable support from the very start. His amazingly fast, generous and always thoughtful responses to the drafts with which I bombarded him, preferably during holidays, provided the exactly right context of encouraging expectation. Joy Margheim has been a great help as my copyeditor for the press.

My deepest gratitude, though, goes to my loved ones. I dedicate this book to John, Caspar, and Floor.

Earlier versions of some of the material in this book have previously appeared in print, and though most of it has been heavily revised, I am grateful for permissions from the publishers to draw on it here: "Aesthetic and Social Engagement in Contemporary French Literature:

The Case of François Bon's *Daewoo*," in *The Autonomy of Literature at the Fins de Siècles (1900 and 2000): A Critical Assessment*, ed. Gillis J. Dorleijn, Liesbeth Korthals Altes, and Ralf Grüttemeier (Leuven: Peeters, 2007), 261–84; "Slippery Author Figures, Ethos, and Value Regimes: Houellebecq, a Case," in *Authorship Revised: Conceptions of Authorship around 1900 and 2000*, ed. Gillis J. Dorleijn, Ralf Grüttemeier, and Liesbeth Korthals Altes (Leuven: Peeters, 2010), 95–117; "Sincerity, Reliability and Other Ironies—Notes on Dave Eggers' *A Heartbreaking Work of Staggering Genius*," in *Narrative Unreliability in the Twentieth-Century First-Person Novel*, ed. Elke D'Hoker and Gunther Martens (Berlin: Walter de Gruyter, 2008), 107–28.

Why Ethos?

*[D]etaching the utterance from [its] surrounding context is like
focusing on the semantic content of a compliment without stopping to
consider whether it is being said earnestly or ironically.*

DAVID HERMAN, *Basic Elements of Narrative*

Houellebecq's work and persona provide for a book like mine almost
too good a case.[1] Let me explain what I mean through some brief comments on *Atomised*, the author's breakthrough novel, and its reception.[2]
Atomised tells the story of two half brothers, Bruno and Michel, left to
the care of their grandparents by their mother, who went off to discov-
er the thrills and deceptions of self-actualization, spurred by the spirit
of May 1968 in France. While Bruno is obsessed with sex, which brings
him more solitary suffering than pleasure, Michel, just as lonely and desperate, withdraws into the realm of science. His genetic discoveries lay
the basis for cloning that will allow humans to reproduce without sexual intercourse. At some point the reader realizes that what mostly reads
like conventional narration by an omniscient narrator is in fact the narration of one such clone, who observes, from around 2080, the gloom
of the late twentieth century with the commiseration of a new and lib-
erated humanity.

Not only was Houellebecq's novel understood to question—but how
ambiguously!—the achievements of feminism, sexual and social eman-
cipation, and the culture of individualism, offering cloning as a solution
to all human misery; his work also raised suspicion regarding its success: Was that success due to the book's literary quality, whatever might
be meant by that, or rather to some scandal effect and effective hyping?

Hailed as the renewal of the novel of ideas, rejected as mere branding or as the breviary of political reactionism, on all sides *Atomised* elicited debate about the author's or the narrating voice's deep-down ethos.

In a kind of public trial, Houellebecq's former colleagues at the magazine *Perpendiculaire*, for instance, found him guilty of defending in his novel disquieting antihumanist positions, yet paradoxically also with a disturbing artistic haziness (Tordjman 1998). They ominously concluded, "Let those who, today, separate aesthetics from politics take their responsibilities in the face of the future" (*La Revue perpendiculaire*, 1998). For others, instead, the novel presented a superior irony in its ambiguous montage of provocative theses; some in turn concluded that the author was *au fond* dead serious, although the text's "theories are asserted by half-wits" (Thomas Clerc, in *Libération*, September 9, 1999).[3]

The commotion occasioned by Houellebecq's work had some piquancy. A few years earlier, Western critics had expressed their astonishment at the fatwa ushered against Salman Rushdie because of his *Satanic Verses*: How could Islamic religious authorities confound a literary character's assertion and that of the author, literature, and public speech, completely missing the autonomy of the aesthetic domain? Now, here, right in the midst of pervasive postmodern aestheticization, was the occasion to reflect on the moral and ideological positioning of the novel *and* its author, a concern that gained even more momentum after 9/11. For narratologists, the additional piquancy of such a case is that it put center stage the author, with his or her ethos, stance, and intentions, this author that some loud-voiced or too-rashly-understood thinkers had apodictically discarded as irrelevant.

But what exactly is meant by *ethos*? Why would this notion, which I borrow partly from Aristotle's *On Rhetoric*, be relevant for the interpretation of literary narratives and for theorizing the role of narrative in culture? In the following I hope to show the interest of the rhetorical notion of ethos for a theory of narrative interpretation and to explain the timeliness of such a focus on ethos for narratology and, more generally, for a theory of narrative.

Ancient Rhetoric and Persuasion through Character

Aristotle's treatise *On Rhetoric* elucidates what makes persuasive discourse effective and stipulates what means of persuasion can best be used in specific situations in the public domain. For the purposes of this book, the treatise's interest resides in Aristotle's subtle analysis of the various—rational, emotional, and social—components of persuasion and of the implied interactive mechanisms. Such elements can also be traced, arguably, in the ways in which literary narratives are invested with meaning and value by their authors, publishers, critics, or readers.[4]

Aristotle, as mentioned, distinguishes three main means of persuasion: *ethos*, *pathos*, and *logos*. While *pathos* is the appeal to emotions and *logos* invokes objectivating, rational arguments, *ethos* pertains to character effects that coincide to create a trustworthy image of the speaker: "[There is persuasion] through character whenever the speech is spoken in such a way as to make the speaker worthy of credence" (Aristotle 2007, 1356a.38). These three kinds of proof together form a "pragmatic triangle" (Eggs 1999, 45), which connects orator (through his ethos), addressee (implied and anticipated in the pathos appeal), and discourse itself (through its argumentative force, or logos). Ethos and pathos are tied to a specific communication situation, with its own norms and expectations, whereas logos "convinces in itself and by itself": its force of argument lies precisely in its independence from the context and from subjectivity effects (Eggs 1999, 45).[5]

Ethos itself also comprises three components in Aristotle's view, namely "practical wisdom and virtue and good will" (2007, 1378a.112). Good sense, or practical wisdom (*phronesis*), involves the capacity to gauge a situation adequately, for instance by applying general principles to a concrete situation.[6] Good sense includes the idea of knowledge and expertise acquired through experience. Persuasion secondly requires the audience's belief in the speaker's good character or virtue (*arete*), in particular his honesty and sincerity.[7] "We believe fair-minded people to a greater extent and more quickly [than we do others]," Aristotle notes, "on all subjects in general and completely so in cases where there is not exact knowledge but room for doubt" (2007, 1356a.38).[8] Given the sociopolitical and judiciary context to which Aristotle's observations pertained, it is not surprising that he defined ethos normatively as virtue. Virtue, though, is not necessarily a matter of what we now might consider actual moral character. It means that the speaker, "[t]o be convincing, . . . must exhibit that quality of character that a culture, and not the individual, defines as virtue. . . . The effectiveness of an ethical appeal thus depends on one's ability to gauge society's values and to display them . . . in one's speech" (Kinneavy and Warshauer 1994, 174–75). In fact, classical rhetoric oscillated between being a pragmatic training in communicative skills, meant to help create an effective impression of reliability and virtue, which of course could be deceptive, and a normative ethics of discourse, advocating actual sincerity and good—which would mean civic—character.

Eunoia, finally, translated as goodwill, refers to the means for convincing an audience of the speaker's good intentions. This leaning toward the audience, it has been remarked, requires an emotional quality (pathos), as well as an appeal to common ground (Eggs 1999, 36). Indeed, to display *eunoia*, the speaker needs to know his audience and to estimate what kind of style and argument appeals to this particular public.[9] The recognition of the importance of a speaker's ability to anticipate how audiences may construct his image and intentions in response to specific clues, and given their own character and norms, calls to mind the recursive intention and character attributions analyzed in current cognitive theory, as adapted by narrative scholars (Butte 2004; Zunshine 2006; see chapter 1). But Aristotle's rhetorical theory pays more attention to concrete situational and socially coded aspects of this process of attribution in his own historical context, that of the Athenian state.

A speaker's ethos may be conveyed indirectly through pathos- or logos-based appeals, among others. Emotions, indeed, can strongly enhance a discourse's persuasive force, if they impart the sense that the speaker is authentically engaged in the views he seeks to convey. Pathos may even be more powerful than argumentative content, Aristotle notes, as "the hearer suffers along with the pathetic speaker, even if what he says amounts to nothing" (2007, 1408a.210), a remark worth pondering with the current media training of our politicians in mind.[10]

On the side of logos, a speaker's authority is often strengthened by invoking maxims and other generalizations, since audiences "enjoy things said in general terms that they happen to assume ahead of time in a partial way" (1395b.168), though Aristotle astutely adds that one should stick to the kind of wisdom that befits one's age and status (such little remarks convey Aristotle's sharp sense of the codes and roles that constitute social reality). All three ethical means—ethos, pathos, and logos—whether directly or indirectly expressed, buttress each other and cooperate to warrant the reliability and authority of the speaker, and hence of his discourse. In what looks like a feedback loop, it is indeed the discursively produced effect of trustworthiness or reliability that, for Aristotle, grounds that same discourse's effectiveness. Ideally, speakers need only to hint at recognized signals of authority and ethos topoi to make their audience jump to attention and adopt the expected receptive attitude.

Aristotle theorized that a speaker had to convey his ethos through discursive means alone.[11] Other rhetoricians, however, Cicero prominent among them, insisted on the importance of the *prior ethos*, the image an audience already has of the speaker on the basis of his reputation, previous deeds, or generally known character traits, an extension that seems indeed appropriate (more on this below), the more so in our own times of increased mediatization.

Ancient rhetoric, in any case, keenly captured and systematized a variety of factors involved in persuasion, from the display of emotions to good sense and the commonality of knowledge and norms. Its fine-grained grid takes on renewed relevance in the light not only of current institutional sociology, discourse analysis, or communication studies but also of cognitive research on mind reading, on empathy and emotion, and more generally, on the need to fine-tune and calibrate worldviews and values in culture.

For a theory of narrative and literary narrative interpretation, some seminal insights regarding the components and persuasive force of ethos stand out, though they are not unproblematic, as we will see: the insight that discourse through its whole form is likely to be understood as expressing its enunciator's character; that the ethos an audience attributes to a speaker on the basis of his discourse is likely to determine deep down what message is conveyed, superseding actual semantic content; hence, that to strategically fashion one's discursive ethos is crucial; and that ethos effects rely on psychological and moral codes, whether truly shared or strategically or deceptively deployed.

If, however, one expands the analytical perspective to literary narrative, one should not forget that what counts as an appropriate ethos and as grounds for ethos attributions changes over time and depends on the communicative situation and genre at hand. Moreover, as recent rhetorical and narratological perspectives emphasize, we need to heed the complexity and layeredness of narrative transmission, an issue that will be addressed in part 2.

In connection with literature, the notion of a *prior ethos* also requires additional distinctions, such as: from what kind of clues would one infer an author's prior ethos? Can these clues be traced back to the author him- or herself, or to others who contribute to the fashioning of an author's image? What credit do we grant these various mediators? The notion of prior ethos, moreover, should be complemented with its a posteriori counterpart, as readers may be confronted with manifestations of the author *after* their reading experience, which may lead them to reconsider their interpretation and, in particular, the way in which they constructed the authorial image and ethos. This sort of reassessment happened for me in the case of Dave Eggers. What I learned about his social activities as well as his own later works retrospectively somewhat changed my view on the irony I had sensed in *A Heartbreaking Work of Staggering Genius* (more on Eggers in chapter 7).

Still, with its keen, pragmatic perspective on the ways in which discourses secure processes of meaning and value attribution and play with anticipations on character, intentions, and worldviews, ancient rhetoric confronts narratology with challenging insights and questions, as this book aims to demonstrate.

Ethos Puzzles

Uncertainties about a source's ethos commonly arise when people with different backgrounds, conventions, and values interact, or when there is hesitation about how to frame the kind of game one engages in. Is James Frey's *A Million Little Pieces* fictional, nonfictional, or something in-between? Our answer to this question of generic framing defines the extent to which the author's authenticity and sincerity become at all important.

But do (professional) readers of literary narratives always construct an ethos for authors, and how and why would they do so? Are there particular conditions under which it is more appropriate for interpreters to attribute an ethos to authors, rather than to narrators or characters? Can and should narratology account for diversity in literary interpretations, venturing beyond *de gustibus non est disputandum*? Given the complexity of the inference and framing processes involved in ethos attributions, and in processes of interpretation generally, it may seem quixotic to try to detect any sort of patterning in them. Yet this is what this book aims to do.

We can go some of the way, I believe, in formulating hypotheses about factors that guide readers' ethos attributions. Assumptions about the authorial or narratorial ethos can spark off, or reinforce, readers' decisions about how to frame the kind of work they have at hand, as well as the kind of interpretation and evaluation regimes that would be appropriate. Vice versa, the work one reads may suggest outlines for an authorial figure, which reinforce or contradict clues one has gleaned from one's previous readings of other works by this same author or from his or her media appearances. More powerfully, the way in which readers construct this ethos—of the author or of the narrating voice(s)—can completely alter the work they read. The circularity of this argument is deliberate and, I believe, unavoidable. Interpretation is a dynamic bricolage, building on hints and hunches that are confirmed, dismantled, and recursively recontextualized in the process of reading and retrospective reflection.

In fact, signaling and deciphering sincerity, deception, or irony and classifying speakers regarding their authority, reliability, and expertise have been the core business of storytelling since humankind's very first stories. Whole literary genres, such as satire or the engagé novel, are defined by their assertion mode and ethos, as are types of literary authors, narrators, and characters, from the ironist and the unreliable *Picaros, Madmen, Naïfs, and Clowns* (Riggan 1981) to the *doctus*, prophet, or gadfly. Literary narratives often stage characters engaged in the hazards of ethos deciphering, with sometimes dramatic consequences. Thus literature spells out codes of conduct and exemplary paths for ethos projection and attribution, helping to shape, transmit, and question culture-bound folk semiotics and hermeneutics of ethos.

However, audiences or readers will not just reenact or judge characters' motivations and intentions. They also establish, even unconsciously, a narrator's or author's ethos, which then may help them to "get" his or her tone and assess how the represented actions and perspectives are to be taken: as exemplary, or perhaps as ironically, or indignantly, staged? Even just framing a text as literary, and as fictional, suffices to create uncertainty about the degree to which an author would endorse the narrative as his or her own act of assertion, an uncertainty that extends to the authority and impact one grants to the expressed worldviews.

Take, once again, Houellebecq's *Atomised*. This novel's narrating voice refers to various scientific grids—sociology, biology, and ethology, for instance—when explaining the characters' individual experiences, grids that are likely to confer scientific authority to the representation. Or, anticipating another of my cases, consider Dave Eggers's *A Heartbreaking Work of Staggering Genius*, in which the narrator, Dave, who conspicuously resembles the author, multiplies tokens of sincerity. To decide whether Houellebecq's frameworks for explaining human behavior are to be taken seriously or whether Eggers sincerely endorses the views on ruthless sincerity voiced by his narrative avatar, readers are likely to build on their image of the authorial ethos and intention, inferred from the novel itself as well as from the author's other works and his para- and extratextual manifestations (Heinen 2002). In both works, the authority, authenticity, or sincerity of the narrating voices is signaled with much insistence yet so flagrantly contradicted by other aspects of the telling that their ethos becomes itself a central riddle. How do we know that we can trust sincerity or authority clues? There's always a hole in the bucket, a loop—and a leap of faith—in the reasoning, though our experiential knowledge often feels as solid ground.

The importance of the ethos we attribute to writers, in terms of their authority, authenticity, reliability, irony, and the like, also appears from its central role in debates about conceptions of literature and about writers' function in society, and not just in outright moralistic approaches. Throughout history, the social functions of literature and of the author have been invested with changing, but always strong, norms and values, extending in particular to the author's or artist's ethos.

For example, in the introduction to his book on literature and evil, Georges Bataille, an ardent defender of literature as the exploration of evil if ever there was, emphatically sets the condition of a ruthlessly sincere commitment for any representation of transgressive experience to be aesthetically and ethically justified (Bataille 1957). Such often tacit ethos stipulations mark the border between serious art and commercial, scandal-skirting provocation or kitsch, as controversies about Houellebecq, Frey, and many other writers and artists demonstrate. In the recent past, the works of Marilyn Manson, Rammstein, Andres Serrano, or Robert Mapplethorpe raised similar categorization dilemmas, which critics solved by, among other actions, taking a stand on the artists' ethos.

Debates about the author's status and responsibility, and about literature as critical reflection and authoritative discourse in society, have recently flared up with renewed intensity in many Western countries. In reaction, it seems, to what was perceived as postmodern "anything goes" irony and disengagement, writers, like their fellow artists working in other mediums, have voiced their social or ethical commitment through their literary works, often alongside forms of social activism. Motivations for writing, such as wanting to make suppressed voices heard, to disclose history's forgotten facets, or to defend causes such as homosexuality, are now widely recognized as central concerns of literature, rather than as exogenous, "heteronomous" ones. An author's protestations about his or her social mission usually require as a backing that she or he radiate a convincing ethos of sincerity, experience-based authority, and so on. This is quite another ethos than the one required, for instance, for writing verse as "aboli bibelot d'inanité sonore," a phrase that eloquently captures Mallarmé's view on poetry's autonomy as a work of art, freed from meaning, usefulness, and its own maker. The following chapters should, however, nuance such facile dichotomies.

Claims of literature's and the writer's social mission should be understood against the background of broader developments. These include, to start with, the diminishing prestige of what we have come to call literature in the current media landscape. The popularity of visual and audio media, such as cellphone cameras or blogs, with their suggestion of immediate, unmediated communication and of other art and entertainment forms, such as film or games, affects the status of literature. The role of literature in the educational system has, perhaps consequently, dramatically shrunk in many Western countries. But do these other modes really outplay literature's age-old function of articulating individual or collective experience (Fludernik 1996) or its role in cultural self-reflection (Donald 1991, 2006) or in exercising the mind through a play with patterns (Boyd 2009)? To consider the continuities between traditionally conceived literature and these new forms of narrative and their common, or respective, anthropological functions perhaps serves to give back to literature, on fresh grounds, its role in society, particularly in education.

The kinds of developments I just recalled in any case prompt writers to propose new arguments, or revitalize traditional grounds, in order to demonstrate the relevance and legitimacy of literature and of their own writing. To this end, they often have recourse to ethos topoi that enjoy broad recognition all over current society: real-life experience, firsthand experiences of suffering, a testimonial position, and so on. These topoi all suggest some form of indexical connection between representation, the represented, and the one who represents, an observation that merits further consideration. In Charles Sanders Peirce's sense, indexical signs are the more concrete ones, building on what we may infer through believing our own eyes or by touching, rather than on the mediation of symbolic signs, as with the disciple Thomas, who had to put his hands in Christ's wounds in order to believe. Writing, in such authentications, takes its authority and credibility from the (claims of the) writer's own physical or other proximity to what he or she speaks about.

Literary works also increasingly borrow their authority and legitimacy from nonfiction genres, such as documentary or autobiography, which, once aesthetically marginal, have now moved to the center of literary culture. But many of the texts discussed in this book precisely problematize or ironize such expected ethos topoi, drawing attention to mechanisms of meaning attribution.

Though author images have always functioned in combinations of a commercial logic and that of disseminating aesthetic, moral, or intellectual values, the foregrounding and exploitation of the author's persona, the effect of his or her actual *presence* (auratic connotations intended), have gained unprecedented momentum thanks to the availability and impact of broadcasting media and podia. In the experience economy sketched by Joseph Pine and James Gilmore (1999), marketing strategies exploit codified effects of presence and authenticity, core ingredients of an author image that sells, while authors' names and postures are fashioned and exploited as a kind of branding.

Yet debates about authors still prominently evolve around ethical issues. This is well attested by painful cases of writers who were taken to embody the moral conscience of a nation—an ethos that included both the author's work and his or her identity as a person—but were exposed as frauds, in the eyes of some, when their political past was unearthed. Christa Wolf and Günter Grass, in formerly Eastern and Western Germany, respectively, are good cases in point. A recent case is the journalist-writer Günther Walraff, known for his relentless critique of German capitalism and his undercover investigation strategies, whose "authentic documentary" research came under suspicion as a result of revelations by one of his former collaborators. The commotion around James Frey's *A Million Little Pieces*, or cases such as the Wilkomirski affair, similarly bring to light tacit implications of generic and discursive contracts (are their works fiction or nonfiction?).[12] The sanction makes the norm appear.

The vehemence of audience reactions should prompt literary theorists to reconsider the idea of the autonomy of the literary field and of the work of art, staunchly proclaimed or implicit in many conceptions and theories of literature, including narratology (more on this in chapter 3).[13] The kind of attention and authority we grant to literature, and to the writer, is clearly negotiated within a specific cultural context, in relation to other media and genres, and vis-à-vis what counts as grounds for authority and authenticity in various settings. To analyze ethos attributions thus leads from discussions about a text's meaning into debates about the social status, authority, and responsibility of literature and writers and into the heart of meaning and value negotiations that weave the fabric of culture (more on these notions of negotiation and values in chapter 1).

Ethos in Narrative Theory and Criticism

Within literary and narrative studies the interest in ethos attributions is not new. In the currently flourishing ethical, ideological, and rhetorical narrative criticism and theory, the ethos of the (implied) author, narrating voices, and characters is a central concern, though usually not under this explicit label (the controversial notion of *implied author* will be discussed in chapter 5). Narratologists, moreover, are more prepared than ever to expand their scope beyond the boundaries of the text, taking into account social and historical contexts in which literary works are written, circulated, and read, as well as the role of the author. In narrative theories that build on insights from the cognitive sciences, attention to the reciprocal attribution of intentions and beliefs, broadly captured in the notion of Theory of Mind, can be argued to include, implicitly, the deciphering of the ethos of the various narrative subjectivities involved. Rich work has also been done in discourse analysis and institutional sociology of literature, on which I elaborate in chapter 2.

There has, though, been relatively little interest in the ways in which textually induced authorial intention and ethos interact with extratextual ethos clues readers may have gleaned from all kinds of sources (with exceptions: e.g., Lanser 1981, 2005, 2001; Jannidis 1999; Heinen 2002; Herman and Vervaeck 2009). Nor have many narratologists been eager to sort out how ethos constructions, presupposed in statements about a narrator's unreliability or irony, for instance, are intertwined with expectations and framing acts resulting from generic cues and reading strategies. Few narrative theorists, moreover, fully address the issue of interpretive diversity, so well attested in cases such as Houellebecq's, or the fact that some works and genres particularly trigger authorial ethos constructions or debates about a narrator's reliability.

With exceptions, again, even cognitive narratological approaches have remained conspicuously silent about these issues pertaining to the pragmatic framing of assertions and their uptake. This is the more curious, as the frame theory many of them adopt would eminently equip them to conceptualize interpretive diversity and the role of framing factors. These are some issues and lacunae this book seeks to address, joining forces with congenial attempts to open up the investigation to the whole chain of literary communication and its context and to dynamize descriptive and interpretive heuristics.

Narratologists have been deeply divided over the need to take both authors and interpretation on board for various reasons, some more principled, others more contingent, as we will see in part 2. Depending on their conception of literature and of narrative theory, narratologists position themselves on the one or the other side of a divide.

On the one side of the divide, following the pathbreaking work of the Russian Formalists, the development of literary studies into an autonomous academic discipline went hand in hand with the evacuation of interpretation, of authorial intention, and of the pragmatic, moral, and existential dimensions of the literary experience. These dimensions were often considered to characterize the ordinary response to literature, from which literary scholars ought to set off their own analyses.

Happily thriving in critical, educational, and ordinary reading practices, notions connected to that of ethos, such as authorial intention and values, as well as the practice of personalizing reading, were dismissed as obsolete, at least in some branches of literary theory. While New Critics famously outlawed the recourse to the authorial intention, structuralist narratology, through authoritative voices such as Algirdas Greimas's or Gérard Genette's, ruled that texts should be analyzed severed from their makers, recipients, and concrete sociohistorical contexts, as pragmatic considerations might endanger scientific objectivity. This was not an inevitable choice but one that corresponded, I believe, to a particular conception of literary discourse as the autonomous play of language forms, which could almost do without players. The reification of the literary work also secured narratology's sense of being a scientific discipline with a clear object and well-defined boundaries, almost like an object in the natural world.

Meanwhile, on the other side of the divide, rhetorical and intertextual approaches were quite successful in maintaining on the scholarly agenda questions of authorship and ethos (see chapters 3 and 5). Wayne Booth, and after him, rhetorical narratology, famously foregrounded issues of (un)reliability, irony, and authorial stance, crystallized in the much-debated notion of the implied author. Booth is often criticized as if he had proposed a theory (in the hard sense) of narrative fiction (see chapter 4). In fact, he emphatically defended hermeneutics as the perspective symmetrically required by textual rhetoric. To analyze any narrative's worldviews and value positions, in his view, cannot but engage the reader's active appropriation and requires first and foremost careful argumentation. Mikhaïl Bakhtin, whose influential work was translated into French, English, and German only in the seventies and eighties, called attention to the dynamic polyphony of discourses and value perspectives staged in the novel, both foregrounding and relativizing the author's role in the orchestration of such polyphonic effects. These kinds of approaches kept pulling on the fences raised by structuralists around the autonomous text and against interpretation, which was associated with unscientific subjectivity.

In those same decades, between roughly the sixties and the eighties, poststructuralist and deconstructive approaches, often entwined with a Marxist inspiration, on their own grounds questioned personalizing conceptions of literature, as well as the notion of the author as the text's originator and prominent voice. Mallarmé's dream of the author's disappearance or dispersion in discourse was programmatically relayed through Maurice Blanchot's notion of the dispossession of both authors and readers in the literary experience. Jacques Lacan's post-Freudian unmasking of the illusory coherence and autonomy of selves, as well as the zeitgeist's libertarian zeal against any imposition of authority, formed part of the backdrop against which Roland Barthes and others opened up literary texts to their intertexts and to "the murmur of language" (*le bruissement de la langue*): a backdrop against which Michel Foucault, Frederic Jameson, Terry Eagleton, and others also scrutinized the inscription of texts in supraindividual structures of power, mediated through discourse, and engaged in fierce struggles for predominance. Feminist thinkers and writers, such as Julia Kristeva, Hélène Cixous, Judith Butler, or Gayatri Spivak, explored what it means to say that "I am there where it/id speaks" (*Je suis là où ça parle*; Cixous, Gagnon, and Leclerc 1977, 488) or how subaltern voices could be heard through their silencing. Philosophers of deconstruction, some of them from a feminist or postcolonial angle, criticized the foundational concepts of ethics, which underlie habitual understandings of ethos: the assumptions of shared values, of an autonomous self, of the evidence of communication, and of the author as the authoritative source of meaning, and of course the concept of morality itself.

These approaches all variously question the idea of the author as the one personalized source or subjectivity, expressed by, and accountable for, the work we read. Yet this does not make irrelevant the ideas that discourse conveys an ethos or that readers may bring such an interpretive expectation to bear on their readings. The subjectivity and ethos that are at stake may be collective ("the ruling classes" or "the subaltern") or even constitute unadopted discursive subjectivity and ethos effects (more on this notion in chapter 5).

Indeed, neo-Marxist, neo-Freudian, feminist, ethical, or postcolonial theories in some way kept holding authors or "texts" (an indication of agency perceived as more neutral) responsible for the conveyed ideologies and ethics[,] and the reader for his or her own positioning. While "teasing out [the] warring forces" at work in texts, to borrow a particularly felicitous expression of Barbara Johnson's (Johnson 1980), deconstructionists arguably seek the contours and the fissures of the author's ethos, complementing their close reading of literary works with the scrutiny of all kinds of authorial ethos expressions, discursive and nondiscursive, literary and nonliterary, synthesized in the author's name.[14] Nuancing his own timely dogmatisms, Barthes himself keenly diagnosed the reader's desire for the author, as an element of the strongly affective undercurrent of reading and writing: "But in the text, in a certain sense, *I desire* the author: I need his or her figure (which is neither his or her representation, nor his or her projection), as he or she needs mine" (1973, 45–46; emphasis original; for a nuanced assessment of Barthes's position, see, for instance, Bennett 2005).

Proclamations of the author's death have by now been sufficiently exposed in their lively polemic contexts, and the author, or rather the author-function (to borrow Foucault's term), has made a triumphant comeback as a subject of investigation. There is, meanwhile, a manifold historical, sociological, narratological, and discourse analytical tradition for investigating this author-function.[15] Authors are definitely *in*, as are their ideological and ethical stances and, more often implicitly, their ethos. Yet within narratology the return to the author and to the personal engagement of the interpreter, with the intention attribution and interpretive activity it implied, is not always explicitly thought through in its epistemological consequences, which I hope to help clarify.

In 1999 Simone Winko convincingly analyzed the "death of the author" as literary scholars' reaction to literature's loss of symbolic capital and diminishing prestige, and as an attempt to ascertain their disciplinary specificity by highlighting specialized, formal, noninterpretive knowledge. The return of the author, and the ethical and narrative turns that preceded it, seems part of a symmetrical, somewhat contradictory legitimization attempt. Most narratologists' discursive ethos indeed still signal scientific discourse, as opposed to both ordinary reading and erudition. But the anxiety of not being scientific enough now seems shot through with that of not being hermeneutic enough and of failing to shed light on the human condition, as attested by the wave of publications by narrative theorists addressing the crisis in literary studies (e.g., Harpham 2005; Todorov 2007; Marx 2005). This crisis was imputed to developments in the theoretical realm, such as formalism and deconstruction, among others, and extended in a sweeping gesture to broader movements in arts, philosophy, and society more generally, in particular postmodernism, accused of an irresponsible lack of social relevance.

There appears to be a renewed urgency to legitimize both literature and literary studies—criticism *and* theory—by foregrounding the ability of both to elicit reflection about values, rationality, or morality, reflections considered vital to culture at large as well as to individuals, a concern that I share. The search for legitimacy perhaps paradoxically also explains the rising popularity of cognitive sciences in the humanities. Cognitive sciences promise a scientific framework and methods that bridge the divide between C. P. Snow's two cultures. Current research on the role that reading narrative fiction can play in developing empathy or as an exercise in mind reading and moral imagination might help give back to the humanities, on new grounds, social, philosophical, and intellectual relevance and status.

Narratology and, more broadly, narrative theory clearly constitute a domain in which contradictory strivings meet and mingle. In light of current cognitive, anthropological, biological, sociological, and psychological insights, it seems imperative that the humanities articulate the relevance not just of narrative, which receives much attention currently, but also of interpretation, as sites for the transmission of and reflection on meaning-making practices.

We live not merely in cultures of instrumental knowledge but in cultures of interpretation, as Yves Citton rightly notes: "At the heart of what we mean by knowledge, information, the flux of facts or communication, it seems important to recognize and analyze a very specific type of operation, which an old tradition articulated through the notion of 'interpretation.' . . . To interpret is neither to know, nor to communicate. . . . To put issues of interpretation center stage again should lead us to revise fundamentally and simultaneously our view on social interactions, our mapping of forms of knowledge, [and] the structure of our higher education institutions" (Citton 2010, 8–9).

This was very much the program nineteenth- and twentieth-century hermeneutics set for the humanities, interwoven with values and assumptions of commonality that aged less well, allowing the baby to be thrown out with the bathwater all too easily. I don't want to defend a utopian view of the human capacity for reason, of which history and literature themselves, not to mention theorists ranging from Nietzsche to Adorno and Horkheimer, should have cured us. But the importance of cultivating the capacity for interpretation, for perspective taking, and for critical reflection on the paths through which we attribute meaning and value has hardly diminished. Ideally this competence requires the triad of empathy, reflection, and argumentation, as well as the active cultivation of the conditions, mental and institutional, that foster this triad. It is with the importance of interpretation in mind that I would like to reconsider narratology, and ethos attributions, in this book.

PART 1   *Ethos, Narrative, and the Social Construction of Meanings and Values*

THE QUESTION OF HOW and why readers would attribute an ethos to literary characters, narrators, or authors is part of the more general issue of how people make meaning from and with texts. Within the humanities, such issues are traditionally the province of hermeneutics, which encompasses the theory, the method (or the "art"), and the practice of interpreting texts. Alternately, interpretations and their underlying processes are studied from the perspective of literary and aesthetic phenomenology, the sociology of literature, discourse analysis, the reception history of literary works (*Wirkungsgeschichte*), or empirical research on actual readers' responses. Current literary and narrative studies instead show a marked tendency to turn to cognitive theories, which often claim to theorize and to analyze meaning-making processes in more scientific ways.

Since structuralist times, scientificity has often been considered to come proportionally to one's distancing from interpretation, and from hermeneutics more generally. Narratologists or narrative theorists thus frequently display an intriguing disregard for hermeneutics' long history of dealing with issues of interpretation and its underlying mechanisms, not just in normative ways but also analytically.[1] Just as curious is the blindness to the interpretive and normative dimensions that sneak back into "more rigorous" narratological methods and concepts, including the cognitive ones, as well as the lack of systematic interest in the social dimensions and, hence, the diversity of interpretive processes.

The first part of this book sets issues of ethos attribution in a broader cultural and social context. In chapter 1 I will, first, draw together several insights pertaining to culture as "distribution of cognition," in which narrative art and interpretation both can be considered as practices of "metacognition" (Donald 2006). Second, I will zoom in on cognitive and hermeneutic approaches to what, in the cognitive context, is called meaning making and in the hermeneutic context, interpretation.[2] Chapter 2 engages with the social fabrication of meaning and value in the case of literary narratives and with the role of authorial ethos in this process, as a complement to narratology's orientation toward texts or individual interpretive processes. I hope to show that the French institutional sociology of literature and discourse analysis provide a fruitful contextualization of the ways in which meanings and values that are read into literary texts get socially negotiated. Both chapters together build the broader framework for my critique, in part 3, of narratology's approaches to ethos attributions in narratives and for the alternative perspectives that this book explores.

1 Literary Interpretation, Ethos Attributions, and the Negotiation of Values in Culture

And they [housewives, over tea] talked and talked, repeating the same things, going over them, then going over them again, from one side then from the other, kneading them, continually rolling between their fingers this unsatisfactory, mean substance that they had abstracted from their lives (what they called "life," their domain), kneading it, pulling it, rolling it until it ceased to form anything between their fingers but a little pile, a little grey pellet.

NATHALIE SARRAUTE, *Tropisms*

The following chapter brings together insights from different theoretical frameworks. My intention is not, however, to suggest that such an eclectic juxtaposition amounts to a theory. My aim is, rather, to point out between these quite different frameworks transversal echoes that shed fresh light on narrative, interpretation, and in particular, ethos attributions. While this chapter's wide-angle perspective seems to lead us away from the more concrete issue of ethos attribution in the context of literary narratives, it actually speaks to the broader relevance of my study, explaining why it is important to debate the authenticity of James Frey's narrator or Houellebecq's irony. These broader perspectives should also help me clarify what kind of approach narratology might develop toward the issue of ethos in narrative.

Narrative Art, Play, and Interpretation as Cultural Metacognition

Beyond differences in theoretical frameworks, methods, and argumentation styles, and despite daunting controversies over definitions and approaches, there is some consonance across disciplines on both sides of Snow's divide that culture involves or even amounts to what has been called the "social construction of reality" (Berger and Luckmann 1966). From the perspective of evolutionary psychology, Merlin Donald in turn defines culture as "a distributed cognitive system within which worldviews and mental models are constructed and shared by the members of a society" (Donald 2006, 5; Donald first developed his theory of culture in his *Origins of the Modern Mind*, published in 1991). From yet another angle, labeled as New Historicism,Stephen Greenblatt describes culture as "a particular network of negotiations for the exchange of material goods, ideas, and . . . people" (Greenblatt 1995, 229). As does Donald, Greenblatt highlights the role of artworks in the circulation of what he calls social energies. What these various understandings of culture have in common is the—admittedly very general—idea that culture requires the transmission and negotiation of ways of doing things, of preferences, values, and worldviews; and also the idea that narratives, and the arts, play a central role in this process.[1]

Both phylogenetically and ontogenetically, before such more complex practices as art, a central means for achieving cooperation and attunement of cognitions is play. The idea that art emerged from play has been defended by many, from Friedrich Schiller to Johan Huizinga or Donald Winnicott. Usually it is the imitative dimension shared by play and art that is highlighted, in connection to the faculty, broadly shared among species, to learn through imitation, which was already observed by Aristotle. The significant difference between animal and human play, however, is "the innate human capacity for self-observation," or metacognition (Donald 2006, 6): only humans engage in play as a mimetic *representational* activity, allowing it to become a form of metacognition. Thus, while we can watch puppies and kittens play-fight, we won't see them suddenly stop the game, disputing the rules, the impersonation of the thief, or the sense that yesterday's game was a much better one.

From an evolutionary perspective, art is indeed often considered to develop from and to improve on play. In his "biological" theory of narrative, Brian Boyd (2009, 95) interestingly argues that, through art as through play, humans coordinate their attention, they practice by imitative action the skills needed for survival, and they fine-tune their goals and their mental models. Art is described as a "set of activities designed to engage human attention through their appeal to our preference for inferentially rich and therefore patterned information" (Boyd 2009, 85; 101). In this description, two elements stand out. The first is this capacity of art to engage people in joint attention. This idea would partly explain why art is such an effective vehicle for the distribution of cognitions, as religious and worldly authorities, as well as their opponents, have always recognized. Likewise, arguably, practices of sharing interpretations of artworks organize joint attention, allowing cognitions to be transmitted, confronted, and negotiated by individuals and groups.

Second, Boyd's description of art as engaging us in "inferentially rich and therefore patterned information" interestingly thematizes the pleasure and interest our minds seem to take in complexity itself, admittedly in different degrees. This pleasure seems akin to what the German psychologist Karl Bühler called *Funktionslust*.[2] This eloquent term refers to the pleasure taken in exercising a mental or bodily function (Bühler 1965, 157). Such function-oriented pleasure can be observed in repetitive movements in animal and child play but also in adult behavior, from a good physical workout to riddles or crosswords that engage the pleasure of puzzling and pattern-seeking minds (on the latter, see Ramachandran and Hirstein 1999).

Like play, *representational* art centrally involves "shared ludic pretense" (Schaeffer, 1999; the notion will be discussed in chapter 3). Ludic pretense requires knowledge and acceptance of the game's often tacit rules from all participants. Hence the importance of the correct framing of an activity and of the adequate gauging of other people's intentions and ethos, as we will see in relation to generic framing and the attribution of an ethos to authors, narrators, or characters in narratives.

Language further expands, and epitomizes, the emergent human capacity for metacognition, as it allows humans to articulate individual and collective experience in efficient conceptual form, saving that experience for collective use and allowing its transmission. Along this line, our daily conversation has been singled out by Berger and Luckmann as "the most important vehicle of reality maintenance." Conversation, they argue, "ongoingly maintains, modifies and reconstructs [our] subjective reality" (Berger and Luckmann 1991, 172). Nathalie Sarraute's evocation of the tea-drinking housewives endlessly "rolling between their fingers this unsatisfactory, mean substance that they had abstracted from their lives" captures this work of reality maintenance (though perhaps not in its most inspiring form).

In what has been labeled the narrative turn, scholars from various disciplines foregrounded, more generally, the role of narrative and narrative art in this process of social construction of reality (e.g., Bruner 1990; Donald 1991; Herman 2002; Ricoeur 1984–88). From myths to history, from epics to gossip, stories arguably help weave the social fabric and shape what we experience as reality. As David Herman puts it, stories are a "basic human strategy for sense-making"; as such, they support the social process by which "the meaning of events is determined, enable the distribution of knowledge of events via storytelling acts more or less widely separated from those events in time and space, and assist with the regulation of communicative behaviors, such that the actions of participants in knowledge-yielding and -conveying talk can be coordinated" (Herman 2003, 8). This characterization, which could easily be extended to Berger and Luckmann's notion of conversation, also ties in with the idea proposed by evolutionary scientists such as Merlin Donald, that narrative constitutes a fundamental mode of metacognition.

Now, what about narrative *art*? In narrative art, representation operates in a double mode. Narrative art does not just offer instructions for imagining a story world. It also displays for metacognition paths for meaning making and for reasoning about values and meanings. This double functioning is, I believe, well captured by the literary scholar Marie-Louise Pratt when she characterizes literary texts as "display texts." In such texts, "a speaker is not only reporting but also verbally displaying a state of affairs, inviting his addressee(s) to join him in contemplating it, evaluating it, and responding to it. His point is to produce in his hearers not only belief but also an imaginative and affective involvement in the state of affairs he is representing and an evaluative stance toward it. . . . Ultimately, it would seem, what he is after is an *interpretation* of the problematic event, an assignment of meaning and value supported by the consensus of himself and his hearers" (Pratt 1977, 136).[3]

Such a "display" of ways of speaking, acting, thinking, and assigning meaning to actions and behavior is found in the earliest fictional narrative of which we have written trace, the Gilgamesh epic, up to the works of Houellebecq or James Frey. For example, Gilgamesh's testosterone-driven behavior, which threatens the social order, is a matter of comment from multiple perspectives within the story world. His self-centered values are also firmly redressed in later developments of the plot. In later episodes, when Gilgamesh roams the underworld like a haggard clochard, desperate from having lost Enkidu, his soul mate and companion in adventure, his behavior is exposed as unmanly and unkingly by other characters. Elsewhere in the epic it is the ruthless wrath of the gods that becomes a matter of debate, leading to a kind of charter for responsible behavior.

Literary narratives thus make "available for circulation, debate and reflection the descriptions and discussions of [cultural] hierarchies of relevance and the clash between plans at different levels" (Johansen 2002, 299). Within literary studies, the ways in which literary narratives achieve this reflexivity have been the concern of scholars as different as Mikhaïl Bakhtin and Victor Voloshinov, with their notion of the polyphony of the novel and the impregnation of discourse with social values, Boris Uspensky, with his analysis of the role of narrative transmission, or Wolfgang Iser or Alain Rabatel, with their work on narrative as the organization of perspectives on perspectives. It is also a central interest of rhetorically oriented scholars, from Booth to James Phelan. My own book means, in turn, to contribute to this investigation by focusing on interpretive pathways and framing acts, zooming in on the role of ethos attributions in these processes.

This capacity of narrative art to configure experience and to solicit concentration of attention and concertation is of critical importance if one considers, with Donald, human cultures as "massive distributed cognitive networks involving the linking of many minds, often with large institutional structures that guide the flow of ideas, memories and knowledge." As a kind of "cognitive engineering," art would play a "crucial role as a collective vehicle for self-reflection and as a shared source of cultural identity" (Donald 2006, 4).

Art's and narrative's roles in metacognition deserve some further attention. In art, Donald observes, metacognition takes a concrete, mimetic form, rather than, say, that of analytic discourse.[4] To understand this proposition, which will prove relevant for my later discussion of narrative mimesis or of kinds of ethos appeals, we need to make a brief excursion into the four kinds of cognition that, according to Donald, defined human evolution—and would still characterize our different modes of cognition. (Similar models have been proposed, in anthropological or psychological perspectives; see, among others, Cassirer's philosophy of symbolic forms and Piaget's work on the cognitive development of the child.)

The modern mind, Donald proposes, evolved through four stages, afforded by specific modes of cognition. The first stage, which humans share with primates, is tied to episodic memory. Higher primates can learn and memorize, but only by direct, literal imitation (Donald 1991, 124–61). The second stage, the mimetic, distinguishes *Homo erectus*. It refers to our ancestors' capacity to represent events independently of their real occurrence, by mimicking them. "The mimetic imitation is *about* the action imitated," van Heusden adds, and this aboutness expresses difference, and the capacity for distancing. It is precisely this uncoupling of perception and memory that allowed the development of imagination (van Heusden 2011, 125).

Donald's third stage, the mythic stage, is connected to an increasing capacity for schematization, which culminated in the emergence of language. Language allowed humans to conceptualize and to narrate (though there is a sense that narrative precedes language): The memory required for group survival can be expressed and transmitted, among other means, through stories and other forms of narration. At this stage, myths constitute the defining narrative practice. The fourth and last stage is the theoretical and most abstract one, characterized by graphic symbols, which allow external memory storage and theoretical thought (Donald 1991, 269–360).

These four stages are cumulative, as the later stages necessarily build on the previous ones, and they are recursive. With the mimetic, mythic, and theoretical stages, Donald points out, human culture developed its distinctive capacity for metacognition (Donald 1991). From a semiotic perspective, Van Heusden notes, "[w]ith each new stage, the semiotic complexity of the world, including the self, social interaction, and physical environment, increased" (van Heusden 2011, 135). And so does, arguably, the capacity for metacognition, or in a more widespread vocabulary, the capacity for (self)reflection. Metacognition is itself a recursive process, which can also pertain to representation as a cognitive process: "One can represent the representation process mimetically (in a parody, for example), one can conceptualize the representation of reality—

as when we explain to someone else what a specific sign means . . . , and we can theoretically analyze the representation process" (van Heusden 2007, 137).

Now, to hypothesize about evolutionary stages is definitely not this book's concern, nor its author's expertise. But the distinction between more concrete and more abstract modes of cognition and representation as well as the ideas of metacognition and increasing complexity will prove fruitful in my own, much more pedestrian, argument. For instance, I will propose that in reading strategies, or in conceptions of mimesis underlying different narratologies, or also, pointedly, in the ethos requested from committed writers opposed tendencies can be observed toward concreteness, or instead toward abstraction. Whereas Sartre's writer-intellectual drew his authority from analytic capacities, from his philosophical and political training, for example, writers who insist on their social mission currently tend to display signs of authority that belong to a much more concrete range: one has been physically on the trauma scene, one is connected by actual descendance or by emotional ties to the figures whose story one evokes, and so on (more on this in chapters 2 and 5). At the risk of aggravating the case for eclecticism, it is tempting here to think about the three kinds of semiotic processes—indexical, iconic, and symbolic—distinguished by Charles Sanders Peirce. The appeal to (physical) contiguity in the mentioned ethos appeals could be considered to exploit indexical modes of signifying. Donald's theory of cognition in any case raises questions about what it means for a society to cultivate such more physical and concrete, or rather more abstract, grounds for one's authority as a speaker.

But let's get back to the issue of language. The choice of medium indeed has significant implications (e.g., Ryan 2004). Though language also requires and presupposes perception, and may well exploit visual or audial iconic and indexical expressivity, as a semiotic system language necessarily involve abstraction, which is inherent to conceptualization. Verbal art is unique in its capacity to articulate human experience, from perception to most abstract thought, through shared concepts also displaying this conceptualization, and verbalization itself, for intensified perception and scrutiny. In literature, all our language uses, from how we stammer our love and pain to the sciences' formalized knowledge about the world, can become objects of representation (see also Carey 2005, van Heusden 2007). Language, this abstract sign bearer, accumulates for its users the affective, evaluative, and ideological charge of situations in which it functions. As a means for communicating one's ethos, however, language should not be overrated. In live interactions people just as well sniff out each other's ethos from their bodily bearing; those physical clues may actually carry more weight than the ethos they infer from a person's words. Intriguingly, such a sense of embodied ethos is often perceived to adhere even to written narrative voices or style, and this effect is partly what the notion of ethos is meant to capture (as will be discussed in chapter 2). Another risk is that of overemphasizing language's semantic-representational dimension, especially in literary narratives, to the detriment of the syntactic (in the sense of compositional) and more abstract compositional dimensions. As Boyd (2009) also suggests, in art people join attention over a particular activity. But even in representational art, the prominent point of the activity may sometimes be in the *joining* or in the *patterning*, before, beside, or beyond semantic content. This issue would require more development than can be provided here.

Insight into metacognition should prove relevant for explaining the importance not just of narrative but also of interpretation (for a discussion of this notion of interpretation, see the section on hermeneutics in this same chapter). Indeed, as an explicit reflective processing, the interpretation of literary narratives gives yet another spin to metacognition. In words that I fully subscribe to, Johansen observes: "[P]art of the specific kind of contemplation that literature instigates is carried over in the interpersonal reflection on it. Because literature articulates, and re-articulates, the subjective experience of and attitudes with regard to the common lifeworld, discoursing on literature is a way both of sharing what is personal, without sharing personal experiences, and a way of establishing, or failing to establish, a common understanding of parts of the lifeworld by viewing it through the perspective offered by the text" (Johansen 2007, 127). Active, intensified interpretation of artworks could belong to these rare institutionally trained and protected occasions for cultivating the verbal articulation of one's values and worldviews and the confrontation with competing perspectives. In a further turn of the screw, the metahermeneutical analysis of narrative interpretation practices reconstructs conventional paths along which meaning may be constructed. This reconstruction is not claimed to be "objective," though it seeks to objectivate interpretive processes, exposing them to reflection. My repetitive formulation points out the increasingly reflective character of these various levels of meaning-making processes. This brief discussion also foregrounds the interconnectedness of narrative and interpretation, raising the question of the extent to which they can really be differentiated or should be perhaps be considered as metacognitive activities at different levels of reflexivity.

The Interpretation of Literary Narratives and the Negotiation of Values

Donald's notion of *distribution of cognition*, which functions in a broad theory of culture, does however not sufficiently convey the sense that, even in organic societies, people may have different experiences, depending on their social roles and biographies, and that this is increasingly the case in complex societies. As Machiel Keestra also notes, cognitive science approaches to narrative or culture tend to emphasize "sharing and convergence of representations. . . . Discussions of divergence are being offered in the cognitive scientific literature, but mostly in the contexts of blocked or failed imitations, and are considered secondary." Hermeneutic approaches would instead emphasize "the indeterminacy and openness of action understanding due to preunderstanding, action configuration, and the processual nature of understanding" (Keestra 2008, 127, 129). However, in many current forms of narrative theory, cultural poetics, or cultural and literary "critique," all of which I consider as forms of hermeneutics, this presumed focus on indeterminacy has given way to a more militant one, namely, on culture as the locus of a power struggle and negotiation, which is also a struggle over, and negotiation of, cognitions.

Let me stop briefly here to specify this notion of negotiation. To make matters more confusing, the notion has been used in at least three different perspectives that are relevant for this discussion on culture, art, and interpretation. First, in its most general sense, the notion of negotiation operates in global perspectives on culture, such as Donald's idea of culture as "distributed cognition" or Greenblatt's description of culture as a "network of negotiations for the exchange of material goods, ideas, and . . . people" (Greenblatt 1995, 229–30). Much more than Donald's distribution of cognition, Greenblatt's notion of negotiation highlights the interest-driven, dynamic, even polemic element of such cognitive distribution processes. The negotiation, however, remains very general, and the subject doing the negotiation is not really specified.

In a second step, negotiation becomes a notion for designating how literary works themselves constitute scenes in which the tensions of their times are represented and dealt with. Greenblatt, in particular, gives a prominent role to literature (and "great writers," as "masters of these [cultural] codes") in this respect (Greenblatt 1995, 229–30). In his *Shakespearian Negotiations*, for example, Greenblatt (1988) reconstructs how *The Tempest* stages and condensates contemporary conflicting views about the colonial enterprise and the exotic "other." Greenblatt proceeds to show this "negotiation" by bringing Shakespeare's play in resonance with all kinds of contexts that speak through their discursive traces, from laundry lists to literary or philosophical works or court archives.

Third, negotiation has been used to describe the mental gymnastics involved in individual textual interpretation: a reader, or an analyst, has to cope with input of very different kinds and provenances, and with conflicting clues, from which meanings of texts are to be constructed. This is also the sense retained by Herman and Vervaeck (2009, 2011), an understanding that I perceive as very close to my own emphasis on readers' hermeneutic activity. Herman and Vervaeck speak of the "reader's balancing act," composing between "all the elements that influence the reading—the text, the context, his own disposition and the author's self-presentation" (Herman and Vervaeck 2011; the authors also point out the congenial use of the notion of negotiation in Heinen 2002 and Jannidis 2002).

As it is used in the subtitle of this book, the notion of negotiation brings together mainly the first and most general sense and the third, that is, readers' active interpretive work. I trust that it will be clear from the context which of these meanings is intended.

Rounding off these global considerations, some suspicion must be voiced about the consonance I see between theories of the metacognitive function of art and narrative, such as Donald's, and the basic tenets of humanities research. Do we not appreciate what seems familiar, rediscovering the humanities' concerns, supported by what counts as science, while that part of the theorizing may not really differ in kind from hermeneutic reasoning?

Donald himself recognizes that "neither brain imaging technology nor neurobiology has solved the problem of how to measure, let alone model, these abstract chains of meanings of the specific states of awareness they induce," adding that "[i]t is unrealistic to expect that a common pattern of neural processing will ever suffice to 'explain' our individual reactions to art" (2006, 11–12). Recognition of the limitations of cognitive sciences with respect to the experiential and social dimensions of art leaves the stage open for humanities scholars, suggesting complementarities and possibilities for cooperation (see, below, Gallagher's similar remarks).

Research on culture, narrative, and narrative art from these cognitive perspectives, in any case, raises questions that narratologists and art theorists or sociologists might feel challenged to pursue. If we take all forms of art, figurative or nonfigurative, as metacognition, which kinds of cognition and semiotics would be exercised by the various forms? How are different forms of metacognition—the more concrete and the more abstract or analytical—spread over time and across cultures? Which media and genres foster more concrete forms of cognition, or rather, the more abstract ones? What part do institutions such as education systems play in the distribution of particular kinds of (meta)cognition? Under what conditions is there *conscious* reflection, and how do particular media and particular devices affect this process, for instance by requiring specific kinds of perceptual and conceptual processing?

These questions are all relevant for investigation about the kind of ethos cultivated by writers, upheld in conceptions of literature, and postulated by narratologists, critics, and other mediators. With these broader perspectives in mind, but more modestly, this book explores some conventions and tendencies in ethos attributions, as well as their role in the interpretation and evaluation of literary narratives. Before embarking on that enterprise, I would like, in the following two sections, to discuss some cognitive views on meaning making and, alternately, hermeneutic perspectives on interpretation. Through this juxtaposition I hope to clarify how my own approach to ethos and, more generally, various narratological approaches, can be positioned.

Elements of a Cognitive Theory of Meaning Making

Cognitive sciences cover a broad and heterogeneous conglomerate of approaches that investigate how the human mind or brain works, drawing from and variously crossbreeding neurobiology, psychology, linguistics, philosophy, ethology, and anthropology, often from an evolutionary perspective. These approaches share an explanatory approach to questions of the mind, modeled on the natural sciences but also the social sciences. I do not claim to have an insider's insight into the whole range of cognitive research on meaning making. My discussion is limited to the use several narratologists tend to make of a restricted number of concepts and models borrowed from cognitive theories, which intersect with theories of interpretation anchored in hermeneutics.[5] Yet, as I hope to show in part 2, borrowings from cognitive sciences have affected narratologists' aims and methods less fundamentally than might have been expected, at least in approaches whose focus remains typological or rests on "describing" and interpreting individual texts.

Scholars in cognitive psychology, linguistics, and artificial intelligence assume that our brains record knowledge in standardized mental structures. Equipped with such memorized experience, we can handle complex information, make inferences and selections, adjust our initial hypotheses about the kind of situation, event, or person with which we are involved, and decide about our course of action. This shared knowledge, as we saw, forms the condition for culture. Various models and concepts have been proposed to account for memory's role in processing experience, such as frames (Minsky 1977), schemata, scripts (Schank and Abelson 1977), mental models (Johnson-Laird 1983), or prototypes (Rosch 1977). All of these concepts indeed refer to the idea that memory somehow stores experience knowledge in schematized forms, reactivating and recombining these in new situations.

The process of meaning making itself is taken to combine top-down and bottom-up processing: top-down, since we approach new situations or divergent information with hypotheses suggested by our memorized experience; bottom-up, as we process an element that differs from what we know and expect by trying to integrate it in familiar frames, scripts, or schemata that we consider to be appropriate.

Adopting such cognitive frameworks, narrative theorists have suggested that readers make sense of texts, including literary texts, and are able to grasp the outline of situations, plot, character types, or themes by having recourse to frames, scripts, schemata, prototypes, and other mental models. Some of these we would draw from everyday life, others from our literary socialization and experience.

The general idea that people resort to standardized and memorized mental models is widely accepted. It is already implied in the working of sign systems itself. (These concepts, in their functionality, also recall the phenomenology of the meaning-making process proposed by Iser [1978] and his notion of repertoires, as well as the hermeneutic circle, about which more below.) But how do people select and delimit the frames, scripts, and schemata required for understanding any artifact, communication, or situation? These frames, scripts, and schemata are not directly observable in texts, nor do they lay waiting for the analyst's use like neat piles of towels. Not coincidentally, the most commonly cited example is that of the restaurant script, which most people will meet with nods of recognition. As soon as contexts are less clear in their framing indications, readers need to select between alternatives according to the relevance context they construct for the case at hand. Moreover, some kinds of texts, and some kinds of reading strategies, require that we hold in mind alternative, conflicting framings and oscillate between them, as this may result in pleasurable ("aesthetic") mental activity. Other kinds of texts, such as scientific works, demand the reduction, or at least a clear mapping, of ambiguities.

This is where we need the concept of an overarching or macro frame, for which Erving Goffman's notion of a *frame* seems to do the right work, except for the risk of terminologic confusion and—again—of eclecticism.[6] Goffman understands frames as tools that allow us "to label 'schemata of interpretation' that allow individuals or groups 'to locate, perceive, identify, and label' events and occurrences, thus rendering meaning, organizing experiences, and guiding actions" (Goffman 1974, 21). As Werner Wolf writes in his useful overview on the notion of frames, framing is about choosing "the correct tools." Framings "help us to navigate through our experiential universe, inform our cognitive activities and generally function as preconditions of interpretation" (Wolf 2006, 5).

Every frame can itself be reframed (cf. Emmott's [1997] notion of recontextualization). We will encounter this phenomenon, for example, when analyzing Dave Eggers's novel, which seems at first coded as autobiography, a framing with consequences for our interpretive disposition and ethos attributions. This initial generic framing may be superseded by that of metafiction, or essayistic fiction, which casts a new light on the thematized and apparently performed ethos of sincerity.

Goffman also points out the importance of what he calls "frame borders" and "framing keys" (Goffman 1974, 43–44). In the case of literary texts, such keys are in the first place (conventional) paratextual and textual markers, signals of fictionality, for instance, or of genre. Ethos topoi and authorial posturing can also, as I hope to show, function as framing keys, cuing readers to interpret a work as an engagé novel, for example. Textual and paratextual framing keys play an evident part in readers' framing acts, as a basis for their interpretations, but one should not forget that such keys themselves are signs, which must be selected as such by their interpreters.

Language allows metacommunication about frames. This, arguably, happens not just when, in a real-life situation, we check through words whether we have properly understood a candlelight dinner, but also in literary interpretations, when people debate over framing Frey's book as being yes or no autobiographical, which has consequences for the kind of experience and point they expect the work to afford.

In order to avoid confusion, I will usually signal when I use *framing* or *frames* in Goffman's sense, rather than in Minsky's cognitive sense. These two different understandings, however, are not deeply heterogenous. As Werner Wolf also remarks, "[A]ll of the different approaches to 'frames' [he refers to Goffman's as well as to cognitive understandings of the notion] converge in one frame function, namely to guide and even to enable interpretation. . . . [S]ince interpretation always involves concepts, one can argue that frames as 'keys' to interpretation are at least 'metaconcepts': concepts that regulate the application of other concepts" (Wolf 2006, 3–4). Goffman's notion of "framing" is quite central for my approach to ethos constructions, as it foregrounds the acts of selection that form the core of processes of interpretation, determining also what kind of value regime would apply to the case one has at hand (this notion of value regime is explained in chapter 2).

Further concepts and assumptions that are broadly used in cognitive psychology, linguistics, and narrative theory are those of inference and the underlying capacity for mind reading. Both notions, and the processes to which they refer, are relevant as well for analyzing processes of ethos attributions in the interpretation of narrative texts. In daily life, as when we read literature, we are constantly engaged in assessing not just what utterances semantically mean but also to what extent the expressed or implied views may be endorsed, and by whom exactly (this is important when quoting, or irony may be at stake). Inferences are sparked by what an audience perceives as clues, which may be discursive or nondiscursive.

The notion of "folk psychology" has been proposed for the shared knowledge that would form the basis of character inferences (Dennett 1987; Gallese and Goldmann 1998; Ravenscroft 2010). More specifically, we would memorize knowledge—about people's character, for instance—in generalized, typified or prototype, form (see also chapter 3, on character in narratology).[7] Inferences about other minds presuppose, as is currently widely assumed, a capacity for mind reading, also called "Theory of Mind" (Premack and Woodruff 1978; cf. Gallagher and Frith 2003). According to this theory, we read people's behavior and "attribute states of mind to ourselves and others all the time" (Zunshine 2008, 67). Mind reading is the "default way by which we construct and navigate our social environment." Hence the "intensive sociocognitive scrutiny"—and, I would add, ethos conjecturing—that fills our days and our fictions (Zunshine 2006, 71).

From an evolutionary perspective, Theory of Mind carves out a plausible function for fiction, and for fictional narrative in particular (Zunshine 2006, 72). The cognitive "workout" comes accompanied with the bonus pleasure that literary works "regale us with something we hold at a premium in everyday life: perfect access to other people's minds via observable behavior," offering the "illusion of superior social discernment and power" (Zunshine 2006, 72). Literary works also offer, one might observe, the more melancholy, yet just as familiar, confrontation with characters' and our own opacity, obtuseness, inconsistency, and duplicity.

Literary works offer rich material to exemplify Theory of Mind and psychological inferences at work, as Zunshine, among others, has forcefully demonstrated. As it is understood by literary scholars, this notion of Theory of Mind seems, in fact, to rediscover a familiar, age-old function attributed to literature, expressed in the idea that literature affords and requires from writers expertise about the "human soul," social interaction, and even morality. However, narratologists should perhaps keep in mind that Theory of Mind is a general theory about the functioning of the mind, which has not been devised to account for the ways in which singular literary works are read and interpreted.

Another critical note pertains to what I call the continuity thesis, often adopted in cognitive narratology. As will be discussed in part 2, Alan Palmer and others plausibly argue that a key frame for understanding narrative is the ascription of consciousness to fictional characters according to everyday psychological inference processes (Palmer 2004, 15).[8] Psychological inference processes arguably also include hypotheses about characters' ethos and about the complex interplay of perspectives, which qualify how we infer a particular character's ethos. Yet some generic contracts or reading strategies may make readers' lifelike imagination of characters' fictional minds problematic, or even irrelevant, as will be discussed. In fact, with all its plausibility, the continuity thesis risks promoting one particular mode of reading, reading for verisimilar human character, as well an unreflected conception of psychology, the interpreter's own (more on this in part 2).

At this point a first reflection on inferential meaning making as a relatively automatic process, versus interpretation, is in order (a second follows in the section on hermeneutics). Conflating the two has problematic consequences, as other literary scholars have also pointed out (e.g., Jackson 2003, Easterlin 2012, Ryan 2010). I merely wish to point out that cognitive theories of literature often carry with them the sense that inferences and meaning making can be accurately reconstructed or even described. Yet if one considers the complex inferences that are at stake— activities such as constructing narrative emplotment, or character, or mind reading—it should be clear that such inferential work goes way beyond the automatic inferencing or attribution of semantic meaning to words: it includes sophisticated synthesizing, as well as the complex computation of perspectives on perspectives, bringing cognitive investigation close to interpretation, perhaps too close for comfort.

To wrap up this discussion on the cognitive (narratological) analysis of meaning making, I would say that cognitive concepts of frames, mental models, inferences, or Theory of Mind do not by themselves guarantee a more scientific and rigorous heuristics for establishing the—or one's—meaning of a text. Nor do they account in sufficiently subtle ways for framing acts and relevance building that play a central role in readers' interpretive processes. Frame theory, however, will be directly relevant for my approach of ethos attributions, but as heuristic and metahermeneutic notions, offering a vocabulary and tentative conceptualizations of such interpretive processes, rather than as self-evident tools for description.[9] Moreover, the usefulness of these key notions, in combination with Goffman's theory of framing, lies in the stimulus they offer to investigate routes and routines that underlie interpretations and evaluations of narratives, seeking out why these may differ.

Hermeneutics: The Return of the Repressed

The following excursion into hermeneutics likewise aims to selectively recall several insights concerning the processes of interpretation and how interpretation functions for the individual and for human culture. I aim not just to bring to light some striking parallels with the cognitive frameworks mentioned in the previous section but, again, to point to some methodological caveats.

Like cognitive sciences, hermeneutics comes in many guises, from Friedrich Schleiermacher's marriage of philology and theological exegesis to the twentieth century's hermeneutics of suspicion. Hermeneutics refers not just to individual, subjective practices of interpreting and evaluating texts, or artifacts more generally. Philosophical hermeneutics, or metahermeneutics, always also strives to gain insight into the processes and conditions of how people interpret. While this interest often leads to normative programs that stipulate the conditions for correct interpretation—a claim that has elicited heavy epistemological and ethical critique—hermeneutics also includes a reflection on the cognitive—and social—processes that underlie interpretation, which has a more general relevance, often overlooked in narratology.

The domain of expertise claimed by hermeneutics is indeed that of interpretation, specifically, the interpretation of texts, considered as expressions and representations of human experience. Hermeneutics' definition of its own aims and methods, it is well known, was spurred by the rapid and influential development of the natural sciences in the nineteenth and twentieth centuries. Take the art of interpretation envisaged by Schleiermacher (1768–1834), one of the founders of hermeneutics.

Schleiermacher's reflections read like a demanding scholarly discipline when he rules that interpretation should proceed through two stages:

1. The grammatical or "historical" interpretation, which has an objective and a subjective aspect. The objective perspective understands a work as the "product of the language." This understanding comprises philological expertise of the vocabulary, genres, writings, and history of the period, as these constitute the whole within which texts must be understood, with all their peculiarities.[10] The subjective perspective considers discourse as the product of the soul and requires knowledge both "of the author's inner and outer life" and of his character and circumstances (Schleiermacher 1985, 83).

2. Psychological interpretation, which also has an objective and a subjective aspect. The objective component refers to the comparative-historical method, which allows the classification of a text and its author according to genre or type and, through comparison, offers a way to grasp a text's uniqueness. The subjective perspective is the "divinatory" interpretation, that is, the interpreter's attempt to understand the author through intuition. To interpret, for Schleiermacher, means to "put [one]self both objectively and subjectively in the position of the author" (1985, 83).

Schleiermacher also famously described understanding as a circular process, referred to as the hermeneutic circle. This circle actually runs, loopwise, through several circuits. The first circuit refers to the fact that when we read, say, Houellebecq's *Atomised*, our understanding of individual elements contributes to our idea of the whole, but it is our intuition of the whole that makes these elements signify. Moreover, to understand a work, we need to place it in its historical context (or, one might propose, in any other context that is relevant), which in turn the work represents or helps us to understand.

The systematic to-and-fro process of interpretation, which keeps connecting (new) parts to (new) wholes, would allow the interpreter to "understand the text at first as well as then even better than its author." For literary scholars, this statement constitutes perhaps Schleiermacher's most well known words (1985, 83, 87). It also earned the hermeneutician much scorn in later days. Yet against widespread associations of hermeneutics with naïve empathy and intention attribution, one should at least acknowledge that Schleiermacher's "divinatory understanding" or intuition of the author results from rather strict analytical procedures, systematic knowledge, and comparison. Sure, he also abundantly celebrates the interpreter's intuitive capacities, placing him in close company with the creative genius himself.[11] But how different, really, is his *divination* from the *inferences* cognitive scientists so easily speak about, and rely on, themselves, when working on individual texts? Schleiermacher's reconstruction of the requirements of interpretation, in fact, might be considered to make explicit the kind of specialized knowledge—specifying frames, scripts, mental models, and framing competences—scholars at a particular time estimated indispensable for expert understanding of texts. This hermeneutics is indeed normative in the kind of expertise it required. Current hermeneutics would instead insist on cultural diversity and struggle and consider other expertise as relevant: sociological models of culture and art, for example, new psychological insights, understandings of the workings of ideology, and so on. But the general model of interpretation lined out by Schleiermacher—with its emphasis on both intellectual or knowledge-based and empathic engagement—has not, to my sense, been fundamentally outdated in cognitive approaches to the assignment of meaning, including to literary texts.

Scholars also criticized the central role Schleiermacher grants to language, which would downplay other modes of cognition and communication (see Pettersson 2009, 19). Schleiermacher's emphasis on language, however, ties in with his focus on interpretation itself, as a language-connected practice of reflection. "Hermeneutics and rhetoric are intimately related in that every act of understanding is the reverse side of an act of speaking, and one must grasp the thinking that underlies a given statement" (Schleiermacher 1985, 74). Not only is "[s]peaking . . . the medium for the communality of thought" (74; one may, of course, object that it is not thought's only medium) but, through language, we can reflect on our thoughts and check, support, or contest this communality of thought. This emphasis on the importance of language and interpretation resonates with particular appeal, I find, in light of ideas such as Donald's about culture as "distribution of cognition" or Berger and Luckmann's on the social construction of reality.

The processes involved in interpretation are further explored by Schleiermacher's pupil Wilhelm Dilthey (1833–1911), who must be credited with proclaiming "understanding and interpretation [as] the method throughout the human sciences" (Dilthey 1985b, 152). [12]

Two further points will be explored here. First, I would like to stress that despite its idealist overtones, Dilthey's work displays a keen phenomenological-psychological and anthropological interest. His descriptions prefigure several of the popularized insights of cognitive theories of meaning making and of culture discussed in the preceding section. "[T]he life of the mind," Dilthey argues, is "based on the physical." While science "unravels the conditions under which mind occurs" and finds "among observable bodies . . . that of man," "experience is related to man in a way which cannot be further explained." With experience, he notes, "we step from the world of physical phenomena into the realm of mental reality" (Dilthey 1985a, 151). Most contemporary cognitive scientists would contest the dualism underlying this last claim, yet Dilthey had a point in emphasizing the qualitative difference of reflecting on human experience from the inside. This issue has taken on central importance again in current cognitive studies, crystallizing in the question of the status of consciousness and of the sense of self, adding to the inquiry recent insight into how the brain works (see, e.g., Gallagher and Zahavi 2008; Nagel 1984).

In the idealist, Hegelian, vocabulary of his time, and with a distinct sense of culture as socially constructed and distributed, Dilthey describes the "objective mind," constituted by "the manifold forms in which what individuals hold in common have objectified themselves in the world of the senses: Its realm extends from the style of life and the forms of social intercourse to the system of purposes which society has created for itself, custom, law, state, religion, art, science and philosophy." In this shared "medium," which surrounds our daily processes of elementary understanding, the "human child before it learns to talk is already wholly immersed" (Dilthey 1985b, 154).[13] Individuals cannot but interpret "life-expressions" against the background of such experience-based and socially shared knowledge. This "elementary understanding" is developed on the basis of "experience (*Erlebnis*) and self-understanding and the constant interaction between them" (Dilthey 1985b, 154).

Dilthey's description of the process of understanding itself, with its circuit of induction-deduction, seems to anticipate, or at least to be congruent with, the cognitive description in terms of frames, mental models, and inference mechanisms. In everyday life, he notes, we make inferences by assigning "life-expressions" to a type of gesture or action or range of usages, categorizations based on analogy reasoning or relations of expression (Dilthey 1985b, 163, 154–55; cognitive sciences, here, emphasizes the role of memory). Once we have made bottom-up inductions about, say, the character of a person, we use these inductions deductively, top-down, to fine-tune our expectations and orient our further selection of signs in order to understand that person.

Normally, Dilthey states, people understand each other because they share experience of elementary "life-expressions." (From a cognitive perspective, we would speak here of shared frames and mental models, as well as other people's intentions and minds.) Ethos and mindreading in this light serve an evident social function: In the "interest of practical life," especially because of "trade and commerce," social life increasingly pointed to "the need to gain insight into the people surrounding us so that we can make sure how far we can count on them" (Dilthey 1985b, 154–55).

In some cases, however, this regular inference process is blocked, as when people hide their "inner states, ideas or intentions" by an "inscrutable attitude or by silence," or when they intend to deceive. Such crises in this elementary meaning-making process are often occasioned by works of literature, either because they belong to another culture and time or because of other interpretive difficulties. In such cases "higher forms of understanding" are required, which is where interpretation as an expert *and* intuitive, empathetic practice comes in (Dilthey 1985b, 154–55).

In passing, Dilthey suggests a plausible hypothesis for explaining what has been considered art's proclivity for challenging routinized perception.[14] It is only, he writes, "when the person encounters . . . a difficulty or a contradiction of what he already knows [that] he is forced to really examine the matter." Deviant experiences thus lead to heightened (self) consciousness: "A change in a state of mind thus becomes conscious of itself. . . . [E]xperience is followed by judgment about what has been experienced in which it becomes objectified" (Dilthey 1985b, 152). Dilthey's observation suggests one example of how Donald's metacognition would, concretely, be obtained. It also indicates why it might be fruitful, for a culture, to have such practices that challenge our standardized inferences.

Actually, and this is the second point I want to make, Dilthey's formulations, at times, are more cautious than those of many a cognitive narratologist, when he acknowledges that "deduction from an inductively arrived insight [can] only achieve expectations and possibilities," not absolute certainty. Such uncertainties increase, he adds, with the "inner distance between the particular life expression and the person who tries to understand it," or when the context is underdetermined. In such cases there are only "probable inferences" (Dilthey 1985b, 157).

Yet the observation about interpretive difficulties that may arise is also one of the moments in which Dilthey's idealism interferes with what, until that point, looked very much like a phenomenological approach, which shares with the cognitive models discussed earlier the attempt to understand the elementary processes of meaning making. Here Dilthey claims that it is the special nature of the artwork, together with the interpreter's capacity for empathy, that explains why a "great work of art" cannot deceive or withhold its meaning from us. "Truthful in itself it stands—fixed, visible and permanent; this makes its methodical and certain understanding possible. Thus there arises in the confines between science and action an area in which life discloses itself at a depth inaccessible to observation, reflection and theory" (Dilthey 1985b, 154).

The pathos of the section mimetically conveys a sense of the very special revelations that art would occasion. Dilthey's hermeneutic discourse and the kind of knowledge strived for itself seem to shift from an analytic-theorizing mode of cognition and discourse to a mimetic one. In Dilthey's view, from those inaccessible depths we can actually intuit the author's intention. First, this is because "[n]o truly great work of art can wish to give the illusion of a mental content foreign to its author." This rather looks like a petitio principii, which might also be understood as a rhetorical celebration of the commonality of values and experiences. Second, it is because the interpreter has the capacity for empathy (*Einfühlung*; Dilthey 1985b, 159), as Schleiermacher had already argued—with, however, a heavy requirement of scholarly expertise, which nourishes expert-intuitive understanding.

Both founding fathers' emphasis on intuition and empathy elicited supercilious comments, especially from humanities scholars who sought affiliation with the harder sciences, giving them grounds to cast the whole of hermeneutics in a rather caricatured light. The hermeneutic model would glorify the interpreter along with the artwork and its genius creator, reinforcing the discipline's prestige and promoting one particular set of values and worldview, that of the ruling class. Meanwhile, by an ironic twist, basic tenets of hermeneutics—the idea of the "communality of thought," empathy—are now central issues in many cognitive approaches also within narratology. I hope that my brief presentation at least mitigates the idea that hermeneutics is *hopelessly* intuitive. Rather, Schleiermacher and Dilthey are quite analytical in defining the knowledge and mental capacities that ground intuition itself. From a frame-theoretical perspective, their work offers grounds for conceiving of intuition as the competence for creative combination of a mind nourished by a multiplicity of frames, scripts, and mental models that might be relevant. This memorized knowledge would range from linguistic expertise to broader contexts and interpretive frameworks, such as conceptions of selves, or morality. This knowledge would also include interpretive skills themselves, which afford multiple, and often alternative, strategies for constructing relevance, meaning, and value for artifacts, behaviors, or whatever social practices one is scrutinizing. For educational concerns, for instance, this emphasis on erudition and analytic knowledge might usefully complement the somewhat narrow trust on innate (emotional) empathy as a sufficient basis for "rich" and socially relevant interpretation.

In Dilthey's view, hermeneutics "always defended the certainty of understanding against a historical skepticism and willful subjectivity," yet the kind of scholarly understanding that is reached "cannot be represented by a logical formula," nor can its "final, and quite subjective, certainty" claim absolute validity, even though it often *feels* otherwise (Dilthey 1985b, 162). In my understanding, the normativity and subjectivity that can be observed in the work of these hermeneuticians appears just as well in more recent approaches, which arguably qualify as cultural hermeneutics (e.g., Greenblatt's cultural poetics, Mieke Bal's and others' cultural analysis, or ethical or postcolonial criticism). In these current "critical" approaches this normativity is clearly an object of analysis, but it often also inheres to the analytic approach itself. This is no flaw, I would argue, but a constitutive aspect: hermeneutics is the domain of reasoning about values and about value-laden interpretive pathways. Hermeneutic reflection is always undertaken from some kind of value position. There are, however, differences in degrees of reflexivity and objectivation (which is not to be confounded with objectivity).

Cognitive scientists as well as narratologists might actually find some non-negligible caveats and complements in later hermeneutic reflection as well. In this context two more points deserve to be highlighted. The first concerns the insight that making meaning of a text often requires much more than mechanical inference or faultless intuition. On this point Gadamer's work has been most relevant. Questioning assumptions of the communality of thought, which would allow interpreters to intuitively grasp the original author's intentions (or allow cognitive narratologists to make safe inferences), Gadamer indeed emphasized that, as an interpreter, one needs to negotiate the gap between the horizon in which a text has initially been conceived and one's own. Somewhat vague, the notion of horizon at least comprises the idea that understanding involves a preunderstanding (*Vorverständis*) based on our prejudices (*Vorurteil*; Gadamer 1991, 270, 281–82, 302).[15] When we understand a work, we establish a "dialogue" with a text that at first seems strange or different to us. In that dialogue, a "fusion of horizons takes place" (Gadamer 1991, 397). One comes out of that experience, Gadamer assumes, enriched by the confrontation with the otherness of the text.

I do not wish to comment in detail on Gadamer's hermeneutics but only want to point out this principled assumption of a gap between the "horizon" of the text (and its author) and that of interpreters. Interpretation, then, is mental work that brings into play, and often challenges, conventions and habitual understandings (which could perhaps be described in terms of specific frames, mental models, and so on). One's horizon is never just personal, in Gadamer's view, as it is steeped in tradition and determined by one's sociohistorical condition. The prejudices that characterize one's own position are not something one should or can get rid of: "They are simply conditions whereby we experience something—whereby what we encounter says something to us" (Gadamer 1977, 9). These conditions constitute the ground for a *pre*judgment "that is rendered before all the elements that determine a situation have been finally examined" (Gadamer 1991, 270). "Prejudice" thus seems to hover between (a) the cognitive notion of frames, as the schematized memory of practical experience, (b) framing acts in Goffman's sense, that is, the mental acts by which we classify a situation, (c) Sperber and Wilson's "relevance frames," as these prejudices form the "conditions whereby... what we encounter says something to us" (Gadamer 1991, 270), and (d) ideological positioning. Gadamer's reflection on interpretation in any case calls attention to several elements. First, an interpreter's understanding of a text is already preconstructed by his or her interpretive "horizon." Second, interpretive horizons and "prejudices" are not automatically shared by authors and audiences. Third, the interpreter's dialogue with the text is on the one hand determined by traditions, shared with others; on the other hand, it is uniquely determined by the interpreter's personality and experience. From this last insight, it follows that acts of understanding have an inevitable event character (such an understanding of interpretation as an individual act grounds Gadamer's stance against method). This event character receives an even stronger ethical coloring in more recent ethical approaches, such as Derek Attridge's (or also in Phelan's rhetorical-ethical approach to narrative fiction).

From here, two possible paths ensue for hermeneutic inquiry, which can also be retrieved in narratology. In the one path scholars embrace the idea that there is a "method," *pace* Gadamer, for analyzing these "horizons" and prejudices. In line with Schleiermacher, but often adding an emphatic critical orientation to the hermeneutic inquiry, various forms of narrative or cultural poetics and cultural and discourse analysis seek to specify *expert* frameworks, which would help—heuristically—to understand how people understand and to reconstruct patterns in the ways in which texts, and meaning attributions, operate in a given society. Alternately, such approaches stipulate, normatively, how the understanding of texts proceeds most fruitfully.

The other path pursues the idea that interpreting is an individual act, engaging an interpreter's whole perceptive, emotional, intellectual, and moral constitution. Interpretation, and arguably also the reflection on how we interpret, then become means for self-understanding. This line leads, beyond scholarly aims, to personal development and self-reflection. This is also the line explored by Paul Ricoeur (even though, in *Time and Narrative*, he went very far in seeking to understand what reconstruction of knowledge and knowledge procedures could be achieved on the basis of the various methods in the humanities available in his time).

Ricoeur's model of narrative interpretation, which assumes a strong connection between interpretation and ethical (self-)awareness, has interesting potential for a more practical application. In his model, interpretation proceeds through three steps: Mimesis I, which comprises the *preunderstanding* of human action we find in our daily cultural environment (this level seems to correspond to what Dilthey called elementary understanding, and to what cognitive scientists refer to in terms of frames, schemata, etc.); Mimesis II, by which Ricoeur designates the narrative configuration a reader encounters in a particular text; and Mimesis III, which is the active appropriation of the text's configuration by the reader, on the basis of his or her preunderstanding (Ricoeur 1984–88, 1:52–87). To assign an ethos to Houellebecq's character Bruno, the narrator in *Atomised*, thus involves our own appropriation of the novel's configuration of the character, on the basis of our own preferences and their underlying values and worldview.[16]

Ricoeur's model to some extent captures the active and increasingly reflective process involved in the configuration of experience through narrative and its interpretation. "Mimesis," he writes, "is an action about action. What it prefigures in the first stage and configures in the second, it transfigures in the third. To transfigure is still to do something" (Ricoeur 1991b, 150). A central issue at this stage is that in Ricoeur's view, like for Gadamer, the "interpretation of a text culminates in the self-interpretation of a subject who thenceforth understands himself better, understands himself differently, or simply begins to understand himself" (Ricoeur 1981, 158). This idea has, not unexpectedly, been questioned (Strawson [2004], in particular, attacked the assumptions of coherence, continuity, and consistency that would underlie Ricoeur's notion of narrative identity. Instead, Strawson argues, our "selves" may well be experienced in much more episodic and fragmentary ways.) I'm not so sure, though, that for Ricoeur the identity-constituting experience afforded by reading fiction, or his own concept of narrative identity (on which I will not elaborate here), necessarily implies coherence and cohesion in one's sense of self. On the contrary, he explicitly discusses the loss of such a cohesive self as an experience we may, or even should, have while reading literary fiction. He even observes that in reading we may well be drawn into empathic engagement with experiences that eschew emplotment and coherence or transgress accepted norms (Ricoeur 1990, 236–37). But his work indeed defends the idea that a conception of selves as endowed with intentionality, agency, and responsibility presupposes a narrative structure. It is through narrativizing that we achieve the "synthesis of the concordant and the discordant," weave patterns of causal and temporal relations between disparate events, and draft a sense of self as to some extent continuous (Ricoeur 1991a). Beyond the existentialist undertones, this may well be the kind of notion of self that is required if one wants to uphold at all an idea of subjects as morally responsible and the idea that to reflect on ethos attributions is at all relevant, for narratologists as well.

Though it appears questionable that just any consumptive reading of any literary narrative would by itself lead to a heightened sense of self or a better understanding of oneself, there is still a point to Ricoeur's argument. Ethos riddles, often staged in literary narratives, for example, offer rich occasions for readers to test out their own stances and to reflect on them (the effect of such a reflective exercise, however, may just as well be that we feel confirmed in our values and reading habits). But the idea of a heightened self-awareness through interpretive activity seems a fruitful one. Practices of interpretation, in a social or educational setting, in dialogue with others or oneself, involve enhanced efforts for analyzing and synthesizing our "feelings" and responses to an artifact and for augmenting our interpretations. Such practices offer occasions for the concentrated shared attention that Boyd points out as crucial for social cognitive fine-tuning. While the conditions under which such experiences could become ethically relevant need to be further specified, the idea of the metacognitive function of interpretation itself seems important enough to be tested empirically, in the light of its potential also in an educative, or any reflective, setting.

Hermeneutics, as mentioned, has been easily reduced to a caricature. Divinatory understanding, the fusion of horizons, and narrative identity were dismissed as un- or prescientific notions, if not as ideologically, ethically, and epistemologically suspect cultivations of outmoded conceptions of the self and of sloppy subjectivity and intuition (not to mention idiosyncratic Heideggerian neologisms, which I have not even addressed).[17]

In turn, the rejection of hermeneutics sometimes looks like a case of repression. Structuralist, poststructuralist, or deconstructionist approaches each had their own interest in obliterating any continuity with the hermeneutic tradition. This tradition was associated with everything that, on the side of Scylla, counted as the opposite of serious science or, on that of Charybdis, smacked of the authoritative imposition of meaning.[18] It also proved strategic, in a science-dominated context, to forget how much reflection hermeneutic tradition fostered on issues of meaning making, not only regarding its role in culture or in the development of individual and collective identities but also regarding the kinds of suspicion, and of rationality, required.

Hermeneutic philosophers self-consciously argued in the past that their approach is not in the strict sense a science. This position need not imply that interpretations become a matter of mere individual taste or biographic hazards. Instead—ideally—metahermeneutic reflection emphasizes that procedures for reasoning and criteria of rigor need to be defined intersubjectively. Many assumptions in hermeneutic conceptualizations of the interpretive process could well prove valid through empirical research, and this is the challenge lying out now, in cooperation with cognitive and social sciences.

In a kindred perspective, Gallagher defends the relevance hermeneutics and cognitive sciences could have for each other. On the one hand, he claims that cognitive sciences definitely provide progress in how to understand matters studied in hermeneutics: "[I]n our [now-cognitive] attempts to explain how we understand others we do not have to appeal to an obscure universal human spirit, as Schleiermacher, Droysen, and Dilthey did. We now have the means to see the meaning of a universal human spirit in the behavior of the infant and in the activation of common brain areas, and to give a hermeneutical account of empathy that is closely tied to these natural phenomena" (Gallagher 2004, 9; I hope to have shown, however, that this "spirit" was also understood in rather more specific terms; see the discussion on Dilthey).

On the other hand, Gallagher emphasizes that exact, scientific computation models of the kind developed within cognitive studies fail "in what Gadamer calls 'hermeneutical situations'. These are precisely situations that are ill-defined, ambiguous, and not open to rule-following or methodological solutions." Such situations require a mode of processing, Gallagher notes, that Aristotle captured in his "concept of *phronesis*— usually translated as 'practical wisdom' or sometimes, as 'prudence' in its original sense—that is, an ability to know the right thing to do and how to do it" (Gallagher 2004, 6–7). I cannot but agree with this observation, which also tones down somewhat the high-strung expectations narratologists tend to have for their recourse to cognitive sciences.

This is not to advocate a return to nineteenth-century hermeneutics, with its normative ideas about the genius of the critic in dialogue with the author-genius, however inspiring such high-level encounters may sound. But I do think we should recognize the extent to which issues addressed in hermeneutics remain fundamental for all sciences of culture (the *we* is meant very broadly, to include, e.g., university boards). Hermeneutic reflections reveal some striking parallels with cognitive insights in procedures of meaning making. They display on these issues, however, a far sharper awareness of the historical and cultural complexities of interpretation, beyond "meaning making."[19]

At the very least, within the humanities itself the rapport of the discussed cognitive models and concepts with hermeneutic debates needs to be clarified (cf. Donald's own observation on this issue, cited above; see also Gallagher 2004; Gallagher and Zahavi 2008; Jackson 2003 reflects on these issues from the position of a constructively critical outsider).[20] In fact, rather than making interpretive work obsolete and epistemologically suspect, cognitive research on culture and narrative could well help explain how we share experiential knowledge about the world and interpretations of human experience through narratives and narrative art, and why that is so important for a culture. The humanities then appear to be the place where social processes of meaning making and pathways for interpretation and evaluation are not just preserved and transmitted but critically analyzed, and their presuppositions, justifications, and consequences weighted.

It seems vital—not just for the institutional survival of the humanities but for the metacognitive function that would characterize human culture—that scholars and other mediating agents in the humanities rethink the relevance of interpretation, as well as how we practice and teach it (see Citton 2010). Cognitive sciences, to the extent that they are interested not just in the human brain but in the social dimensions of mind, and in culture, may provide arguments for such a stance.

Cognitive research to some extent, as we will discuss in later chapters, allows us to understand better how we attribute an ethos to characters, narrators, or authors. Yet these models do not, I propose, offer *scientific* tools for textual analysis-cum-interpretation. On any approach cherishing such claims, a therapeutic dose of Gadamer or Ricoeur would not be wasted. In my view narratology, as a collective singular, cannot and should not avoid interpretation. It involves interpretation in two distinct ways: as a task for which it develops heuristic tools, and as an object of study, which corresponds to what I called its metahermeneutic task.[21]

Between objectivity or universal validity and mere subjectivity there is a zone in which relevance and meaning-making paths are laid out and contested, for which the skills of both interpretation and reasoning are vital.[22] It is from this perspective on interpretation as a fundamental cultural practice, one that itself needs to be constantly scrutinized and monitored, that the following chapters will bring together various approaches in order to get a better grasp on the role of ethos attributions in the interpretation of literary narrative. This should bring the inquiry more down to earth as well.

2 Ethos as a Social Construction

Authorial Posturing, Conceptions of Literature, and Value Regimes

Sois indéterminé! [Be undetermined!]

NATHALIE HEINICH, *Etre écrivain*

Who or what determines the credit granted to Houellebecq's work and to himself, as a writer? Is it appropriate to ask about the sincerity or authority of his novel's denunciation of the rotten state of Western culture? What clues would we have to answer this question, or does trust come before the clues? What is the role in such an ethos attribution of clues derived from an author's public image? Drawing on a combination of approaches and models, this chapter engages with the social fabrication of meaning and the literary value of narratives and with the role of authorial ethos in this process.

I will first recall some sociological and historical perspectives on authorial ethos, habitus and postures, developed by Bourdieu and Viala, or in their wake, by Meizoz and others. Second, I will briefly sketch the relevance of considering conceptions of literature and literary value as factors in ethos attributions. Third, I will explain that French discourse analysis, especially the work of Amossy and Maingueneau, provides a timely reactualization of the Aristotelian notion of ethos.[1] Last, I will briefly discuss Boltanski and Thévenot's model for conflict analysis, which holds interesting potential for the analysis of competing interpretive practices and value regimes. Though not all of them are new, these perspectives nevertheless form a challenge to narratology, as they highlight various socially mediated framing acts, which I take to underlie the ways in which people attribute meaning and value positions to literary texts.

Throughout the chapter I will illustrate the argument by reference to various writers and their works. A more detailed discussion of the construction of Houellebecq's work and persona by two French critics closes off the chapter, which should demonstrate the heuristic relevance of the proposed frameworks.

The Production of Meaning and Value in the Literary Field

The approaches discussed in this chapter all share an interest in what I would call the relays, formats, and conditions that make meaningful experiences of literature possible. These conditions encompass institutions, such as schools, publishing houses, or literary journals, as well as agents, such as authors, publishers, critics, or censors, as analyzed by Bourdieu in his theory of the literary field (Bourdieu 1993a, 1996). The field conditions also include what could be considered as specific cognitive operations and models circulated in and by these institutions.

Who speaks, from where, with what authority are questions that fascinated Bourdieu, like many critical thinkers of his generation, from Foucault to Jameson. In Bourdieu's view, authority is determined by the institutionally defined position of a speaker and by the authorization rules that prevail for specific genres and in a particular (literary, religious, political, etc.) field. A writer thus may display tokens indicating that he should be regarded as an "authorized spokesman . . . [who] can act on other agents . . . because his speech concentrates within it the accumulated symbolic capital of the group which has delegated him and of which he is the authorized representative" (Bourdieu 1991, 111).

Bourdieu's perspective has consequences for his understanding of the value attributed to literature. Literary value, from this angle, appears as a form of belief (*croyance*) resulting from social processes of value attribution and negotiation in which institutions and agents play their role. Literary critics in particular act as prominent arbiters and gatekeepers of what counts as good literature. In Bourdieu's line, the value of Houellebecq's work, for instance, does not reside in any intrinsic aesthetic properties but results from the manner in which it was published and marketed and from the degree to which critics with varying authority and signature praised or demolished it, advancing their own ethical or aesthetic norms and conceptions of literature. Critics, and of course writers themselves, indicate paths along which readers are led to process a work as belonging to this or that category of valuable or valueless objects (more on value attributions later).

Established French critics such as Dominique Noguez, for instance, were highly instrumental in setting out a reading of *Atomised* as the work of a visionary author and thus as a work to be taken seriously from a literary-aesthetic and social perspective. Houellebecq himself also points out ways for reading his work through his authorial *posture*, a notion that gained renewed interest in recent years. *Posture* has been defined by Jérôme Meizoz, after Viala and Bourdieu, as an author's "mode of self-presentation," his or her "personal way of investing or endorsing a role, even a social status," through which he or she "replays or negotiates his [or her] 'position' in the literary field" (Meizoz 2004, 51; for an English presentation and illustration of the notion see Meizoz 2010). A posture allows an author to mark his or her position in the literary field, defining "the horizon for his/her reception," an idea that is central also in my own perspective (Meizoz 2008, 2).[2]

Postures build on a repertoire engrained in the memory of the literary field, ideally–but not always, I'd like to add—shared by authors and their audiences. Every aspiring author thus is "socialized into the practice of literature" and legitimizes his writing "by reference to these great ancestors from which he borrows beliefs, motifs, forms, and postures." Examples of postures are the "writer-as-citizen," or the Romantic "unhappy genius, [which] has very ancient roots in the European social imagination" (Meizoz 2009).

Writers mark or express a posture through all kinds of signals: through their style of writing and choice of genre, register, and themes; through the whole gamut of paratexts, from the book's presentation, its mention of biographical details, or its use of the author's picture, to interviews with the author, letters to other writers, or an author's essays about his or her own or other authors' writing; through an author's public self-fashioning, in which nondiscursive clues play a considerable part, from one's physical bearing and way of dressing through one's general behavior or specific actions (Meizoz 2004, 2009; Heinen 2002). Houellebecq's puzzling silences during broadcast interviews come to mind, which might incite interpreters to attribute to him the posture of the somewhat unadapted genius or, alternately, of a weirdo posing as a genius.

A posture elicits expectations regarding an author's ethos, and conversely, ethos clues suggest a posture. As I will argue in chapter 6, for instance, the posture of the engagé writer conventionally requires a displayed ethos of authenticity. Dave Eggers's writing programs with underprivileged people arguably provide a strong backing to his posture of sincerely committed writer.

But who actually creates an author's posture, and where should it be located? Posture, like ethos, results from an interactive process, Meizoz argues, as both are "co-constructed by the author and various mediators (journalists, critics, biographies) serving the reading public. Posture begins from the moment of publication—at the publisher's therefore—and involves the very presentation of the book (size, cover, etcetera)" (Meizoz 2010, 84–85). These various agents strategically or polemically devise ethos and posture constructions, anticipating the one on the other, while the analyst seeks to describe this whole interactive process. Whatever ethos an author attempts to project, she or he can never be sure that it will be received in exactly that way (Meizoz 2009, n13). Writers, moreover, are often skillful in exploiting tensions between the postures and ethos of protagonist, narrator, implied author, and the writer as a person. These positions should not be simply amalgamated, which is where narratological distinctions of levels in narrative communication come in (Meizoz 2009).

In contemporary media culture, writers get ample occasion to self-consciously "play out the mediatization of their persona and include it in the space of their works; their writings and the posture through which these are made public are presented conjointly as one single performance" (Meizoz 2007, 19–20). This is clearly not a new phenomenon, as Meizoz's own work on Rousseau demonstrates, but one that is substantially fostered by the availability of new media and podia. Houellebecq, for instance, would extend the ambiguity counted as a value in the aesthetic realm to his own person, in the public domain. In Meizoz's view, the author thus blurs the boundaries between art and life in a pervasive aestheticization, characteristic for postmodern culture (Meizoz 2007). To my sense, however, such cases should instead be analyzed as occasioning category uncertainties that interpreters may solve differently, depending on their conceptions of art and normative expectations and on what domains they perceive to be blurred, for instance, art and commerce, art and kitsch, or art and propaganda. Boltanski and Thévenot's model of competing value regimes, presented further below, should help clarify this view.

The perspective opened up by Viala and Bourdieu and elaborated by Meizoz, Diaz, and others provides fruitful avenues for researching ways in which a writer's authority and value are socially established and negotiated by readers or by professional interpreters through "ready-made formats for being-a-writer" (Meizoz 2008, 2; see also Diaz 2007). Research has focused on individual posturing strategies as well as on "the social, collective history of the typical and exemplary . . . postures and authorial scenographies, offered for imitation to a whole group, a whole school, a whole generation at a certain moment" (Diaz , in Amossy and Maingueneau 2009, par. 5).[3] Rich work also resulted on particular ethos components of postures, such as the writer's responsibility, a notion fraught with culture-bound values, or his or her commitment as a public intellectual (e.g., Sapiro 2011). Such research is relevant for understanding the conventional basis on which expectations regarding an author's ethos, as well as our actual ethos attributions and consequent evaluations, rely. Insights of this kind seem particularly useful for narratologists working on narrators' unreliability or (implied) authors' stances, as will be discussed in part 2.

In their time, Bourdieu's constructivist views concerning the fabrication of literary value within the literary field may have been intended to debunk both the prestige of high culture and that of traditional hermeneutics, which assumed in one sweep the singular value of the literary text, of its maker, and of the critic as the expert reader. This polemical thrust has now somewhat subsided, and from a cognitive perspective the emphasis on the mental, interactive, and conflicting nature of value as belief is almost self-evident. Concepts such as posture and ethos might be understood as mental models, conventional paths along which writers classify themselves and in turn are classified by others, with consequences for the interpretation of their works. A posture, in this perspective, connects schemata (conceptions of literature, including ideas about its function in society and about constellations of roles; genres as macroframes, implicitly suggesting a communication contract), scripts (how to be—and behave like—a writer, on both the public and the private scene), and mental models (writer postures and ethos types: the writer as guide, prophet, outcast, genius, enfant terrible, etc.). As familiar models, these activate, top-down, particular interpretive and evaluative regimes and thus help audiences classify the kind of writer one has at hand. Such classification suggestions are particularly helpful for new, ambiguous, or generically hybrid works, as we shall see in chapter 6.

These various mental models arguably form clusters, so that one element functions metonymically for the whole: a picture of Houellebecq on a cliff, with infinity as the horizon, frames him as a tormented romantic writer, which typically includes an emphasis on the writer as the social outsider, whose authority to criticize society derives from his marginal, hence autonomous, position. Suggesting a different classification, a picture of Houellebecq in a scientist's white coat, in a lab, by loose metonymic association conveys a scientist's impartial ethos, transferred to the author's depiction of Western society.

An important point on which the sociological approach differs from the cognitive perspective, though, lies in the sociologist's emphasis on institutionally established and protected, but also competing, interpretive pathways (which might perhaps be understood as cognitive macroscripts). The social space thus appears as a locus of struggle over cognitions, in which individual interpreters negotiate what makes meaning, for them, among conflicting options.

Controversial cases such as Houellebecq's, however, also reveal the methodological vulnerability of these approaches to ethos and posture. In Meizoz's understanding of posture as a dynamic co-construction by various agents, what is left out is what entitles the analyst to present his or her ultimate "re"-construction as the correct one. How, indeed, do interpreters discriminate, in their analysis of an author's posture, between sincere expression and irony, parody, and cunning self-fashioning and branding strategies, except by already postulating the authorial ethos they are analyzing? Moreover, how would they judge an author's ethos, mitigating between the many agents besides the writer him- or herself who are instrumental in mediating a particular author image? And how should one explain divergences in ethos or posture attributions on the reception side? Posture, ethos, habitus, and their dynamic co-constructions require a hermeneutic and argued reconstruction rather than mere description of the codes on which such sign projections and readings rely. The (meta)hermeneutic expertise that is demanded in this argued reconstruction includes insight into historically evolved conceptions of art and literature and historical and sociological knowledge about the literary field (complementing Schleiermacher's grammatical understanding).

Bourdieu's own approach, moreover, typically oscillates between a deterministic and a dynamic view of human conduct. On the one hand, authors are not free to invent a posture or an ethos, as the roles they adopt in the literary field tap into a habitus, which Bourdieu defines as a person's "subjective incarnation" of "objectively given conditions" (Bourdieu 1993b, 86). An ethos thus corresponds to "[p]rinciples of choice [that] are embodied, turned into postures, dispositions of the body. Values are postures, gestures, ways of standing, walking, speaking. The strength of the ethos is that it is a morality made flesh" (86). On the other hand, authors have some leeway for agency and may strategically adopt the tokens of an established writer posture, coin an antiprofile, or engage dialectically with their own prior posture. Meizoz, for his part, gives the example of Rousseau, who took to cultivating as his trademark what used to be his handicap, his lack of social capital. As grounds for a writer's authority, the anticourtly posture of a rough-hewn person, sincere and authentic, grew to be widely popular among writers starting out, like Rousseau, from a low social capital position (Meizoz 2010).[4]

The interest of the notion of posture, like that of ethos, as Meizoz rightly claims, lies in its attempt to leave behind the "old division of tasks between specialists of the text's inside and of its outside" and to "articulate the rhetorical and sociological dimensions, that is: agents' discourses, as well as their position taking within the literary field . . . by which a voice and a figure stand out as singular" in that field (Meizoz 2009). Like that of ethos, the notion of posture for me has primarily heuristic value: it sharpens the analyst's eye for what may be perceived as clues set out or unwittingly conveyed by the author or by mediators and invites argued reconstructions of the connections between readers', including the analyst's, perceptions of the author image and their modes of classifying, interpreting, and judging that author's works.

For instance, to anticipate my more elaborate case study at the end of this chapter, for one critic Houellebecq is definitely the prophet of our age, who sacrificed his own personality on the altar of art. So if he appears on TV as amorphous, badly dressed, clumsily holding a cigarette between the wrong fingers, brooding for five long minutes over a stammer that only gradually becomes a sentence, this is a sure sign of genius (bright but unadapted to social life) and of a most sincere ethos, which enhances the quality of his literary work. For another critic, on the basis of mostly the same clues, Houellebecq is just as evidently the perfect fraud. He incarnates the perversities of our times, ruthless commercialization and cunning branding, and shamelessly exploits sex, violence, and fake spirituality as the attractions of best-selling literature. Both critics need only hint at a well-known posture, evoked *pars pro toto* by one or two significant details, and their own readers will fill in the picture.

Now, my reader might say, these are literary critics, not narratologists or literary sociologists, who would remain far more neutral and rigorous in their descriptions or analyses. Moreover, the object of attention here is the author, not the narrative structures of his works. But can a narratologist setting out to describe dual voice or the presumed narrator's unreliability in *Atomised* avoid making inferences about the author's ethos? Let this be a bit of a cliff-hanger, to which I will come back in part 2.

Conceptions of Literature and Authorship

As mentioned, conceptions of literature play a central part in the conditions in which literature functions in culture at particular periods in history. As normative constructions defining the nature and function of literature, conceptions of literature can be considered to set out cognitive grids for how to make meaning of literature, rallying interpretive communities. Such conceptions include definitions of textual properties and literary techniques through which texts are expected to have specific effects on their readers (see van Rees and Dorleijn 1993, 3; 6). They also include norms regarding the role of the writer, for which some useful heuristic distinctions have been proposed, to which, I propose, must be added ethos expectations.

Van Rees and Dorleijn point out the heuristic value of Meyer Howard Abrams's distinction between four "theories of poetry," as Abrams calls them, which focus alternatively on the author, the audience, the represented reality, and the text, resulting in four conceptions of literature: the mimetic, with requirements such as verisimilitude, or truthfulness; the pragmatic/rhetorical, with an emphasis on decorum; the expressive, with demands of sincerity and so on; and the autonomist, with values such as complexity, unity, and the like (Abrams 1953, 10).

The usefulness of Abrams's model, I would argue, lies in its generality, due to its connection to the basic elements of communication (the same role could have been played by Roman Jakobson's—in fact, Bühler's—six functions of language). In my own analyses in part 2, which focus on the interpreter's side—that is, on the narratologist as an interpreter—mimetic and expressive conceptions of literature often appear to feed into one reading strategy, joining demands of factual exactitude and an ethos of sincerity. Such a mimetic-expressive cluster is often set off against an autonomist/aesthetic conception of literature, with a wholly different set of ethos expectations, with ambiguity and irony—and devices such as narrators' unreliability—as leading values.

From her research on writers' self-definitions, which, par excellence, express conceptions of literature, Nathalie Heinich draws some useful additional heuristic distinctions. She distinguishes two kinds of calling: the professional, insisting on the required métier (professional competence), and the vocational (as in postures of an author as genius, prophet, saint, hero, or spokesman) (Heinich 2000, 64). Both kinds of calling, I would say, may be expected to be supported by particular ethos clues, which could be inventoried. Heinich, moreover, observes two regimes to which writers subscribe or according to which they are classified by others: the regime of singularity, which highlights the unique personality, marginality, or originality of the writer, and the opposed regime of community, through which writers ally themselves with the collective good, however defined.

Each of these postures, let me add, runs a risk: while aligning with community may threaten one's claims to originality, achieving singularity often requires deferring to some generally accepted function or value (Heinich 2000, 240, 153). Specific ethos clues, in my view, are likely to buttress each of these posturing regimes. Thus, in order to convincingly highlight his or her singularity, a writer often displays topoi of authenticity and truthfulness. Authentic real-life experience was what James Frey, deceptively, promised his readers. Alternately, to convincingly align with a particular community, ethos topoi emphasize that the writer is an authorized and reliable spokesman who has the required inside knowledge. Unsurprisingly, the latter posture often foregrounds thorough and truthful documentation as backing for an ethos of personal commitment (this will be further developed in chapter 5).

Heinich furthermore opposes person-centered and a work-centered approaches to literature (Heinich 1997). In the former, I expect a writer's personal ethos of honesty, sincerity, integrity, irony, playfulness, and so on, to ground a work's impact. Such personal ethos clues are likely to be much less prominent in work-centered approaches. Yet there are, I believe, appropriately effaced-author postures, such as the writer as hermit, whose authenticity is unadulterated by the media's meddling (see the discussion on authors in chapter 4). This posture has been attributed, for instance, to Jonathan Littell, upon publication of *Les Bienveillantes* (*The Kindly Ones*), a two-pound work of fiction on Nazi atrocities told from the perspective of one of the perpetrators, or rather, a lucid yet deeply complicitous onlooker. The work exploits almost sickening shock effects. Many critics mention in passing that Littell keeps away from the media, interpreting this as an authentic ethos of reserve, which consolidates the work's value as a serious configuration of actual history. Some critics instead denounce this posture as commercially strategic or criticize the author for not taking responsibility for his acts of representation. (In my view, Littell's work for a humanitarian aid organization or his recent clandestine reportage from besieged Homs, in Syria, written for leading newspaper *Le Monde* and published as *Carnet de Homs* in 2012, strongly support an ethos of commitment and concern.)

For my own purposes, the relevance of research on conceptions of literature, like that on authorial postures, lies in the attention it draws to historically evolved, and contested, argumentation paths and frameworks through which we attribute intentions, meanings, and value to literary works.

French Discourse Analysis, Narrative, and Authorial Ethos

The following section explores in more detail the notion of ethos itself, discussing the perspective of what, to simplify, I will call French discourse analysis. Developed by Dominique Maingueneau and Ruth Amossy, among others, this brand of discourse analysis significantly contributed to making the Artistotelian notion of ethos operational for all kinds of discourses, in particular for literary narrative.[5]

Dissatisfied with thematic or narratological approaches to literature, which neglect the material and pragmatic conditions in which texts circulate, Amossy and Maingueneau, like Meizoz, aim to build bridges between (literary) texts and their contexts, which remains one of the key methodological puzzles for literary theory. To this end, they consider the notion of ethos to be particularly useful. Besides elements of institutional sociology, rhetoric, and argumentation theory, from Aristotle to Perelman, their approach integrates insights from linguistic pragmatics (speech act and enunciation linguistics) and *sociocritique*.[6] While their approach is for me in many respects congenial, as I draw on many of the same formative theoretical influences, my perspective is more explicitly (meta)hermeneutic. Rather than the illusive and elusive ethos of the actual author, what interest me are the dynamics of value and meaning attributions and negotiations by interpreters and their implicit or explicit justifications.

Ethos as Index and Stereotype

In line with Aristotle, Amossy defines ethos as "the image of self built by the orator in his speech in order to exert an influence on his audience" (Amossy 2001, 1). Audiences construct their image of the speaker or writer on the basis of his or her whole way of speaking or writing (ethos, here, as for Aristotle, primarily results from the text's expressivity itself). "Thus," Amossy writes, "a style punctuated with exclamations allows one to deduce the temperamental or excitable character of the speaker, while a concise and blunt manner of speaking which shows no concern for conventional politeness may indicate a person of integrity who does not deviate from the truth" (Amossy 2001, 8; this expressivist perspective, about which more later on, brings the notion of ethos close to that of tone, which in fact is often used to translate the Greek *ethos*).[7]

Building on Perelman's work on argumentation as well as on Aristotle's, Amossy emphasizes what could be called the recursivity of ethos inferences. In order to persuade, a speaker anticipates on his or her audience's values, expectations, and norms, including those regarding the speaker's ethos, and adapts his or her speech to these anticipations, setting out clues that steer the audience's response (Amossy 1999, 133).

In this process, Amossy writes, even though the speaker's image "remains ultimately singular, the reconstruction is effected with the aid of cultural models which facilitate the integration of data into a preexistent schema" (Amossy 1999, 133). Hence the role of stereotypes in ethos projections and attributions: "The stereotype allows the speaker to make hypotheses about the modes of reasoning and the sets of values and beliefs characteristic of a group. . . . An orator would be unlikely to make the same speech in front of Communist Party militants or wealthy executives, of chador-wearing Muslim women or American feminists" (Amossy 2001, 7–8; see also Amossy and Herschberg-Pierrot 1997).

Recast in terms of cognitive theory, one could say that ethos attributions rely on recursive mind reading (e.g., Zunshine 2006) and involve the relay of mental models and of scripts for processing situations. "In a cognitive perspective," Amossy specifies, "the stereotype allows for generalization and categorization, thus helping the individual to make sense of the environment as well as to make previsions concerning the future" (Amossy 2001, 8). Mental models of characters, for instance, are such stereotypes, which define ethos expectations. This kind of cognitive processing yields, besides the stereotypical ironist, braggart, or honest man, author postures, with their standardized ethos expectations (see further elaborations in chapter 5).

Character models, in my view, indeed subsume not just psychological traits, but also a particular rapport to one's assertions and a particular degree and kind of authority. Dave Eggers expends much effort in the multiple paratexts of *A Heartbreaking Work of Staggering Genius* to fend off being stereotyped as just one of those postmodern writers whose irony corrodes whatever they speak or think about, a stance that would determine his audience's reading attitude. Yet the "formal gimmickry" characteristic of his writing seems to activate precisely such a stereotype. Such tensions between discursive and thematized ethos, and that of the author as private and public person, intensify readers' search for the author's "true" communicative attitude, perhaps sensitizing them to the importance, and the hazards, of even identifying a discourse's source(s) and the extent to which assertions can be considered endorsed by the author.

Ethos Topoi

In order to establish their authority in an interaction situation, speakers refer to culturally recognized grounds for rhetorical credit, or ethos topoi (Eggs 1999, 42; Amossy 2001, 132). As Ernst-Robert Curtius recalls, the notion of topos goes back to classical rhetoric. Quintilianus, for instance, defined *topoi* as *argumentorum sedes*, storehouses of arguments, or of trains of thought, phrases that would delight a cognitive scientist. Orators were trained to memorize their speeches along such topoi, projecting their arguments onto concrete spaces. Curtius enlarged the notion to "common-places," which, one could say, metonymically condensate such trains of thought and worldviews (1979, esp. 70, 105).

For Aristotle, whose context was public speech in the Athenian state, ethos topoi belonged to good sense, virtue, or goodwill, as I recalled in the prelude to part 1. Other kinds of clues become relevant if we extend rhetorical analysis to different times and places and different kinds of discourses. Moreover, salient ethos effects seem to be attached to four main kinds of grounds: the ethical (morality), the alethic (truth), the epistemic (expertise and knowledge of various kinds), and the sociopolitical (power).[8] These various sorts of ethos effects can be conveyed by all kinds of clues and carriers, textual or extratextual, written, oral, visual, auditive, or physical, including one's behavior, one's car, the color of one's nail polish, or the way one decorates one's apartment. Any facet of human expression can indeed be taken as a signal for an ethos, on the basis of associations one has learned to make, captured in cultural codes and probably in biological responses as well.

On that matter one could argue that persuasion through physical effects of character, such as the authority or the goodwill elicited by physical stature, frailty, sexiness, or timbre of voice, should be reckoned as a fifth ethos ground. This would, however, mean taking a medium, that is, the body as sign bearer, as a categorization criterion, whereas for the four other cases the criterion lies in the kinds of grounds used for persuasion. I think, rather, that bodily ethos effects might effectively back up, or undermine, any of the other four kinds of ethos.[9]

Morality and truth, as ethos grounds, often operate together. They underlie all three of Aristotle's ethos components—good character, goodwill, and *phronesis*—and characterize the speaker's rapport to him- or herself, to others, and to the object of discourse and its intended effects in the world. Topoi indicating morality and truth pertain in particular to a speaker's (in)sincerity, (dis)honesty, (ir)responsibility, or (in)authenticity.

Knowledge, as an ethos ground, can comprise institutionalized, professional knowledge and expertise but also practical wisdom, experience, or skills of any kind, often connected to a professional habitus. For instance, when François Bon's narrator in *Daewoo* in a long scene makes clear to the reader that he knows how to make the women he interviews confide in him despite their habitus of restraint, the suggested communicational skills may help establish his authority as a spokesman in the eyes of the reader. Nineteenth-century realist and naturalist writing features narrators who express their expertise in matters of the human mind and society through topoi such as the comparison of the narrator or writer to the scientist or the doctor, importing into literature a socially highly validated authority, based on knowledge and skills. Orientalist writers, in turn, would insist, or have their narrators insist, on their personal experience as travelers. Firsthand subjective experience, rather than abstract knowledge, is also the dominant topos in testimonial literature.

Finally, power, as an ethos ground, includes institutionally grounded authority but certainly also physical power and attraction, as politicians well know, preferring the media to portray them in full swing: President Obama running up some stairs, with his panting advisors in his trail; Silvio Berlusconi, full of lust and hence full of energy to run his country, though one might consider this inference a category mistake.

Ethos and Embodiment

Among the implicit ethos clues, bodily ones are indeed often very effective (Meizoz 2007, 2010; Maingueneau 2004, 219–20), an idea that merits some elaboration. In semiotic terms, I would propose, we tend to perceive physical expressions as indexical and so as natural signs, which involuntarily express one's inner being, emotions, or thoughts, avoiding the mediation of language and, hence, rhetoric's deceits. Signs written in or expressed by the body often work as decisive proof for an ethos. François Bon's narrator can't sleep, he notes, after having talked to some of the women who lost their jobs, a physical reaction that for many readers authenticates his claim of engagement. More dramatically, for a writer of testimonial Holocaust literature, an arm marked with an Auschwitz number is a fundamental ethos guarantee, as is any sign of physical torture for political witness writing.

As embodied minds, less distant than some believe from animals that sniff out each other's dispositions, we are likely to be particularly sensitive to the nonverbal communication of intentions, moods, and character disposition. The body is our visible, audible, tangible, and even smellable exposure par excellence, so we have every reason to learn to decode its expressivity and, regarding ourselves, to check this expressivity. Cultures unsurprisingly discipline the body into conventional expression in the name of conceptions of self, good manners, and self-protection.[10] Clearly, despite associations with naturalness, our bodies are codified sign bearers; like all conventional signs, those of the body become exploitable for ludic pretense or deception. Who can tell how honest Tony Blair really was, protesting his innocence in the Iraq interrogation with his hand on his heart, a conventionally natural token of sincerity? (more on sincerity in chapter 7).

Pursuing Bourdieu's observations, Maingueneau argues that embodied ethos effects also paradoxically obtain in written discourse, including in written literature (Maingueneau 1999, 78). Such effects may be achieved through reference to social codes of physical expression, of which Balzac's or Jane Austen's works are rich founding groves. In Balzac's *Le Père Goriot*, for instance, bodies (and surroundings) are plethoric metonymic and metaphoric sign bearers, confirming a character's ethos, which Balzac's authorial narrator also explicitly qualifies. Madame Vauquer's opulent but smudgy forms famously speak to her sensuality, greed, and stinginess, which together translate into an ethos that is redundantly confirmed by the greasy plates, cutlery, and furniture of her boardinghouse.

But a bodily ethos may also be expressed through discourse itself, on the basis, still, of codified chains of associations. Readers readily translate textual rhythm, punctuation, syntactic structures, and so on into emotions, moods, or mental dispositions that sketch out an ethos. Meizoz gives the example of Rousseau's autobiographical *Les Rêveries du promeneur solitaire*, in which style and tone convey a sense of leisurely strolling that rhetorically transforms the author's unasked-for solitude into a blessing. The sentences meander along with the walker, iconically and indexically proving the authenticity of their author's stance. But one may object to Meizoz's obediently empathic reading; a suspicious reader like Voltaire might unmask such a serene rhythm as wishful mimicry, like that of animals who parade fierce colors to set off aggressors. To decode ethos clues is a complex calculation, taking into account a kaleidoscopic interplay of perspectives. Suspicion often roots in the prior ethos one has constructed for the writer or speaker. Let me illustrate this point with a brief digression.

A Cautionary Tale: Christine Angot's *Sujet Angot*

> It isn't working, what you're writing now. Sorry. But these sexual things you talk about, these guys, that's not you. . . . It's intellectual, artificial, what you're doing now, I'm sorry. But above all: you're not in it enough. You should be in it. You. You, Christine Angot, you. You should be in it, you. Not just a hodge-podge of what others may think of you. What you jotted down in the café, on the phone. That, that will never make a book by you. What one may think or say about you. You should be in it, you. . . . [M]oreover, you're making a bad book. Because you're not in it, you. That's what we want, we here, your style. Unique. Not just a portrait by omission. You must be in it. These things with these guys, all that, that's not you. . . . That's not interesting. . . . What we want, we here, that's your unique style. And you yourself, what you have to say, just as unique. You. Who you are. You. You who are unique. I could speak hours about that, me. (Angot 1998, 10–11)

This quotation is a fragment of the long letter written by Claude to his former wife, "Christine Angot," in Christine Angot's autofictional "novel" (as the cover indicates), *Sujet Angot*. The letter reads both as a portrait of Christine, rendered through the eyes and words of her ex, and as Claude's self-portrayal through his manner of writing, speaking, and thinking. But Claude's style is also very much characteristic of Angot's own writing, and of course, it is Angot who is listed as author of the book. (I trust that the stylistic features to which I want to draw attention remain sufficiently salient in my English translation.) So whose discourse, and whose ethos, do we read into the text, and how do we decide this, with what consequences?

Issues of ethos play a role on almost every level of the narrative and of its reception, as we shall see in more detail in chapter 6. For now, I'd like to concentrate on some ethos effects that might attach to Claude's, and Christine's, discourse and character. In particular, narrator Claude amply comments on Christine's body, which in one breath he connects to her style and her being; the one confirms and warrants the others, in a circular ethos effect. This body of hers, he writes, is characterized by its "fine joints" and smooth surface (*lisse*). This neat and harmonious body is also compared to a "small newborn squirrel," a nicely apprehensible, diminutive, and presexual form, by which Claude defines, and confines, the authenticity of Christine's body and person. (The comparison resonates significantly with Claude's remark that he feels physically and sexually diminished since Christine is gone.) Christine's style as well is most authentic when it sticks to what Claude considers its fundamental characteristics. To know Christine intimately, both bodily and stylistically, in turn grounds Claude's self-proclaimed authority to judge, and warrant, the authenticity of her person and her writing. The rules of this implicit contract are strict: if she does not stick to her image, that is, to his image of her, then "I will not be your reader anymore," implying that she would lose him as the litmus test for, and warrant of, her authenticity (14).

Claude's own writing, in turn, expresses a very embodied ethos indeed, torn between logos and pathos. While he keeps arguing about Christine, Claude depicts himself as wallowing in tears, a sexually diminished and abject body. With their obsessive repetition of the second-person pronoun and Christine's name, and their emotional punctuation and syntax, the tone and style of Claude's letter buttress the authenticity of his sense of loss and diminishment. But again, whose style are we deciphering in the body of his text? Claude's writing conspicuously resembles the writing Angot displays in almost all her work, the characteristics of which are self-consciously commented upon within the text.

At some point, indeed, Claude quotes Christine's reaction to a critic who dared define Angot's intentions and identity on the basis of her style. Claude's unmarked quotation of the critic's qualification of Angot's writing unexpectedly slides into his own jointly aesthetic and erotic appreciation of Christine's/Angot's body: "The sentence is, deliberately, halted, there is no narrative continuity. . . . she pursues her autobiographic undertaking. Everyday life is omnipresent, the 'refusal of narrative' claimed by Angot, [is] extremely effective. One must recommend *Les Autres* [a book published by Angot in 1997] for the virulence of Angot's prose and subject material. One of the things about you I find most beautiful, Subject Angot, are your breasts, which make your body beautiful" (84).

How then, between Christine's breasts and her style, between eros and ethos, and between Claude's and Angot's agency as narrators, can we hope to capture any of these discursive subjects' ethos? And how different are we, readers, from this abject ex and this poor ironized critic when we hunger for the author and seek to define and confine her ethos? Angot's writing grooms us into realizing how natural, how crucial, yet how tricky it is to read an ethos in a body, or in a text.

Whose Master's Voice and Ethos?

The idea that discourse expresses through its mode of saying the character of its speaker, which my little tale exposed as somewhat problematic, remains a fundamental assumption in French discourse analysis's approach to ethos, as well as in Meizoz's and others' perspectives on authorial posturing. Yet, as might be expected given their pragmatic orientation, discourse analysts prove well aware of the complexities of the "polyphony of enunciation" (Ducrot 1984, 193–94, 199; Maingueneau 2004, 205). Narratological distinctions are called in to sort out narrative levels and voices to which expressive discourse features might be attributed (see Meizoz 2009, for instance, where he imports the notion of implied author, together with the methodological problems it raises).

To establish the origin and the degree of endorsement of an utterance is indeed far from being a straightforward issue, whether in literature or in everyday utterances. Even in what looks like a most simple case, that of a speaker who speaks in his own name, in a nonfictional genre, Maingueneau (2004, 205) proposes to distinguish, in line with the linguist Oswald Ducrot, between the speaker as a "biographical subject"— the person belonging to the actual world, which Ducrot terms *locuteur-lambda* (say, Barack Obama, or Dave Eggers, as a real person)—and the "inscriptor" or "enunciator," staged in and characterized by discourse, which Ducrot names *locuteur-L* (this is the image of President Obama conveyed by his speech or that of Dave Eggers conveyed by the preface to *A Heartbreaking Work of Staggering Genius*; further distinctions regarding authors in their role as a text's origin are discussed in chapter 5).

This dissociation of speaker images, Ducrot notes, is especially operative when one speaks about oneself, as ethos effects attached to these different subject positions may be played out against each other. Thus, locuteur-L may discursively convey a sense of modesty or auto-irony yet by implication signal that, given one's excellence as locuteur-lambda (the actual person), locuteur-L's modesty may be a polite way to protect the feelings of one's audience. Such tensions, or possibly strategic orchestration of different self-presentations, should be heeded in analyses of ethos effects. These remarks also incite us to reconsider the idea, widespread in structuralist narratology, that in everyday communication speakers endorse their utterances, whereas in literary or fictional communication the work-as-utterance is severed from its origin.

There is another interesting implication of Ducrot's and discourse analysis' assumption that audiences will construct a discursive ethos even before and independently from attaching it to an individualized source. This idea seems fruitful for cases in which sentences produce subjectivity and ethos effects that cannot readily be attached to a source. These are what I call, somewhat paradoxically, *unadopted* subjectivity and ethos effects. Such effects are frequently exploited in experimental writing, but they can also result from anonymous graffiti on a wall. I will come back to these issues of enunciation and ethos effects when discussing characters and discourse in the novel in chapter 5.

Generic Scenes and Framings

Another contribution of French discourse analysis, which I perceive as particularly congenial given its attention to framing acts, is Maingueneau's distinction of three levels in our understanding of a text:

A discourse's global scene (*scène englobante*), which defines at the most basic level its pragmatic status as fiction or nonfiction, or as a literary, religious, philosophical, or any other global discourse type. These classifications determine in particular a text's expected rapport with reality. They also determine, I would like to add, the relevance of conjecturing about the author's ethos.[11] The label "fiction" conventionally—but only to some extent, I propose—makes the question of the author's ethos, for instance her endorsement of the expressed worldviews, less relevant than for a work labeled as nonfiction.

A discourse's generic scene (*scène générique*), which pertains to generic conventions. Since genres are perceived as differently ranked within particular cultural contexts, by choosing a particular genre, writers signal their alignment with specific expectations, unless they actively contest these; conversely, their choice of genre contributes to their own posturing. A generic scene (or framing, which is the phrase I will use myself) typically includes, I propose, expectations regarding the authorial or narratorial ethos. Thus, autobiography or historical fiction conventionally elicit expectations of commitment to factual truth.

A discourse's scenography or scenographies, which refer to the concrete communication situation(s) that are evoked. For instance, a narrative can be staged as confession, as a letter, as an apology, and so on, scenographies that raise particular ethos expectations. (Maingueneau 1999, 103–7, 204, chap. 17, 190–202)

These three terms plausibly suggest a succession of embeddings, with the "scène englobante" as the outer matryoshka, enfolding the "scène générique," which in turn frames the "scénographie." However, sometimes scenographies that are part of a fictional world (such as an autobiographic scenography or that of historical witnessing) can be so suggestive that they trump diverging indications of a global scene (for instance, that of literary fiction). Readers furthermore may feel cued for competing scenographies or lack the sensitivity for tacit global framings, just as they may conflate a narrator's voice and the author's. Literary texts often exploit tensions between levels and kinds of generic framing, eliciting uncertainties about which interpretive and evaluative regimes would apply.

In *Sujet Angot*, for instance, Claude's letter to Christine evokes a scenography that suggests intimacy and foregrounds their relationship as a relevant theme and sincerity and honesty as relevant ethos traits. But this letter is inserted in Angot's novel, whose generic scene remains unclear: should we read the book as the real Claude's authentic biography of Christine, as Angot's documentary use of his authentic material, as her fictionalized autobiography by proxy? Decisions about genre are intertwined with the decision about the global scene (is this fiction, or nonfiction?). The adopted framing determines to what extent whose ethos would be relevant (the characters', the narrator's, or author's?) and according to what expectations and norms we would construct and judge it, as we will see in chapter 6.

What about Literature?

In its analysis of ethos, French discourse analysis does not make a fundamental distinction between literary and other discourses. Mechanisms of ethos projections by speakers or authors and of ethos attributions by readers or audiences occur for all kinds of discourses: that of the scientist, the church minister, the politician, the mother admonishing her kids, or of Christine Angot, staging her avatars in a complex specular game. On the other hand, quite evidently, discourse analysts express a keen sense of the pragmatic and institutional conditions for ethos effects, attached to specific discourse types and genres, including literature. These pragmatic conditions, however, deserve further scrutiny, to which this book aims to contribute.

In this context, Maingueneau's reflections on the need for literary discourse to secure its legitimacy are of particular interest. Literature, he argues, traditionally belongs to a class of discourses that lack direct pragmatic grounding and so qualify as paratopy (Maingueneau 2004, 34–35). Unlike, for instance, a report, speech, or conversational narrative, literary narrative is not anchored in a concrete communication situation: one can pick up a novel or a poem anytime, in any place (although particular genres, such as eulogies, necrologies, or some fables and tales, find their legitimization from their precise social contexts). This speaks to literature's adaptivity but also to its precariousness. Literary texts usually require additional legitimization, which ethos effects as well as authorial posturing may contribute to secure.

While for Booth a rhetorical approach to literature was evidently sensible, given literature's acknowledged role in conveying worldviews, Maingueneau's approach belongs to an era in which literary writing no longer enjoys unchallenged prestige. Authors face an increased need to secure attention and authority. Why should we read Angot's or Eggers's novels, a comparatively demanding activity, rather than exchange our latest experiences through Facebook or follow a celebrity on her blog? "Experientiality," the core business of narrative, according to Monika Fludernik, no longer has narrative fiction as its privileged domain, invested with highest symbolic value. It is indeed highly instructive to look more closely at how writers insert in their works, prefaces, book covers, or interviews topoi that connect their writing—their own act, and the work—to culturally validated social functions. Literary criticism and educational systems relay such topoi, which are attached to particular postures. The writer as the archivist of that which society tries to obliterate, as the spokesman for those whose voices are suppressed (François

Bon), as the doctor or scientist who diagnoses the ills of his time (Balzac, Houellebecq) are some of these ethos insurance strategies.

To summarize, French discourse analysis fruitfully calls attention to processes of ethos construction and to the culturally validated or contested grounds for attaching authority and value to texts, textual voices, and authors. It also proposes a relatively fine-grained approach to the author function. Thus, it complements and challenges narratological frameworks for establishing the stance of "implied" authors, textual points of view, or the (un)reliability of narrative voices, as I will argue further in part 2.

This approach, however, also presents some methodological ambiguities, most of which I signaled on the way. First, the assumption of the indexicality of discourse with respect to its source, as we have seen, is both sensible and problematic, if only because the ethos conveyed by an utterance needs not be that of its technical speaker. This potential dissociation has been signaled by Maingueneau, among others, but deserves further elaboration, as it plays a decisive part in effects of irony, authentication, and authority, as I hope to show. There is an unavoidable circularity, or loop effect, in processes of induction and their subsequent confirmation or correction: it is indeed our constructions of the various subject positions, with their character and ethos, that in cases of ambiguity allow us to decide who is speaking, or that may trigger our suspicion that dual voice or irony are at stake. Conversely, such ethos attributions help define the contours of a character or narrator (more on this in chapters 5 and 7).

Second, it is not always clear whether the analysis aims to establish a speaker's or author's actual, unconscious, or strategically displayed ethos. Maingueneau does distinguish a "displayed ethos" (*ethos montré*), an explicitly expressed ethos (*ethos dit*, as in "I am speaking to you as a friend"), a prior ethos (*ethos prédiscursif*), and an effective ethos (*ethos effectif*, the one that the addressee actually constructs; Maingueneau 2004, 204–6). Yet these distinctions are not systematically heeded in his subsequent analyses.

Maingueneau's position on both the analyst's and the actual audience's interpretive work is almost prototypically ambiguous. He firmly defends the claim that discourse analysis belongs to the language of sciences and that its methods depend on scientific knowledge about language, in contrast to more evidently hermeneutic approaches. Yet he also expresses a clear awareness that there is no purely linguistic position here: ethos is always the result of an inference, in which the strategies and interpretive constraints of the interpreter play their role (see, e.g., Maingueneau 2008). Ethos, he stipulates, is not "a static and well-delimited representation, but rather a dynamic form, constructed by the addressee on the basis of the movement of a speaker's discourse" (Maingueneau 2004).[12] But this insight is not systematically integrated into the theoretical framework, nor reflected in its methodological consequences. I hope, however, to have made sufficiently clear the rich potential of this discourse-analytical notion of ethos, together with that of authorial posturing. Both notions, and the frameworks to which they belong, offer a hermeneutic heuristics for seeking out an author's textual and extratextual ethos; they also point to the relevance of the meta-hermeneutic analysis of divergent interpretations and ethos attributions, and of their underlying topoi.

Literature, Value Regimes, and Value Transfers

The previous section has defended a connection between acts of generic or discursive framing, ethos and posture clues, and ways of securing the relevance and value of discourses and of literature in particular. I would like now to come back to the issue of value assignment. Processes of value attribution, as I've already mentioned, play a central role in Bourdieu's sociology of literature, according to which the literary field functions according to a double logic: "the logic of the market (a work of literature is a commercial object among many others)," and that of art, which needs to deny the logic of the market and present "literary value [as] a symbolic, not a practical value" (Viala 2006, 81–82; Bourdieu 1996).

Within the literary field, this symbolic value has been defined with respect to two poles: the autonomous pole, in which aesthetic values are dominant, and the heteronomous one, in which political, commercial, or other nonaesthetic values prevail.[13] This rather rough binary remains fairly unchallenged in more recent work. Heinich, for instance, still insists that the opposition between art and money is the fundamental law governing the functioning of literature and art in society (Heinich 2000, 30). At least in France, many writers and critics express some uneasiness about the combination of the two. The same holds for success in the media, which—again, in France—often leads to a denial of artistic quality within the small circle of literary connoisseurs. Houellebecq would combine both vices: he earns too much and gets too much media attention, which together suffice, for many a critic firmly grounded in an autonomist artistic credo, to discredit both the work and its maker.

Rather than articulating any law, I take these oppositions to express normative conceptions of literature attached to specific social and cultural conditions, conceptions that are subject to change. Moreover, this bipolar conception of the literary field pays insufficient attention to how, in the actual evaluation of literature, conventionally aesthetic values interfere with values functioning in other domains of life. The complexity of value attributions seems more dynamically addressed in Boltanski and Thévenot's (1991) work on the role of value definitions in conflicts.

Boltanski and Thévenot closely examine the ways in which people in all kinds of conflict-solving processes set out to classify situations or actions under contest and to establish what value regimes or justifications are appropriate. Within contemporary French society, they distinguish roughly six domains, also called Cities or Worlds (I will maintain the latter term, and will use capitals to refer to such terminology). Each of these Worlds has its own value hierarchies on the basis of which actions and states of affairs are evaluated.

These six Worlds comprise the Inspired World, with the arts as prototype, in which creativity and originality, for instance, are leading values; the Domestic World, instanced by family life, which cherishes, for instance, respect for tradition, mutual love, and support; the World of Opinion, instanced by the media, with fame as a leading value; the Civic World, that of politics or of the juridical system, with responsibility, justice, or the common good as recognized values; the Industrial World, which encompasses all spheres of work, in which values such as efficiency, zeal, and technical skills are prominent; and finally, the World of Commerce, with rentability as a dominant value (Boltanski and Thévenot 1991, 201–60).

These Worlds do not correspond to actual social domains but to ways in which a particular artifact or behavior is discursively framed. If one speaks of running a university or an art school like a business, this classifies these institutions as belonging to the World of Commerce, activating a corresponding value regime, with efficiency and rentability as leading values. Quite a different framing results from calling universities creative laboratories, for instance, or from speaking of their management in terms of running a family. These modes of speaking place them, respectively, under the regimes of the combined Industrial and Inspired Worlds and of the Domestic, with quite different axiologies and justifications for courses of action.

In cases of conflict, Boltanski and Thévenot suggest, agreement is achieved through a rise in generality (*montée en généralité*). This means that participants reach out for an overarching value that might be recognized by the different parties involved. The proposed mechanism amounts to processes of generalization, which underlie value attributions more generally. For instance, Heinich points out how, in the case of literature, writers or their critics often translate claims of singularity, required to impress audiences with the author's originality and unique value, into values that can be generalized, if not universalized. Hence the appeal to topoi, such as expressing common human experience, the heroic sacrifice of personal life and of material success, or the suffering, solitude, or marginality to which a writer consents in the name of a higher goal (Heinich 2000, 130; Meizoz 2009).

Processes of value justification or negotiation also often involve what Boltanski and Thévenot call transfers of misery, or of greatness, from one World to another (Boltanski and Thévenot 1991, esp. 184). We will see further on how one critic, Jean-François Patricola, invokes Houellebecq's miserable personal history (he was abandoned by his mother, and so on) and transfers this misery from the Domestic World onto the author's literary work, supplanting the value regime that conventionally holds within the Inspired World.

From my own perspective, the interest of Boltanski and Thévenot's framework lies, in part, in its means of affording an understanding of debates about literature as the articulation of framing conflicts and uncertainties, which mostly relate, I propose, to uncertainties about a work's genre and its author's ethos. In what World should Angot's *Sujet Angot* or Dave Eggers's *A Heartbreaking Work of Staggering Genius* be categorized? According to what value regime should they be judged? Should we apply to Claude's portrait of Christine, and to Angot's book overall, Domestic values, the sort of everyday moral norms associated with how one deals with loved ones or ex's? Or should we categorize this work as fiction, as primarily belonging to the Inspired World, in which ambiguity and even the provocation of widespread moral norms may count as a value? The kind of analysis I have in mind does not, however, seek to put a work in one neatly definitive generic box nor to define the one World to which it rightfully belongs. Rather, it proposes, metahermeneutically, to reconstruct actual or potential categorizing acts of critics or other readers, virtual or actual, whose framing acts determine what value regime, and even what ethos expectations, are considered appropriate.

Richly stimulating, Boltanski and Thévenot's approach also raises many questions and reservations, due in part to the fuzziness of their terminology. Their notion of World is far from clear, as is its relation to that other spatial metaphor, Bourdieu's concept of field. The latter at least has the advantage of comprising field-related normative conceptions and institutions that can be, up to a point, empirically analyzed. The idea of distinct value regimes corresponding to different realms of social life, though heuristically interesting, also raises the methodological problem of how to access the suggested value hierarchies, if not on the basis of a rather fragile and very much ad hoc induction. Like Bourdieu's field model, Boltanski and Thévenot's approach on the one hand suggests general relevance; on the other hand, it is explicitly rooted in the French situation. But in contrast to Bourdieu's, which strived toward systematicity and rigor, Boltanski and Thévenot's models have a flavor of "bricolage." This is a deliberate effect, as, in their view, heavy epistemological claims are not warranted in a domain that consists of people's experiences and social processes of meaning and value attribution, to which there is no direct access.

The fruitfulness of Boltanski and Thévenot's approach for my metahermeneutic purposes lies in their calling attention to actual justification and negotiation strategies of authors, critics, and other agents who are discursively engaged in interpretations and evaluations of literature: what kind of value regimes are considered to be relevant, and what arguments are invoked for their classification and evaluation? The validity of such analytic "re-"constructions is not guaranteed by any objective proof but rests on the analyst's reasoning. Another advantage of Boltanski and Thévenot's model is that their work speaks to the fact that the literary field, and writers themselves, are exposed to heterogenous, often contradictory, values and norms, way into the field's supposedly autonomous core. I will in particular investigate the relevance of their model for interpreting controversial or hybrid works, which raise uncertainty regarding the World to which they belong and regarding which value regimes apply.

Finally, by detailing some of the framing acts through which we attribute meaning and value to literature, and by insisting on the struggle over such categorization acts, Boltanski and Thévenot bring a necessary complement and dynamic to narratology's or discourse analysis' models for analyzing posture and ethos, as I hope to show in part 2. But let me now first demonstrate the heuristic value of some of these concepts in a somewhat more lighthearted case study.

Frustratingly Unclassifiable: Houellebecq, a Case

Between 2002 and 2007 alone, some twelve book-length monographs on Houellebecq were published, mainly in France, Germany, and the Netherlands. In the following pages I would like to reconstruct how two critics, whom I take to represent exemplary positions in the Houellebecq reception, proceed to construct the value of his work in relation to his posture and ethos. To this end I have chosen Dominique Noguez's *Houellebecq, en fait* (The factual Houellebecq, 2003), and Jean-François Patricola's *Michel Houellebecq; ou, La provocation permanente* (Michel Houellebecq: The Ongoing Provocation, 2005).

Both Noguez and Patricola hold a position in the literary field as critics, writers, essayists, and editors, the first with more notoriety than the other. Noguez, a well-known writer and critic indeed, is a friend of Houellebecq's. He even acted as a witness when Houellebecq faced trial in September 2002, accused by Muslim organizations of inciting religious hatred and racism. Noguez's witty essay on the hypes created around "great writers" (the "Grantécrivain") did not prevent his own book from looking suspiciously like a hagiography, as Patricola sardonically notes. The latter, by contrast, intends his book as the démasqué of a literary and moral impostor. As we will see, both critics rely on conventional arguments, topoi, and writerly postures in their defense or demolition of the value of the writer and, *eo ipso*, his work. I will highlight in particular the ways in which Noguez and Patricola shift between value regimes, their implicit classification of the Worlds in which Houellebecq's work functions, and their transfers of greatness or misery between domains. Like most responses to Houellebecq's work, both essays show a striking tendency to focus on the person rather than on the work.

By way of background, a few details on Houellebecq's position in the literary field may be useful. His debut occurred in what Bourdieu calls the field of restricted production, through poetry published in small, specialized literary reviews, an essay on Lovecraft (1991), and a collection of essays, *Rester vivant* (1991), followed by a second collection, *Interventions* (1998). Success of a cult nature came with his first novel, *L'Extension du domaine de la lutte* (1994). This novel was refused by all of the larger publishing houses before being recommended by Noguez to the publisher and critic Maurice Nadeau, generally recognized as a discoverer of new talent. Nadeau's acceptance of the manuscript certainly contributed to the author's recognition in the literary field. *Particules élémentaires* (1998), published by Flammarion, was Houellebecq's national and international breakthrough.

Several factors contributed to this success, beginning with the work's provocative stance on sensitive issues, which included, as mentioned, the devastating impact on Western society of the May 1968 events, women's liberation, and sexual freedom, with cloning as a hardly less provocative solution. The attention of the trendy cultural magazine *Les Inrockuptibles* certainly helped to launch this unclassifiable author, precisely by adopting him as "one of theirs." In addition, the trials in which Houellebecq has been engaged contributed their scandal effects. In fact, with *Plateforme* (2001), public attention did not rise to the expected level until a stir caused by the author's statements in the media: the magazine *Lire* featured an interview in which he characterized Islam as the "plus con" of monotheist religions (Sénécal 2001). This prompted the French Human Rights League and the MRAP (the movement against racism and for friendship between peoples) to bring Houellebecq to court.[14] During the trial the attack on the Twin Towers occurred, justifying in the eyes of some the timely denunciation of Islamic fundamentalism that the novel was held to perform.

Since then, other works have followed, with *Possibilité d'une île* (2005) concluding the novelistic trilogy labeled "Au milieu du monde." *La Carte et le territoire* (2010; *The Map and the Territory*, 2012), the latest novel to date, epitomizes issues of ethos, as if the author wanted to confront—playfully, satirically, seriously, all three?—his critics with all their attempts to nail him down (Korthals Altes 2013).

Portrait of the Artist as "a Softy Who Punches" and a Prophet, Discovered by Noguez

Although at the outset of his book Noguez pledges allegiance to the autonomist credo that an author should be judged on the merits of his work, he justifies his extensive focus on the person Houellebecq by pointing out the ad hominem attacks to which both the author figure and the private person have been subjected. In order to shift the debate to the Inspired World, and establish the author's greatness in this realm, he first needs to construct him as a real writer.

In a classic move, Noguez first firmly roots Houellebecq in literary tradition. In just the first two and a half pages, Houellebecq is put on equal footing with some thirty highly literary authors, with many more to follow, an overdose that would blow over anyone contesting Houellebecq's status as a literary writer. The next move—and the next flourish of expertise that guarantees Noguez's own authority as a literary expert—is to demonstrate in over sixty pages of technical analysis the originality and literariness of Houellebecq's style, *pace* Houellebecq's adversaries, who reproached him for having none, a deadly sin in France. Besides establishing the author's singularity, Noguez grants him the ethos of a craftsman, through the topos of the *poeta faber*. (This topos is actually contradicted by Houellebecq himself in his essays, where he emphasizes writing as a vocation, not a métier, preferring apparently to be put in the box of romantic genius aesthetics). This demonstration allows Noguez to claim Houellebecq's literary expertise, hence his greatness in the Inspired World. The way is subsequently cleared for a comparable claim to be made about the author's role in the Civic World without endangering his literary quality.

Houellebecq's work is then indeed presented as a benefit for the community, fitting the familiar posture of the writer as public intellectual. Noguez combines for Houellebecq, somewhat syncretically, the postures of the prophet and misunderstood messenger of an unwelcome truth, the analyst-expert in possession of intellectual-scientific analytic tools, the guru whose wisdom plunges deep roots in mysterious grounds, the visionary guide of the people, and the engagé writer, prepared to pay with his person. Duly magnified are the corresponding ethos topoi of heroism and personal sacrifice.[15] French culture in its entirety is staged as subjected to censorship and political correctness (19, passim), against which the writer has the courage to stand up, taking personal risks. The carefully constructed ethos of personal honesty and heroism reinforces claims of expertise and vision (252).

Noguez's Houellebecq thus fully represents the authoritative posture of the writer-with-a-mission, a "great thinker" and "maître à penser" (59). This "sharp analyst of our times" (30) stands "in the midst of the world" (15), unlike so many others, who remain aloof in their ivory towers (Noguez herewith echoes the subtitle Houellebecq gave to his trilogy, "in the middle of the world"). Countering accusations of nihilism and antihumanism, Noguez casts Houellebecq's novels as "novels of ideas" (84), conveying a "messianic plea" for more love (220).

Houellebecq is even presented as most definitely a moralist, or rather a "new moralist," the newness lying in the lack of fixed beliefs (160). The fact that Houellebecq does not hesitate to change his opinions (as fast as his clothes, the French would say) may be grounds for reproach to Patricola and others, such as Houellebecq's former companions at the review *Perpendiculaire*. For Noguez, such ideological flexibility is a sure sign of a real thinker, which is certainly an intriguing thought. The line seems to be thin between what would appear as opportunistic opinion swapping according to norms of the Civic World and as interesting ambiguity from the perspective of the Inspired World.

One path for generalizing Houellebecq's singularity, and for amplifying in the Civic World his greatness in the Inspired World, is to present him as an ordinary person. For Noguez, precisely the fact that his personality seems "dead" and lacking a "sur-moi" (*Über-Ich*) makes Houellebecq the right medium to express without inhibition what everybody feels (the Elkerlyck topos). Moreover, it confirms his sacrifice of his personality on the altars of Art, Truth, and Universality (18; passim), which is, as Heinich points out, another topos connoting a particular writer posture.

There are two more problems that Noguez needs to neutralize, which he partly does by being fairly discreet about them. First, Houellebecq's involvement with media and genres (pop music, comics, shopping magazines, science fiction, erotic film), conventionally considered low-standard or clearly nonartistic genres, which might discredit both his prestige in the high-art world and his credibility as en engagé writer;[16]

and second, his commercial and media success, definitely killing in the Inspired World (that is, in France and for some leading critics, not necessarily for broader audiences).

Houellebecq's multimedia exploration, in turn, undergoes a generous positive generalization through the valorizing label of "transécrivain" (something like a boundary-crossing writer; 14). Noguez does not go into much detail regarding the aesthetic quality of Houellebecq's films or poetic and lyrical performances. Instead, he stages these as an almost exotic, adventurous, and timely undertaking: the old medium of literature is revitalized by taking it out of the ivory tower into the real world of today, reaching out to new and young audiences, and bridging the gap between underground and high culture. This is the posture of the new-style engagé writer. Yet a true classical writer Houellebecq remains.

Noguez's careful presentation of Houellebecq's own rapport with the media and with money is well tuned to the ethos of honesty and civic responsibility and to the canonical figure of the writer with a mission. A personal ethos of sobriety and generosity is suggested, which by implication undermines potential accusations of greed. Noguez moreover presents his friend as a perfectly authentic person, uninterested in publicity. There is nothing striking about Houellebecq, except precisely his lack of flashiness or of a "sound-bite" personality. On the contrary, this is a writer who resists the high-tempo and banalizing format of TV shows and interviews, imposing on them instead his own slowness and singularity, as if signaling the triumph of the individual over the mass media: "[H]ere is a man who has achieved an extraordinary degree of freedom regarding other people's opinions. . . . That's his strength. That's what makes him uncontrollable. What people won't forgive" (198–99).[17] Thus Houellebecq's popular and commercial success can be viewed as fully in harmony with the moral qualities of authenticity, honesty, and sincerity required for his status as engagé writer and, more broadly, with his authority as a public intellectual.

In support of Houellebecq's ethos of authenticity, Noguez adds ethos arguments from the Domestic World. He is a faithful friend, as Noguez can testify, a person without showy airs, trustworthy, of genuine goodness. These ethos grounds support his greatness in the Industrial (professional) and Inspired Worlds, established by autonomous literary arguments, as we have seen, as well as in the Civic World. Hence, Houellebecq is an authentic, sincere writer with a mission, a posture he is justified to adopt. He is ready for posterity as an artist, a writer. Justice should be done to this person's noble calling and socially important mission.

Portrait of the Artist as an Impostor: Patricola's Houellebecq

Jean-François Patricola, as his book's cover copy points out, is a writer, biographer, translator, and essayist whose works include an essay on Blanchot, the epitome of a conception of literature as high and impersonal art. He is also the founder of a literary review and publishing house, L'Estocade, and of the art publishing company Abécédaire. His book on Houellebecq was published at a publishing house whose name, Ecriture, suggests autonomist concerns. His monograph defends the thesis that Houellebecq's success is due to marketing and publicity strategies rather than autonomous selection mechanisms based on literary quality. (Patricola pinpoints with particular ferociousness Noguez's responsibility in the "creation" of Houellebecq as a literary phenomenon.) Houellebecq therefore belongs to the Worlds of Commerce and Opinion and not to the Inspired one, in which he would be exposed as an impostor. The book, significantly, opens with the media stir caused by the amount of money paid in advance in summer 2005 for an unpublished book by Houellebecq, which Patricola significantly compares to a soccer transfer, suggesting the appropriateness of classifying Houellebecq's work in the World of Commerce. Patricola's own rhetoric clearly aims at creating an alliance between him and his readers through witty chapter titles, catchy phrases, and an appeal to common (moral) sense through rhetorical questions and gnomic formulas.

Houellebecq's work, which, in an autonomist conception of art, one expects to provide the basis for a negotiation of his value as a writer, is dispatched in a few pages, as Patricola denies it the qualities required for greatness in the Inspired World. Instead, he frames Houellebecq's work in the Civic World, exposing it to real-life moral criteria. He concedes that Houellebecq's points about society's immorality are perhaps accurate (35). Yet he judges the work's ethos as nihilistic and depressing, partaking in the very immorality it depicts.[18] Substituting a Domestic value regime for an Inspired one, Patricola attributes Houellebecq's bleak worldview to his personal history (he suffered abandonment in his youth, and so on), disqualifying the work as an "objective" representation of society.

Besides shifting the interpretation and evaluation regimes from literary to nonartistic ones, Patricola sets out to deny both author and work any greatness in the Inspired World, tackling successively some of this World's core values. Houellebecq has no originality. He merely rewrites the opening of *L'Etranger* or uses the naturalist, "much exploited method" of Paul Bourget or the "trite" format of the *roman à these*. His writing verges on plagiarism (149, 182). His thematics belong not to the Inspired World but to those of Opinion and Commerce. (Apparently, for Patricola themes can either be aesthetically appropriate or not, not exactly autonomist *doxa*.) "Like all stars," Patricola adds, Houellebecq capitalizes on fashionable themes such as sex and violence and political incorrectness. Such work should get the audience the author deserves and addresses. With an undeniable talent for sound bites, Patricola casts Houellebecq as a "writer for schoolkids" (153) and for the in-crowd of *Inrockuptibles*, the "*Paris Match* of the underground" (37).

These systematic value denials are completed by the denial of craftsmanship: the author lacks basic narrative skills (170). According to Patricola, Houellebecq ignores the fundamental distinction between author, narrator, and characters, among other tokens of clumsiness. Ironically, most of Patricola's own argument demonstrates precisely that amalgamation.

As for Houellebecq's personal ethos, Patricola denies him loyalty (to his two earlier publishers, who made his success, as well as to former friends and colleagues), honesty (which he traded for commercial and media success), and authenticity (his autobiography is a carefully crafted imposture and a clever marketing strategy; 101, passim). His biographical misery is compared to that of Auguste Comte, to whom Houellebecq himself often refers. Comte ended up mad, a fate that may very well become Houellebecq's, Patricola foresees (162). Patricola projects all this domestic, moral, and psychological misery, with much glee and indignation (of course, I am the one to construct here the critic's ethos), onto the functioning of Houellebecq's writing in both the Civic and the Inspired Worlds.

The moral norm is writ large and offered for sharing as evident common sense: for Patricola, Houellebecq is a writer who lacks a high-standing personal, civic, and professional ethos and is not worthy of literary consecration. Even more, Patricola suggests, literature and society should be protected against this fraud and loser.

Patricola goes on to deny Houellebecq any claim to a canonical writerly posture. Exit the *poète maudit*, a mere posture Houellebecq "consciously mimics," with his Dark Romantic poses adopted before the camera, in the media (41, 67, 70), and in his "sulphurous" writing. An imposture even, as he infringes a fundamental literary "law," brought to awareness by a rhetorical question ("Which moral principle is infringed here?"; 22), before being nailed down: "[A]t posterity's gate, money and temporal glory are harmful" (26). This reads like a gnomic reformulation of Bourdieu's "reversed economy" thesis.

Greatness in the Worlds of Opinion and Commerce morally precludes greatness in the Inspired World, as suggested by the fact that, for truly literarily valuable Dark Romantic writers, from de Sade to Genet, consecration came posthumously. Patricola's list is much longer, as if to confound this impostor and his credulous believers, just like Noguez piled up ancestors to demonstrate Houellebecq's truly literary affiliation. Unlike Houellebecq, these real writers stood the test of financial misery and absence of recognition, as well as the test of time, classic ways to translate singularity into accepted, generalizable value.

Exit also the posture of the writer with a mission: the inconsistency of Houellebecq's ethos, both in his work and in his public pronouncements, morally disqualifies him for this role, Patricola argues, strategically downgrading both the object and the agents of the consecration. Teasing out, not unconvincingly, I must say, the mechanisms of value creation utilized by publishers, critics, other agents, and the author himself, Patricola aims to show to what extent even the inner circle of the literary field is at the service of opinion and of commercial values, squandering its autonomy (10). By blurring the conventional distinction between author, narrator, and characters, Patricola argues, Houellebecq himself called for a heteronomous reception, forcing the audience to focus on his person instead of his work and hence exposing his work and authorship to the Civic value regime rather than to that of the Inspired World, if I may paraphrase his argument in Boltanski and Thévenot's terms. In such a case, to adopt an autonomist attitude would make one a "hedonistic consumer," clearly a danger for civic society: "What does this posture mean, of a nihilistic writer who opts for euthanasia of the living?" (235). Framed as a Civic risk, this attitude justifies the critic's demand for moral and ideological clarity about the author's—and his narrator's and characters'—"posture . . . on the literary and political or social platforms" (25; see also 252–53).

Patricola unsurprisingly finds greatest fault with Houellebecq's rhetoric of ambiguity, which "throws back the reader on himself." This leads him to an exasperated, and unwittingly funny, outburst: "Where does Houellebecq position himself, with respect to humor?" (286). All this makes Houellebecq a false "author-with-a-message," since his message is not clear—or if it is, it is nihilistic—and his vagueness (*flou*) is no more than a strategy to be successful with as many audiences as possible (54, 144). These claims suggest that Patricola measures Houellebecq against the conventional posture of the engagé writer or ideologue, a figure associated with an unequivocal ethos of sincerity, expressed in a Sartrian, transparent form. Houellebecq's proliferation of postures and the resulting "slipperiness" of his ethos are not redeemed as aesthetic irony and ambiguity but instead condemned as plain dishonesty and framed as belonging to the Civic World. This normative stance coexists somewhat unhappily with the autonomist norm to which the critic himself could be expected to pledge allegiance, considering the positioning suggested by his own activities in the literary field (see the introduction to this section). His lengthy and very rhetorical justification of the legitimacy of his approach perhaps reflects this uneasiness.

In my cavalier paraphrase of both Patricola's and Noguez's (de-)constructions of Houellebecq's literary value, the triteness of the topoi may seem depressing. Let's not forget, though, how much conviction gets invested in such ethos negotiations in the heat of discussions about works or artists that really stir public opinion. At stake is not just the literary value of a particular writer's work but fundamental values and entire methods of interpreting and evaluating. My discussion should at least have brought to light how postures and ethos mutually reinforce each other and function as cognitive frames and mental models, which allow details to cohere and make sense.

As this example demonstrates, debates about controversial works offer rich material to investigate more precisely the cognitive strategies readers or critics develop in order to make sense of how they feel authors appeal to them, as well as the diversity of actual norms underlying readers' negotiation of values and meanings. Such debates, moreover, allow us to reconstruct how critics, writers, and other agents in the field aim to keep alive the frame borders, as Goffman would say; in this case, the rules of the game we play when we engage in literature.

Together with chapter 1's wide angle on narrative interpretations as a practice in which a culture transmits and adjusts not just worldviews but also modes of cognition, the framework provided in this chapter challenges narratology's take on ethos clues and attributions, a challenge that will be explored further in part 2.

PART 2   *Ethos in Narratology*

The Return of the Repressed

THE CONTROVERSY SURROUNDING FREY'S *A Million Little Pieces*, sparked by his passing off as factually correct and honest a memoir that rather creatively invented its truth, raises some central questions. What might the consequences be of framing a work as fiction, or rather as (to some extent) factual, and of experiencing our reading of such a novel as a communication with a fictional character, or rather with a narrator, or even an author? In what respect would our ethos attribution change? What made readers expect Frey to be authentic and truthful in his narration of his character's tribulations? Can and should narratology account for the role ethos attributions play in interpretation and evaluation of literary works and for the diversity and the patterns they demonstrate? These are among the issues that I aim to clarify in part 2 of this book, along with the question of how narratology might be enriched by the approaches presented in part 1. My discussion does not aim for exhaustive coverage of all that has been written on these subjects but picks out issues and perspectives that I take to be particularly valuable or critical given my focus.

To concentrate on ethos indeed brings out fundamental but contradictory presuppositions and aims in the heterogenous bulk of work that falls under the label of narratology. Chapter 3 discusses this striking lack of consensus within narratology, beginning with the question of whether issues of ethos are even relevant objects of study. Answers to this question usually demonstrate an allegiance not only to a particular conception of literature but also to a particular understanding of narratology's position between science and literary interpretation. Chapter 4 then addresses controversies on five concepts that are bound to play a central role in any attempt to define and analyze ethos attributions within narratology: literary narrative as communication, its layered or embedded character, intentionality, fictionality as framing, and the idea of reading strategies. Chapter 5 concentrates on the attribution of ethos to characters, narrators, or rather to authors: to what extent is such an orientation—on characters, or rather on narrators or even authors—relevant to the analysis of narrative interpretation? What frameworks does narratology, or do narratologies, have on offer to help theorize and analyze ethos clues? How can these frameworks be complemented with the institutional, historical, and other conventional framing factors explored in the first part of this book? Besides Frey's novel, I will engage with Alain Robbe-Grillet's *Djinn*, Philip Roth's *The Human Stain*, and Samuel Beckett's *Not I*, as well as some other literary examples, to illustrate and test the heuristic relevance of the framework.

3 Narratology between Hermeneutics and Cognitive Science

> *Hermeneutics is not . . . something one can do without (it is coextensive with all criticism), but merely something one can acknowledge or not.*
>
> JONATHAN CULLER, "Prolegomena to a Theory of Reading"

As has been amply observed, the current proliferation of narratologies did not exactly increase disciplinary consensus on terms and procedures. Concepts that involve ethos attribution, such as those of the implied author or the (un)reliability of narrators, play a central role in rhetorical, ethical, and other forms of critically engaged narratologies, yet there is not much agreement about even these core concepts. This should not come as a surprise, since such concepts bring into the open fundamental divergences of opinion and uncertainties about what narratology is or should be.[1] The appeal to cognitive sciences has not really solved this problem, it seems.

This chapter zooms in on narratology's history of hybridity, always oscillating between developing general models of narrative and proposing tools and justification paths for interpretations. These various aims can be set out on a model, which, I argue, ranges from ambitions of scientificity to that of serving interpretation, with, somewhere in between, what I call a metahermeneutic intent.

A History of Hybridity

Interpretation was, right from the start, narratology's bone of contention. Classical structuralist narratology, which aimed at being a "science of narrative" (Todorov 1969, 10) or at least a descriptive "poetics," evacuated the flesh-and-blood agents involved in literary narrative communication and the activity of interpretation itself. For narratologists such as Greimas, Genette, or Tzvetan Todorov, James Frey's intentions, for instance, would have been of no relevance in describing the meaning structures of *A Million Little Pieces*, since, as Gerald Prince sternly put it, "[n]arratology is not primarily the handmaiden of interpretation" (Prince 1995, 130); but note the "primarily." For some, the aim was rather, in line with the Russian Formalists, to contribute to a systematic and historical poetics, comprising the description of literary—or, broader, textual—devices and conventions. This interest was sometimes combined with attention to normative reading conventions, as in Culler's and Peter Rabinowitz's work, a perspective that I would define as metahermeneutic, as it seeks to understand and modelize the interplay between textual and interpretive conventions. In practice, structuralist as well as "poststructuralist" or postclassical narratology's relation to interpretation has remained ambiguous until this very day. The test of narratology's relevance is often taken to lie in proposing tools that are used, first, heuristically, to guide the analyst's textual analysis, and then to explain and justify the analyst's interpretations. On closer scrutiny, moreover, the ideal of objectivity in textual description and analysis is hard to maintain, as has been pointed out often enough.[2]

From structuralist to rhetorical and other forms of critical narratologies—feminist or postcolonial, for instance—the shift was decisive, though its epistemological consequences were not always acknowledged. In rhetorical approaches, attributions of an ethos to characters, narrators, and authors became central concerns, since their reliability, sincerity, authenticity, or irony constitute grounds for ethical judgment, as outlined in Phelan's 2007 book *Experiencing Fiction: Judgments, Progressions, and the Rhetorical Theory of Narrative*. Emphatically repersonalizing textual analysis and reinstating ethical concerns alongside or over aesthetic ones, these approaches adopt an unmistakably hermeneutic stance, in contrast to the metahermeneutic (Genette) or outright scientific (Greimas) aims of structuralist narratology. In rhetorical and "critical" narratologies, author, reader, and critic are held accountable for their acts of writing and interpreting. Interpretive acts are now described in terms of events, highlighting their singularity—which does not mean, however, that these acts of meaning assignment are not shareable. Quite the contrary: an important function of such criticism is to propose shareable pathways for reasoning, and to demonstrate these in a compelling mode in interpretive and analytical practice.

Let us consider, for instance, how Phelan discusses James Frey's case. By inventing major events while presenting his text as referential (a "memoir"), Phelan argues, Frey "violate[d] the ethics of referentiality." Phelan concludes that the work therefore loses "its reputation for being an honest confrontation of the difficulties of addiction and recovery and its status as a worthy aesthetic achievement. . . . [I]ts inventions made the book more embarrassing than compelling" (Phelan 2007, 216). Here the narratological-rhetorical model functions clearly in the service of criticism, used to analytically ground interpretation and judgment of the author's writing from both moral and aesthetic perspectives. Yet despite their evidently hermeneutic orientation, rhetorical or ethical narratologies are often still understood as theories of narrative, in the sense of a body of hypotheses that aims at general or clearly circumscribed validity. In fact, their aims and validation procedures are mainly of a (meta) hermeneutic kind, resting on appeals to folk psychology, morality, and cultural history, offered for sharing.

In the wake of the reader-oriented approaches that gained momentum in the early seventies and of the epistemological discussion raised by both structuralism and poststructuralism, some scholars turned the spotlight on interpretive activity itself. In a landmark volume edited by Susan Suleiman and Inge Karalus Crosman in 1980, *The Reader in the Text: Essays on Audience and Interpretation*, Culler, for instance, called for a reorientation of "poetics" from its Genettian focus on the typology of textual structures and literary devices to the "conditions of meaning" and "literary competence."[3] Rather than the production of "scientifically valid" interpretations, the diversity of interpretations itself became an object of study, as well as shared—or not shared—semiotic conventions (Culler 1980, 49–50). In a similar move, Stanley Fish (1980) famously proposed the notion of interpretive communities. For Fish, what are perceived as textual structures vary according to readers' interpretive habits, and it is these socially shaped interpretive habits that should be object of study. Culler's and Fish's metahermeneutic orientation opens up to research the whole sociohistorical domain of conventions and their markers, as well as of interpretive practices and the values they enact.

More recently, narratologists have taken their lead from cognitive, linguistic, and psychological research on processes of meaning making.[4] As in the heyday of structuralism, the cognitive turn seems to ally narratology with the aims, rules, and methods of scientific inquiry. Partly, hermeneutics disappears from the stage, dispatched for instance as "a myriad of contradictory theories," which have left us "with much confusion and no consensus as to the nature of the text, the reader, and the reading experience" (Bortolussi and Dixon 2003, 8).[5] Partly, hermeneutic insights are respectfully, or simply without much ado, integrated into what seems to count as more "rigorous theory," as when Fludernik (1996) builds on Ricoeur's notions of Mimesis I, II, and III.

Drawing, as we saw in chapter 1, on frame theory, Theory of Mind, and linguistic pragmatics and aiming, like structural narratology, for general validity, approaches along cognitive lines propose hypotheses for reconstructing and explaining the process of meaning making. Such frameworks usually underline the role of context, of readers' own norms and values, and of the frames and cognitive operations involved in the readers' mental activity. But the reconstruction of how, in general, people make meaning of the textual "object" often gives way to an unreflected recourse to the analyst's own inferences and, ultimately, his or her interpretations of a particular text, presented as generally valid (exceptions include, among others, Herman 1999, 2002; Herman et al. 2010; Jannidis 2004; Patron 2011).[6]

The challenge of addressing the diversity of processing *and* interpretation strategies has indeed been picked up by, among others, David Herman in the pragmatic-cognitive approach he proposes under the acronym of CAPA. This model encompasses "[c]ontexts for interpretation (including contexts afforded by knowledge about narrative genres, an author's previous works, or Frey-like confessions); storytelling Actions performed within those contexts, and resulting in texts that function as blueprints for world making; Persons who perform acts of telling as well as acts of interpretation; and defeasible Ascriptions of communicative and other intentions to performers of narrative acts—given the contexts in which the persons at issue perform those acts and the structure that their resulting narratives take on" (Herman et al. 2012, 227–29).

Herman's more flexible approach refrains from typologies of the kind developed by classical narratology and from the functionalism that often seems presupposed (of the kind: "this device produces that effect"). As a general model, and given Herman's own discursive ethos, the CAPA model aims at being part of a cognitive science of narrative and of its interpretation, rather than confining itself to the more basic stages of meaning making. One might, however, also argue that the CAPA model is metahermeneutic. Indeed, the model theorizes the various ways in which people may process different kinds of texts and set out to interpret them; it registers the factors that, theoretically, can play a role in people's acts of meaning ascription and interpretation. As soon as the model is used to make sense of a particular text or to reconstruct how other readers, including narratologists, proceed to interpret a concrete narrative, it arguably turns into, respectively, a hermeneutic or metahermeneutic heuristic.

Yet Another Mapping

As this rapid overview suggests, the explosion of developments within narratology might be mapped according to the role of interpretation, moving from "hard" theorizing to the interpretation of individual works. Along this spectrum exist fundamental—but often unacknowledged—differences of aim, point, method, and validation.[7] Very roughly, such a scale would encompass the following orientations:

1. A *theory* of narrative, coupled to a theory of meaning making, covering the whole range from simple decoding to complex interpretation. This theory addresses questions such as: How do people make and share meaning through narrative? What cognitive structures and procedures characterize narrative as a tool for thinking and the various narrative genres that circulate in a culture? What kind of interpretive pathways do specific groups of readers follow ("interpretive communities")? To what extent are such structures dependent on media and genre? Or, regarding ethos: How do people discern ethos clues, and what role do ethos attributions play in various kinds of interactions? Here *theory* refers to a systematic body of hypotheses specifying the conditions under which they are valid and under which they might be eliminated as inaccurate. An example of work along this line is Amy Coplan's (2004) discussion of empathic engagement with nar-

rative fiction, in which she seeks to balance often-made claims of narrative theorists against empirical evidence. Such a theory might help *explain* individual cases of meaning making and interpretive differences and analyze cognitive and social processes involved in interpretation. Methods derived from theory, however, do not yield scientifically valid analyses or interpretations of individual works, as this is not their aim, though their insights might feed into heuristics for (meta)hermeneutic approaches.

2. A *metahermeneutic narratology*, analyzing from a metacritical perspective conventions by which people make and interpret literary narratives or through which they attribute an ethos to narrators or authors (this expands on what Genette and Culler termed *poetics*). Normative or prototypical conceptions of narrative and interpretation, or of literary conventions, with their historical and culture-specific dimensions, are part of this model's object. Metahermeneutic validation proceeds via reasoning and does not itself include empirical testing through the methods of social science, for instance, though it is perfectly compatible with it. A good recent illustration is *The Implied Author: Concept and Controversy* (Kindt and Müller 2006), which teases out the presuppositions, procedures, aims, and claims of approaches employing the notion of the implied author.[8] By its own reasoning procedures, metahermeneutic narratology still belongs to hermeneutic in a general sense. Its divergence from actual text interpretation lies in its higher degree of generality and distancing: it can certainly concentrate on one particular text, but the focus then lies on reconstructing interpretive processes and conventions.

3. *Hermeneutic programs*, such as critical ethical, feminist, or rhetorical narratologies, in which the adjective—ethical, feminist, and so on—defines the relevance frame, which in turn determines what textual elements become signifying in the first place and how they are taken to signify (as expressing an author's stance; or as author-independent clues for world making, for instance). The substantive—narratology—determines the allegiance to a particular understanding of narrative and to text-bound argumentation. Such programs stipulate what and how one should analyze and interpret, on grounds established outside the theory itself, such as

an emancipatory sociopolitical agenda or insights from psychoanalysis, ethics, cognitive sciences, and the like, which shed new light on literature. Such programs typically include all kinds of norms: about what kinds of discursive subjects should be inferred (personalized voices, or rather "implied authors"; sociolects; or anonymous discursive vectors of subjectivity) or norms about what literature, selves, or morality should be and do. Hermeneutic programs also defend particular interpretive methods rooted in these normative conceptions, advocating, for instance, the neat hierarchizing of minds or voices in an attempt to determine the author's views and constructing coherence, or instead teasing out the warring forces, as in deconstructive hermeneutics. Such a program also holds criteria and procedures for determining validity. These usually encompass argumentation and rhetorical seduction in various mixtures, as well as an implicit or explicit appeal to values and presuppositions shared by the interpretive community they address and help constitute, among other ways through the use of catchwords such as *subversion, aura, agency, dialogue, spectral, embodiment, ethos.*

4. *Narratological hermeneutic practices*, finally, can be traced back to such explicit or implicit hermeneutic programs. Narratological concepts and procedures then may function first as a heuristic, second as a justification vocabulary, and perhaps occasionally, as an authority effect. At minimum, recourse to narratology expresses allegiance to a form of close reading, hence attention to textual form and argumentation. This makes such practices themselves most interesting for a metahermeneutic perspective, as they demonstrate ways in which we interpret narratives.

Narratologists mostly do not opt for one of these orientations exclusively but combine them. In her or his analysis of a particular work, a scholar might indeed want to test, or to use heuristically, the model she or he devised. For instance, Phelan's rhetorical narratology, as developed throughout his publications, shuttles between all these conceptions of narratology or narrative theory. With all its metahermeneutic relevance, as I see it, the ultimate goal of his "theory of aesthetics," in which his rhetorical narratology is inscribed, is to share a hermeneutic program.

Confusion about the aims of his approach explains what I take to be an exemplary misjudgment about Phelan's approach's claims to generalization in Michael Eskin's overall quite positive review of Phelan's *Living to Tell about It: A Rhetoric and Ethics of Character Narration*, published in 2007. Eskin remarks that "the [normative] psychological core of Phelan's narrative ethics makes it vulnerable—in the state of its present conceptualization and application—to criticism for the dearth of empirical evidence necessary for the vindication of its claims" (Eskin 2007, 803).

In my view, it is indeed only "insofar as Phelan endeavors to lay out a *general theory* of engaging with narrative" that the normativity of his approach is a problem (Eskin 2007, 803; my emphasis). For Eskin, there seems to be no middle path: either one's approach is fully generalizable, something close to the nomothetic stance of the hard sciences, or it remains *merely subjective* reading, as its theoretical assumptions cannot but be "tentative, not to say unreliable, as far as their general validity is concerned." The pursued rationality and generalization, I think, are of a more hybrid kind: Phelan's approach certainly aims to examine general characteristics of narrative rhetoric. His hypotheses could be reformulated in such a way that they could be tested empirically and hence, if necessary, amended. But he does not strive for such testing. His approach needs not meet the criteria of a general theory of narrative. Instead, his program is hermeneutic, to the extent that he offers a method of reading that corresponds to the kind of values he, and his solicited community of readers, attribute(s) to literature and to criticism. It is also metahermeneutic, to the extent that Phelan makes his own readers aware of how they might (not) want to interpret.

Like Booth in his time, Phelan is crystal-clear about the presuppositions of this hermeneutic program and about the steps to follow when one analyzes and evaluates a particular work. The relevance of his approach cannot be separated from the scholar's agenda and values, which in this case combine aesthetic and ethical concerns. The critical test to which this approach should be submitted lies in the discussion of arguments and presuppositions.

The hermeneutic character of much that goes on in narratology is not in itself a weakness, as often gets suggested in times dominated by a reductive model of knowledge and science. Quite the contrary, I believe, as long as there are no misunderstandings about the kind of systematicity and the kind of knowledge that are produced. Greater awareness of the value- and presupposition-laden nature of concepts and methods, and of the primordial significance of argumentation in interpretation, arguably increases epistemological lucidity. This awareness should encourage research on differences in conceptions of literature, of criticism, of selves, of language, and so on, and on the sociocognitive functions of this diversity. Far from embracing total subjectivity, such metahermeneutics articulates shared grounds for commonality *and* disagreement. There is no reason to dismiss interpretive processes or their analysis because of their unavoidable *relativity*: metahermeneutic reflection precisely *relates* interpretive argumentations to their underlying value-laden conceptions and pathways.

Narratology's hermeneutic orientation also draws full attention to the semantic potential of textual form, subjecting it to shared attention, as Boyd also suggested (see chapter 1). It thus practices itself the attention to particulars that constitutes a central element both of the art experience and of ethical reflection. In light of the theories of narrative and interpretation in culture proposed in part 1, narratology thus can contribute, both as a heuristic and as analysis of interpretation modes, to keep alive and sharp cultural practices of interpretation and metacognitive reflection on values in worldviews, on the expressivity of narrative form, and on the more complex meaning-making procedures involved in the engagement with narrative art.

4 Key Concepts Revised

Narrative and Communication, Embeddedness, Intentionality, Fictionality, and Reading Strategies

> *[I]s narratology a tool, a method, a program, a theory, or is it indeed a discipline?*
>
> JAN CHRISTOPH MEISTER, "Narratology," in *The Living Handbook of Narratology*

Should the debunkers of Frey's "fraud" have done their narratological homework better? Would any of the current branches of narratology, each of which claims to analyze how we make meaning from narrative texts, have helped explain the bewilderment that for some readers, like Oprah, followed from Frey's exposure? Perhaps, to the extent that narratologies offer heuristic procedures and concepts to tease out stances conveyed in narratives. Not really, or not yet, because narratology, though concentrating on textual features, insufficiently takes into account the conventions through which these features are invested with narrative functionality and meaning.

The following chapter tries to sort out some issues that, like interpretation, seem as fundamental to narratology as they are controversial: literary narrative and communication, the embeddedness of narrative voices, intentionality, fictionality as a form of framing, and reading strategies. One's stance on these issues determines how one speaks about the ethos of characters, narrators, and authors.

Literature as Communication

A focus on ethos, with respect to narrative, inscribes itself in a rhetorical perspective on literature, which considers literature as a form of communication. In line with linguists such as Sperber and Wilson, I will assume in a rather minimalistic way that literature belongs to "ostensive-inferential communication"; this is the process whereby "the communicator produces a stimulus which makes it mutually manifest to communicator and audience that the communicator intends, by means of this stimulus, to make manifest, or more manifest, . . . informative intention, and communicative intention" (Sperber and Wilson 1995, quoted in Walsh 2007, 24).[1] This assumption carries with it the idea of a communication contract, a concept nicely captured also by Doležel when he describes a text as a "set of instructions [submitted by author to reader] according to which a fictional world is to be recovered and assembled" (Doležel 1988, 489). Genre indications arguably form a crucial element of such instructions, determining the kind of communication contract in which the reader feels engaged. Such assembly instructions, however, can be unclear or deceptive, creating for the reader a categorization problem, which triggers the search for clues as to the author's ethos and intentions.

On the idea of literature as communication, as well as on the questions of who is involved in communicating and which aspects of this communication should be objects of theorizing and in which disciplines, communities of scholars have been split. The grounds for this division lie in different understandings of the notion of communication, as well as in competing normative conceptions of literature and of narratology. The various models and metaphors that define literary (non)communication bespeak their allegiance to such value-laden conceptions. Literary writing, indeed, has been variously defined, not just by writers and critics but also in different narratologies, as a dialogue with an actual, personalized, implied, anonymous, or collective author; as not involving communication at all; as a rather spectral communication, with both author and reader declared dead or absent, dispossessed of themselves, or disseminated; or as a mere "echo chamber" in which heterogeneous sociolects resonate. Such different understandings have consequences for whether, and how, one would construct an ethos for the author of a narrative.

Despite their different signatures, (neo)structuralists such as Genette, Todorov, Seymour Chatman, or Schmid, speech act theory and rhetoric-oriented scholars such as Booth, Phelan, Pratt, Susan Lanser, or Michael Kearns, and cognitive narratologists such as Herman or Palmer all assume that literary narrative is appropriately treated as communication.

There are, however, important differences in what is meant by communication and who is considered to communicate.

For Genette, whose stance has been influential, whatever their importance in actual literary communication, the real author and reader do not belong to literary narratology's concerns. Neither do the author's ethos-fashioning or a reader's interpretive acts, since narratology concentrates on *intra*textual communication.[2]

Instead, rhetorical, ethical, feminist, and other critical narratologies usually defend a more inclusive communication process, the "triangle" of author, text, and reader (Phelan 2005, 18). Their author is mostly the "implied" version, and connections to the biographical or public author are hardly explored, while their reader is mainly the scholar him- or herself, who makes the text speak (more on the implied author in chapter 5). In these approaches, the ethos and intentions of (implied) authors are primordial concerns, at least as much as those of narrators or characters, including issues such as their sincerity, authenticity, irony, or reliability.

In contrast, pragmatic and cognitive communication approaches emphasize that narratology should include real authors who engage in communication with real readers. Meanwhile, their analyses tend to remain on the brink of analyzing more concretely how (real) authors or readers would come in.

In another camp, literature is definitely not viewed as communication, least of all between author and reader. One argument for this position lies in the commonsensical idea that, evidently, there is no author present whose intentions and meanings a reader could check. A stronger argument holds that in literature the basic speech act would be not communication but invention (Hamburger 1968; Banfield 1982; Walsh 2007; Nielsen 2011; Patron 2009, 2011). Furthermore, communication models oriented from sender to receiver, such as Jakobson's or Genette's, would wrongly suggest that reading is a matter of the reader passively receiving a predetermined message. Communication models might also foster reductive reading strategies, in which (implied) authors, narrators, and characters are responded to as if they were real persons. Though reassuringly mirroring the reader's perception of him- or herself as an autonomous and whole subject, such an understanding would be particularly inadequate as a response to more experimental narratives, which often aim to shatter such illusions of coherence and autonomy. Some of the sharpest critiques of the communication model target the idea that it is the narrator who communicates through telling or reporting. Instead, it is argued, it is the author who invents and narrates, which may include inventing a personalized narrator figure (Walsh 2007; Patron 2011; Nielsen 2011).

The noncommunication conception of literature has also been justified by referring to texts that problematize or block meaning making processes, as in what recently have been called unnatural narratives (Richardson 2006; Alber et al. 2010).[3] Experimental deviations from conventions of narrative communication, however, do not necessarily mean that it has become irrelevant for one's interpretation to conjecture about authorial or narratorial communicative intentions and about ethos effects in narrative transmission. Precisely in cases of interpretive difficulties about communicative intentions, hypotheses about an author's ethos may be expected to serve as a decisive orientation and backing. It is likely, for instance, that for many readers Samuel Beckett's posture, inferred from pictures of his ascetic, witty face or from what is known about his dedication to writing, reinforces an authorial ethos that promises a profitable reading or viewing of his works, despite their initial strangeness. Writers' vitae, like those of saints, are effective ethos and posturing devices, commanding authority and qualifying the kind of authority involved. Even Mallarmé, whose work is the epitome of an autonomous, noncommunicative conception of literature, carefully cultivated and effectively communicated a posture of self-effacement and modesty that contributed to increase the value of his works, which then transferred back to their author (Bakken 2011). Models of (literary) narrative, as communication or rather noncommunication, that hold sway in narratology thus appear imbued with normative conceptions of literature. It may be expected that if one describes literature in terms of dialogue or communication, one would theorize to some extent a personalized implied or real author figure, by whom one feels addressed and for whose ethos one has particular expectations. Alternately, an approach rooted in conceptions of literature as *fictio*, or as intertextual echoing, is likely to be much less personalizing or even antipersonalizing, though the author may be reinstated as the agent responsible for the orchestration of the echoes. From a hermeneutic, or metahermeneutic, reconstruction, these various ways of framing the literary experience become themselves objects of investigation, in their connections to interpretation modes and evaluation regimes and to ethos attributions.

Ethos Attributions and the Embeddedness of Voices and Minds

Whatever their stance on the inclusion of the real author and reader, narratologists have sought to create models conceptualizing the multiplicity of levels involved in literary communication and the hierarchical relations among them (e.g., Genette 1988; Chatman 1978). Such models usually involve the by now established distinction between extradiegetic narrators, that is, narrators who are not contained in another narrator's tale, and (intra)diegetic ones, who are contained in another narrator's telling. In Genette's canonical formulation, "[t]he narrating instance of a first narrative [*récit premier*] is therefore extradiegetic by definition, as the narrating instance of a second (metadiegetic) narrative [*récit second*] is diegetic by definition, etc." (Genette 1988, 84). This distinction was complemented by an ontological one, between hetero- or homodiegetic narration: in the former case, the narrator does not belong to the world she or he narrates; in the latter, she or he does.

Beyond their typological aim, at stake in these distinctions is usually the attempt to anchor, in formally describable textual features, potentially epistemological, ontological, and rhetorical or ideological effects. These effects include, prominently, the distribution of truth, the establishment of what counts as real within the fictive world, and the exploitation of the hierarchy of narrative levels for persuasive, if not ideological, aims.

The distinction of narrative levels is certainly significant for the analysis of ethos attributions in narrative. Among other distinctions, readers' negotiation of the potential effects of embedding appears to be of decisive importance for how they would "calculate" the play of perspectives in their engagement with a narrative. Their focus also determines whose ethos one would be tempted to reconstruct and consider most relevant.

The Genettian model of nested or embedded narrative communication, however, like others inspired by it, is in several senses problematic, as has been pointed out often enough. As mentioned, the model starts by excluding the real author and real reader, a strange move, as any facet of a narrative requires a real reader in order to come to life. The model's symmetry, likewise, is confusing, as once again it is the interpreter who constructs all the positions located in the model, to which there is no independent analytic access. Rather, it is on the basis of the mental models of possibly relevant subject positions, which function in a way like a "prior ethos" for characters, narrators, and authors, that readers are able to detect voices, a fortiori, as effects of dual voice or discursive irony, as I shall argue in chapter 7.

Beyond this, the distribution of authority among narrative voices, as perceived by readers, does not necessarily follow the formal hierarchy of levels. A character whose perspective is, according to Genette's model, overarched by a narrator's may be presented with ethos clues, such as good sense, goodwill, virtue, or other qualities, that make that character stand out as *the* subject position to which readers should relate and whose views they should find compelling. From *Le Grand Meaulnes* to *The Human Stain* or Balzac's series of works featuring the charismatic scoundrel Vautrin, numerous are the novels in which heterodiegetic or homodiegetic narrators and their authors transmit to readers their fascination for a character, whose rhetorical power is guaranteed by the narrator's own—often explicitly thematized or discursively performed—affect.

The ways in which readers negotiate the interplay of narrative voices and perspectives, and how they connect these to the views, intentions, and ethos they attribute to the author, are something that empirical research on different kinds of readers should help establish. Until then, a well-argued (meta)hermeneutic reconstruction is, I believe, the most we can achieve.

Narratologists also tend to adopt essentializing positions on the degree to which heterodiegetic versus homodiegetic narrators can and should be omniscient, authoritative, and reliable. Conventions regarding the authority of narrators or characters, however, may change. Heterodiegetic narrators in nineteenth-century realist and naturalist novels often grounded their authority in impartial analysis: a logos-based ethos, steeped in scientific rationality, which was held in high esteem in the surrounding culture. Currently, the pathos-based firsthand experience of a homodiegetic narrator is often considered more authoritative, and even more truthful in the end, as it acknowledges the partiality of one's vision.

Models of narrative embedding, moreover, might pay more attention to the narrative distribution of authority and knowledge. This authority is not by definition attached to particular forms of narrative transmission, though it draws on historically evolved conventions and ethos topoi. Such conventions, and various degrees of familiarity with them, explain why readers may trust omniscient narrators who drop heavy hints regarding their expertise and analytic capacities or may feel prompted to become resisting readers in the face of such authority implications; why readers trust a first-person narrator, whose scars or stammering seem to testify to the truth of his tale; or why they are allergic to such all-too-obvious authenticity claims.

What makes embeddedness interesting for the analysis of ethos attributions is, furthermore, the idea that a literary narrative is a conjunction of separate ontologies: a story world with its own laws, the world in which the story is purportedly told by a narrator, and the world of the extra-textual author (for a thorough analysis of the relation and interplay between such ontologies, see Patron 2009). As Didier Coste and John Pier note, "It is not by coincidence that Genette's study of paratext—the 'undecided zone' between the interior and the exterior of the text occupied by prefaces, epigraphs, notes, interviews, etc. which constitutes a space of transaction between author and reader—is titled *Seuils* (thresholds), the very term employed to describe the transitions between narrative levels" (2011, para. 18). Metalepses infringe the boundaries between these ontological levels. They also play a decisive role in processes of ethos attribution, as they operate as frame switches, requiring readers to suspend an immersive reading, concentrated on the story world, in favor of the "fiction-effect" (*effet-fiction*; Calle-Gruber 1989).[4] Instead of being engrossed in imagining the minds of characters and their reciprocal ethos computations, the reader's attention is reoriented to another communicative circuit, the one connecting the narrator/author-reader, and to other interpretive and evaluative regimes. I will come back to this idea in the section of this chapter on fictionality and in later chapters.

To figure out subjectively tinged perspectives on states of affairs, and perspectives on these perspectives, is as crucial in our reading of literary narrative as it is in any real-life interaction. In this respect, despite their problematic aspects, narratological models of embedded communication are indispensable for their heuristic potential. They allow more precise discussion among interpreters, helping clarify, say, the fact that one interpreter takes the "I" in Frey's *A Million Little Pieces* as evidently the real author, while for another this is at most an avatar of the author, functioning within a fictional framing. Narrative communication models, however, would have to be complemented with the roles of author and reader. Phelan's author-text-reader "triangle" should perhaps be tilted, as the narrative communication situation is necessarily the interpreter's construction. (This idea will be substantiated in chapters 6 and 7, with respect to genre and irony). Understood as a more flexible heuristics, narrative models of embedding could prompt questions about how readers construct the rapport between the narrative voices and perspectives they infer or about the processes of narrative mediation and the play of perspectives these foster.[5]

Authorial Intention

The ethos we construct for characters, narrators, or authors qualifies the intentions we attribute to them. Intention is another issue on which narratologists have fiercely disagreed: should narratology be concerned with intentions at all, and if so, whose intentions would that be?[6] Establishing the author's intention has been considered the primary task of many hermeneutic approaches. Structuralist narratologists instead dismissed it from their concerns, as for them, authorial intention stood for undesirable interpretation and speculation anyway.

Anti-intentionalism spread its dogma with astonishing ease in the early years of structuralism, encouraged, from another angle, by William Wimsatt and Monroe Beardsley's (1946) denunciation of the "intentional fallacy." This condemnation persisted, on the tide of a hybrid combination of factors, such as autonomist conceptions of literature and, in structuralism, the desire for a neatly defined, almost palpable object that could be subjected to scientific scrutiny: the work. In the wake of deconstruction, intentionalism remained suspect. It seemed to postulate the author as a conscious, autonomous, and stable originator of the text and smacked of the desire to control meaning. Anti-intentionalism, in turn, seems of late to have fallen into decline, as the recrudescence of rhetorical, ethical, and critical narratologies and the current return of the author demonstrate. The foregoing little narrative, which casts intentionalism or anti-intentionalism in terms of rises and declines, should by itself have made clear the normativity underlying such theoretical perspectives.

Another controversial issue is the question of who is doing the intending. Eco (1990) summarized the options, distinguishing between *inten-*

tio auctoris (which is primordial, in the view of E. D. Hirsch), *intentio operis* (arguably, Wimsatt and Beardsley's position), and *intentio lectoris*. In an extreme form, the latter corresponds to Barthes's idea of *texte scriptible*; a more moderate form perceives the text itself as intentional but considers that it is the reader/interpreter who does the intention attributing, in backwards reasoning.

For some scholars it is the actual intention of the real author that the critic should aim to reconstruct (actual intentionalism; Hirsch 1967). For others, authorial intentions remain the reader's hypothesis (hypothetical intentionalism; on the respective claims, see Iseminger 1996). Still others defend a moderate intentionalism, which navigates between giving textual clues, authors, and readers their due (see, e.g., Levinson 1996; Spoerhase 2007; Herman 2008).

A narratology that proposes a method for analyzing what was labeled the implied author, or narratorial unreliability, cannot but adopt, tacitly or explicitly, one of these conceptions of intentionalism. Alternatively, taking up a metainterpretive stance, narratology could analyze how different conceptions of literature result in granting different roles to intention and ethos attributions.

In my view, narratology can safely embrace the minimalist idea that to write or read literature implies, for readers and authors, the assumption that one engages in meaningful action, presupposing a global intentionality. This assumption predisposes readers to adopt an overall constructive interpretive and evaluative attitude. In other disciplines, such as linguistics or communication studies, as well, many scholars have adopted a similar assumption, which, according to Michael Kearns, qualifies as one of literary fiction's "Ur-conventions" (Kearns 1999).[7]

Such a general intention attribution includes what has been nicely called "the principle of charity."[8] Readers will do their best to make sense of narratives with strange gaps in information transmission (whole murders eluded), implausible narrators (horses, unborn babies, needles), ontological inconsistencies (houses that can expand or shrink, in narratives that strongly cue a realist reading), apparently pointless stories (about individuals without qualities, engaged in nonactivities), and ethos incongruities (sincere ironies, ironic sincerity).[9] Intention or ethos attributions are, anyway, forms of reasoning backwards, reconstructions of reasons a subject may have had, given the kind of result we have.[10]

In the case of literature, there are some additional qualifiers for that global intentionality. As Stein Haugom Olsen notes, "[O]ne gives the work the particular type of attention literary interpretation represents because one assumes that the author has honored his commitment" (Olsen 1987, 51). Specific expectations regarding intentionality attach to particular discourse types and genres. Without knowledge of such categorical intentions, which determine how we frame (in Goffman's sense) the practices we engage in, "one is powerless even to begin to sort out [the text's] meanings by casting about for readings that could most reasonably be attributed to its contextually situated marker" (Levinson 1996, 176–77, 188–89).

To such overall intentionality attributions belong conjectures about the ethos of a maker, however hazy and little personalized the interpreter's idea about such a maker may be. I do not start reading Beckett's *Not I* without expecting to be in for a worthwhile read, which I believe to have been the author's sincere communicative intention, expectations I do not have when I leaf through the telephone book in search of a number. This is not the same as conjecturing about the exact meaning intentions Beckett may have had in writing his work. The same applies for anonymous texts or those that evolved over a long span of time, with unidentified, collective, or multiple successive authors.

Some episodes in the Gilgamesh epic, for instance, made me perceive a switch in generic tone and discursive ethos. To give but one example: the description of Gilgamesh's ghastly journey in the underworld, after the death of his beloved Enkidu, appears to me to call for the audience's empathy with the bereaved king, as the text zooms in on Gilgamesh's distress. But in a late episode the tone seems quite different: Gilgamesh, who has been so desperate for immortality, at last obtains the plant that should grant him eternal life. Relieved and relaxed, he jumps in the water for a refreshing swim, and a snake is quick to steal the plant. From the scene's intimacy and its expedient, matter of fact, telling—an anticlimax to the long building up of this journey to immortality—the reader I am infers a much more jocular ethos. But it is risky, clearly, to make statements about narratorial or authorial ethos for textual fragments that one accesses in translation and for which one has so little background knowledge. Even more importantly, our current access to the Gilgamesh material in edited editions stimulates our drive to read *a text*, to which we attribute narrative and generic coherence, and a particular communicative intention, whereas what we read are retrieved fragments, some of which belong together, others don't. This story material circulated over centuries and huge areas, and was adapted to all kinds of genres, tones and functions. Moreover, ethos topoi, including stylistic ones, are very much culture-bound. So let this be a reader's rather than a scholar's reflection (for a more detailed narratological analysis of this epic, see Korthals Altes 2007).

Framing a work as literary by intention exposes it to particular expectations and interpretive and evaluative procedures. In Western cultures this may comprise, by convention, intensified attention to form, so that any aspect of form, especially perceived deviances, may become signifying. If Frey, for instance, is taken to have intended his work as nonfiction, this generic framing elicits a mode of processing and evaluating in which personal, authenticated experience becomes salient. The activated cognitive frames are those of "real-life experience," including referential truth. Judgment about whether the narrative is well or badly written comes later, although this may still be an important criterion for selecting nonfiction for publication. In current times, to be "well written" would probably mean, for this particular genre, to be written "grippingly," that is, with pathos, rather than referring to stylistic innovation. If instead one ascribes to Frey the intention of writing a literary memoir, emphasis may fall on the work's imaginative, compositional, and/or stylistic qualities, or also on the work's power to evoke generalizable human experience. Readers will search for ethos clues that confirm the authority required for tone of these kinds of writing, sparked off by intention and genre attribution. Conversely, ethos clues can trigger hypotheses about intention and genre.

Maingueneau's distinction, discussed in chapter 2, between scenography, generic scene, and global scene also is useful here. Frey's *A Million Little Pieces*, some would argue, deceives with respect to categorical intentions of documentary-autobiographic writing. This framing intention is suggested not only on the level of the narrative's scenography (a former addict and criminal telling his own life story), but also through the work's paratextual generic framing (memoir), which conventionally is held to express the author's intentions. In order to make up for the turmoil created by the presumed generic "contract breaches," Frey later had to multiply statements that seemed to "merely" specify the initial authorial intention but in fact very much looked like a strategic generic reframing of the work.

Literary works often make their readers do some cognitive gymnastics by setting out ambiguous or contradictory framing clues concerning ethos and intention attributions. Yet, with Carlos Spoerhase, one may ask where, for various groups of readers, lie the "thresholds for deciding to invest cognitive effort" or to bring it to an end (Spoerhase 2007, 416, 109). Further research on such thresholds seems particularly relevant for readers' tolerance of ethos and genre ambiguities, as attested in the cases of enfants terribles such as Houellebecq and Angot or artists such as Serrano; or, for that matter, the case of the Danish performer-writer-artist Claus Beck-Nielsen, who managed to stage his own death, get erased from official registers, and be buried according to church rituals (Iversen 2011). Such writers and artists have in common the fact that their persona and works challenge conventional categorizations, raising questions about their ethos and intentions: Serious or playful performance? Serious or mock social commitment? Critics can be particularly nervous about the risks entailed in such categorizations of ethos, tone, and genre, which bring into play their expert judgment and position them as members of an intelligent interpretive community, much like the segregating positioning effects produced by irony.

Another question is, of course, whether recuperation through aesthetic charity, implied in the reader's interpretive attitude, operates as an immunization strategy, making it impossible to speak of a work's flaws. This, again, is a point at which interpreters may be expected to have recourse to an author's ethos. Together with generic framing, this attributed ethos determines expectations regarding artistic-technical perfection or moral deficiencies, or how likely it is that perceived deviances were aesthetically or ethically intended. Such ethos attributions are often decisive arguments in the evaluation of works that risk being classified as kitsch or shocking.

Once again, Houellebecq is a good example. Some critics inferred from his presumed lack of literary style the weakness of his aesthetic intentions: He would merely echo and even plagiarize existing discourses, mixing them in a commercially effective cocktail. The author was actually accused of lazy plagiarizing of whole chunks of Wikipedia in his most recent novel, *La Carte et le territoire* (2010; *The Map and the Territory*, 2012).[11] At the risk of too much charity, I credit Houellebecq's work with an artistic intention, taking the author's manner of quoting sociolects rather as "playgiarizing," to borrow Raymond Federman's felicitous *mot-valise* (Federman 1976).

So in the broad sense discussed in this section, intention and ethos attributions are part of any reading of literature and of any communication. They belong to our classification of the kind of practice we're engaging with. But depending on the reading strategy—and the kind of narratology—one adopts, the intentions and ethos of the author may become explicitly acknowledged and highly relevant, or not.

Literary Narrative, Ethos, and Fictionality

Fictionality is another controversial issue regarding which the stance one takes affects how one theorizes ethos attributions. At stake are usually the distinction of fiction (its relation to truth and reference, its mode of assertion) and its markers, the functions of fiction, and the relation of fictionality to literariness.

In debates about fiction, and about literary narrative fiction in particular, two main positions can be roughly distinguished, as pointed out by David Gorman: a semanticist one and a pragmatist one, which need not be conceived as exclusive to one another (Gorman 2005, 164). Semanticist theories, whether philosophical, linguistic, or literary, look for something distinctive in fictional discourse itself. This might consist of the ontological status of fictional beings and fictional sentences, that is, their lack of denotation. The semanticist position includes possible worlds theory (Doležel 2010; Pavel 1986; Ryan 1991). Pragmatists instead focus on the "production and reception of fiction," including "the intentions and conventions involved, and the social role that fiction plays" (Gorman 2005, 164–65).

Rather than focusing on philosophical issues of truth and reference, I am concerned from a pragmatic perspective with the issue of fictionality as an overarching framing (in Goffman's sense). What does it entail to frame a text or a practice as fiction or nonfiction? What happens when, alongside and in competition with the fiction frame, alternative framings seem called for? Together with more specific generic framings and, of course, readers' reading strategies, classifying a work as fiction determines to a great extent which interpretive and evaluative regimes are considered adequate, what kind of communication contract would apply, what weight a reader assigns to authorial ethos, and which kinds of ethos constructions are likely. Conversely, hypotheses about an author's ethos may suggest a classification in terms of fiction/nonfiction. Most of the following observations on classifying texts as fiction are assumed to hold as well for generic framing, to which, given its importance, I devote a separate chapter in part 3.

Among the research expressing a marked interest for pragmatic considerations, Jean-Marie Schaeffer's is particularly interesting. Building on John Searle's idea of pretended illocution and adopting a broad cognitive perspective, Schaeffer (1999; 2010 for the English translation) proposes to consider fiction, as did Aristotle, as an inherently human capacity, through which we learn about the world and seek to understand it. In a discussion interview on the Internet forum *Vox Poetica*, Schaeffer notes, "Mimetic learning, far from being a secondary or marginal phenomenon, constitutes in fact one of the four canonic learning modes, alongside the cultural transmission of explicit knowledge, individual learning by trial and error, and rational calculus." It is through mimetic immersion in play, for instance, that children incorporate "exemplifying models. . . . Once assimilated in the form of . . . mimemes, these imitation units can be reactivated any time" (Schaeffer 2010, 120; see also Boyd 2009, discussed in chapter 1).

Fiction, Schaeffer observes, is found not just in literature or film but indeed also in children's games, in daydreaming, in planning, in forming scientific hypotheses, and so on. Like children's play, literary fiction belongs to what he calls *shared ludic pretense*. Unlike deception and lies, ludic pretense is self-consciously fictional. It operates under an implicit contract, acknowledged by all communication participants (Goffman's and Bateson's notion of framing resonates here).[12] Fiction results "from a decision, even a communicational pact, with respect to the usage one decides to make of certain representations, in this case, a usage that consists in bracketing the question of their denotational force" (Schaeffer 2002; see also Schaeffer 1999, 212).[13] The issue, then, is not "to know whether these representations do or do not have a referential scope, but to adopt an intentional stance in which the issue of referentiality does not count" (Schaeffer 2002; note the parallel with Walsh, below).

Narrative fiction combines three mimetic mechanisms, according to Schaeffer: shared ludic pretense, mimetic immersion, and mimetic/analogic modelization. Schaeffer's notion of mimesis thus is not restricted to the idea that fiction imitates reality but includes imitative representation of our modes of representation of reality (Schaeffer 2002, 2010). To the objects of mimesis, in fiction, belong the mental processes and patterns through which we perceive and make sense of events, situations, or characters, besides these events or actions themselves. For instance, Houellebecq's *Atomised* does not just re-create a historically adequate late twentieth-century France. It engages readers with the ways in which various characters, including the narrating voice(s), perceive their/this reality in quite idiosyncratic ways: Bruno, in terms of sexual opportunities; Michel, in terms of scientific description, which makes him feel a stranger in daily social life.

With the imitation of cognitive processes, ludic fiction builds on, extends, and challenges more or less widely shared "socio-constructive" modes of representation. Fiction proposes models for perception and cognition, and develops what the Austrian writer Robert Musil so aptly named "*Möglichkeitssinn*" (a sense of potentiality; Musil 1978, 16). It seems likely to assume that it is precisely because of fiction's mimetic and inventive capacity that society submits it to strict, though often tacit, regulation.

This broader understanding of fictional mimesis should allow us to leave behind the somewhat problematic distinction, defended in recent years, between natural and unnatural narratologies, by jettisoning the narrow conceptions of mimesis on which they build. I will come back to this issue in the following chapter, when discussing the mimetic dimensions of fictional character.

In Schaeffer's view, then, fiction is a "framing [*dispositif*] which the author and the audience (or participants) will recognize as such, rather than . . . a property of a text/film/game" (Schaeffer 2002).[14] It follows from this viewpoint that for Schaeffer there are no necessary and sufficient textual signals of fiction (cf. Cohn 1999; Zipfel 2001). Instead, what stands out is the importance of mastering communication codes, so that one is capable of categorizing and reading kinds of sociocultural situations.

Precisely because signals of fictionality are as fragile as they are determinative, Schaeffer emphasizes the social need and ethical responsibility for keeping alive the often-tacit rules of communication contracts. This especially holds in the case of literary fiction and very much concerns the attribution of an ethos to writers, narrators, or characters. "It is rather easy to masquerade a deceptive story as a true story," Schaeffer observes, but "every time an author makes it impossible for a reader to recognize this boundary, he commits a moral crime" (Schaeffer 2010). This is quite a statement, one made, however, in the midst of an interview in which the moral dimensions of literary hoaxes were at stake. While I fully share Schaeffer's pragmatic understanding of fiction as a contract with social and moral dimensions, I don't think we should want less ambiguity in literature. In line with Schaeffer's own argument, I'd say that what deserves to be developed, rather, is readers' hermeneutic capacity, which includes the capacity to argue for their interpretations, as well as their ability to discern *playing with frames* from deceptive cuing. Schaeffer's moral norm for paratextual framing would probably seem evident to many of Frey's readers and likewise to many rhetorical or ethical narratologists. Yet one can imagine good grounds for arguing the aesthetic *and* ethical appropriateness of uncertainties about framing intentions, as a device that precisely makes literature a cognitive—and ethical—challenge.

Nielsen (2011, 90), for instance, argues that Frey's book wasn't presented exactly as nonfiction, since the genre memoir, under which it was presented, arguably allows different readings: If we read it "as *fiction*, we will read with the assumption that the author has created a world that we should trust." If instead we read it as nonfiction, it does "make sense to say that the author is lying or exaggerating and to compare the described events and world to the real events and world. In fact, any reading that regards the book solely as fiction or solely as nonfiction will miss something," either "some of its most essential messages about addiction and how to overcome it" or "some of the premises [of fictionality] that are clear and visible in the narrative itself." Nielsen's comment, with which I wholeheartedly agree, illustrates the assumption that framing a work as fiction or nonfiction programs a particular interpretive and evaluative regime. In my view, though, the investigation can be extended to more specific genre expectations, as well as to framing habits belonging to reading strategies, as I hope to demonstrate in part 3.

Independently from Schaeffer, whose work has been translated into English only recently, Richard Walsh defends a rather similar pragmatist position, with a somewhat more polemical tone. He rejects definitions of fiction built on the suspension of truth and referentiality, which consider fiction to deviate from the norms of language use, and reverses their main proposition: "[F]iction is no longer seen as narrative with certain rules (of reference) in abeyance. Rather, nonfictional narrative is seen as narrative under certain supplementary constraints (connoting historicity, objectivity, etc.) that serve to establish a rhetoric of veracity." For Walsh, as for Schaeffer, fictionality is "neither a boundary between worlds, nor . . . a frame dissociating the author from the discourse, but . . . a contextual assumption by the reader, prompted by the manifest information that the authorial discourse is offered as fiction" (2007, 39).

Classifying a text as fiction or nonfiction is not "a matter of empirical taxonomy," Walsh (2007, 40) furthermore declares, nor does it entail a particular kind of reference or relation to truth. The distinction of fiction, rather, is rhetorical. Fictionality, Walsh writes, in terms that I fully endorse, "determines the terms in which [a text] solicits interpretation" (7). Classification of a text as fiction sends the reader on a search for relevance, rather than for referentiality and truth. Or, in Walsh' gnomic formula, "Relevance supersedes truthfulness in communication" (26; Walsh borrows, as I do, this notion of relevance from Sperber and Wilson 1995). This "assumption of relevance, which is there even before an audience starts making sense of a narrative, sets off the audience's search for how to 'maximize' that relevance by seeking out possible contexts in which an utterance would receive a satisfying meaning" (Sperber and Wilson 1995, 142, quoted in Walsh 2007, 26).

For Walsh, as for Schaeffer, conventional textual signals are not sufficient to mark a text as fiction, nor are they necessary, unlike contextual and paratextual clues (Walsh 2007, 44–45). I find myself questioning, however, Walsh's observation that "the concrete evidence" provided by a narrative's frame of presentation or paratext, which designates it as fiction, makes this categorization "independent of such uncertain or inscrutable contingencies as authorial intention or reader response" (45).

Half a page later he adds with more caution, "[I]f the text is to function as fiction, there must be some frame that situates it as such, beyond any fictional paratext or behind any deceptive paratext (*for some readership, if not for all*)" (46; my emphasis). Yet he does not pursue the latter issue.

The idea that fiction is textually marked, with signals that can be to some extent objectively described, as is assumed in Dorrit Cohn's work on the distinction of fiction, needs to be qualified. Although some textual elements may be obvious as fiction markers, they are, quite obviously, conventions that are effective in a particular culture; such signals require particular contextualizations, in order even to turn into signs. Many of the examples in this book provide framing signals that, by convention, are perfectly clear (Bon's work's documentary character; Frey's or Angot's autobiographic framing clues). But the extent to which these framing clues are correct, or perhaps misleading, or just playful pretense, needs to be decided by the reader, who will have to negotiate his or her information about the author and his or her experience with the genre as well as textual clues, in order to decide. The "rhetoric of veracity" so rightly called for by Walsh demands (meta)hermeneutics as its complement.

Walsh's notion of relevance, moreover, appears somewhat too general to fulfill its task. The assumption that relevance trumps truthfulness, for instance, holds for many kinds of communication, such as political speech or polite "face-saving" in conversation. To consider such cases as a form of fictionalizing hardly captures the more significant point, which lies, I believe, in grasping the kinds of norms involved in a particular framing of a situation.

Cases of hybrids and frauds are in this respect particularly interesting. Indeed, what if paratextual and intratextual signals are contradictory, underdetermined, or deceptive and the communication contract is not clear, or erroneous? I fully agree with Walsh (2007, 36) that "hybrids like nonfiction novels in no way compromise the specificity of [fiction's] rhetorical regime," which resides in that demand for relevance rather than truth. But this does not help us understand why readers, including professional ones, often react so strongly to mixed or deceptive cues. Apparently, truthfulness for some (groups of) readers does constitute relevance, as in the case of Frey's *A Million Little Pieces*.

For Walsh, "[t]he distinction between mutually exclusive communicative intentions [the fictive and the assertive] and the relativity of informative intentions, can accommodate the range of borderline cases that vex definitions of fiction: historical novel, roman à clef, fictionalized memoir, historiographic metafiction, hoax" (2007, 36). For me, the point of hybrid or uncertain cases is precisely that the puzzlement they elicit reveals mostly implicit conflicting norms underlying communication contracts, which centrally include expectations regarding the authorial ethos.

Such expectations and contracts are more tenacious than is assumed by critics who claim that postmodern literature has done away with generic boundaries. They are also more fragile and multifaceted than many theories of fiction, including Walsh's, seem to recognize. Cases of works that are taken to convey racist and other socially dangerous attitudes immediately question the limits of literature's autonomy. In Boltanski and Thévenot's terms, they raise questions about what "World" they should be classified in, the Inspired one or the Civic, or perhaps the Domestic. Intriguing transfers of ethos may also result from morally or ideologically disturbing information about an author that may arise after the publication of his literary work. Such information works as what I call a "posterior ethos," which may affect retrospectively how one would frame his or her work (see, in chapter 5 Chatman's quite contrary statement about the irrelevance of Céline's political positioning).

A pragmatic approach might analyze how, in such borderline cases, audiences are cued for competing ways of establishing relevance, as I aim to show for generic hybrids in chapter 6. It is not, I believe, the task of a metahermeneutic narratology, nor that of narrative theory, to help us solve framing dilemmas, as this brings into play our own ethical and aesthetic norms and interpretive habits. Narratology can, however, help analyze such dilemmas and the ways in which they get resolved.

One last and important point, related to the previous one, is that of the accountability of authors of narrative fiction, which Walsh, in contrast to Schaeffer, does not extensively confront. Yet accountability is perfectly compatible with Walsh's rhetorical pragmatic perspective and with his elimination of the authorial, hetero- and intradiegetic narrator in favor of the author (more on this in the next chapter). As we have seen, theories of fiction tend to emphasize, among other rules of the literary or ludic fiction games, the suspension of truth and reference. Literary fiction often implies, by convention, that "a speaker [in this case, the author] can no longer be held responsible . . . , thus is not accountable for the possible falsehood of what he or she says" (Gorman 2005, 164). This holds not just for falsehood but also for the potential damage to real people, that is, the moral reprehensibility or controversial nature of assertions attributed to a character or a narrator or, in cases such as Frey's, the moral discomfort of readers who, given its authenticity suggestion, used his book as an encouragement to overcome their own addiction.

However, rough-and-ready distinctions of fiction in terms of "as if" or nonserious assertions or of authors' nonaccountability do not sufficiently take into account readers' complex negotiations of the text's connection to factuality and expectations regarding the author's ethos and accountability, as court cases from Flaubert's or Baudelaire's to more recent public trials such as Frey's demonstrate. The autonomy and impunity of the aesthetic are fragile achievements, which moreover are far from being accepted by all social groups. Moreover, the chorus claiming primacy for morality in art becomes louder and louder, not just in the Anglo-American countries, in which it has always been rather strong. It is one of the tasks of metahermeneutics to investigate such negotiations of the function, legitimacy, and status accorded to literary fiction in a particular culture.

Hence, with all its uncertainties, the classification of a text as fiction and regarding genre plays a decisive framing role for readers' interpretations and evaluations. Such a classification partly determines whether assessing an author's ethos is at all relevant. Explicit textual and paratextual signposting does not suffice for unambiguous categorizing, as such signals may be conflicting, indeterminate, or ironically mentioned. Reading strategies, in turn, affect which clues are selected and how they are weighted.

The blurring of generic and fact/fiction boundaries that would characterize postmodern writing paradoxically demonstrates the importance of such classifications as cognitive frames involving conventional expectations about kinds of relevance, authorial ethos, and interpretive and evaluative regimes (more on this in chapter 6).

Ethos, the Reader, and Reading Strategies

Two issues will stand central in this section: what reader do I have in mind, and what is understood by reading strategy? Regarding the reader, I'll be brief. I do not claim to know, predict, or set out to test how different kinds of actual readers react to a particular work and construct an ethos for narrators or authors. I do, however, propose hypotheses about patterns in reading strategies. My assumptions and hypotheses spring from various sources, besides self-reflection: exchanges with students and reading groups, the analysis of reception documents (i.e., articles or books about authors and their works, by professional academic and journalistic critics), and phenomenological, cognitive, and social science research on reading, though my forays in these domains remain limited.

As regards the notion of reading strategy, I am aware of its problematic associations with voluntarism and consciousness. Notions such as habit or disposition might have been more adequate, yet I retained the notion of strategy, in homage to the mind's inventiveness whenever confronted with disconcerting information. In my view, reading strategies build on normative conceptions of literature and hermeneutic programs and form scripts or methods for seeking out the kind of relevance expected from the reading experience. But perhaps we can achieve more precision and go beyond mere individual differences in understanding what reading strategies entail.

Structuralist narratology did not devote much attention to actual readers, nor did it do much to systematize readers' interpretive approaches. Meanwhile, it practiced an autonomist interpretation itself, in which the text (to some extent) was severed from its context and its author and considered as a tightly knit structure (with Roman Jakobson and Claude Levi-Strauss's analysis of Baudelaire's "Les Chats" as classic example). Engagé narratologies are typically more explicit in defending their particular mode of reading, well aware of their axiological underpinnings. Examples are Judith Fetterley's resisting reading, Hillis Miller's or Barbara Johnson's deconstructive reading, and Phelan's, Lanser's, or Kearns's rhetorical reading.

From the rhetorical angle, more reflection has been proposed on reading. Rabinowitz's (1998) oft-quoted distinction between authorial and narrative audiences, meant to refine the notion of the implied reader, seems indeed important and could be extrapolated to actual readers' strategies. Some readers obediently follow the text's rhetoric, attributed to a narrator, where others seek to join what they construct as the author in his or her rhetoric.[15]

Another fruitful line of approach resides in Phelan's model for analyzing fictional characters: he distinguishes between their mimetic, thematic, and synthetic functions, a model that occasionally seems to describe, rather, reading strategies (and rightly so, in my view), as when Phelan observes that there is an "impulse of readers to preserve the mimetic" (Phelan 2005, 4). This distinction will be discussed more amply in the following chapter, as it captures a switch in the prisms through which literary narratives are read and interpreted.

Several other perspectives seem relevant for analyzing the connection between reading strategy and ethos attribution. In the first place is research on conceptions of literature (see chapter 2) and, more generally, the awareness of historical-cultural factors that influence our "horizon of expectation" and explain the reception history of works. Expanding on Hans Robert Jauss's "aesthetics of reception," Iser's phenomenology of reading drew attention to the normative frames and the repertoires of standardized knowledge, norms, and beliefs that underlie reading acts (Iser 1974, 1978). These perspectives suggest the fruitfulness of sociological, historical, and psychological research into conventional reading paths. They also draw attention to interpretive diversity. In actual practice, as has often been noted, Iser tended to foreground his own reading.

Stanley Fish (1980), by contrast, addressed head-on the diversity of interpretations, through the notion of interpretive communities, characterized in part by their reading strategies. While this notion was criticized as imprecise, as well as for suggesting more homogeneity within an interpretive community than warranted, it is widely used and works as a shorthand reminder of interpretive diversity.

Sociological and psychological research, in turn, has sought to tease out, through empirical testing, factors that would determine differences and patterns in audiences' receptions of literary works (see, for instance, Andringa and Schreier 2003). A frequently made distinction is that between, roughly, two reading strategies, which work as macro-framing acts, involving not just a particular way of making meaning but also a relevance frame and a value regime. The one is a mimetic-realist, psychologizing reading strategy, which foregrounds characters and interprets these as if they were real people. The other is the aesthetic strategy, sensitive to the work as *fictio*, to the semantic potential of its form, and to the complexities and ambiguities of meaning. Along similar lines, S. J. Schmidt opposed readings according to the *factual convention* (*Tatsachenkonvention*) with readings based on the *aesthetic convention* (*Polyvalenzkonvention*), in which reading literature means being on the lookout for ambiguous and multiple meanings (Schmidt 1991, 89–92; this distinction often resurfaces, e.g., in Schneider's 2001 analysis of ways of constructing fictional character).

Differences in reading strategies have been explained by the kind and degree of general education, reading experience, and resulting competence, which would distinguish expert from nonexpert readers. These factors would determine in particular the decisive capacity for dealing with complexity, for instance with the multiplicity or ambiguity of frames (Schmidt 1991).[16] Such an explanation may have to be nuanced, however, as differences in interpretive strategies and in tolerance for ambiguity or complexity also seem to connect to character disposition, which cuts right through the literary competence distinction (see Tsur 2006 on the cognitive style of literary critics, which one might extend to narratologists themselves). It seems plausible to expect a strong interrelation between the tolerance for and appreciation of complexity, ambiguity, and the role granted to a personalized author figure and corresponding ethos attributions. But clearly such a hypothesis also needs empirical testing. In this book I will use the notion of reading strategy as shorthand for the hypothesis that readers, expert or nonexpert, adopt conventional paths, or scripts, for making meaning of literary texts and interpreting them.

All in all, I hope to have clarified in this chapter some advantages of a metahermeneutic narratology, which investigates conventions that intervene in meaning-making processes. Such conventions affect not just what kind of reading experience one is in for, and so the kind of relevance one takes a literary work to have, but also one's expectations regarding ethos. The following chapter explores in more detail such expectations, conventionally attached to characters, narrators, and authors.

5 Whose Ethos?

*Characters, Narrators, Authors, and
Unadopted Discourse*

> *What critics talk about when they talk about literature is the problem
> of authorship . . . this uncanny, undecidable author.*
>
> ANDREW BENNETT, *The Author*

Dance for me.

They've been together for about six months, and so one night he
says, Come on, dance for me, and in the bedroom he puts on a CD,
the Artie Shaw arrangement for *The Man I Love* with Roy Eldridge
playing trumpet. Dance for me, he says, loosening the arms that
are tight around her and pointing toward the floor at the foot of the
bed. And so, undismayed, she gets up from where she'd been smell-
ing that smell, the smell that is Coleman unclothed, that smell of
sun-baked skin . . . and, with him keeping an eagle eye on her, his
green gaze unwavering through the dark fringe of his long lashes,
not at all like a depleted old man ready to faint but like somebody
pressed up against a window-pane, she does it, not coquettishly, not
like Steena did in 1948. . . . He says, Come on, dance for me, and,
with her easy laugh, she says, Why not? I'm generous that way, and
she starts moving, smoothing her skin as though it's a rumpled
dress, . . . What's the big deal? Plunge in. Pour fourth. If this is what
he wants, abduct the man, ensnare him. Wouldn't be the first one.

She's aware when it starts happening: that thing, that connection. She moves, from the floor that is now her stage at the foot of
the bed she moves, alluringly tousled and a little greasy from the
hours before, . . . scarred in half a dozen places, . . . another bruise,

blue-black at the turn of her unmuscled thigh, spots where she's been bitten and stung. . . . She moves, and now he's seeing her, seeing this elongated body rhythmically moving, this slender body that is so much stronger than it looks . . . and he's seeing her, every particle, he's seeing her and she knows that he's seeing her. . . . She knows he wants her to claims something. He wants me to stand here and move, she thinks, and to claim what is mine. Which is? Him. Him. He's offering me him. Okey-dokey, this is high-voltage stuff but here we go. And so, giving him her downturned look with the subtlety in it, she moves, she moves, moving like this to that music and the formal transfer of power begins. And it's very nice for her, knowing that at her slightest command, he would crawl out of that bed to lick her feet. . . .

But now I'm naked in a room with a man . . . and it's calm and he's calm. . . . I can do that for him. . . . He says, dance for me, and I think, Why not? Why not, except that it's going to make him think that I'm going to go along and pretend with him that this is something else. . . . You know what? I see you, Coleman.

Then she says it aloud. "You know what? I see you."

"Do you?" he says. "Then now the hell begins."

. . ."What is it, Coleman? What does matter?"

"This," he says.

"That's my boy," she replies. Now you're learning. (Roth 2000, 226–34)

The scene I so extensively quote is a fragment from Philip Roth's *The Human Stain*. When I read these pages, my imagination moves in and out of the consciousness of two lovers responding to each other. The woman who dances is Faunia, a janitor at the college and Coleman's much younger mistress. She's a somewhat strange, independent woman, bruised by life. The man who lies in bed, watching, is Coleman, former faculty dean and classics professor. He's a man in his seventies who lost his job, his wife, and his status, in a doubly ironic plot twist. This master of words lost everything for one imprudent phrasing, for saying something understood to be derogatory toward blacks. Yet this "Jewish" professor is actually a light-skinned black American who managed to enter the Navy as a white man and ever since has passed for white.

In fact, the two of them are three. The third in the game is the character-narrator Nathan Zuckerman, familiar to Roth's readers as the author's misanthropic alter ego, a writer living far from the big city. It was Nathan to whom Coleman turned, as a scribe of sorts, when fate came crashing in on him and of whom he demanded that his story should be written in accusation of those who so narrow-mindedly had pronounced judgment over him. Nathan complied with this demand only after Coleman's funeral, when he had a fuller vision of the complexities of the life of this formidable man whom he had come to see as his friend. He also starts to write only once he is free to play with the narration's genre and objectives, but I will not discuss that here.

Scenes like this one in the novel convey a strong sense of presence, drawing us into empathizing with the characters, as we are given to read their very embodied minds. Narratologists would be quick to classify Nathan as an unreliable narrator. Indeed, if we trust the text's instructions for world making, Nathan was not there on the bed, watching Faunia dance from exactly Coleman's eyeline, spelling her naked body's signs. Nor could he know what Faunia thought and saw from where she stood dancing, gazing back at Coleman. This intimate scene, one may infer, so vivid and *present* in its sensuous detail and tempo, must be Nathan's retrospective imagination: his fiction. The text provides good psychological grounds for such an interpretation. For instance, we may consider that Nathan's imaginative narration feeds off his fascination with the older man's vitality and his need to warm his own impotent self at the fire of the couple's desire (the text insists on Nathan's worrying about the side effects on his temperament and sex life of the prostate cancer operation he's recently undergone). Nathan even describes how, after a long period without any contact, he went to spy on the couple at night, not unlike Faunia's deranged and stalking ex, imagining for us from this voyeuristic angle the warmth of their intimacy (see, e.g., 202–3). Meanwhile, as if contagiously, his writing transfers this affect, this fascination, onto me, the reader.

In such a psychological reading, we smooth away any oddities in the narrative structure: we narrativize it, Fludernik would say (Fludernik 1996). The experience of the characters forms the core of our imaginative engagement, and their ethos keeps us puzzled within the greater context of the story world. For instance, we follow Coleman's oscillations between deceit and authenticity and navigate Nathan's evolving attitudes toward this man, with his unruly way of life, and toward his own writing. We may also feel inclined to criticize Nathan's lack of professional ethics. How, indeed, does his own practice of fictionalizing relate to the narrating voice's ironic comments on public rumor, which creates and breaks a person's character?

We may also, instead, shrug our shoulders at the lack of verisimilitude marking Nathan's omniscience: unnaturalness, after all, is fiction's right. Roth might simply adjust Nathan's narrator function as he—the author—thinks fit: at times individuating Nathan, at times not, depending on the needs of plot, of expressivity, or perhaps with reflective, metafictional aims. In the dance scene, thus, the implausible narrative perspective could well serve other functions, besides characterizing Nathan as a narrator. The oscillation of narrative perspective between the two characters might expressively convey the intimacy of the lovers' inter-mental rapport, which to some extent abolishes the boundaries between them (on this notion of the inter-mental, see Palmer 2004). The section might also iconically suggest Faunia's swaying, reinforcing the indolent mood of the moment, or it might express how body awareness, memories, and scraps of inner dialogue come in waves in her consciousness. This alternate framing of the elements in the novel may peacefully coexist with one's psychological-mimetic engagement in the story world.

For the reader I am, though, the artifice of this narrator-character is so heavily signposted that it works as a frame-switch trigger. On several occasions, as mentioned, the narrating voice brutally reminds the reader how limited his, Nathan's, actual knowledge of Coleman's life and personality is. Such remarks work as wake-up calls for a reader like me, making me realize how these "gripping" and "lifelike" characters are being constructed under my nose by Nathan-the-writer, precipitated by my willing suspension of disbelief. Mimesis then changes object, and the novel's point becomes another: *The Human Stain* now displays narrativizing in action, teasingly teaching me a lesson about our own voyeurism and hunger for story and romance. This other framing makes me reflect more intensely on how, like Nathan, people know what they know about each other, especially about each other's ethos and intentions. This issue is also pinpointed in the metafictional title of the novel's first chapter, "Everyone Knows." My interest consequently moves to another communication circuit, in which the intentions and ethos of the author are priming, rather than Nathan's as a character-narrator.

The verisimilitude of the narrating first person now gets provocatively exposed as an artifice. It is not to Nathan's psychology that I would impute the desire to play narrative tricks on his (implied) readers. I don't find ground in the story world for this suspicion, while metanarrative awareness, even playfulness, is definitely something I credit Roth with, on the basis of his other works, their frequent staging of a narrator-character with many similarities to the author, and so on. As it is the author whom I hold responsible for the *fictio* I read, other kinds of ethical questions ensue at this point, in regard to Roth's portrayal of women, for instance, the scope of his irony and metafictional play, or other choices of form, theme, and stance.

This example highlights some initial questions on which the following chapter will expand: Is it always relevant to read for character and to attribute an ethos to characters? Why would readers conjecture about a character's ethos, rather than about a narrator's or an author's? What are the consequences for ethos attribution in adopting the one or the other communication circuit (or narrative level) as the most relevant for our interpretation of a text? And last but not least, is it narratology's task to offer analytical frameworks for such issues, which so clearly involve interpretation?

Exploring answers to these questions, this chapter will focus consecutively on characters, narrators, and authors. Even if readers are often happy, at the slightest hint, to amalgamate narrative voices on various levels (say, equating Nathan-character and Nathan-narrator with Roth himself), this separate discussion allows me to tackle ethos-related issues and conventions that have come to be attached to these different categories of narrative personnel. Ultimately, I hope to shed fresh light on and ask new questions about some persistent and thorny ethos-related issues within narratology, such as narrative (un)reliability, the usefulness of distinguishing narrator and author (implied, hypothesized, or real), and the author's accountability. This chapter does not attempt to give exhaustive coverage of the narratological research on characters, narrators, or authors. I merely wish to point out lines of thought, issues, and positions that are relevant for my focus on ethos attributions.

Characters and Ethos Attributions:
The Psychological Temptation

Why would narratology pay special attention to fictional character, and why should we focus on their ethos? One answer is that the representation of actual or fictive human (or anthropomorphic) experience is quite generally considered to constitute a key interest of narratives. Characters would be primordial vehicles for readers' empathic involvement in fictional narrative. And to assess a character's sincerity or authority is likely to affect our empathizing. Empathizing occasioned by stories, in turn, has been taken to be instrumental for developing the moral imagination required for ethical awareness (see, e.g., Johnson 1993; Keen 2007; Nussbaum 1990). Another possible answer is that in our engagement with narrative art, characterization itself, together with its underlying mechanisms, may become the object of attention. By the effort and patterning they require, such reframing exercises arguably contribute to what Donald called metacognition.

While this second answer is not widely shared, rhetorical, ethical, and cognitive narratologists seem to agree on the first, which highlights the importance of characters as the focal point for one's reading engagement.[1] For Phelan, for instance, it is fully appropriate to deliberate about characters' ethos, including their moral attitudes, and even to judge them as if they were real people. Cognitive narratologists, for their part, seek to elucidate the particulars of such lifelike processing of characters in narratives.

The position just sketched corresponds to what I called the continuity thesis, that is, the assumption that we read fictional or literary minds (much) as we decipher real people.[2] The continuity thesis comes in (at least) two versions. A cautious version is represented by the following statement: "[N]arrative characters are represented *much as* real people are, readers must use their real-world knowledge and beliefs concerning the relationship between dispositions and people's behavior" (Bortolussi and Dixon 2003, 153, 140–41; my emphasis). This version seems almost self-evident, corresponding to what Dilthey called elementary understanding, as discussed in chapter 1. It leaves open the possibility that real-life people, like literary characters, may eschew our grasp. It also allows for the idea that representing and understanding literary characters may involve additional procedures, such as determining what generic and other pragmatic codes apply or evoking the option that a narrator's thought report could be ironic. The stronger version assumes that literary characters *should* be, and actually are, understood and responded to as if they were real people, that it is the experientiality of characters that defines narrativity, and also that the analyst has unproblematic access to what texts mean.

Monica Fludernik and Alan Palmer are among the most prominent scholars associated with this "continuity thesis." In her influential *Towards a "Natural" Narratology*, Fludernik, for instance, defines narrative as "the quasi-mimetic evocation of 'real life experience'" summarized in the notion of "experientiality" (1996, 12). For Palmer "[e]vents only have significance when they are experienced by actors," for which characters are the likely candidates (2004, 30, 177). Narrative, for Palmer, is in essence the presentation of fictional mental functioning. Cognitive theories of meaning making are invoked to explain these observations. Readers would make sense of fictional narratives by drawing on their everyday experiences with people and their actions, stored in memory in schematized form (frames, schemata, scripts, and mental models; see chapter 1).

It is not my aim to discuss here the innovative elements of both scholars' work, Fludernik's on experientiality as the core of narrative, for instance, or Palmer's on "fictional minds" (especially his exploration of "the social mind in action" or his justified critique of structuralist approaches to literary character). My point concerns the predominantly mimetic-psychological reading of character that Palmer especially defends, if I understand his work correctly, although it is also prominent in Fludernik's notion of "narrativization" as a form of "naturalization."[3]

Both scholars seem to have a strong case, at first glance, as the mimetic impulse is powerful and widespread, and not just among nonprofessional readers. A good illustration of the mimetic impulse among professional readers would be Bruce Morrissette's rehumanizing interpretation of Alain Robbe-Grillet's experimental fiction. Morrissette, a renowned specialist of the French Nouveau Roman, countered Barthes's canonizing (and canonized) reading of Robbe-Grillet's writing as "objectal" (*chosiste*; i.e., as attempting to represent a world of things without human experiences; see, e.g., Morrissette 1975). Morrissette, for his part, spotted various sorts of existential concerns and an indirect staging of individual consciousness in Robbe-Grillet's world of things and in his play with form and narrative convention. However, the point of Robbe-Grillet's *La Jalousie* (Jealousy) or *Les Gommes* (The erasers) may not for all readers lie in eliciting empathy with jealous or obsessed story-world "experiencers." One's interest may reside, rather, in the work's play with literary conventions (I will later discuss, along similar lines, Robbe-Grillet's *Djinn*).

The popularity of the continuity thesis might lie in the role it plays in a broader argument about the relevance of both literature and literary theories. The emphasis on the continuity between literary or fictional and everyday narrative stands in a polemic relation to conceptions and theories of literature that cultivate literariness. Formalist and structuralist insistence on literature's form and, later, postmodern imperatives of metafiction or irony have been held, pell-mell, responsible for the anemia from which both literary studies and literature itself would presently suffer. The current cognitive turn at long last would relegitimize on scientific grounds the mimetic-psychologizing mode of reading as the natural, anthropologically justified approach to narrative, including fictional narrative. To foreground the existential dimension of the narrative experience—on the level both of the literary representation and the reader's engagement—is not by chance a basic tenet of many approaches within the ethical turn as well. I agree that the humanities, in cooperation and complementarity with social and cognitive sciences, should claim the domain of representing and interpreting human experience. Yet there are significant risks and losses, I believe, in an unduly narrow conception of literary mimesis, which finds expression also in such mimetic-psychologizing concepts of character.[4] In allegorical writing, in writing under constraints, from Roussel to Perec, in narratives constructed on the model of games or puzzles, in the loop fiction cherished by Borges or Cortazar, or in metafiction, the experientiality of characters and their "minds in action" hardly seem to be the narratives' primary point, though one evidently needs "folk psychology" to make sense of them at all (see also Ryan 2001, 89–99, 175–99, on immersive versus game-like involvement in narrative fiction).[5]

As a general claim, the continuity thesis also risks foreclosing reflection on the functions of fiction. For instance, empathizing with characters fulfills additional and even different functions from that in daily life. A judge may need a certain capacity for empathy with a murderer in order to pronounce judgment, but he or she stands under the obligation of judging, and so of acting. In fiction, as discussed in chapter 1, mind reading is not there just to trigger readers' empathizing. It is also "on display." As Schaeffer puts it, "[I]n most of its forms, fiction does not imitate reality [read here: characters, minds], but our modes of representation of reality" (Schaeffer 2002; see further discussion of the continuity thesis in chapter 4).

Approaches insisting on the continuity between artistic narrative and everyday understanding of people also risk ruling out the semantic potential of narrative form, even with respect to the evocation of "experientiality." This is a sad paradox, since complexity and strangeness of form can be most instrumental in rendering the enigma of perception and experience. Ethos riddles, as we will see, can have the effect of eliciting cognitive and ethical questioning in the reader. In addition, the pleasure we may take in our skillfulness in understanding intricate form may also appear like the *Funktionslust* of puzzling and pattern-seeking minds (this notion has been explained in chapter 1). The diversity of readers' experience of narrative is evacuated as well, and with it, the recognition of the importance of analyzing the sociological and mental conditions for this diversity. Thus, in this book I try to capture how interpreters' reading strategies and framing acts may affect the importance characters and their experientiality have for them.

All of these observations are relevant with respect to the analysis of ethos attributions as well. More awareness of the need to account for different functions characters may have, I find, is found in Phelan's work (as mentioned in chapter 4, where reading strategies were discussed). Literary characters, Phelan proposes, can be considered according to three functions, or "spheres of meaning" (Phelan 1989; with Sperber and Wilson [1995], I would be tempted to speak here of relevance frames):

Mimetic, when characters are recognizable "images of possible people" (2). Coleman's intriguing personality, in Roth's novel, is such a mimetic character effect.

Thematic, when characters are taken as representing "some proposition or assertion" (3), for instance, when they are considered as representatives of a particular social group, or as incarnations of an ideology or of abstract or thematic issues. Thus I would consider Coleman a typical Philip Roth protagonist, prototypically atypical as a university professor, as a black American, or as a male chauvinist.

Synthetic, which refers to the "artificial component of character (3), as when characters are perceived as narrative constructs. This the case where I realize that I have access to Coleman only through Nathan's narration, so as the product of the latter's imagination, or that having the events in the story world narrated through Nathan is at times hardly verisimilar, although the mimetic character effects are stark (which itself reads as the triumphant display of the power of fiction).

A brief comment on Phelan's use of the word *mimetic*, however, is in order here. The notion, as I argued in previous pages, is a little awkward, since thematic and synthetic dimensions can be considered just as well as forms of literary mimesis, understood now in a less limited sense. In its thematic function, Coleman's character is part of an iconic representation of real-life contexts or of abstract issues, such as the social conditions of life for black and Jewish Americans. Characters' synthetic functioning, in turn, is mimetic in that it exposes processes of meaning making and interpreting at work: Nathan performs acts of narrative patterning and imagining that I may understand on a more global level as an iconic *mise en abyme* of writing, reading, and imagining. But given that this use of *mimetic* is fairly widespread, I will adopt it myself, adding usually something like *realist*, *psychological*, or simply quotation marks in order to signal that it refers to the narrow conception of the mimetic.

In light of my emphasis on the interpretive impact of framing acts, Phelan's three functions of character might be stretched a little and made to designate three reading strategies, characterized by their modes for framing character. In a mimetic reading, thus, we ascribe an ethos and intentions to individual characters, with whom we engage as if they were real people. To this end, (folk) psychological and moral frameworks are fully appropriate. Alternately, in thematic or synthetic framings of character, the narrator's or also the author's communicative intentions and ethos with respect to character representation move to the foreground. More abstract forms of cognition and patterning seem involved.

Thematic interpretations, for instance, connect character to frameworks involving various kinds of conceptual knowledge (history, religion, anthropology, politics . . .), generalizing a character's meaning or taking it to function within an argument. A synthetic reading of character requires analytic attention to the means of representation themselves. Characters are, again, made to function in patterns of a more abstract kind, modeled on games, puzzles, music's abstract composition, and so on.

Some texts, Phelan notes, privilege one dimension over the others. In fact, whole traditions of writing, as well as of criticism and theory, are built on the idea that characters are significant not because of their individual psychology but rather through their allegorical (thematic) or structural functions.[6] Yet on the whole, according to Phelan, these three functions of character peacefully add up. My attention in this book goes to the cases in which these interpretive strategies can be constructed as not coexisting peacefully at all. Conflicts between various framings of narrative are brought to the fore precisely in the understanding of character. As my Roth example aimed to show, a text may be perceived as cuing readers for a mimetic construction of character, only to recontextualize this reading strategy itself in a critical or humorous way (which is, again, a matter of ethos attribution). Mimesis then might turn upon itself, confronting the reader with his or her own reading and worldmaking strategies. Such interpretive mechanisms have been amply described in theories of metafiction and *mise-en-abyme* (see also the analysis of Eggers's novel in chapter 7).

Let me give another Robbe-Grillet example here. Robbe-Grillet's *Djinn: Un Trou rouge entre les pavés disjoints* (1981), a typical Nouveau Roman, at first reads as a thriller. On a mysterious errand, the narrator-protagonist encounters a young attractive woman named Jean (American pronunciation) and, later on, a boy and a man called Jean (French pronunciation). However, the characters soon mutate into one another like variants conjured up by the gendered potential of their name in different languages. The novel teasingly elicits a mimetic-psychological and realist model for character construction, hitting the notes of erotic suspense and film noir. Expecting danger, I'm caught looking with the protagonist at a sexy silhouette, which suddenly appears to be a puppet. I realize how I have been producing, like a puppet on a string myself, the expected eroticized and thrilled responses to conventional clues.

To read a work like *Djinn* for a character's ethos seems, to put it mildly, beside the point, despite the fact that folk psychology and mind-reading strategies form a basic response on which the novel plays its tricks and puns.[7] Such a work makes readers perform what looks like a frame switch. One moves from what Rabinowitz (1998) called the position of narrative audience, adopting the story world on the narrator's conditions of verisimilitude, to that of an authorial audience, with a concurrent shift in communication circuit. This frame switch has consequences for whose ethos and what kind of ethical questions become relevant and for what interpretive and evaluative regimes one considers appropriate. The *point* of the narrative experience changes accordingly, from an immersive-psychologizing or thematic reading to, for instance, metafictional reflection or play.

In any case, to justify one's mimetic-psychological framework for character analysis through cognitive research on meaning making seems overly hasty. There is no consensus about how exactly cultural factors and biologically "natural" ones intersect, nor about the precise impact of the pragmatic conditions under which we engage in reading fictional narratives and their characters. For now, more prudently, it appears justified to expect a metahermeneutic narratology to map factors that intervene in readers' construction of characters and to account for the observation that readers do not always read for character.[8]

One might object that my counterexamples are all of a particular, experimental and/or postmodern kind. To some extent this is correct. However, I would like to note that nonmimetic, or rather other-mimetic, functions of character representation have been cultivated all along in the history of the (verbal) arts. Keeping in mind Schaeffer's observation that literary fiction also represents our cognitive operations, I would argue that it is just as natural for narrative art to focus on mediality and narrative means of representation as it is to represent characters engaged in actions and in experiencing (see also van Heusden 2007).

Narratology's Heuristics for the Analysis of Characters and Their Ethos

Following these general considerations, let us examine some narratological frameworks for analyzing narrative character, from the perspective of ethos attributions and interpretive strategies. Once again, one may expect narratologists' conceptions of literature and narrative to affect such analytic frameworks and even to determine the extent to which they attend to matters of ethos.

Structuralist models for character analysis had been firmly set on rejecting as unscientific the analyst's empathic/psychological involvement with characters-as-if-real-persons. Instead, as discussed, they focused on literature's devices and conventions, as they developed over time and as they can be systematized beyond the uniqueness of individual works.[9] With literature considered as a "combinatory of possibilities," narrative characters were defamiliarized, laid bare as artifices grounded in conventions. They have been described as bundles of semantic traits engaging in oppositions and combinations (Bal 1977; Hamon 1983; Rimmon-Kenan 1983) or as actantial-cum-thematic roles (Greimas and Courtés 1979).

Ethos aspects could perhaps be treated in terms of such traits or role characteristics, something like + or – *trustworthiness*. The analyst would, however, soon stumble against the difficulty that one needs to assess first how any information about a character should be taken. This means assessing the authority of one's various sources of information and checking the appropriateness of our inferences. This is where Genette's hierarchy of voices and narrative levels becomes relevant, or Doležel's heuristics for determining a narrator's authentication function (more on the latter in the subsequent section on the narrator).[10] Yet, as Margolin rightly notes, "There is no algorithm for deciding whether any or all of the above conditions [of reliability of information] are satisfied by a given text even though readers make such decisions semi-intuitively all the time" (Margolin 2009, 26).

Genettian poetics also paid significant attention to narrative voice. *Voice* was defined by Genette, though, in a technical-grammatical rather than an expressive-rhetorical sense. The latter is definitely more relevant for an analysis of ethos effects in narratives, as the section on discourse analysis in chapter 2 should have made clear.[11]

Narratological concepts and models for character analysis and narrative transmission received new prominence within stylistic, ethical, and rhetorical approaches. In a more explicitly hermeneutic orientation, these approaches enlisted the structuralist framework in the service of exploring narrative representation of consciousness and the rhetorical effects of narrative structures. Rich heuristics ensued for the analysis of voice as a discursive expression of subjectivity.[12] The investigation included effects of free, indirect discourse and (un)reliability, the interplay of value perspectives in narrative transmission, and the selective authentication and "authorization" of various narrative "voices" and levels.[13] For all of these issues, arguably, the determination of the ethos of characters, narrators, and even (implied) authors is a central concern, though usually not under this explicit label. The work done in this field is evidently fruitful for the analysis of ethos attributions. I expect most of it to be well known to most of my readers and will not expand on it here (see, for instance, most of the quoted works of Bahktin, Booth, Kearns, Phelan, Lanser, Rabatel, Rabinowitz, or Suleiman).

Let me just note that concerns about characters' or narrators' ethics, and about the narratologist's individual response, were integrated with the structuralist framework with intriguingly little ado, despite the latter's stance against interpretation. This syncretism illustrates the point I made in chapter 3. Indeed, in Genettian poetics as in a rhetorical narratological perspective, the determination of focalization or of narrative voices (or of hierarchies or blending of voices) involves basic interpretive decisions: the analyst perceives dual voice, for instance, by matching discursive clues with his or her mental models for who could be speaking or thinking. Such mental models prominently include the various narrative voices' ethos. It is because the reader's memory has assembled an image of Faunia and Coleman—and of their honesty, truthfulness, irony, authority, and so on—that one attributes to one or the other the sentences one reads, together with the views they imply, even when there is no formal textual indication of who is doing the thinking. But as soon as one senses Nathan's possible unreliability or the artifice of his character-narrator role, one cannot be sure anymore how to interpret the strongly expressive features of Faunia's way of thinking, not to mention her ethos.

Seeking alignment with a more scientific and rigorous approach, narratologists turned to theories of human cognition for their models for the analysis of character in narrative. Two tendencies, I believe, appear in current cognitive research on characters (which may combine within one and the same scholar's work). On the one hand, there are models for character analysis that integrate elements from cognitive theories of meaning making, such as the notions of frames and mental models. Yet, like classical narratology, they still seem to pursue typological aims and tend to stay clear from experimental analysis. On the other hand, there is research that draws on experimental psychology and seeks to account for readers' emotional involvement in narratives and (fictional) characters, an issue that classical narratology conspicuously failed to address.[14] Such work might ultimately confirm, or lead to amending, narratologists' assumptions about the rhetorical effects of particular textual devices. I will not, however, discuss this more empirical work on affective or perceptual involvement, despite its evident relevance for ethos attributions, for the simple reason that I have only started exploring it. My focus instead will be on narratological models for character analysis that seek to integrate cognitive understanding of understanding, as exemplified in Palmer 2004 or Schneider 2001 (and to some extent in Eder 2008 and Jannidis 2004).

For character analysis, as mentioned, cognitive narratologists build on the idea that people are capable of ascribing intentions, beliefs, or character traits to each other on the basis of memorized and schematized experiential knowledge. In one of the more extensive studies on character, Schneider thus defends the fruitfulness of the notion that mental models constitute a framework for analyzing literary character. Let me briefly elaborate on some methodological aspects of Schneider's approach.

Mental models, he recalls, encompass "set(s) of assumptions about human behavior that meet with a high degree of agreement," among which are included culturally and historically defined "implicit personality theories." These models allow "efficient top-down processing and labels for the designation of person types or psychological dispositions" (Schneider 2001). Mental models of character, Schneider proposes, form package deals with conventional situation schemata and action scripts. This is, I believe, a fruitful idea, which seems similar to the metonymic connections I evoked between ethos stereotypes and characters' typical actions (see chapter 2; in line with Amossy's work on stereotypes, I suggested that from a "villain" or an "innocent girl," for instance, a prototypical behavior is expected, as well as specific kinds of authority and relationship—one of adherence or, instead, of distance or dissimulation—between words, intentions, and actions).

In everyday life, as in literature, Schneider notes, character models tend to turn into normative paths for "evaluations of human behavior as socially acceptable or unacceptable." The habitual becomes the required behavior (Schneider 2001).[15] The same seems likely for ethos expectations.

However plausible, thus far this approach in terms of mental models or frame theory does not ask the basic question raised in the previous section, namely: is it always productive to interpret literary characters in this "naturalizing" mode? Moreover, Schneider's framework needs some nuance and specification, which he himself sets out to deliver, raising new, and interesting, questions along the way.

First, addressing the potential objection that, like people in real life, literary characters tend not to fit into preestablished molds, Schneider proposes to distinguish between "categorized" and "personalized" characters. The first kind allows for routine and stereotypical casting—corresponding, one might suggest, to Dilthey's "elementary understanding." The second requires intensified processing (the distinction also recalls Edward M. Forster's famous distinction between flat and round characters). Schneider's distinction arguably would also apply to ways in which readers would construct a character's ethos.

But is this distinction so easily made? To consider a character categorized or personalized is to some extent a matter of interpretation, and also of one's experience of life and of literature.[16] Many readers might consider Faunia, in *The Human Stain*, as a personalized character, riddled with lifelike contradictions. She comes from a well-to-do background yet claims not to be able to write. Having learned hard lessons, she rejects the idea of love yet in many respects acts lovingly toward her elderly lover. For me, instead, she appears very much categorized, precisely through the way in which she is "personalized" in her stereotyped complexity, and as a rather stereotypical male fantasy. The riddle Faunia holds for me shifts to another narrative level as I start conjecturing whether Roth was aware of his character's stereotypical features and might be writing ironically. But about whom or what would he be ironizing? About Nathan, the character-narrator? About Coleman, through whose eroticizing eyes Faunia is presented? About the author's own indulgent self-irony? About the reader's tendency to typify, or his or her complicity with this male gaze and/or with its ironizing function? Schneider's descriptive tool instead appears to be a way to label, retrospectively, our variegated interpretive constructions of character.

Second, rising to the challenge to present formal criteria for his distinction, Schneider proposes complexity of style as a possible trigger for a personalized processing of literary character. Given the importance of style as indicator of ethos, this seems a promising trail. If I may paraphrase Schneider's argument as I understand it, stylistic refinement in the evocation of a character would iconically and indexically suggest that character's psychological complexity. Complexity and nuance would get transferred from the description to the described.

One could object, however, that stylistic ethos effects are not so securely attached to an enunciator, as has been discussed in chapter 2. Whose way of thinking and ethos would be characterized in Faunia's first-person discourse in the dance scene quoted at the outset of this chapter? "He wants me to stand here and move, she thinks, and to claim what is mine. Which is? Him. Him. He's offering me him. Okey-dokey, this is high-voltage stuff but here we go." Are these sentences discursively characterizing Faunia's way of thinking and perceiving, or Nathan's, while he engages in imagining this woman's mind, who herself would imagine her lover's thoughts and feelings? Or does the section display the author's creative use of style to convey effects on all kinds of levels simultaneously? Stylistic virtuosity, in fact, may even stand in the way of psychological-empathic reading, redirecting the reader's attention toward another communication circuit, in which the narrator or the author as craftsman stands central.[17]

Schneider's approach remains, in fact, close to its structuralist forebears in its typological inclination. In order to address the range of effects characters may have for readers, the model should be dynamized, for which frame theory in fact is eminently equipped. One might, for instance, include in the framework the idea that readers apply various overarching framings for characters (and their ethos) depending on their reading strategies. A frame-based model could also benefit from including analysis of expressive textual features that have been, until now, considered in terms of voice, style, or tone, which in this book have been connected to their rhetorical appeal, as conventional signals of an ethos. Yet again, the rhetorical-textual perspective needs to be tilted, foregrounding readers' interpretive frameworks in which textual elements may work as clues.

Rather than offering a more scientific approach, models such as Schneider's, in my view, offer interpretive heuristics and argumentative pathways to explain and justify retrospectively the analyst's own construction and interpretation of narrative character; alternately, they can be useful for metahermeneutic reconstructions of interpreters' various routes for making sense of characters. But in my view, this kind of model needs to live up to its constructivist perspective and focus on factors that affect readers' framing acts, such as reading habits and normative conceptions of literature. Rigor of a more scientific kind could also be obtained by exposing the framework's assumptions to empirical research on actual readers' responses. In turn, empirical research on reader response could benefit from more awareness of the various factors, textual and reader-bound, involved in character construction, from style, tone, or the choice of first-, second-, or third-person narration to reading strategies and normative conceptions of selves, literature, and communication.

Unadopted Ethos Effects

The last question I want to address in this section on character is whether ethos attributions might occur for discourse that cannot be ascribed with precision to an individualized subject, which is how traditional characters would be conceived.[18] What I have in mind are texts in which discourse may be felt to produce subject and ethos effects even when there is no clearly individualized character to which these can be ascribed, or when such ascription to an individualized source would be impeded.

Although it may read as oxymoron, I would like to call such phenomena unadopted subject and ethos effects. Such effects occur in particular in experimental fiction, in which language sometimes seems to speak by itself, for instance, through shreds of discourse (analyzed also in Richardson's 2006 work on Beckett, for instance). But the effect I mean can also result from graffiti on a wall. Elliptic, fragmentary, or anonymous utterances may convey an ethos through their discursive form, if one opts for a particular interpretive mode. Any stylistic feature can be taken as expressing the contours of a subjectivity and an ethos, from argumentation or emotion markers up to the use of metaphor or adjectival or verbal modalization (see Kerbrat-Orecchioni's [1980] or Fludernik's [1993] masterful inventory of subjectivity markers in discourse that may coalesce into an ethos; think also of Ducrot's acknowledgement of an "inscriptor" or "enunciator," staged in and characterized by discourse, or locuteur-L, independent from the actual speaker, as I have briefly recalled in chapter 2.)

Fludernik, I think, is interested in the same phenomenon when she observes that in experimental literary discourse "embodiment can be reduced to consciousness or perception with the setting dwindling to rudimentary implied contiguities. But consciousness there needs to be, because this is the locus of experientiality" (1996, 311). This is circular reasoning: one postulates that narratives are "the locus of experientiality" and uses the premise to explain as a consequence ("consciousness there needs to be") something that is included in the premise. From another perspective, this circularity seems perfectly admissible, as everything indeed may become expressive of subjectivity to an interpreter intent on finding "experientiality." Yet, at the risk of being repetitive, let me emphasize that to engage in an individualizing reading of experientiality, and in individualized ethos attribution, may not be the (only) point of a narrative experience.

Take Beckett's *Not I* (Beckett 1990). This play stages Mouth, "hanging about 8 feet above stage level," with a "cloaked figure" standing silently on its left side. Beckett's text defies the construction of individualized characters, if only through its title, which meanwhile quite obviously points out individual identity as a theme. Uncertainty reigns, and is heavily thematized, about who says what, what the story is, whose story it is, and what aspects of discursive ethos might be at stake in the denial of enunciation: *Not I*. There is uncertainty as well about whether the main "event" dramatized in the narrative lies in the told or rather in the act of telling and what the connection between telling and told would be.

However, the elliptic, halted, and rambling monologue (or perhaps montage of monologues) contains fragments of (life-)narration, which readers are likely to "narrativize" by calling upon familiar schemata, scripts, and character models: Was there perhaps a traumatic experience, which explains the disrupted and dissociated telling mode? Has *she* been raped? Hints at a socially underprivileged background, lack of agency and of verbal articulatedness, physical and moral suffering, and so on conjure up familiar sociological and psychological scenarios and characters.

Moreover, the telling itself, with its emphasis on personal pronouns and its metanarrative comments, is fraught with frequent, and strong, emotion markers, which are likely to spark off readers' imagining of an emotional deictic center. From the very first lines of the play, two, if not three, such deictic centers might be inferred, to which all the textually suggested and reported perceiving, suffering, and thinking could be attributed: Mouth, a "tiny little thing," and an older *she*; audiences' habits of constructing textual coherence might lead them to amalgamate the latter with the former. Yet readers' efforts to assemble coherent outlines for character and plot are regularly interrupted by the phrase "Who? Not I," which some might take as a typical case of avowal through denial.

With its discursive characteristics, the telling itself may work as an important index for *an* ethos, before any specific attachment to the speaking Mouth, for instance, or to the figure referred to as *she*: ". . . out . . . into this world . . . this world . . . tiny little thing . . . before its time . . . in a godfor– . . . what? . . . girl? . . . yes . . . tiny little girl . . . into this . . . out into this . . . before her time . . . godforsaken hole called . . . called . . . no matter . . . parents unknown . . . unheard of . . ." (Beckett 1990, 216). Not only does discourse thematize the painful outburst of inhibited speech, it seems to iconically perform the same process, confirming through its discursive ethos the authenticity of the emotions that are evoked. Tonal cues, to use Molly Hite's felicitous expression, convey a sense of discourse's "affective connotations, and thus value" (Hite 2010, 250). Readers might attribute such affective valences to the narrating Mouth, qualifying its attitude toward its subject, "she." The expressive effects of this halted narration itself may work as a clue for readers to amalgamate Mouth and this *she*, whose experience is associated with that same fragmented, halted, and emotionally charged quality (*Not I = I*).

Meanwhile Mouth's discursive ethos also displays a sophisticated mastery of language. This discourse is also very much logos oriented (if we keep in mind Aristotle's distinction between means of persuasion) in its meticulously precise vocabulary and its complex, even if elliptic, syntax, in which argumentation markers abound. There is in fact a huge gap between the intellectual and verbal competences displayed by this voice and the kind of figure and voice one would construct for *she*, presented as hardly articulate. Thus, arguably, while there are strong clues for equating Mouth and *she*, as well as conflating both dramas of the advent of speech, just as convincing are the discursive clues for holding them apart.

The text thus cues readers for a built-in uncertainty of representations, which, once again, may work as a signal for a frame switch. As a reader, I feel on the one hand cued for a psychological "narrativization" of the evoked and performed situations, as well as for imagining a personalized character and narrator, with her or his own ethos. On the other hand, rather than simply understanding the halted narrative form as an "authentic" index of individual trauma, social incapacity, or individual pathology, one may be inclined to read *Not I* as a more abstract work of art: a dynamic composition, for which uncertain and unadopted discursive subjectivity effects, with their quite strong ethos and pathos appeal, constitute the material. Experientiality is then evoked in less personalized but still affect-loaded form, through discursive emotion slots, more like the orchestration of moods in music. But perhaps phenomenology and experimental psychology are better equipped to help analyze such effects than narratology.

Narrators and Ethos

Narratological debates about the narrator usually revolve around questions of why readers would want to establish a source for fictional narrative discourse, how the narrator stands in relation to the author, and how fully a narrator can be personalized, or to issues of truth, authority, and (un)reliability in narrative transmission (see, among others, Margolin 2009; Patron 2009; Walsh 2007). I will argue that, beyond textual clues, generic framing and reading strategies also may incline readers to imagine and attribute an ethos to a personalized narrator or, instead, to a less personalized narrat*ion*, or to equate this narrator or narration with the author.

Since Plato, mediation by a teller has been considered characteristic of narrative fiction, while the dramatic mode relies on showing. Within narratology, the role of the narrator has been defended as a structural one, though its function has been variously conceived. As a cornerstone of structuralist narratology, the narrator became invested with the important function of marking the distinction of fiction as a mode of assertion. Genette, as we saw in the previous chapter, proposed as the law of literary fiction that "A *is not* N," whereas in factual narrative "A = N."[19] To explain his thesis, Genette resorts to speech act theory, in particular to Searle's understanding of fiction as pretended assertion. I will not enter into detailed discussion of these analyses here, only elaborating on their implications for a focus on ethos. Following Genette, literary fiction, as an assertion, is uncoupled from factual referentiality and from its source, the author.

As a consequence of Genette's "law," narratology could push aside as irrelevant the point of view and/or intentions of the real author, as well as his or her ethos—his or her reliability or authority, for instance. Fictionality thus would interrupt everyday expectations concerning the idea that a way of speaking indexically expresses its enunciator, as well as this source's accountability.[20] Instead, the narrator became the last instance to which intentions and values were attributed. At the same time, interpretation was to be kept at bay. A sound descriptive methodology would suffice to establish the relevant communicative levels, types of narrative transmission, and the resulting hierarchy of perspectives on the basis of which the reliability of narrators and characters could be established. Both moves are unwarranted, as has been argued earlier in this book, as well as in many others (see Schaeffer 2010; Walsh 2007; Patron 2009).[21]

From a rhetorical perspective, in turn, literary narrative has been described as "someone telling someone else that something happened" (Margolin 2009; Phelan 2007). Though narrators are taken to do the telling, it is now the implied author whom, in the last instance, the interpreter holds responsible for the ultimate narrative act (more on this in the next section, on authors). This move marks an incipient questioning of the boundaries between fiction and real-world assertion, posing on new grounds the question of the author's accountability. Rhetorical approaches thus have greater latitude to analyze tensions between ethos constructions that pertain to different levels of literary communication. Their formal analysis quite naturally also leads into ethical reflection, which had been ruled out in structuralist narratology.

Current cognitive and psychonarratological approaches often, though not always, support the idea that every text, including fictional ones, has a narrator. However, the narrating figure is now understood somewhat differently, as a "textually projected and readerly constructed function" (Margolin 2009, 351–52). On a general level, people "must of necessity maintain a representation of the other [communication] participant, together with certain aspects of their mental state for communication to proceed (deixis, information about knowledge and mental state, intentions and goals), in order to understand the function of the speech acts": this "participant" is the narrator, Bortolussi and Dixon argue (2003, 77). This understanding of the narrator seems to coincide with that of the inscriptor or enunciation subject postulated in French discourse analysis (Maingueneau 2004). One's representation of "the other participant" would include his or her ethos.

But this is not the role Genette had in mind for the narrator, which for him incorporated fundamental pragmatic conditions of literary functioning. Unsurprisingly, for Bortolussi and Dixon the distinction between narrator and author, like that between fiction and nonfiction, loses its urgency. To "construct a representation of the author" is just as natural as constructing a narrator. Anyway, "there is no clear method for determining the precise relationship between the [point of view of the] author and [that of the] narrator, and readers are left to draw whatever inferences they can" (2003, 76; 61). While I agree that there is no foolproof method for describing readers' inferences about this relation between author and narrator, this relation does not therefore lose its analytic relevance. Quite the contrary, it becomes a challenge in its own right to reconstruct why readers would, or would not, imagine a narrator.

Against the thesis that in fiction the narrator must be distinguished from the author, the commonsensical argument is often invoked that readers feel no qualms in equating narrator and author—indeed, that even professional critics are often caught in this act. From a linguistic point of view, critiques of the all-narrator assumption have been severe. Banfield famously ruled that if there is no linguistic evidence for a narrator figure, one should refrain from postulating it (Banfield 1982).[22] From a pragmatic-narratological perspective, Walsh observes that in the structuralist view "the narrator . . . functions primarily to establish a representational frame within which the narrative discourse may be read as report rather than invention" (2007, 69). To his sense, this is a completely dysfunctional idea: "[F]ictions are narrated by their authors, or by characters. Extradiegetic homodiegetic narrators, being represented, are characters, just as all intradiegetic narrators are. Extradiegetic heterodiegetic narrators (that is, "impersonal" and "authorial" narrators), who cannot be represented without thereby being rendered homodiegetic or intradiegetic, are in no way distinguishable from authors" (84; see his chapter 4).

Refraining from postulating a narrator allows analysts to get rid of some artificial problems created by the concept itself, Walsh claims. These problems include: (1) the obviously wrong idea that a narrator invents the fiction we read, which is different from having a fictive source of narrative transmission (see also Hamburger 1968; Patron 2009; Herman et al. 2012); (2) the problem, signaled by fictionality theories, that the narrator thesis cannot account for the author's work as a serious "act of representation" (Walsh 2007, esp. 84; Schaeffer 2010); (3) the problem that narrators are often only intermittently noticeable as voices with subjectivity markers, making it more economic not to posit a narrator alongside the author, who arguably does the overall narrating; and (4) the problem of the closed border postulated between fiction and an author's real-world discourses.

Although I agree with most of Walsh's critiques and welcome his reinstatement of the author's agency, I do not subscribe to all of his solutions. As I see it, the issue of delays, or relays, in fictional narrative assertion is crucial, if one focuses on literature's rhetorical and reflective functions. What is at stake, as Walsh himself notes, is the kind of standing we attribute to a discourse, as well as the kind of interpretive and evaluative regimes we consider appropriate. For Walsh, structuralist understandings of the narrator tuck the "telling" role safely away between the ontological borders of fiction, thus dismissing the issue of fictionality itself. Yet does he not himself discard it too easily by sticking to an either/or typology: either a text has a homodiegetic narrator or it is the author who narrates? Should not a pragmatic-cognitive approach explore precisely how readers decide that *fiction* is the appropriate reception frame? The frame borders of fiction are not always clear, and the same holds for communication contracts.

To dismiss en bloc the relevance of an authorial narrator, as distinct from the author, obliterates the required interpretive calculus. Moreover, by trading the concepts of heterodiegetic or extradiegetic narrator for that of author, does Walsh not run the risk of fostering exactly the personalizing, psychologizing reading he seemed intent on avoiding? I wholeheartedly side with David Herman when he writes that there is no "one-size-fits-all answer" to the question of whether reasons for telling should be ascribed to narrators rather than authors:

[R]ather, the structure of a given narrational act, the profile it manifests as it unfolds in a particular context of storytelling and story interpretation, determines the nature of the inferential pathway that leads back to the agent or agents who performs/perform it. The pathway may be relatively direct, as in (some) autobiographical narration, or relatively indirect, as in first-person or homodiegetic narratives that feature unreliable tellers—with an intermediate position being occupied by texts that, like McEwan's [*On Chesil Beach* is Herman's tutor text], are narrated heterodiegetically. The pertinence of the concept of "narrator" varies across these and other storytelling situations. (Herman et al. 2012, 47–48)

In line with this more pragmatic formulation, and borrowing terminology from Lanser, I will propose in the section on authors some hypotheses concerning the conventional procedures for attaching or detaching narrators from authors. But first I want to come back to some other issues at stake in the debates about the necessity of positing for fiction a narrator distinct from the author.

Truth, Authority, and Reliability

In the construction of narrative truth, the narrator's role as well as his or her authority and reliability have received intensive attention. Doležel, in particular, addresses the issue of readers' sense of truth in fiction by drawing on possible worlds theory. I only want to comment here on his idea that "[w]e have to introduce a generalized, graded authentication function that can formally express the world-constructing force of all available narrative modes. The function assigns different grades (degrees) of authenticity to fictional entities, distributed along a scale between 'fully authentic' and 'nonauthentic.' Consequently, it provides world constituents with different ranks or modes of fictional existence" (Doležel 2010, 152).

In his earlier contribution on the subject, Doležel defined three main models for such authentication processes: (1) a binary model, in which an anonymous narrator possesses "authentication authority" that characters' speech acts do not have; (2) a nonbinary model with "subjectivized" third- and first-person narration, the authentication authority of which is relative: it depends on the authority of that third- or first-person narrator; and (3) a model without authentication (Doležel 1980). Doležel's typology, however, seems to beg the question of how readers assess the degree of subjectivity and authority of a narrator in the first place. Subjectivity in narrative acts is only to some extent a matter of formal linguistic signaling. Moreover, the authority attached to first- or third-person narration rests on conventions that change over time. In the currently fashionable genre of semifactual literary narrative, for instance, I-narration is often invested with the authority of the witness or of firsthand experience, while an omniscient narrator might become suspect precisely because of his or her claim to objective knowledge (see also Walsh 2007; Nielsen 2004).[23]

Related to issues of truth and authority in fiction is, of course, the concept of the unreliable narrator, one of the most debated ethos issues in narratology, a "problem . . . as complex and (unfortunately) as ill-defined as it is important," Yacobi already observed in the early eighties (1981, 113). "Determining whether a narrator is unreliable is not just an innocent descriptive act as this objectively changes value judgment or projection governed by the normative presuppositions and moral convictions of the critic, which as a rule remain unacknowledged," Nünning also notes (Nünning 1999, 60). I could not agree more, as his formulation captures the whole idea behind this book.

Since Booth devised the notion of unreliable narration in 1961, it has received exhaustive attention, especially since the 1980s, with renewed interest in the ethical dimensions of literature, and more recently in conjunction with cognitive approaches that hold the promise of solving some stubborn critical problems. Here is, first, Booth's definition: "For lack of better terms, I have called a narrator 'reliable' when he speaks for or acts in accordance with the norms of the work (which is to say, the implied author's norms), 'unreliable' when he does not" (Booth 1961, 158–59). This definition, it has been amply noted, simply displaces the question: how, then, do we know the norms of the work, or of the implied author? (more on the implied author in the following section).[24] Despite numerous amendments, the notion remains as contested as it is popular.[25] Nünning (1999, 2005, 2008) helpfully lists the main critical points. There is no *method* to establish the unreliability of the narrator other than to "read between the lines" or to note the "secret communication behind a narrator's back." Indeed, "the only yardstick [Booth] offers for gauging a narrator's unreliability is the implied author," a notion at least as contested, theoretically and methodologically, as that of unreliability itself (Nünning 2005, 91; 2008, 30–45). Moreover, the procedures for establishing unreliability would rest on the problematic assumption that there is a reliable view on the world and on selves, a shared sense of psychological, moral, and linguistic normality, which constitutes the default setting of narrative. Instead, Nünning notes with a touch of provocation, "no generally accepted standards of normality exist which can serve as the basis for impartial judgment. In a pluralist, postmodernist and multicultural age like ours it has become more difficult than ever before to determine what may count as 'normal moral standards' and 'human decency'" (Nünning 1999, 64): But does not cognitive narratology, including Nünning's increasingly cognitive approach, try to reconstruct precisely such "accepted standards," reformulated as "frames" (Nünning 2005; 2008)?

Rather than on the basis of such implicit norms or the mere intuition of the critic regarding an implied author, detection of unreliable narration can proceed on the methodologically more solid basis of definable textual clues, Nünning argues in one of his early articles on this matter (Nünning 1997, 97). Such textual clues include verbal tics of the narrator, linguistic expressions of subjectivity, textual inconsistencies, conflicts between story and discourse or between characters' utterances and actions, and other text-internal contradictions or inconsistencies (see also Nünning 1999; Olson 2003).

In his later syntheses on narrative unreliability, Nünning distances himself from his earlier, still very much text-based, approach and notes that, in fact, the "term 'unreliable narrator' does not indicate a structural or semantic feature of texts, but a pragmatic phenomenon that cannot be fully grasped without taking into account the conceptual premises that readers and critics bring to texts" (Nünning 2008, 45). Nünning brings in pragmatic and frame theory. Bypassing Booth's postulation of an implied author and his all-too intuitive rhetoric-hermeneutic approach, such pragmatic and cognitive approaches are expected to "present a possible way out of the methodological and theoretical problems that most theories of unreliable narration suffer from because cognitive theories can shed light on the way in which readers naturalize texts that are taken to display features of narrational unreliability" (Nünning 2008, 46; 2005).

Readers are considered to bring to their reading activity schematized knowledge, which allows them to fill in what counts as standard behavior or evaluation, against which a character or narrator then appears unreliable (Nünning 2005, 98ff; 2008, 47–49). These frames can be "referential," that is, drawn from everyday experience, hence they would normally be responsive to verisimilitude. These referential frames include social, moral, or linguistic norms, relevant for the period in which the text was written and published, as well as readers' knowledge of pertinent psychological theories of personality or their own models of psychological coherence and normal human behavior.[26] The activated frames can also be "literary." These literary frames include conventions of genre; intertextual references; character prototypes, such as the picaro or the trickster; and "last but not least the structure and norms established by the respective work itself" (Nünning 2008, 48; the idea that a literary work would establish by itself its structure and norms is intriguing, in light of Nünning's own emphasis on readers' framing acts). Research can now also extend to historically *changing* norms about selves or trustworthiness, explaining how, over time, a narrator's reliability may have been differently constructed (Nünning also refers to Zerweck 2001, 151; and Vera Nünning 1998, who foreground the importance of changing historical contexts in which [un]reliability is assessed). In my view, this historicizing brings the investigation into metahermeneutic grounds, like Tamar Yacobi's very adequate proposal to explore the various strategies readers adopt for dealing with a narrator's incongruities; to decide that a narrator is unreliable is one among several such strategies (Yacobi 1981).

A question arises, however, regarding how exactly the recourse to cognitive frame theory functions here. Nünning clearly distances himself from what he considers Booth's underformalized and overly intuitive approach, placing himself, as I understand, on the side of methodological rigor. The aim of his own framework seems to be threefold, but the different objectives seem somewhat internally conflicting: to offer (1) a cognitive sciences–grounded explanation of how readers detect unreliability in general—as a general framework the approach seems plausible, but it would require further empirical testing; (2) a cognitive theory–based method for a more objective assessment and analysis of unreliable narration, an approach that also includes narratological lists of textual, extratextual, or paratextual signals, which are considered to be describable—this is where, in my view, the suggestion of methodical rigor is unwarranted, in light of Nünning's own frame theory account of readers' interpretive activities; (3) a systematic hermeneutic (or metahermeneutic) reflection on the interpretive steps involved in assessing the reliability of a narrator—here one might use any expert framework and reading strategy; what counts is analytic relevance and persuasive argumentation.

To the extent that the recourse to cognitive theories suggests a more scientific procedure, one might also expect a turn toward empirical research, investigating what frames readers actually activate, for example in order to establish the reliability of a narrator. Instead, Nünning's discussion of McEwan's short story, "Dead as They Come" (2008: 51–56), which was meant to illustrate his cognitive-rhetorical framework, exemplifies meta-hermeneutic exploration: it reconstructs his own negotiation of textual clues, background norms, and (textual and authorial) intentions detected in the perceived textual rhetorical steering (51–54). In that respect it might not really be fundamentally different from Booth's rhetorical-hermeneutic reconstruction of how readers would detect irony and stand in need of arguing for their interpretation.

There is one last issue I want to address in connection with unreliability. It pertains to the suggestion that the effect of narrator unreliability lies "in redirecting the readers' attention from the level of the story to the discourse level occupied by the speaker, and in foregrounding peculiarities of the narrator's psychology" (Phelan 2005, 495–96). As mentioned, such a redirection seems to correspond to what I called a frame switch, to which, according to Goffman's understanding of framing, belong the following elements (see chapter 1): the idea that one's framing of a situation involves selecting what becomes significant; the idea of frame borders and framing keys; and the idea (which I added in chapter 2) that particular evaluative regimes are attached to particular framings. In my view, the redirection Phelan speaks of need not always foreground "the narrator's psychology," as I've contended earlier in this chapter. Any suspicion regarding narrative telling modes does, however, prompt us to ask about the author's communicative intentions and ethos (this will be discussed in more detail in the case studies in chapters 6 and 7).

For now, in an intermezzo of a more essayistic kind, I would like to reflect on what happens if we start suspecting the reliability of conventional heterodiegetic authorial narration.

An Unreliable Narrator, or Author?

David Mitchell's *The Thousand Autumns of Jacob de Zoet* (2010) tells the story of an overzealous clerk appointed by the Dutch East Indies Company to eradicate corruption from the small Dutch enclave on the island Decima, near Nagasaki, in the early nineteenth century. Japan, grimly ruled by a shogun, is shut off from the outside world aside from this tiny conduit, through which scientific, medical, and technological knowledge seeps into the country. There are many framing clues that suggest that this novel should be considered to be a historical novel. Like most works in this genre it also seems to conform to conventional realist aesthetics. Indeed, *The Thousand Autumns* invokes lifelike characters, which calls for a processing along everyday psychological and moral frames. Moreover, historical fiction is usually marked by a tacit contract of global correspondence to historical truth. In this particular case, author, publisher, and many critics joined in emphasizing the number of historical figures, details, and historical analyses that found their way into Mitchell's fiction. The book is announced as a "panoramic novel," which "transports us in the year 1799." The images printed in the book include reproductions from referenced historical sources showing the reconstruction of the actual historical Dejima, among other scenes. The author's note and acknowledgments consolidate the impression of historical accuracy. Mitchell provides his readers with relevant historical information and refers to his stay at the Netherlands Institute for Advance Study (NIAS), a famous research intitute in the Netherlands, which allowed him intensive contact with various experts in Dutch universities and archives. Even when Mitchell points out that he took some liberties with historical truth, such a caveat paradoxically underlines this assumed commitment to global factual accuracy. Like many historical novels, moreover, the fiction seems serious in its intention to address themes from which "we might learn" or that are relevant with regard to the present, such as the clash between East and West or the intertwining of commercial, political, military, and intellectual interests. A non-negligible consecration came from the Historical Novel Society (HNS), devoted to promoting historical fiction, which praised the novel for its vividness (http://historicalnovelsociety.org/reviews /the-thousand-autumns-of-jacob-de-zoet-2/).

In any form of *writing history* the authentication of the narrating voice is a critical issue. *The Thousand Autumns of Jacob de Zoet* is narrated in third-person mode by a nonpersonalized authorial narrating voice. Expert knowledge courses through the narrating voice's richly technical vocabulary and stylistic expressivity, which portrays characters in their ways of thinking and socio- or idiolects that could well be accurate for the depicted time and place. Thus the discursive ethos of this mode of telling also conforms to what may be expected from a historical novel: expertise, stylistic richness, *couleur locale*, and vivacity. The confirmation of my expectations makes me trust this narrative transmission as a regular instance of traditional authorial narration (many critics pointed out Mitchell's return to more conventional writing in this novel, after his more experimental writing in works such as *Cloud Atlas*). Though this heterodiegetic narrating voice often makes room for the free-thought report of the protagonist, the clerk Jacob De Zoet, this "inside view" does not endanger the overall generic pact ("historical novel") I at first consider appropriate for this novel.

Yet readers may find themselves sensitive, as I was, to some excesses that appear incongruous in this generic framing. While stylistic expressivity is fine in a historical novel, this particular novel seems one big virtuoso exercise in *skaz*, beyond realistic motivation.[27] While historical novels frequently represent characters that recount their lives, making for a sociologically and linguistically diverse picture, this novel keeps pouring out personal histories in expressive idiolects.[28] And while historical novels often combine with features of the adventure novel or romance, this one undergoes curious switches in its manner of telling: whole episodes suddenly read like a samurai film script or a manga with a tinge of the Murakami initiation-cum-fantasy novel; the style and overall posture of the narrating voice follow suit. Am I still reading a historical novel when the narration gets off trail with the protagonist's Japanese counterpart, who sets out with his samurai to liberate his beloved, sequestered in the mountains? Black cats are there to signal danger, as in a fairy tale.

In my experience with Mitchell's novel, such quantitative and qualitative oddities of style and telling disrupt the coherence of the generic frame I expected to underlie the narrative transmission: a conventional framing that was supported by the global sense that the story was told through a traditional authorial narrator, whose perspective—and instructions for world making—I was to trust. Significantly, in their reviews of Mitchell's novel, some critics have voiced uneasiness regarding what they perceived as some lack of balance in composition, style, or tone. This novel in any case is not, for me, the straightforward historical novel it appears to be at first glance. I read it, rather, as a pastiche of various genres, sampling these with flourish and contagious pleasure in its play with language and with narrative forms. The book could even be read as an "exercise de style" such as Raymond Queneau's, around the question of how to make art from historical material, in what genre, with what tone and style, and from whose perspective. As Mitchell demonstrates, contemporary writers can choose among the graphic novel, the samurai film, Sir Walter Scott's or Victor Hugo's respectable examples, or even poetry as they attempt to catch the fleeting present. Why not sample these modes, rather than choose between them? The solid and trustworthy authorial narrator, however, suddenly comes to be a manner of telling on display, rather than just doing its work and *telling* (interestingly, in his review of Mitchell's novel, Dave Eggers does not prove sensitive to this effect, noting instead, "This new book [*Thousand Autumns*] is a straight-up, linear, third-person historical novel, an achingly romantic story of forbidden love and something of a rescue tale—all taking place off the coast of Japan, circa 1799. Postmodern it's not"; http://www.nytimes.com/2010/07/04/books/review/Eggers-t.html?ref=davidmitchell).

Triggered by the incongruities I just mentioned, I find myself shifting from wondering about the narrator's intention or ethos to wondering about the author's. Should I take the novel's style and generic mannerisms as straightforward instructions for world making or rather as—parodic? playful? deceptive?—echoic mention (to anticipate my discussion of irony in chapter 7)? Is Mitchell counting on my willingness to follow him—as the text's "composer"—blindly from the conventions of the historical novel into the well-trodden mountain paths of a samurai story or Romanesque fantasy, or does he count on my complicitous awareness of his play with narrative convention? Is Mitchell perhaps just being commercially clever, making sure to captivate different audiences by combining the attractions of erudite historicity and romanesque suspense? Is the authorial narrator here merely a trick to lure me, as a reader, into trusting the novel's realist fiduciary pact? Is it appropriate, here, to speak of an unreliable authorial narrator, or even an unreliable author? Depending on how I construct the author's prior ethos, I will take the mentioned textual "excesses" as signals of irony, playfulness, or parody, or instead, as plain weaknesses (the author is not consistent in his historical-realist perspective; he indulges in clichés; his style is overbearing; and so on).

On the basis of my reading of Mitchell's previous works, such as *Cloud Atlas*, for my part, I credit him with the intention of seriously exploring literature's potential in two senses: first, as the representation of what Fludernik called experientiality; in this case, of experiences attached to a specific—culturally and psychologically rich—historical situation; and second, as a playful reflective treatment of literature's means for representing such experience. In its play with generic framings and forms of narration, Mitchell's fiction provides a good example of the idea that to classify a work as unreliable in its apparent generic framing and its narrative mode requires a complex exercise of ethos attribution. His novel also exemplifies a wide range of today's artworks, which adapt like a mobile by Alexander Calder depending on the reader's or viewer's aesthetic experience and inclination.

To wrap up this section on the narrator, let me side with Herman's observation that "the pertinence of the concept of 'narrator' varies across these and other storytelling situations" (Herman et al. 2012, 48). The pertinence of the concept of narrator also depends, I hope to have argued, on the reader's interpretive strategy and generic framing. It would be better, perhaps, to speak of narra*tion* as a function rather than an agent and as a device adopted by the author. As Tillotson observes, "A narrator is a method rather than a person; indeed the narrator never is the author as a man [*sic*]; much confusion has arisen from the identification, and much conscious art has been overlooked" (K. Tillotson, *The Tale and the Teller*, 1959, quoted in Kindt and Müller 2006, 50). Narrators, moreover, are not necessarily anthropomorphic and "continuous." It pays off, however, to keep this layer in narrative transmission distinct from that of the author, if only in order to be able to ask about Mitchell's, or Roth's, narrator/narrating voice's possible unreliability and, subsequently, about the author's ethos.

Authors and Ethos

As my brief interlude on Mitchell's novel or, in chapter 2, on the two critics bickering over their Houellebecq aimed to demonstrate, an interpreter's idea about the author is likely to influence how one perceives a narrating voice's—or even characters'—discourse: for instance, as unreliable, cynical, ironic, or as seriously intended. This section contends that a narratology that does not include the extratextual author expels a potentially important factor in the meaning-making and interpretive processes it aims to describe.[29] I start by explaining why we need to distinguish among various facets of the author and formulate some conditions under which readers are likely to include conjectures about the author's ethos in their interpretations of a work. I then discuss in more detail two particularly significant issues concerning the author: his or her posture and the idea of implied author. I will propose some hypotheses about how these facets of authorship intervene in ethos attributions in connection to reading strategies and generic framing. Integrating insights from part 1, I thus aim to complement narratology's approach to literary communication and its heuristic potential for hermeneutic and metahermeneutic aims.

The Multifaceted Author

Are some conditions likely to stimulate the attribution of an ethos to an author, rather than, say, to a narrator or character? Can we say more about how such ethos attributions would proceed and about their functions? Empirical psychological research on actual reading behavior, while still relatively scarce, seems to provide some confirmation of what we might already assume from the immense popularity of writers' biographies and from the way literature is discussed on an everyday basis: that in various degrees readers tend to include conjectures about the authorial ethos in their overall interpretations of a literary work (Claessens 2009). But, as said, more research is required if we want to be more affirmative.

As I indicated in chapter 2, there is ample sociological and historical research on authorship. Such research has concentrated, among other topics, on the role of the author's name and posture in the marketing of literature, in the circulation of his or her work, and in the attribution of meaning and symbolic value to it. It is by now quite well established, for instance, that the (name of the) author functions in ways comparable to branding and that marketing mechanisms have an increasing grasp on the mediation of literature. While expert journals used to function as the primary gatekeepers for established conceptions of literature, nowadays public media, talk shows, photo shoots, interviews, blogs, Facebook, and live performances all have become sites for the fabrication of a work's meaning and literary or other value (such as its ethical, historical, or informative value). The attribution of values occurs according to a much further democratized plurality of tastes and through channels that often operate outside of the traditional literary spheres. Rather than focusing on the work, these media tend to zoom in on the author *live*, as a private person or in his or her public role as the writer.[30]

Changes in the processes of selection and distribution of literary artifacts and of meaning attribution may also be expected to foster other kinds of ethos grounds. Indeed, authority and authenticity grounded in a sense of communion, or in direct, "visceral" experience and sensation, seem currently to be appreciated more than those rooted in literary-artistic craftsmanship and tradition. This foregrounding of the author perhaps speaks to a pervasive demand for presence and concreteness, a longing for the *real*, which seems exacerbated in our overmediatized everyday life. Broad audiences—and not only "popular" ones—hunger for an author's word made flesh, for discourse endowed with the author's lived experience and presence.[31]

My own perspective in the next section focuses less on the marketing dimension of the author's name and posture than on the ways in which author images and self-fashioning cue readers to a certain *kind* of experience, as well as to particular pathways for attributing symbolic value, authority, and relevance to the literary work. Such framing clues are all the more important if we keep in mind Maingueneau's suggestion that literature is characterized by its paratopy: as a type of discourse, it belongs rightfully nowhere and needs to validate its right to speak (see my brief discussion of this notion of paratopy in chapter 2). Effects of pathos and ethos attached to an author's public image seem to take on symbolic value, which then transfers back to the work, in a feedback loop interlocking value and ethos, work and person.[32]

From a metainterpretive perspective, building on Foucault's seminal 1969 essay regarding the author function as well as on Maingueneau's (in fact Ducrot's) distinctions, I expect the following facets of authorial image to be most relevant for meaning-making processes:[33]

1. The author as a biographical, "flesh and blood" person and as citizen (in fact these are already two different roles, which, in

Boltanski and Thévenot's terms, resort respectively under the Worlds and values regime of the Domestic and of the Civic). This is Michel Thomas, who adopted *Houellebecq* as a pseudonym, or James Frey, with his actual personal history.

2. The author in his or her social role as a writer, for which the notion of authorial posture was introduced. This is Houellebecq as the visionary author, photographed in a dark, romantic pose on a cliff, or as the media star, with flushed cheeks and unsteady gaze, surrounded by women on a book launch. This is the James Frey who in interviews justifies aesthetically the marketing and framing of *A Million Little Pieces*.

3. The image of the author constructed on the basis of a writer's previous oeuvre, which may be considered to function as a *prior ethos*, in light of which a (new) work is classified, interpreted, and invested with value—or divested of it. Besides the author him- or herself, literary historians and critics, among others, contribute to the construction of this oeuvre-based ethos. Such an ethos need not be monolithic or consistent, and it is constantly actualized in the *Wirkungsgeschichte* of an author's work. This is the kind of authorial ethos to which Dorrit Cohn gestured when she argued that the narrator in Thomas Mann's *The Confessions of Felix Krull* should not be equated with the author, as their views and modes of assertion were too different (Cohn 1999).

4. The author image that the analyst or reader constructs on the basis of peri- and epitexts. These have a complicated status regarding authoring and authorizing: who speaks in them, and with what (possibly strategic) dialogic inflections? Interviews tend to pull the interviewee into the interviewer's preset frame, so ethos attributions on the basis of the author's own statements should be made with an awareness of such filtering effects. Writers often exploit the convention that it is "the author" him- or herself who speaks in pre- or postfaces, authoritatively cuing readers for a particular framing of the work, as well as of a particular authorial posture and ethos. But precisely this convention allows writers to play with readers' framing habits and to multiply conflicting framing clues. In *A Heartbreaking Work of Staggering Genius*, for instance, the question typically arises whether we should take

the nearly one hundred pages of authorial paratext as expressing Dave Eggers's actual views on literature or whether the *parergon* already requires an aesthetic framing, one in which ambiguity and irony might prevail. Hesitation about how to classify the authorial voice is intertwined with uncertainty about the tone and genre of the text.

5. The image of the author that the analyst or reader constructs on the basis of the text she or he reads, which has been termed the "implied author"–alternately the abstract, inferred, or hypothetical author (see Kindt and Müller 2006; Heinen 2002). As an interpretive construction, this implied author subsumes the worldviews and values the text as a whole is taken to express. This is the only author dimension that has been extensively discussed in narratology, and I will come back to it below.

6. The author as narrator, a subject that has been touched upon in the previous section and on which we need to elaborate.

But why neglect Ockham's wise rule, since readers and narratologists alike often don't bother to make such distinctions? The proposed distinctions, moreover, are far from being clear cut. Where, for instance, should we locate the Dave Eggers who organizes writing groups for the underprivileged: under authorial posturing or under the civic or biographic person's activities? From a metahermeneutic point of view, though, there are good reasons to maintain such distinctions, however precarious: They draw attention, heuristically, to the different grounds and argumentation patterns, and the different value regimes, used to establish meaning and relevance for literature. Each of the authorial facets, moreover, is produced in a different discourse genre and by different agents, besides the author: editors, translators, critics, publisher, and so on, agents who may have different strategic aims. Each of these discourse genres and media moreover projects a different kind of authority: Patricola's rabiate monograph weighs differently in my own interpretation of Houellebecq's work than would a thorough academic analysis.

In addition, different reading strategies are likely to attribute different weight to the various author facets: a personalizing/mimetic reading strategy probably attaches greater importance to information about James Frey's actual life than an autonomous/aesthetic one.

So, even though somewhat counterintuitive, these distinctions at least make us aware of the mediated and often contradictory nature of "the" authorial ethos—an ethos that must be reconstructed hermeneutically if the narratologist is to avoid taking his or her readerly intuitions at face value.

When Is Conjecturing About the Author's Ethos Relevant?

While I have defended the idea that in all communication situations ethos attributions occur, these become salient for assigning meaning to literary narratives only under particular conditions.

Exploring how literary texts, and certain genres in particular, "rely for their meaning on complex and ambiguous relationships between the 'I' of the author and any textual voice," Lanser (2005) proposed five criteria for what she called an "attached" reading, that is, a reading that seeks to connect the worldview conveyed by a textual voice to its author. These criteria are: *singularity*, or the presence of only one character; *anonymity*, which makes it easier to see the author in the narrator; *similarities* between the narrator's character and biographic details and those of the author; *reliability*, that is, compatibility between the values and perceptions of the author and those of the narrator; and *non-narrativity*, by which Lanser refers to a narrating "I" that is not reporting on or enacting events but rather giving voice to certain views (perhaps a term like *opinionating* would have been more helpful).[34]

While similarities between a character's and an author's life experiences or concerns constitute plausible grounds for an attached reading, Lanser's other criteria seem somewhat less convincing. Counterexamples for the anonymity criterion quickly come to mind: Robert Pinget's *Quelqu'un*, Beckett's *Not I*, and Wiesław Myśliwski's *Stone upon Stone* all have anonymous narrators, but I don't see why I would feel prompted to equate them with the author. The reliability criterion also seems problematic; we cannot refer to the author's norms as a given, since these are our interpretive construct. It seems safer to argue that any narrative, no matter its mode of transmission, raises questions about its own relation to the author's worldview as soon as the narrative is considered from an ideological, ethical, or rhetorical perspective, as Lanser's own work compellingly suggests. This idea undergirds the whole tradition of rhetorical narratology.

To Lanser's criteria I would in any case add genre and reading strategies, as both operate as a framing, in which authorial ethos may or may not be foregrounded. Let me briefly develop these two suggestions (anticipating chapter 6, which will be devoted entirely to generic framing and ethos expectations).

If, as for instance Lejeune (1975) proposed for autobiography, we consider genres to be tacit communication contracts or "pacts," expectations regarding the relevance of the author's ethos arguably form one part of such generic contracts. Some genres in particular—including autobiographical, essayistic, documentary, or testimonial fiction and the historical novel—conventionally presuppose a strong fiduciary pact stipulating the relation of the writer to his or her words and that of narrative discourse to what is known as factual reality. Such genres tend to display a battery of conventional clues reinforcing the author's authenticity or, minimally, his or her attempt at truthfulness and sincerity.[35] The representation of extreme historical events, such as the Holocaust, is often expected to conform to strong ethos norms, such as those formulated by Jean Améry or Elie Wiesel, for instance: a writer should demonstrate and foster an attitude of respect for the victims or show restraint in trying to represent the unrepresentable. Other writers, from Martin Amis (with *Time's Arrow*) to Jonathan Littell (*The Kindly Ones*), precisely stretch such conventions to their limits, immediately raising questions as to their own ethos and intentions and their right to address such sensitive subjects.

An intriguing issue, in this context, is also the question of how one could distinguish between works that are generically deceptive and those that would be merely ambiguous or complex, as is constitutively the case for generic hybrids, and what kind of framing would result in each of these cases. Generic hybrids have become so popular that they are now recognized as distinct subgenres, such as autofiction, docufiction, mockumentary, and other such designations. But to label a work as a hybrid risks closing off further investigation of the cognitive work that these genres elicit, as we will see in the next chapter.

A special case that needs to be discussed is that of hybrids that challenge more overarching discursive categorizations (what Maingueneau called "global scenes"; see chapter 2). I am thinking here of writers and artists who turn their own lives and body into a performance. Such practices blur the boundaries between writing, or art, and living, and also, in

Boltanski and Thévenot's terminology, between the Domestic and Civic Worlds and the Inspired one, for instance. Quite obviously, in such cases we cannot avoid paying attention to the author's ethos: the cognitive oscillation such works or performances elicit through their generic hybridity, as well as through uncertainties about the author's ethos, constitutes part of the meaning and reflexive quality the artifacts afford. Far from eliminating the relevance of framing borders, these cases precipitate audiences' desire to make generic classifications and characterize the ethos types involved. In order to even start classifying the work as serious art, for instance, or as a mere provocation or hoax, audiences are particularly likely to formulate hypotheses about the author's categorical and aesthetic intentions in conjunction with their ethos (of sincerity, authenticity, irony, etc.).

To give but one example here, I would cite the literary work of Catherine Millet, a well-known French art critic. As a critic Millet argued against any merging of art and reality. She defended the specificity of the art object, favoring aesthetic "distance" and clear "frame borders," to use Goffman's terms, over modern art's tendency towards dedifferentiation. Aesthetic distance, she writes, is the "screen that prevents the artist's gestures from getting dispersed in the totality of reality" (Millet 1997). In good Adorno tradition, her criterion for real art is its resistance to alterity.

In her own literary work, however, Millet seems to do everything to challenge this credo: *La Vie sexuelle de Catherine M.*, published by the "high literature" publishing house Le Seuil as part of a series titled Fiction et cie., appears to be a hardly fictionalized account of the writer's own intensive sex life, featuring quite nakedly many recognizable public and less public personalities. There seems to be little aesthetic distance here, and much room instead for musing about the ethical and aesthetic borders between real life and art, and also about privacy norms. But it is up to readers—and those represented—to contextualize such a work: as a concrete instance of exhibitionism and privacy infringement or, despite appearances of concreteness, as a conceptual artwork that implicitly thematizes framing acts.[36]

Such cases, in which tacit ethos norms attached to genre are transgressed, reveal via the sanctions they elicit the tenor of the pact. As we shall see in chapter 6, generic contracts, like many a contract in everyday life, are not the less effective for being tacit and informal (see also the discussion in chapter 4 of fictionality as a contract). Yet how does a reader decide whether what later turns out to be erroneous framing was intended as aesthetic playfulness, or rather as deception?

Generic frauds indeed deserve special attention. Boltanski and Thévenot's idea that we classify practices according to the "World" to which they belong, and in each of which certain value regimes apply, becomes useful here. It helps explain why readers feel cued to classify a work as factual, as in the case of Frey's *A Million Little Pieces* or Helen Demidenko's *The Hand that Signed the Paper* (discussed in Rigney 1998). Associating expectations of factuality with an authentic authorial ethos, readers feel that breaking such an authenticity contract turns a work not into fiction but into a lie. Yet the lines may be traced differently, depending on one's reading strategies, and depending, of course, on the strategies through which a work was marketed and distributed. In my view, it is not the task of metahermeneutic narratology to prescribe the (im)morality of such practices but rather to lay open for reflection the norms and interpretive procedures on which readers' divergent responses rest.

Reading strategies are indeed the other factor, which in my view may contribute to an "attached" reading. Such strategies are rooted in normative conceptions of literature and interpretation, setting off a selective search for clues. Certain reading strategies, including those of some narratologists, emphasize the intentions, character traits, and/or behavior of what is construed as the real author; for others, this perspective is anathema, which is not to say that the real author plays no role in such practices of interpretation and evaluation.

We might imagine an axis on which conceptions of literature and its analysis could be located, with its two poles consisting of, on one side, a person- or author-oriented approach and, on the other, a work-oriented reading posture (cf. Heinich 2000). Moralistic and psychological or psychoanalytical conceptions of literature tend to promote personalizing reading attitudes, requiring a writer's personal ethos to be congruent with or symptomatic of the ethos conveyed by his or her works. Hence, for audiences who adopt a straightforward moral perspective, Rousseau's abandonment of his own children affects the authority of his pedagogical work, and Céline's anti-Semitism endangers the value of his literary work. Conversely, in autonomous-aesthetic conceptions of literature any recourse to the author's personal ethos is deemed irrelevant. Chatman, for instance, observes that "It makes no more sense to accuse the real Céline or Montherlant of what the implied author causes to happen in 'Journey to the End of the Night' or 'Les Jeunes Filles' than to hold the real Conrad responsible for the reactionary attitudes of the implied author of 'The Secret Agent'" (Chatman 1978, 149). In a metahermeneutic narratology such statements, which express a particular conception of literature, become part of the object of study.

Let me conclude this chapter by elaborating on two facets of the authorial image and on the role these issues play in the interpretation and evaluation of literary works: the author's posture and the implied author.

The Author as a Role

This section refers to what I discussed in chapter 2 under the term *posture*, in relation to the kinds of Worlds (Boltanski and Thévenot) in which posture components operate. By posture, as explained, I mean a double-sided phenomenon: (1) authors suggest in their literary works and especially in the para- and peritexts of their work, as well as in their public expression, interviews, and media appearances, clues that classify them in a particular social role as writer; while (2) readers and other audiences may perceive in their own ways the kind of author they have at hand and pick to that effect what they consider relevant clues (my emphasis, as indicated, lies on the second perspective; in any case, I take the first to be accessible only through an analyst-interpreter's reconstruction).

Neither classical nor postclassical narratologies have devoted much attention to the question of how, and under what conditions, such authorial posturing rather than, for instance, actual biographical details intervene in processes of literary interpretation and evaluation.[37] Yet, as has been well demonstrated in sociological research, author postures are commonly used at all stages of literary communication, not to mention their function in the realm of literary marketing.[38] Attending to authorial postures places negotiations of literature's meanings and values back into the social-cultural sphere, rather than setting these apart in an autonomous literary domain.

Complementing what has been said in chapter 2 about posturing, I would like to briefly comment on two opposed tendencies that may be observed. The first is a tendency among writers, artists, and critics to question the autonomy of literature and the arts, as well as the boundaries between life and art implied in this construction. Studies of postmodernism, for instance, often signal a pervasive inclination toward aestheticizing. This tendency would be expressed by the extension to the public and private spheres of axiologies prevailing in the aesthetic domain: ambiguity, irony, also the right of transgression and provocation, considered as a prerogative of authors and artists, valid within the autonomous realm of the arts, get extended to everyday life. This seems to be the case, for instance, in Houellebecq's, Christine Angot's, or Catherine Millet's public performances, as was the case for Oscar Wilde and other famous dandies or "agents provocateurs."

In such instances, it is reductive to leave the author's public presentation out of an analysis of their narrative work. The author's persona is quite evidently exploited for artistic and ethical effects, and the ethos effects that particular postures elicit fold back onto the interpretation of the work. But as I argued above, such blurring of Worlds exacerbates rather than attenuates the relevance of frame borders and the normative expectations attached to particular genres. Referring to Donald's distinction of modes of cognition, such works and performances, as well as their reception, become art of a more abstract, conceptual sort, as was pointed out by Nelson Goodman (1978), among others. What constitutes the art experience is the cognitive oscillation about how to frame a particular event of artifact, while the thematic material addressed in the performance or artifact (say, bringing sexual acts in the public sphere, in Millet's case) contributes to defining the "relevance frame."

There is, however, symmetrically, an equally conspicuous pervasive ethicization (to use an ugly neologism) in academic and nonacademic literary criticism and "theory." This tendency extends to a writer's literary work the moral norms brought to bear in everyday life, including the need to adhere to and take responsibility for one's words. It also suggests a direct correspondence between a writer's conduct in real life and the value of his or her work. Such a perspective, in contradistinction to the previous tendency, seems to aim toward more concreteness, more continuity between everyday life and the literary experience and less mediating layers and recontextualizations.

Such broader cultural developments are relevant for narratology, as they form part of the pragmatic conditions within which literature operates and according to which we assign meaning and value to works or their makers and decide what value perspectives and worldviews a particular literary work is taken to express.

The Author "In" the Text: The Implied Author

As discussed earlier, while classical narratatology cordoned off real authors, rhetorical narratology let them in through the back door in order to account for what these critics experienced as the intentional, strategic, or ideological organization of point of view within the text—along with what I have called ethos effects, such as irony or unreliability. I will concentrate here on the notion of *implied author*, a concept that, like that of unreliability, to which it is intimately tied, is still regularly invoked as the foil against which critics determine the ethos of characters, narrators, and authors.

There is no need to rehearse all the positions and nuances in the prolific debate about the notion of the implied author, as this has been done thoroughly by a number of theorists (see the excellent special issue of *Style* on the implied author, Richardson 2011; and Kindt and Müller's [2006] thorough investigation of the concept's origins and the strategic work it was made to do; see also Nünning 1997, 1999, 2005; Heinen 2002; and Phelan 2005, 38–49). My point, which was forcefully made earlier by Kindt and Müller, is that disagreements among narratologists about the legitimacy and the definition of the implied author reflect normative conceptions of literature, of interpretation, and of narratology.

But we cannot wholly avoid revisiting some history, especially when it is still very much with us. Booth (1961, 75, 74, 71) famously defined the implied author as the "ideal, literary, created version of the real man," which readers infer as the "official scribe" of the text. As Kindt and Müller note, the implied author allowed commentators to speak in a synthesizing sense about the point of view of a work, to attribute it to a source, and to characterize its ethos, all while avoiding both reductive biographical interpretation and unbound semiosis. "Given these manifest virtues," Harry Shaw writes, "it is hard not to consider 'perverse' the Genettian kind of narratology that considers the term redundant" (Shaw 2005, 301).

Yet these very same virtues of the concept have also been deemed its vices, not only from a classical-descriptive but also from a cognitive-narratological perspective. These grievances have been neatly summarized by Nünning (1997, 2005) and Kindt and Müller (2006). The critiques to a great extent echo the reproaches to Booth's notion of unreliability, for which the postulation of an implied author formed a basic condition: The implied author concept is ambiguous, as it refers both to the origin of the text and to the reader's post hoc construction of a unifying authorial intention and value position.[39] It also relies on the problematic presupposition of a homogeneous, consistent, and personalized author figure and presumes one single correct interpretation. This ambiguity persists in Phelan's revision of the term: "The implied author is a streamlined version of the real author, an actual or purported subset of the real author's capacities, traits, attitudes, beliefs, values, and other properties that play an active role in the construction of the particular text" (Phelan 2005, 45).

The epistemological status of the notion also remains unclear. Is it a central concept in the theory of interpretation? Or is it part of a quasi-empirical, phenomenological theory of reception, a construct necessarily employed by every reader? Despite its apparently technical nature, there is no precise methodology for defining the implied author as a gestalt subsuming the norms of the text, meaning that, in practice, the critic's own moral, psychological, and aesthetic norms and interpretation are projected onto the author.

The implied author concept clearly belongs to interpretation, and not to description, Kindt and Müller conclude.[40] Yet, as they also note, more than thirty years after Genette tried to bar it from noninterpretive, descriptive, narratology, this hermeneutic concept still thrives under the cloak of a descriptive tool. The persistence of the notion would be precisely due to its fuzziness: the term, with its connotation of technicity, allows analysts to circumvent the taboo on speaking about the biographical author's intentions and values (Kindt and Müller 2006, 10).

As I see it, the main fault of the implied author notion, from both Kindt and Müller's and Nünning's perspectives, seems to be its interpretive and normative character (later Nünning adopts a more nuanced position, partly in response to his dialogue with Phelan, embracing a notion of the implied author as an intentionality constructed by the reader; see Nünning 2008). The implied author also reactivated within narratology considerations about the moral and civic responsibility of the author. Each of these implications constituted, arguably, a breach in the autonomist conception of literature and/or in the objectivist stance that classical and cognitivist narratologies tend to profess.

The appropriateness of the critiques, though, depends on how one views the role of interpretation in narratology. From my perspective, the suggestion that there is a descriptive method for establishing an implied author position itself indulges in what might be called a descriptive fallacy. If one recognizes the hermeneutic character of the concept as it was coined by Booth, who never made a secret of his hermeneutic stance, and if one keeps in mind the insights of both cognitive theories of meaning making (especially the role of frames in making sense of new experiences) and hermeneutics, there is no theoretical ground to sever this author image inferred through the text from readers' other interpretive strategies. Instead of pledging allegiance to one normative conception of literary narrative, a metahermeneutic narratology may instead want to account for the range of conceptions, investigating why, when, and how readers attach or detach a given text to an implied author.

Moreover, if one considers that any discourse genre requires specific interpretive and evaluative regimes—even if one text may be perceived as combining different generic frames—then it is certainly better *not* to amalgamate the real author and the image we may construct on the basis of a work. At least seems justified to differentiate between the author as I infer her or him from her or his work, on one hand, and the biographical person, on the other. This is a clumsy way of speaking, which is why I propose, from a metahermeneutic perspective, to keep the term *implied author*, in full awareness that it is just one interpretive strategy to imagine such a figure. Like a reader's idea about the genre to which a text belongs, his or her conjectures about an author's ethos and posturing can be considered as macrohypotheses for classifying a work and for activating interpretation paths and evaluation regimes. But we need to investigate more closely the relationship between the inferences summarized under this concept of implied author, those that result from clues about authorial posture, which readers may glean from the public domain or paratexts, and readers' other strategies to come up with overall meaning intentions for a text they read. This investigation, however, would require another book. It also would require research cooperation, bringing together narratological theorizing and empirical, reception-oriented research.

Only by recognizing the interpretive and composite character of the author image, including that of the implied author, can narratology begin to address the diversity of readings, which would particularly appear in readers' diverging construction of narrator's and author's ethos, or of a text's irony. To take on board the author's postures, his or her public images and modes of self-fashioning, also allows us to heed, in fairly precise ways, the broader context within which literature's rhetorical dimension operates. Moreover, this broader perspective sharpens the analyst's eye for topoi through which authors secure moral, civic, or aesthetic value and authority for their own writing.

PART 3   *Further Explorations*
                Contracts and Ethos Expectations

BUILDING ON THE FRAMEWORK developed in the first two parts, part 3 elaborates on two key issues. The first, which has regularly popped up already, is that of the framing function of genre, which is explored in chapter 6. Genres can be considered to raise expectations regarding the point of the literary experience and the work's rhetorical aims: for instance, to move, convince, and denounce, in the case of engagé literature; to inform and, often, to testify or denounce, in documentary works; to reflect, in the essay. To the generic expectations also belong anticipation regarding an author's or narrator's ethos and about the interpretive and evaluative regimes considered appropriate. A writer also adopts a posture and expresses a conception of literature through the choice of genre. She or he inscribes her- or himself into the "structured space of positions" within the literary field and offers his or her writing for accreditation (Dubois 1992). But just as texts, or their authors, may elicit interpretive uncertainties through conflicting or indeterminate generic clues, they can withhold or contradict an expected ethos, display it deceptively, or multiply conflicting ethos cues.

The second issue that is central in part 3 is how readers would assess a narrative voice's or an author's sincerity, or rather, its irony. While there is a sense in which sincerity and irony form two sides of the same coin, and each can very well accommodate a dash of the other, I discuss them separately, shedding light on different perspectives that should be fruitful for the analysis of ethos attributions. Both subjects, which are particularly challenging for any analysis of ethos attributions, are developed in chapter 7. Sincerity, as one of irony's "others," will be mainly approached from a culture-historical perspective. I draw attention to the various topoi that might signal sincerity but also to the quite diverse connotations and evaluations attached to this kind of ethos. The other section concentrates on forms of irony that are intimately connected to uncertainties about who asserts, and whose point of view or ethos we would construct as being asserted, an uncertainty that is partly inherent to the fictional or literary communication contract.

6 : Generic Framing and Authorial Ethos

*Every text participates in one or several genres, there is no genreless
text . . . yet such participation never amounts to belonging. And
not because of an abundant overflowing of a free, anarchic and
unclassifiable productivity, but because of the trait of participation
itself, because of the effect of the code and of the generic mark.*

JACQUES DERRIDA, "The Law of Genre"

In this chapter I would like to spell out the interconnection between
generic framing and ethos attributions in more concrete terms. I
shall concentrate on two cases, François Bon's *Daewoo*, as an example of engagé documentary fiction, and Christine Angot's *Sujet Angot*,
which many would classify as autofiction. Both *writing the social and
writing the self* raise particular expectations regarding the rapport between (real) author and narrative voices and about their ethos: in the
case of *Daewoo*, about the narrator's and author's trustworthiness and
authorization as a spokesman, in Angot's case, about the authenticity of the displayed self-reflection. It is not my aim to propose new
interpretations of these works. Rather, I explore the heuristic and
metahermeneutic fruitfulness of focusing on the dynamic connections between genre-bound ethos expectations as framing acts, reading strategies, and textual clues. Clearly, one case does not suffice to
build an argument about specific genre expectations. Moreover, this
research would benefit from being extended, combining metahermeneutic investigation with empirical reception research to test the former's hypotheses.

Writing the Social: The Constraints of *Engagement* in François Bon's *Daewoo*

Debates about the status and relevance of literature have been waged in many Western countries. One common view suggests that literature is currently facing an impending decline. The formerly prestigious art of language has to find a new place in competition with more popular arts and media, along with new strategies to capture the attention of audiences that perhaps have become used to more accessible media and genres. The writing and reading of more traditional literary genres indeed demand leisure time, concentration, and an extended mastery of language, which arguably have become rare in our times.

In France the writer and literature more generally have traditionally been invested with high symbolic value, to the extent that quoting literary authors increases a politician's authority, in a transfer of values from the literary to the civic domain. The posture of the writer as the independent conscience and gadfly of the nation has been so eloquently incarnated by Voltaire, Zola, or Sartre that the French tradition has helped shape, on an international scale, the writer's role as public intellectual.[1] But after a Sartrian overdose and the tide of well-meaning emancipatory writing of the sixties and seventies, literary *engagement* came to be associated, somewhat hastily, with unsophisticated, instrumental writing, wholly opposite to the cult of aesthetic form and self-referentiality that had become the token of high art.

Recently, however, authoritative voices in the literary and broader cultural field have accused "formalist" navel-gazing *écriture* itself of cutting off literature from its native task, which would lie in expressing people's experiences and concerns (Compagnon 1998; Marx 2005; Todorov 2007; a similar view is frequently voiced in ethical criticism and cognitive narratology). Literature in turn now requires the injection of discursive authority borrowed from various other domains: the civic, but also the world of the news and entertainment media. The work of François Bon provides an example of writing that responds to the challenges evoked above but that seeks to reinstate the social mission of the writer right in the heart of his or her reflection on the aesthetic.

With a new book nearly every year, Bon is a prolific writer who publishes with prestigious and select literary publishers (Minuit, Verdier) as well as others targeting a broader public (Fayard).[2] His first book, *Sortie d'usine* (1982), about the world of factories and the working class, already displayed a characteristic style, which remains mimetically close to the parlances of the social milieus it evokes while heavily stylizing them, combining poetic or aesthetic, phenomenological, and critical effects.

Bon often emphasizes that his writing springs from his own life experience but also from his passion for literature and the other arts, lenses through which he discovered the world. Like Eggers, he seems to take very seriously his role as cultural mediator, conducting writing workshops with homeless people and prisoners, whose experimentations in language and narration in turn feed his own writing.[3] His website (www.tierslivre.net) and the site about contemporary literature he founded (www.remue.net) offer dynamic platforms for critical reflection on contemporary culture and society.

As I will be discussing Bon's novel *Daewoo* in more detail, some further specifics about its composition and structure should be helpful.[4] *Daewoo* intertwines short sections belonging roughly to four distinct strands: (1) facts and figures about the history of the Daewoo factories in the Lorraine region, resulting from the narrator's fact-finding; (2) his interviews with the women who lost their jobs; (3) fragments of the author-narrator's earlier play, incorporating but also transforming the words of these women; and finally, (4) reflections on writing and seeing. These strands, heterogeneous in tone and style, are combined in an attempt to "convene this diffraction of languages, of faces, of signs, that one has, over all these weeks, accumulated" (12).

With his denunciation of social violence, Bon stands in the venerable French tradition of literary *engagement.* "Let the novel be memory . . . for those women workers who do not have a place anywhere anymore," the blurb on the back cover announces, raising expectations of committed docufiction and testimony writing. In these genres referential and rhetorical dimensions are primordial; they also require ethos cues that suggest the author's authentic commitment and authority in the matter.[5]

Bon, however, tends to react as if stung by a bee when asked about his writing's social or political commitments, a vehemence that points to the norms associated with the author's posture, as I hope to argue (see, for instance, Bon and Bourmeau 2004). Indeed, however strong the cues for a referential and engagé reading frame, Bon's writing always displays conspicuous signals of literariness, calling for an aesthetic framing of his work. In fact, Bon himself denounces the opposition between aesthetic and social or ethical concerns as utterly sterile. Any attempt to reinvest literature with social relevance, in his view, is necessarily connected with the aesthetic challenges today's writer has to overcome, in particular the concurrence of visual and more popular media.

But how does his work negotiate these possibly conflicting demands? In particular, how does he ensure both the authority of documentary or engagé writing and that of the writer who is to be taken seriously in the aesthetic domain? I hope to show in the following pages some significant connections between generic framing and ethos clues, through my reconstruction of the author's positioning with respect to the engagé novel.

Genre and Position Taking

In connection with the dismantling of the Daewoo factories, one finds on Bon's website—aside from references to the original play, photo series, films, and written, audio, and visual public media—performances, exhibitions by other photographers, and petitions to be signed and political actions to join. Why add a novel to all this multimedia material? The question is all the more legitimate since in an earlier manifesto-like essay Bon demonstratively discarded the novel as a genre: "The novel does not suffice anymore, nor does fiction. . . . One would prefer pure documentary, . . . the silent succession of images . . . , [the] inventory. . . . One should not have to invent [the real], but just try to come near to it" (1998, 12–13; I will leave out of the discussion the intertextuality with Georges Perec's writing, which resonates in this program of making an inventory of the real; even though, with respect to authorial posturing and ethos, such affiliations have strategic and semantically specifying value).

How then should we understand this paradoxical return to the novel, which would reject fictionality and invention, letting reality speak for itself? Bon's argumentation about the novel operates, as said, in a literary landscape polarized between Sartrian engagement and its emancipatory heirs, on the one hand, and the experiments of the Nouveau Roman and *Tel Quel*, on the other. Keeping in mind these tensions, I would like to reconstruct Bon's strategic redefinition of literature—and the novel in particular—as mimesis, stipulating its functions and tasks.

Far from being enslaved to the reproduction of reality, Bon argues, artistic mimesis throughout the history of art sprang from a fascination with the enigma of reality and human experience (*enigma* is a word the author clearly cherishes). It is in that tradition that he places his own allegiance to the real, the visible, and audible (Bon 1998).

Bon's rejection of fiction as invention and his allegiance to the real as the writer's domain strengthen both his socially committed and his aesthetic positioning. On the one side, he postures himself and his narrator as social seismograph and ethnographer, invested with a particular social responsibility because of his skills as a "man of words." As a craftsman whose material is language, Bon is particularly sensitive to the ways in which reality's complexity appears in the diversity of verbal expressions, which conveys both people's highly singular perception and their social conditions.[6]

Specific ethos clues work to reinforce this posture. There are still traces in Bon's writing and posturing of a Sartrian kind of writerly authority, rooted in the writer-intellectual's specific analytical expertise in unveiling the real. But such a logos-based ethos tends to be supplanted by more pathos-based clues, suggesting an authentic, personal, and truthful engagement with the people whose experience the writer seeks to mediate.[7]

On the other side, it is up to the artist to capture and transmit the paradoxical sense of reality's immediacy. Hence the cues for a posture and ethos of aesthetic craftsmanship but also of philosophical, poetic, and political sensitivity, all in the service of a better understanding of reality and an effective transmission of this understanding. In this way, connections are secured between writing traditions and discursive genres often perceived as mutually exclusive: traditional realist fiction, the documentary or engaged novel, and experimental writing, but also between literature and the analytic discourses of philosophy, ethnography, sociology, and political critique.

With this complex conception of literary mimesis and his conspicuous work on style and composition, Bon can safely cast his narrator and himself in the posture of a social witness and truth finder, without incurring the risk of being "classified in the documentary slot, or even in the sociological one"—and, I would add, the engagé one—generic boxes with much less aesthetic prestige (Bon and Bourmeau 2004). As I hope to show, there is more than a suggestion that the writer's social task is to carry apparently antiaesthetic subjects into the novel, revitalizing a genre that some declared moribund, in the same manner that seventeenth-century Flemish painters of everyday life or nineteenth-century writers renovated their art. Bon's handling of these various tasks of literature leads to intriguing reciprocal transfers of value between the aesthetic and social worlds, with the narrator or writer as the mediator of values. To make my point, I will first discuss some markers of more traditional modes of literary engagement, before investigating *Daewoo* more closely in terms of authorial posturing and ethos projection.

Writing to Counteract "Effacement": The Engagé Ethos

In light of Bon's views on writing, briefly sketched above, the very first paragraph of *Daewoo* reads programmatically. The opening sentences announce the militant agenda: "To refuse. To confront effacement itself" (9). The narrator is described in a symbolic hermeneutic posture, on the threshold of the empty factory building, expressing his desire to see and understand in order to tell readers about the human experiences occurring beyond this sight. This role brings the writer close to the journalist, but also the social analyst, and suggests his work's affinity with genres such as reportage and documentary. The text, however, immediately withdraws from our comprehension what was made visible, insisting on its hidden meaning instead. Thus, beyond thorough information and analytic expertise, the writer-reporter's role is enriched with the task of discerning and interpreting the signs that lead to a deeper grasp of reality (a task reminiscent of the hermeneutic scholar's task of "divination," discussed in chapter 1).

Just as programmatically, rather than the transparent language that Sartre claimed for engagé literary prose, these opening sentences display a style that conspicuously draws attention to itself: "Such a stunning presence, sometimes, of all things, there, in front of an open porch which however one cannot transgress. . . . Discrete signs, nevertheless, and opaque, nothing but ordinary" (9).[8] Thus, on the threshold of the book, style works as a frame key (to borrow Goffman's term), signaling that the reader is entering a literary, aesthetic, experience. This keying may correct the posture of rather plain commitment conveyed by the militant agenda on the book's cover.

Despite the author's disclaimers, and the salience of aesthetic concerns, Bon's work and public manifestations display many of the characteristics of literary engagement inventoried by Benoît Denis (2000, 30–50). Let me summarize in terms of topoi Denis's account and briefly elaborate on it. Such topoi, I propose, activate in the minds of readers—at least, of those who share this background knowledge—a familiar authorial posture, which rests on socially recognized grounds of authority and trustworthiness:

> Engagé writing is meant as an act accomplished by the writer on the public scene, which implies taking risks, and springs from a sense of urgency. Its relevance is specific rather than universal (though the latter can very well tap into the former), meant for the "here and now," not for some abstract eternity.
>
> Engagé writing requires a personal investment by the real author, overcoming the aloofness and impunity claimed for the writer in autonomous conceptions of literature. The "engaged writer . . . has explicitly taken on a series of commitments with regards to the collectivity, [and] is in a sense tied to it by a promise, [having] engaged his credibility and reputation" (Denis 2000, 30). In this posturing, which stages the writer as a public figure, the ethos of the work and the extratextual ethos of the author constantly reinforce each other (see also Denis 2000, 47). The author, moreover, will tend to bring to the fore his or her authorization to speak and an urge to speak up as the mouthpiece of a minority, a people, a nation, and so on. Popular arguments for such a writer's authorization, nowadays, would typically include participation (shared experience) and testimony, which convey an ethos of authenticity drawing heavily on pathos rather than on abstract analytical knowledge (logos).
>
> Engagé writing takes a stand on political, social, or ethical issues. It often displays a clear oppositional actantial and axiological structure, which culminates in the *roman à thèse* (Suleiman 1983) or even the pamphlet (Angenot 1982). We will find this oppositional structure also in *Daewoo*.

Readers, moreover, are cued to consider the world evoked in the novel as homologous to and in continuity with the real world, which should make one feel actually concerned. This is achieved, I propose, through both analogic and metonymic means: the scenography implied in a text and its paratextual framing emphasize the exemplarity of the situation, offered for analogous translation into the reader's own experience, and/ or its contiguity to the readers' world, so that, after closing the book, one must extend one's reflection to real-world conditions.

Unsurprisingly, all these elements highlight the pragmatic dimension of the literary work and its efficacy in conveying a standpoint and achieving some kind of intervention in reality, beyond the protected playground of autonomous art. In fact, as Bon rightly observes in an interview when asked about the tensions between engagement and aesthetic concerns, "I don't understand how you can suggest such a binary opposition" (Bon and Lecoq 2002). However reductive, I will adopt the binary for my own argumentation, claiming that it still works in a way that structures Bon's own strategies for authorial self-positioning.

In *Daewoo*, the engagé topoi are indeed conspicuous. Much is done to make sure that readers conceive of the evoked world as the real world, eliciting a generic framing as documentary fiction. Referentiality is secured by the abundant use of documentary material, such as newspaper clippings, figures, and names of actual people. Photographs on the website function as indexical proof: The author himself was there, on the spot, witnessing the dismantling of the Daewoo factories.

Readers are indeed incited to equate narrator and author. Like his narrator, Bon mentions in interviews and on his website how his interest was caught by a short item in the regional newspaper *L'Est républicain* about the closing of the factories. He recalls, like his narrator, how he went on the spot to investigate and was overwhelmed by the impact of what he saw, or rather by the work of "effacement" he could still witness. Hence the necessity and even the urgency of scripting his play, and later the book: "This is not a premeditated book: . . . because of the faces, for the thickness of the shared words, I decide to write," he explains on the back cover of *Daewoo* (where the "I" conventionally will be considered to be the author). Such an explanation, in my view, is not merely factual but works as an ethos topos, like the claim that the author has a mission. Someone has to right/write the wrongs that have been done, or at least to document and denounce them: "If there's no place anywhere anymore for these workers, let the novel be memory," the back cover copy continues. The title (*Daewoo*)—which, again, will usually be taken to be the author's choice, whatever the role of the publisher—explicitly targets the culprit. Writing clearly aims to be an act in the Civic World, and this mission is embraced by narrator and author alike.

The personal investment of author and narrator is underlined by topoi that also establish their authority and legitimacy. The text mentions the writer's "duty to speak": "One is summoned," Bon's narrator writes, as if this were a self-evident norm. He modestly refers to himself in the impersonal form, the writer-reporter's ego effaced by the weight of the cause. "One" has no choice, even though there is some personal cost, felt in the body: a "feeling of being crushed . . . , insomnias" as a result of the depressing inquiries.[9]

The investigation is presented as involving real risks, which testifies to the writer-reporter's true commitment. The grounds of the factories are guarded; the narrator has to sneak in or assuage the guardians, but their watchdog is less easy to persuade. Again, François Bon's own extratextual ethos seems to fully back or even coincide with his narrator's. Not only, as mentioned, does Bon's website "prove" his own presence on the Daewoo grounds, but, more generally, his solidarity with the destitute, attested by his work with homeless people and prisoners, seems to confirm in real-life deeds the textually conveyed posture and ethos of commitment.

Critics also often mention other facets of the topos of expertise and inside knowledge that ground Bon's own authority as a spokesman for the world of labor. Critics in particular refer to what Bon himself frequently points out, that he was trained and worked as a skilled technician, that his father was a mechanic who had a garage and sold cars. He also knows from the inside the world of factories and workshops and has shared in the habitus of the working class. Significantly, Bon positions himself both as an outsider to the literary field and as natively belonging to it through his mother, who as a teacher gave him early access to words and literature, as well as through his own work and disposition. Thus, Bon's writing can be framed as belonging simultaneously to two Worlds, in Boltanski and Thévenot's terms (see chapter 2): the Industrial World, that is, the world of labor, and that of the Inspired or aesthetic. In each of them different kinds of authority prevail.

It befits this Industrial authorial posture, for instance, that writing is not presented as a leisure activity, practiced in isolation, nor according to conventional conceptions of literature's autonomy, but as a profession, with a public dimension and responsibility. Bon's expression "nos métiers de plume" (our professions of the [feather] pen; 83) nicely conveys the connection to the age-old task of the writer as social scribe. The artisanal dimension of writing also establishes continuity between the world of manual labor and that of the writer. Like the worker, Bon speaks about his tools, material, and craft, specifically the craft of using language: "My own working field is very clear: how things get expressed through words, what happens, consequently, to language?" (Bon and Lebrun 2004). Elsewhere he notes, "My work is to acknowledge, through writing, relations and events that occur between human beings." To the writer's profession is attached symbolic authority in society: "It's just as well to benefit, sometimes, from this fear that still surrounds, for some, the capacity to bring words into the light" (82).

This posture of social scribe and spokesman implies not only trust but also accountability. The text of *Daewoo* mentions on several occasions how the narrator is himself seen through the eyes of those about whom, and on behalf of whom, he writes, as well as how he engages with their image of him. In this way, the text itself raises questions about the legitimacy of the narrator's inquiry, placed under the well-intentioned motto of "explain[ing] to one half of humanity how the other half lives."[10] Such an inquiry, however, means poking into people's lives, thereby transforming their experience: this paradox, and the ethical dilemma it entails, is well known to ethnographers. The narrator mentions, for instance, the reticent reaction of a husband whose wife is interviewed: "One does not speak so much anymore about that. One needs to rest, after that" (71; similarly, 72–73).

Quite explicitly, Geraldine Roux, one of the more flamboyant characters among the women the narrator interviews, confronts him with his own blindness to his alibi function. His audience will inevitably seize on his representations of the workers and mold those representations to fit stereotypes, she says: "A worker, who can do nothing but complaining." She has no doubts about his good intentions, but "for the rest, everything remains in its place, one has done what one had to, laid a bunch of flowers at the funeral" (104–5). The novel thus both emphasizes and relativizes the author-narrator's ambition and right to represent the working-class people, in the double sense of evoking them and of speaking for them. Yet, again, such self-critical reflections, which tone down the concrete social effects of literary *engagement*, may paradoxically enhance the writer-narrator's personal ethos of sincerity.

All in all, the effect of posturing, which taps into socially validated roles for writers and immediately activates an ethos, should not be underestimated. It suffices to evoke a few stereotypical features and the whole posture and ethos jump into place, shielding from awareness, perhaps, dissonant details. In the insistent investigator or reporter posture, for instance, both author and narrator replay the emblematic model pioneered by Zola, as critics dutifully picked up. Like Zola, Bon and his narrator typically explore the world equipped with notebook and camera, aiming to register reality as indexically as possible, professionally and truthfully.

Writing under such circumstances requires specific social and professional skills and ethos. Bon's narrator mentions in passing his familiarity with journalistic interview techniques. More importantly, as we saw, the text extensively conveys the narrator's truthfulness. I want to insist here on the transfer of trust from the women to the narrator, which seems to be staged in several scenes. At one point, for instance, the narrator recalls and scenically represents how he manages to make even those women whose working-class habitus hardly inclines them to speak about personal matters talk to him, thus demonstrating their trust in him. I read such scenes as confirmation of the narrator-interviewer's attitude of *eunoia* and the recognition of his good intentions by his audience-interlocutors. The work, meanwhile, emphasizes in several other scenes the lack of trust and respect encountered by the interviewed women, not only from their employers but also from the media that were supposed to inform the world about their unjust treatment. Thus, in contrast, is grounded the narrator-author's superior authorization to speak for the victims.

Paradoxically, even the fact that the narrator is explicitly granted by the women themselves the liberty to rework—read: fictionalize—their words can be interpreted as a token of trust. For instance, in response to one woman's questions, Bon's narrator writes, "I answered that my reason for noting with precision, was also the need to paint freely: that it is only at that price that one is accurate" (103).

This staging, within the work, of the women's trust, and of the narrator's right to speak for them, is the more interesting if we keep in mind that the interviews that form the core scenography of the book, as authentic documentary, have not—not to this extent—actually been conducted. This means that despite the strong clues inviting one to equate author and narrator, differentiation between the two is relevant. During a conference on Bon's work, the author indeed acknowledged that most interviews that feature in the book were invented, which apparently shocked several of the participants (Montfrans-van Oers 2010). Reconstructing the grounds for this reaction in Maingueneau's terms (see chapter 2), it seems that the scenography of *documentary writing*, which is the framing suggested for the narrator's work, has been projected upon the generic scene, which applies to the work as a whole, as well as upon the text's overall discourse type (as in Frey's admittedly much more dramatic case). The preceding detailed analysis picked out the many conventional clues that "justified" amalgamating author and narrator and conflating these different "scenes." The insistent cues pointing to an indexical and documentary stance may explain that at least some readers experienced the "revelation" of invention as a breach of trust and a breach of contract (interestingly, these readers were literary experts; their sense of deception might have stemmed from being faced with their professional failure to adequately classify the text's genre, rather than from moral expectations).

From a metahermeneutic perspective, the literal factuality suggested in works like Bon's appears indeed to be more or less relevant depending on readers' conception of authenticity, their reading strategy, and their generic framing of the work. A broader understanding of documentary and engaged art, for instance, easily accommodates a detour through fiction: the cognitive path from the reading experience to reality then proceeds, one might suggest, along a parabolic process (the exemplary), rather than through indexicality and direct reference. For a reader sensitive to such clues, there are, moreover, sufficient discrete signs scattered over the book to tone down expectations of wholesome factuality.

All in all, a framing of the work as engagé documentary to some extent seems perfectly warranted. The novel displays strong rhetorical appeals to readers to share its emphatically well-informed and sincere depiction of and standpoint on the Daewoo case and its social consequences. The rhetorical posturing and ethos of both narrator and author, respectively staged in the work itself and expressed in the author's public manifestations, seem to confirm the required sincerity and authority and authorize them to speak up and to speak for the victims.

The frontiers between book and life, moreover, seem intentionally porous. The text insists on the concrete links that connect the reader to the depicted world, implicating us and suggesting our responsibility: don't we buy the televisions (like those) they were assembling in the Daewoo factories, with the traces of these women's hands and faces still on their shining screens? The intriguing use of the plural and collective pronouns *vous*, *nous*, and *on* contributes to this sense of inclusion of the reader, who can also move on to Bon's website and engage in action, like signing a petition for the man who had been (unjustly?) accused of setting fire to the factory.[11]

Occasionally, through its oppositional actantial structure and axiology, *Daewoo* even skirts the pamphlet, underlined by a rhetoric that castigates the "wrong side" and credits their victims with authenticity and truthfulness. In some sections the ideological structure definitely supersedes the aesthetic, at least for the reader I am, as when the argument about the wrongs done by the closing of the Daewoo factories is extended to a five-page list of economic sectors with similar problems (150–54) or to a litany of grievances voiced by the actresses (250–55). These sections alone strongly contribute to the narrator-author's posture of denunciator, recalling the Zola of *J'accuse*. But how does this overall engagé rhetoric and ethical stance coexist with the aesthetic framing also elicited by Bon's work, in particular, by his conspicuous attention to writing?

Daewoo *and the Ethics of Aestheticism—or the Reverse?*

Daewoo indeed evokes the lives of the workers and the world of factories and suburbs in insistently aesthetic terms, which may add other dimensions to the reader's construction of the narrator's and author's intentions and ethos. The text, for instance, systematically evokes the low cultural and social prestige of the workers and their world of factories and suburbs as presented in the media, only to highlight their aesthetic potential, often within one and the same sentence.

Thus, describing "[t]he world, here, with the highway on one side and the apartment buildings on the other, [which] does not lend itself to becoming a poem, nor to the creation of fantastic worlds," the narrator adds, "[h]owever, that's what even here had to be forced out: this mystery, which connects a concrete place to the enigma of human lives, sometimes doesn't leave traces. . . . [T]he poetic tension of [one's] prose is the precise movement through which one extorts out of the real this sense of presence" (119).

Bon's work on style does not just convey this "sense of presence" but also, I want to argue, transfers meaning and value from the text to the evoked reality. Such a value transfer requires the intervention of the writer, defining a posture that Bon often adopts not just in his literary work but also in his writing workshops: that of the writer as a mediator of values, who bridges social and cultural gaps precisely through the power of language and imagination.

Together with style and literary invention, literary and artistic references also operate as such vehicles for value transfer. For instance, recalling how he stepped into the empty Daewoo factory buildings, the narrator observes, "One experiences in an empty factory almost the same elation as in a cathedral. And from these arbitrary, but plastically magical objects, for instance, between the two identical halls, this passage through a door of thick plastic, in an iron frame: the pure and abstract image of a red rectangle through which runs a black line, against the grey background of the doorway, with the orange lining, a Rothko" (80). The description represents the factory space in aesthetic-abstract terms. Its rhythm, alliteration, syntax blocks, and punctuation iconically convey some of the rectangular effect of "a Rothko." Style seems to project value onto objects or subjects deemed less prestigious, as does the reference to "a Rothko," which does not just activate a particular visualization but can also be perceived as transferring to the factory space the symbolic value attached to the painter's name.

Another example of this mechanism of value transfer is a scene in which the narrator looks together with one of the workers, Martine S., at a letter written by Sylvia, a syndicate leader who committed suicide. Martine mentions that, at the end of that letter, "'the question mark, she [Sylvia] did not put it at the end of the sentence. It is underneath that she put it.' I answered that it was beautiful like some Nathalie Sarraute, and told her in three words who that was, and why [she was] so important to me, Nathalie Sarraute" (277). In this particular situation, the reference to Sarraute, usually considered to belong to highbrow experimental literature, bridges cultural spheres often perceived as incommensurable. Apparently, "three words" are all there is to intracultural communication.

The aestheticization and allocation of symbolic value actually seem to function in a kind of exchange, rather than in a one-sided transfer: the victims of Daewoo—the women with whom the narrator talks—give him their trust and their words, while his job is to broadcast their experience and transform it into value through writing.[12] In return, the writer stands out as an important relay in the distribution of values and experiences in society. He is the mediator between high and low culture and between social groups, divided by their incommensurable vocabularies. In this light, Bon's aesthetic attitude can be considered to reinforce the ethical or engagé strategy.

But does it really work that way? In several places the aesthetic effect seems to stand proudly on its own, rather than supporting an engagé agenda. The artist's display of virtuosity, already conspicuous in the Rothko example, characterizes several key scenes of the book. The grand description of the fire that destroys one of the factories, for instance, occasions the following reflection on the narrator's artistic aims: "What one would hope to force out of reality, even here at Fameck, is something like a Hieronymus Bosch through words, where there would be darkness, dashes of fresco, strange inventions, and almost palpable faces looming in close-up. Together with the fire in the background, as I could recall it in Hieronymus Bosch (a painter for writers, a sculptor friend one day told me). . . . [T]o find for Fameck this direct force, this presence, without reflection or any hesitation, that is what I wanted for my book" (97). This remark foregrounds the challenges of the aesthetic, such as the excitement of exploring the limits of language and of emulating the intensity of vision in the visual arts.[13]

Wary of any narrow political positioning, the author takes care to counterbalance any reductive foregrounding either of these aesthetic challenges or of his ethical and social commitment. When asked by a critic whether he considers his work as engagé, Bon typically shifts to its aesthetic purport instead, in a conspicuously crafted style: "[H]ow to say [in words] an underground parking garage, if that's what appears beautiful to us?" Or, in the same interview, he redefines engagement as "a wrestling in which . . . , in one's guts, one takes the full impact of the world and its signs" (Bon and Millois 1995). The somewhat clumsy phrasing, for me, discursively conveys an ethos of sincerity, iconically and indexically attesting that the response comes from somewhere deep, from the author's "guts": a bodily lived truth rather than the expression of some prefab conceptualized ideology or political standpoint, which counts as a risk of engagé art.

Against the kind of experimental art that would widen cultural gaps, but also against the tendency to discard literature itself as elitist or obsolete, Bon's writing and public activities, in my view, aim at reinvesting literature with a social function, which is presented as its native task. Writing is conceived of in terms of documenting and witnessing, with roots in real personal and collective experience. Far from a narrowly understood functionality, though, novelistic mimesis includes the aesthetic rendition of how people in different nooks and folds of society configure, in their own vocabularies and scripts, their particular perception of reality. To convey in the performativity of writing such a conception of literature requires a complex ethos projection, which I have attempted to reconstruct in reference to the dialogic context within which formal choices resonate and to topoi associated with the suggested generic frames.

Bon's writing symbolically stages the heartening suggestion that cultural gaps can be bridged, enacting an aesthetic strategy that his texts thereby seek to export into real life. Consequently, the consecration he seeks has to come from two sides. First, it comes from the socially oppressed, whose transfer of trust he stages in the writing itself, a virtual recognition that is more easily ensured than that of an actual audience, on this side of the cultural divide. Second, consecration must come from established literary authorities, in particular literary critics, who on the whole have quite positively responded to his literary enterprise (see Korthals Altes 2007).

As Maingueneau suggests, an author's own ethos management often leads back to the desire to defend both literature's and the writer's social relevance. The infusion of literature with the real, of which Bon's work is just one example among many, seems currently to be one of the most effective means of securing this justification. This observation also suggests one reason why Bon wrote a novel about the Daewoo case: more than a play, the novel allows the writer to give center stage to an auctorial narrator, dramatizing his testimonial act and expert scrutiny of the real as a "man of words." The extent to which one is sensitive to ambiguities in this self-staging depends on the image of the author a reader holds and on one's expectations of documentary or engagé literature.

Writing the Self by Procuration: Autofiction in Christine Angot's *Sujet*?

What the works of Angot, Bon, Eggers, and Frey have in common is that they elicit what Lanser called an attached reading (see chapter 5), folding textual voices back onto their author while raising uncertainties regarding authorial ethos and generic framing. This section concentrates on textual and extratextual ethos effects in autofiction, a hybrid of autobiography and fiction. My case here is *Sujet Angot* by Christine Angot, a marked, and controversial, voice in contemporary French autofiction.

Angot branded her image of pugnacious authenticity through her memorable appearance on Bernard Pivot's literary TV talk show *Bouillon de Culture* on the occasion of the publication of *L'Inceste* (September 3, 1999). This performance, in which she challenged conventions and representatives of the institutionalized literary game, played a pivotal part in her breakthrough after nine years of rather discreet publishing.[14] Whichever genre Angot adopts, from fiction to live performances, her own persona seems to be ubiquitous, publicly aired, moreover, by the French media with her willing cooperation. Angot's persona and work seem exemplary in tearing down the frame borders between writing, real-life experience, and public conduct, a dismantling of borders that raises interesting questions about the authorial ethos.

Autofiction: Rabbit and Duck

Confronted with a book titled *Sujet Angot*, while the cover calls it a *roman*, the informed reader is likely to recognize the paradoxical framing cues that have come to define autofiction. Structuralist or historical studies of autofiction usually studiously list its hybrid generic features (e.g., Gasparini 2008). In my view, such approaches bypass what constitutes the genre's interest, namely, the uncertainties regarding generic categorization, which translate into uncertainties about the point of such works and about what interpretive and evaluative regimes appropriately apply.

Long relegated to peripheral status in terms of literary standards, autobiographic expression has become one of the most popular practices in our culture of narcissism, to borrow Lasch's (1979) increasingly apt qualification. New social media urge us to exhibit a self in its most intimate details and to facilitate its broadcasting, intensifying the conjoined imperatives of transparency and spectacularization. Meanwhile, contemporary science, art, philosophy, and psychoanalysis highlight the precariousness and evanescence of personal identity. Autofiction is the genre in which this self-interrogation is pushed to its highest—ludic or anxious—degree of reflexivity.

Writing the self comes in a multiplicity of genres, including, mainly, autobiography, diary, memoir, autofiction, and the essay. All the forms of self-writing define themselves, to some degree, by what Philippe Lejeune called the autobiographic pact, according to which the author, the work's narrator, and its protagonist are expected to "be" the same person.[15] Like every contract, this one requires the backing of an ethos, primarily here that of sincerity (Lejeune 1975, 7–8).

As a form of *autobio* writing, autofiction cannot avoid drawing central attention to the rapport between writing and the author's "real" experience. Yet as *fiction*, autofiction may be expected to uncouple, to some extent, the work from its author and biographic context, activating a literary or aesthetic reading attitude.

Literariness, as we saw in chapter 4, has been defined in several ways. As Genette proposed, a text can be literary by *fiction*, that is, invention, or by *diction*, so by style or, more generally, attention to form (Genette 1993). Schmidt (1991), for his part, observed that in literature the *aesthetic convention of polyvalence* prevails; ambiguity, complexity, and irony are valued, superseding the *factual convention*, which requires referential truth or verisimilitude. These formulations give some grasp on what it might mean, conventionally, for an autobiography to be literary.

As autobiographic writing, yet writing that exploits aesthetically innovative form, autofiction activates conflicting world-making conventions and interpretive regimes, blending these in uncertain degrees and combinations, putting the reader to work. In Boltanski and Thévenot's terms, autofiction cues readers to classify a given text as simultaneously belonging to different Worlds: to the Domestic World of intimate self-expression and to the Civic World of public speech, since writing here means going public about oneself. In both realms, one is conventionally accountable for one's words, and writing falls under the rules of everyday communication, captured in Herbert Grice's (1989) maxims: be truthful, be as informative as is required (but not more so), be relevant and clear, not ambiguous.[16] Under these terms, discourse calls for a factual, personalizing, folk psychological, and moral interpretive and evaluative regime (corresponding to Phelan's, Fludernik's, or Palmer's mimetic approach to literary characters; see chapter 5). Under such a regime, one might fault a writer for deviations from everyday moral norms.

But as a literary form, autofiction also belongs to the Inspired World. To classify a work as autofiction activates an aesthetic interpretive and evaluative regime, with, for instance, complexity and ambiguity as leading values, which may well supersede moral convention or factual exactitude.

Such norms, which literary scholars produce so readily, are culturally and historically defined and subject to change, as I will argue more amply in the next chapter. These norms also tend to simplify a much messier negotiation of contradictory steps in our interpretation and evaluative processes, as I hope to reconstruct with respect to my own reading.

In its generic hybridity, autofiction encounters conflicting risks that require ethos management. As a genre that is to some extent bound to referential truth, autobiography encounters the risk of factual inaccuracy, because of failing or distortive memory, for instance. Hence the importance of sincerity topoi, which promise attempts at truthfulness without guaranteeing factual reliability. Closely related is the risk of inauthenticity: can the writer avoid destroying by artifice of style and narrative form the very sense of presence, authenticity, and sincerity she or he seeks to convey? Thematizations of the impossibility of being true, sincere, and authentic have unsurprisingly become themselves a powerful topos of sincerity.

Yet another risk is that of irrelevance. How can one justify one's demand of readers to read hundreds of pages about oneself, infringing conventions of relevance and quantity, as captured in Grice's maxims, which particularly apply to the amount of attention one draws to oneself in social interactions?[17] Autobiographies often suggest paths for attributing value to the individual case, countering this threat of irrelevance. Justification proceeds, for instance, by singularizing (the writer's personality is unique and enigmatic, her or his life story exceptional, and so on) or by generalizing (this is everyone's story or that of a particular group of people; my life's enigma stands for that of the human condition; or each life is worthwhile, *I'm okay, you're okay*).

As the more reflexive autobiographical form, autofiction can be expected to scratch where it itches and to create ambiguity exactly on these justifications. As I hope to show, this is indeed the case in *Sujet Angot*, extending to the author's public manifestations, which create similar classification uncertainties regarding the author's ethos.

The Bécassine, or Joan of Arc of Literature

As we know from other artists and writers, in controversial cases more than ever interpreters construct an authorial ethos. It is such an ethos that they hold onto to discriminate, for instance, between art and kitsch or between ironized kitsch or camp and bad taste. In Angot's case, controversies mainly pertained to what was perceived as her uninhibited exposure of her most intimate real-life experiences, not just in her literary writing, but also in her public self-presentation. Such public exhibition brings writing and performing oneself back into real-risk arenas, a classical topos of autobiographic writing. Or is her blurring of the boundaries between life and fiction just fashionable ironic metafiction? Answers to such a question involve the interpreter's own framing decisions and norms, especially concerning the author's ethos.

Angot's intense capacity for disturbance has much to do with her posturing, and especially with her refusal to docilely endorse conventional paths for making her entry in the literary field. As Jacques Dubois rightly observes, the game she plays is "a disruption of the hypocritically consensual game in which cultural television programs excel: [this game] reaffirms the literary space as a space of rivalries and struggles; it brandishes the flag of a literature of Truth and Writing [*écriture*], disqualifying the others" (Dubois 2011). The posture of "literary rebel" or "heretic" (Dubois's terms) that she adopts requires authenticating ethos clues, which, as we will see, the author amply provides. But it is precisely Angot's authenticity, supported by her provocatively antiaesthetic stance, that is staged most ambiguously.

The mental models and types with which Angot has been associated provide insights into the kinds of worlds in which her work and persona have been classified. Here is a young writer who "strikes a right tone," whose voice is "beautiful, direct and without compromise," leading *Le Monde* critic Josyane Savigneau (1998) writes, contributing to the authentic-rebel posture.[18] Others, instead, constructed Angot's directness as "exacerbated narcissism" (Rousseau 1998) and, very institutionally, as a sign of the "degeneration of literary culture" (Drouin 2000). In Boltanski and Thévenot's terms, both "definitions" of Angot's work and persona deny her access to the Inspired World and refuse to transform, as convention would allow, her Domestic misery (the incest she would have been victim of, among other experiences) into greatness in the Inspired World. Instead, her work and public presentation are framed mundanely, as pathological or as bad taste, anything but art.

Her "authenticity" earned Angot some significant qualifiers, which point to the role of gender stereotypes in ethos constructions, especially when these are made to function in valorizing classifications (is this even literature? good literature?) by gatekeeping experts. One critic casts her as "Bécassine," with her "figure of a girl straight from the province, which contrasts with her neurotic novels," a qualification that ambiguously emphasizes her naïveté (Angelo Rinaldi, quoted in Dupuis 2008).[19] Critics also referred to her as a "little girl that one would like to protect" (Jean-Marc Roberts, quoted in Dupuis 2008), or alternatively, as a "young boy," remarking on her "fresh outlook" and her authenticity (Dupuis 2008). Just as ambiguous is the qualification as "Joan of Arc of literature": does that pinpoint her independence and courage or her relentless righteousness and combativity (Dupuis 2008)? Both girl types to which critics refer, with their rustic, domestic ethos of authenticity, make Angot an outsider in the midst of a sophisticated professional world implicitly constructed as male. These images may also activate the posture of the rough-hewn, hence authentic, writer, recalling Meizoz's analysis of Rousseau's typecasting.

Angot fiercely cultivates this outsider position and ethos, which helped her carve out her niche in both the Inspired and the Domestic Worlds, both depicted as inauthentic. But clearly, the author's extratextual ethos and posturing themselves pose categorization problems. Although critics still use their constructions of the authorial image in order to help classify her work, these constructions arguably rest on familiar frames that require elimination of quite some dissonance.

Sujet Angot

While Christine Angot seems to be the central object of the narrative in *Sujet Angot*, she is not at first sight the narrator, though she qualifies as the extradiegetic narrator, who intermittently intervenes in the narration.[20] Even the reader who recognizes the characteristics of autofiction right from the start by the contradictory generic framing keys is in for a surprise. Instead of some version of Lejeune's autobiographical pact, we find a long letter whose narrator is Christine's ex-husband Claude, as explained in chapter 2.

In a later study, Lejeune examined heterodox cases of autobiographical writing, including autobiography in the third person—mostly, he observes, a transparent mask for the *I*. Not so strange a figure, he comments, as there is always distancing involved in autobiography, and "the first person always hides a third person" (1980, 34). The figure we find in *Sujet Angot* is somewhat different, more like an autobiography by procuration, or an auto-through-allo-portrait (Angot exhibits herself while staging Claude portraying himself depicting Christine; I hope my reader is still with me). The issue of the narrative's sources and their ethos, and of the resulting play of perspectives, is in any case amply foregrounded.

One of the rare precursors for this configuration is helpfully mentioned in the text: *The Autobiography of Alice B. Toklas*, by Gertrude Stein. Stein—complacently? ironically?—puts herself in the center of the fictional autobiography attributed to her secretary and partner, who "recognizes important people when she meets them" (quoted in Angot 1998, 34). If picked up, such a signal works as a frame-switch trigger, transferring the reader from narrative to authorial audience. We then are cued for a reading focused on the obliqueness of writing the self, wary of idea(l)s of transparency and authenticity. Such a reorientation means that readers identify another communication scene as the main one. Other ethical perspectives then prevail: Is it the couple of Claude and Christine that stands central? Or rather the couple we readers form with Angot, the author? The frame switch also has consequences for one's perspective on the conception of writing articulated and discursively performed by Claude.

Sujet Angot, at any rate, rather heavily insists on its biographical or autobiographical dimension, activated in the title and supported by the many similarities between characters and events in the book and what is known about Angot's life and her entourage. But the metafictional warnings are written just as big, signaling the dangers of taking literary discourse as a straightforward autobiographic outpouring of emotions. At some point Claude quotes "Angot," who, in a novel called *Sujet Angot*, which of course is not the one we are reading, scorns journalist Carole Vantroys of the magazine *Lire*, who fell into the autobio trap and forgot the distinction between fact and fiction: "Listen to me Carole: fiction-reality, between both, a wall. Okay? So stop it, to mix it all up . . . 'For a long time, Christine Angot published books in which she spoke about herself, books like sobs.' Do you know me? Do we know each other? Who told you I speak about myself? . . . You never heard, during your studies, about the author-narrator distinction . . . ? 'Sobs,' do you realize? If I feel like crying, do you really believe it's your shoulder I'm going to choose?" (52). Nor is it perhaps the reader's all-too-supportive shoulder the author has singled out.

Other clues as well question the (auto)biographic framing. While the adopted scenography is that of Claude's letter to Christine, at some point his monologic narration is exposed as embedded in that of an extradiegetic narrator, who can be imagined as Christine's, the character, or Angot's, the writer. Whether the interpreter chooses the one or the other option depends on how fictional one takes this book to be. Signaling the embeddedness of Claude's narrative minimally draws attention to Christine's/Angot's power to manipulate and ironically expose his discourse on Christine.

These disruptions of Claude's monologue do not stand alone. On several occasions, there are stretches of text that cannot really be attached to one precise origin but, however, convey a strong discursive ethos. For instance, Claude's sentimental recollections of how he loved Christine's "good side" (*côté sage*; 22) take on a sinister echo in what looks like an unmarked insertion from a treatise on pathological sexuality. The section offers a clinical, yet obviously fascinated, description of the obsessive masturbation and subsequent "treatment" of a female patient, X: "X promises to be good" (*promet d'être sage*), followed by free-roaming fantasies about marking her (whose?) parts with a red-hot iron (30).

To whom should one assign these sentences, and the discursive ethos one might infer from them? A narrowly mimetic reading could attribute these sentences to Claude, who is at any rate the apparent narrator of the text that is presented to us. Alternately, attributed to him, the intertextual borrowing could signal his desire for exclusive possession or express his lucid, even self-ironic acknowledgment of his sentiments. More plausible perhaps is an understanding that shifts the communication plane to the extradiegetic narrator, or even the author: Angot, or her fictive avatar Christine, would thus expressively convey the disgust and aggression Christine's unruly body elicits in her ex and perhaps generalize Claude's discourse, placing it in a coercive patriarchal tradition.

Intrusions of an extradiegetic narrator especially occur in sections in which Claude expresses his distress. Suddenly overt, this bracketed voice occasionally reacts on Claude's dialogic prompts: "Do you understand what I mean? [Yes.] Do you think it's right? [Yes]," and so on (120). Whether we read *Sujet Angot* as Claude's one-sided telling or as Christine's ironic exposure of a frustrated ex-husband's discourse, their conflicting perspectives here seem to blend into a genuine conarration of a painful shared experience (this characterization clearly reflects my own ethos attribution). By espousing Claude's pathos, the extradiegetic voice seems to authenticate his writing, as well as its own sincerity and *eunoia*, encouraging a *factual* framing of the book we read.

On closer scrutiny, Claude's monologue might thus become a much more dialogic text, with a built-in oscillation.[21] If the reader adopts the position of narrative audience, real-life psychological and moral frames and norms seem appropriate as a response to Claude's rhetoric, with its accent of authenticity. The point of the text, then, is then something like *him about her.* In his role of narrator and of expert on Christine, one may find Claude authentically pathetic yet evidently unreliable, misled by his sense of loss and angry frustration.

If instead one adopts an authorial audience position, sensitive to the trickiness of the narrative situation, Claude's authenticity or unreliability become mentioned instead of used (see the discussion, in the next chapter, of Sperber and Wilson's analysis of irony as mention). Instead, one might ask what this authorial montage of an ex's pathetic discourse says about the subject one deems responsible for the embedding. The point of the text then becomes *her about [him about her].* The book's composition itself, for which one would hold the author responsible, might then appear unreliable. It lures us into empathic engagement with Claude's pathos, which then appears quoted, possibly manipulated, perhaps even wholly invented. Yet one may still feel solicited to engage emotionally with the text. One would now imagine two (real) people, Claude and Christine, in the painful process of separation, both using writing for exercising their persuasion on each other, and on the reader. The narrative structure, a kind of tug-of-war between two ex-lovers, is likely to make one's sympathy oscillate between the male and the female perspective, the latter enjoying the advantage of superiority in the narrative hierarchy.

This framing, which is still (auto)biographical, raises ethical questions as well, but different ones: How morally acceptable is what may appear as ironic revenge, with the author, or Christine, trumping Claude's attempts to control "sujet Angot"? How narcissistic is Angot's staging of herself through the gaze, desire, and discourse of this ex-husband? Such questioning, and one's answers to it, cannot but be affected by whether or not one trusts the alleged (auto)biographic pact for this somewhat deviant case and by how one constructs the ethos of both Claude and Christine/Angot.

An even more fundamental frame switch occurs if one constructs the work as primarily *fictio*, calling for a more abstract reading strategy. The focus then is no longer Claude's real or verisimilar sense of loss and desire of control, nor Christine's real or verisimilar revenge through ironic framing (which so perfectly corresponds to the author's claim that writing should be an act and intervention in real life). Though the narrative configuration in terms of *fictio* still appeals to readers' desire to know and understand the author, it opens onto other kinds of reading. The kind of ethos one attributes to the author, however, could appear decisive for a more tragic, serious interpretation of the metafictional aspect or for a more ludic, perhaps ironic, interpretation.

This kind of oscillation has consequences for one's perspective on the rather programmatic conceptions of writing expressed or implied in Claude's letter. Would they be perceived as endorsed by the author, given the work's ambiguous narrative structure and the difficulties of authentication that arise?

Ethos and Self-Writing

A medium that reflects on itself is not just a blueprint for building a story world, as it redirects the interpretation to the work's metafictional purport. In *Sujet Angot*, Claude keeps commenting on Christine's way of writing, highlighting its charms and its flaws, as well as its functions. Let me briefly highlight some functions that would seem to programmatically define Angot's own writing.

WRITING THE REAL

Claude urges Christine on to convey real experience, "all we went through" (93). This is what his own writing purports to do and what critics generally admire or reject in Angot's own work. Among the rhetorical means for ensuring this reality effect we find, first, the suggestion that real experience can be imported metonymically in writing by inserting chunks of actually spoken discourse, verbal ready-mades, to which reality would indexically adhere: "Put in Léonore's words [their daughter]. Take my sentences" (93). The reader is to believe that the text we read results from exactly such reality insertions. The pathos attached to these chunks of reality seems to warrant their authenticity ("this is so powerful, emotionally"; 93). The authenticity of the conveyed experience supposedly radiates back onto the narrator's ethos, and Christine's. But let's not forget the warning to the critic, quoted earlier: "Do you know me" from "my" writing, however confessional?

The reality effect is conveyed through stylistic means as well. In a fascinating belief effect, as Bourdieu might have called it, style perceived as raw, unpolished, is conventionally taken as a signal of authenticity and immediacy, as if the rejection of aesthetic convention sufficed to eliminate mediation itself. Claude's style, and Christine's/Angot's, displays many such antiaesthetic effects: ellipses; parataxis in place of coordination; unusual punctuation, brusquely separating words that one expects to be grammatically grouped; a heavy recourse to deictics such as "ça" (this), unelegant according to the stylistic norms of written language in French, which, however, seems effective to conjure up a referent as if by pointing at it. My enumeration catches me in the act of doing what the quoted critic did, namely, reading the author in her style, which earned the critic an ironic rebuff. Turned into convention itself, antiaesthetic style indeed may become a deceptive index.

WRITING AS THERAPEUTIC FACE-TO-FACE WITH FORMLESSNESS

Claude claims to write to help Christine to be, or become, herself as a woman, as a body, as a writer, as a Self (the four guises are mentioned), for which he considers himself a competent helper. But soon he appears to be the one in need of help, since having lost her puts him in a state of utter self-loss. Claude's discourse ends up showing precisely that—complacent, compulsive?—exhibitionism for which Angot is admired or reproached. Toward the end of his letter, he broaches the question of whether his offering of all the "horror, abjection and writing: that of others, our own" (121) to Christine-the-writer should be interpreted as loss of dignity (113), with perhaps a wink, from the author, to Kristeva's insightful essay on abjection in modern literature.[22] Unsurprisingly, Claude's writing ends when the therapy is completed: after all this "[w]riting to stop crying," "the pain wears off" (25).

This therapeutic function of writing, quite celebrated nowadays, is also one that many critics apply to Angot's own writing, especially in reference to the author's "traumatic" incest experience. Claude's exhibitionism, like Angot's own, consequently gets invested with positive value, backed by an ethos of courageous sincerity. Such an ethos, for instance, is suggested by both character's and author's daring drop of decorum and naked pathos (such a reading implicitly frames Claude's, or Angot's, writing as basically nonfictional).

But perhaps the therapeutic virtue of Angot's writing is of a more bracing kind, stemming, rather, from a sharp analysis of tear-jerking mechanisms rather than from dripping self-expression and empathizing.

WRITING AS TRANSFIGURATION OF THE COMMONPLACE

Writing not only would have therapeutic effects. As literary writing, it would transfigure the common, everyday experience—even that of abjection—into art, with the writer as "magician": "It makes me strong and proud, my surrender to your writing. . . . [I]t is far, very, very far from wallowing in misery. Christine wants to use it? But of course! . . . [G]o ahead, Queen, go ahead, Magician," Claude conjures her (113–14).[23]

We have here a topos, one that has been given pregnant form by Baudelaire, for instance (see also Danto 1981, *The Transfiguration of the Commonplace*). Should one take this view on writing as the transfiguration of the commonplace as the author's own credo? In an interview about another of her purportedly nonfictional works, *Les Autres* (The others; 1997), Angot was asked to what extent her narrator's representation of all the suffering and sexual abjection people confided to her actually made for an experience qualitatively different from theirs. She replied (without blinking, I imagine), "The difference is that she [the narrator] makes a book out of it. It's a matter of transsubstantiation" (Angot 1997). Now, transsubstantiation is a rather strong notion, with religious, even mystical connotations. I do find it hard to take this claim at face value in the context of *Sujet Angot*'s specular narrative construction and what I perceive as its mannerist-authentic style. My suspicion of authorial self-parody increases when I read a comment, attributed to Claude, in which he condemns Christine's/Angot's attempt to translate the rawness of experience into words: "This is not how one should say it. This is too direct, you understand, too much message. I have thought this, I write this. This is not you, this. Subject Angot does not do this" (10–11).

Yet the claim might well be seriously intended, right through all the self-parodying. The pathos of Claude's own discourse for me works as a strong prompt for such an intention and ethos attribution. Reading may engage us into experiencing clear oppositional affects. But negations may keep the negated element lingering in one's mind. Booth interestingly proposed that narratives ask their readers to step into a pattern of desire (Booth 1988, 201). In my sense, such patterns of desire may be precisely conjured up through irony or through other devices that seem to present an attitude or thought from a negative perspective. Such negated yet affectively charged thoughts can form strong undercurrents, underneath the actual story line and its apparent argumentative structure. But these, clearly, are more an object for phenomenological or outright hermeneutic approaches.

STYLE, OR WRITING THE UNIQUE SELF

Christine's style, Claude insists, expresses her unique mode of being and thinking. Uniqueness is so heavily stressed that it becomes strange, even grimly coercive ("we want: your style. Unique," "That's you," "that's not you"; see my discussion in chapter 2). Precisely the uncanny resemblance between Claude's writing and Angot's trademark style makes Claude suspect as spokesman for the author, with his candid, pathos-laden claims of stylistic authenticity and expressive indexicality.

Alternately, rather than following the lead of ironic or self-parodying metafiction, one might consider Angot to be exploring how important uniqueness really is, in real life, as in (auto)biographic writing. That same question is also raised in the interviews that constitute a big part of *Les Autres*, in which a host of "others" confide to "Angot" intimate facets of their erotic desire. These voices are likely to appear as authentic on the basis of the interview scenography and, again, the stylistically conveyed speech habitus (idiosyncratic reticence, manners of saying). On closer scrutiny, however, these authentic ways of speaking appear to be, mostly, literary citations. Moreover, the narrator often switches within one sentence from the third person to the third-person plural. This switch may be perceived as a brutal dismissal of the claim of uniqueness each of the subjects may hold. Alternately, the montage of voices in writing may work as a dilution of painful singularity, including the narrator or author in a chorus, sharing the pathos of suffering.

At some point in *Sujet Angot*, Claude—or the extradiegetic narrator?—comments on the evolution in painting from the magnified Self in Renaissance self-portraits to its painful and abject contemporary forms. The (whose?) voice concludes with appropriate pathos: "[M]odern Art and contemporary art [Francis Bacon] have evacuated the pride of the portrait. Instead, we have people's suffering, the emptiness that inhabits them. Of this sin, the autoportrait is all we have left. The artists' faces look at us." (45) What is omitted in this programmatic statement, which aligns Claude's/Angot's (auto)portrait with Bacon as the artist of the faceless and abject self, is the tonic ambiguity of many contemporary self-presentations, including, perhaps, Angot's.

CRAFTING ONESELF AS AN ENIGMA

Spectacularly on display both in writing and in the media, yet ambiguously framed by a rhetoric of authenticity, Angot's exhibitionism entices readers to desire to know and come close to the author. Yet despite all the apparent authenticity and indexical rawness of her writing, "sujet" Angot will not be defined, nor confined. No Aristotelian goodwill here. Having lured the reader into the intimacy of a voyeuristic position (if we read mimetically), into seeking bonding complicity with the author, who turns out to be disturbingly manipulative (if we read metafictionally), Angot/Christine then kicks the authorial audience out of any alliance, except perhaps on pain's common ground. Nor is there any truthful promise of consolation through a healing, identity-constituting conarration of life experience. We have just art, holding up a mirror to us readers, reflecting our own desire for possessing the author, pinpointing her ethos: a writer who postures as an artist, carefully arranging her narrative ambiguity, and that of her own ethos.

This exercise also suggests some lines for further inquiry. For instance, how do various kinds of autobiographic writing suggest their more general value, as literature? What ethos topoi belong to that, and how do they connect to culturally circulated ethos stereotypes? What conventional paths for ethos inference are activated in cases in which generic boundaries are blurred? Narratology, as I have argued throughout this book, cannot offer fail-safe methods for answering such questions. It can, however, help us be more attentive to devices that create interpretive riddles, and to ethos cues that help solve them, within the framework of a particular reading strategy. It can also make us understand better why readers would solve these riddles in different ways.

7 Sincerity and Other Ironies

This book . . . has been in a strange position: many readers . . . who have read too much . . . have felt that the book was too naked, too raw, and much too sentimental: in sum, too earnest. . . . At the very same time, there were those who felt that the front matter was (and is) pomo garbage *and that . . . the entire story is being told with a tongue in its author's cheek, a wink toward the skybox. . . . [H]onestly: everyone who actually reads this dumb book, or any dumb book, will understand it. So I beg of you:*

    People, friends, please: TRUST YOUR EYES, TRUST YOUR EARS, TRUST YOUR ART!

DAVE EGGERS, *A Heartbreaking Work of Staggering Genius*

The epigraph sets the course for this chapter.[1] It features in a short essay on "Irony and Its Malcontents," part of the appendix added by Eggers to the paperback edition of his first book and bestseller, *A Heartbreaking Work of Staggering Genius* (2001; from now on I will adopt the author's helpful acronym AHWOSG for his title). In this book Eggers tells in some five hundred pages the story of an adolescent who loses in a short time both parents, takes upon himself the education of his younger brother, and explores adult life. The cover indicates that the book is based on a true story.

Many critics and readers have responded to the book's autobiographic material, often perceived, as in Angot's case, as raw, authentic, and grippingly told. Many critics, however, also expressed puzzlement and even uneasiness about the book's self-consciously hilarious if not ironic tone, which is experienced as somehow in tension with authentic emotion. In the paratextual comment quoted above, Eggers dismisses two major ethos profiles—too sincere or sentimental or too postmodern ironic—attributed both to his book and to himself, in favor of what reads as a slogan written in capitals, with its three-beat rhythm, repetitive structure, and emphasis on trust and art: "People, friends, please: / TRUST YOUR EYES, TRUST YOUR EARS, TRUST YOUR ART!" But what exactly are we invited to trust? And should we take what looks as a programmatic authorial statement as reliable? Under what framing conditions is such a question relevant?

The present chapter explores the two assertion modes that seem at stake here: sincerity and irony. Eggers plays out these modes against each other, as do many theories of language use. The first section, on sincerity, highlights in an essayistic mode the importance of historically determined values that imbue narrative authority and trustworthiness, complementing the textual bias of classical narratology. The second section discusses a number of theories of irony, illuminating some of its rhetorical, social, and cognitive mechanisms, in particular in the case of literary narrative. I expect that these historical and theoretical perspectives will shed light on narrative ethos attributions more generally. Yet I maintain the claim that they are not fail-safe methods for detecting or describing irony in a given narrative, just as I contended in chapter 5 that there is no method, but only a useful heuristic, for detecting and describing narrative unreliability. The chapter concludes with a more extensive interpretation of Eggers's AHWOSG, a novel that makes readers fittingly oscillate between irony and sincerity. Throughout the whole chapter, besides Eggers's memoir, novels by Knut Hamsun, Houellebecq, and a Russian postmodern author, Prokhanov, serve to illustrate and test the proposed perspectives.

Sincerity, or the Codification of Ethos through History

Literature is a tricky place to search for sincerity or reliability, as narratologists well know. Whose voice do we imagine, with whom is it communicating, how reliable can we trust it to be, if all we have is a reader who on the basis of a text constructs in his or her mind images and voices of paper beings—as well as their narrator or author—and then conjectures about their interplay?

Sincerity has been defined as the "congruence between avowal and actual feeling" (Trilling 1972, 2) and as "a disposition to make sure that one's assertion expresses what one actually believes" (Williams 2002, 96). Eggers's call for trust, quoted at the opening of this chapter, seems to produce such an effect of congruence by its discursive form alone: the insistent repetitions, exclamation marks, and capitals, besides appealing to the reader, conventionally suggest an emotional style, the pathos of which corresponds perfectly to the proclaimed ethos of sincerity—though one might read the exhortation ironically, but more about that later. While the notion of sincerity suggests that a speaker intends to say what she or he believes to be true, it does not maintain a factual truth claim, as reliability would, at least the kind of reliability that pertains to the "axis of facts," as Phelan and Martin (1999) called it in their analysis of different sorts of unreliability.

Cultures, moreover, differ in the value they assign to sincerity as a communicative attitude and moral trait, so what is appreciated as sincerity in the Netherlands may count as bluntness in France. Cultivated as an ideal in many religious, philosophical, pedagogical, and literary traditions of moral self-fashioning and formally required in the juridical sphere and other institutional settings, the use of sincerity is nevertheless restricted in many cultures, both in domestic and professional spheres, since it can strongly increase one's vulnerability or obnoxiousness. While sincerity has been contrasted with various other notions, ranging from prudence and irony to dissimulation or lying, it does not necessarily stand in a relation of full opposition to these postures, as literature often illustrates. Irony, like prudence, can be perceived as a complex form of sincerity, which might be the case for Eggers's tone.

The semiotic capacity of the body, conceptualized as an outside expressing an inside, plays a significant role in the confirmation of an ethos of sincerity and authenticity (as discussed in chapter 2). Signs conveyed by the body are indeed often experienced as natural and true expressions of an ethos, indexically tied to our inner impulses like smoke to fire. Similarly, insincerity is supposed to be expressed by the body. Lie detectors concentrate on bodily symptoms, and jealous lovers scrutinize each other's unconscious twitches and distractions. Conceptions of communication that insist on the faithfulness of bodily expression unsurprisingly tend to share a distrust of language and an ideal of direct and transparent exchange between true interiorities. Without the mediation of language, there would be no rhetoric, hence, no deceit. But we cannot escape our semiotic condition. Symptoms can be faked and even sup-posedly natural bodily signs are used rhetorically, standing in need of interpretation, as proposed earlier in this book.

While in real-life interactions or visual figurations bodies are dis-played as sign bearers for us to (mis)read, literature can only explicit-ly mention these bodily signs or stylistically suggest them, which it lav-ishly does, as we saw in the case of Angot's writing.[2] Let me briefly dwell here on an older example, taken from *Mysteries* (1892; Hamsun 1971).

In this novel by the Norwegian author Knut Hamsun, the riddle con-stituted by the protagonist's ethos plays a central role. The text quite typ-ically refers to a conventional bodily semiotics in order to set out signals of the characters' sincerity or duplicity, which function both within the story world, and so for other characters' mind reading, and for the reader.

Mysteries evokes a small coastal town in Norway in which one day a stranger disembarks, Johan Nagel. While there have been an unsolved murder and a strange suicide case in town, Nagel, the foreigner, is in fact the mystery around which the plot evolves. Where did he come from? What's in the violin case he never opens? (Nothing like unopened boxes to unleash the hermeneutic drive.) Where does he get his money from? What kind of a person is he? Nagel keeps the townspeople hooked by their own curiosity. He especially intrigues the beautiful Dagny, whom he all but stalks and proposes love to, well knowing that she is engaged to another.

While we may feel invited to reflect with a tinge of irony on Dagny's and the townspeople's habitual ways of putting people in neat catego-ries, our own ethos-attribution and mind-reading machinery work full throttle, as they would when "processing" Balzac's Vautrin, Dostoyevsky's Raskolnikov, Danielewski's Zampanò, or character-narrators such as Humbert Humbert, who all too loudly profess their sincerity.

The text quite typically mentions bodily signs from which the charac-ters are expected to infer each other's intentions and ethos. Take the fol-lowing dialogue between Nagel and Dagny, which I have to quote some-what extensively. The protagonist and the young woman walk through a moonlit night:

[T]he beauty and the stillness of the night filled him [Nagel] with such elation that his breath came in gasps and his eyes welled with tears. . . . His words had a spontaneous and sincere ring, as if he were trying to be fair on both sides. His expression, too, was open and candid.

But Dagny stopped abruptly, looked him straight into the eyes, and said, utterly astonished: "But that isn't the way it happened!" . . .

"You will see [Nagel says] that when I gave you my version of the incident . . . , perhaps distorting it a bit, it was purely for my own benefit. . . . I am being honest with you . . . . I would rise in stature, acquiring a reputation for magnanimity and nobility of spirit which I could not earn otherwise. Am I not right? But I can only attain this by being so lowly and crude that I thoroughly disgust you. I have to confess all this to you, because you deserve complete honesty." . . .

She kept looking at him, completely baffled by this man and what he had just said, trying to sort it all out in her head . . . and burst out in loud, ringing laughter: "You're the most shameless person I've ever met! . . . I just don't understand. Why do you plan your moves so carefully and then fail to realize that you are exposing yourself—your own lies?"

He was silent for a moment, and then said, without wavering; "But on the contrary, its part of my scheme. . . . I'm risking nothing if I reveal myself to you, as I just did—at least, not very much. . . . A minute ago, you said you couldn't figure me out. You said it because you were thinking about me, which thrills and delights me. I do have a lot to gain, whether you believe me or not. (Hamsun 1971, 103–7)

Nagel's elation, on which the scene opens, is described through physical effects, which conventionally confirm his sincerity: "his breath came in gasps and his eyes welled with tears." Nagel must be a sensitive person, given his tears, one might infer. The congruence of feelings, expressions, and words is redundantly suggested by reference to Nagel's "open and candid" expression, except of course that the narrator's insistence may raise suspicion. Not much later, "brazenly looking her [Dagny] straight in the eyes, [Nagel] proceeded to tell her how he had planned the whole thing" (Hamsun, 1971, 106). The straight look is, again, a conventional token of sincerity, the eyes functioning as transparent windows to the soul (the topos also characterizes Dagny herself in the same section). Similarly, to speak "without wavering" by convention connotes sincerity: One's voice, our very bodily instrument of self-expression, would necessarily betray one's deep-down feelings and intentions.

Yet these notations regarding Nagel's physical ethos may be perceived to be in contradiction with his discursive ethos. His sentences explicitly thematize a rather involuted, if not crooked, relation between his deeds, words, and intentions. Dagny, at least, has learned at her own expense to pick up signals of dissonance. Should she trust his bodily signs or instead respond to the ethos conveyed by his all too complex ratiocinations? "She kept looking at him [Nagel], completely baffled by this man and what he had just said, trying to sort it all out in her mind."

To help her sort out Nagel's character's riddle, Dagny can resort to several "mental models," which the text hints at without allowing her, or the reader, to choose with certainty: folk psychology, according to which Nagel's welling up of emotion would define him as a sensitive, empathic person or, less generously, as a crook who would play on other people's emotions by feigning his own; or the stereotype of the Romantic artist, with an overly sensitive temperament, a rather new and fashionable model helpfully spelled out by the doctor to the little town's community.

The crisis provoked in Dagny's mind by Nagel's intrusion and unreadability spreads as if by contagion to the habitual mind-reading paths of the whole small community. Familiar people's words suddenly appear difficult to gauge, if not deceptive. Carefully knit social structures start to tear. The novel ends with a scene in which, sometime after Nagel's suicide, Dagny and Martha, the two women he claimed to love, walk along the coast. They walk arm in arm, so as not to slide on the icy slope, all social distance and amorous rivalries abolished, as if united against a common threat. The women briefly evoke how at the party they just left Nagel had been talked about. "After a long silence, Dagny said thoughtfully: 'This was the road he always took.' 'Who?' said Martha." Her repartee firmly reduces Nagel's irruption in their midst, together with his unexplained suicidal plunge into the sea, to ripples in the pond of their provincial existence. Everything and everybody resumed a familiar course, except that, to freely adapt Derrida, society's and reality's structure meanwhile has been exposed as centerless, and the mystery of Nagel's ethos remains entire.

Even Nagel's suicide, which could appear as his ultimate statement, remains riddled with questions. Did he, through this final act, sign with his body the authenticity of his despair? Was his death merely a pathological reaction to the spur of the moment, with perhaps no sincerity involved at all, as there was nobody there to say "here I stand"–Ricoeur's formula for ethical self-affirmation (Ricoeur 1990, 197)?

The question is to what extent a character's or narrator's sincerity can be determined from the text. In the metahermeneutic framework elaborated in this book, several elements appear relevant to how readers would establish sincerity as, indeed, a discourse effect, but not exclusively so. Like Dagny's, the ethos with which we credit Nagel depends on the mental model we construct for him throughout our reading experience, cued by the text. But this ethos attribution very much depends on our own moral norms, on our psychological insight, and our literary experience, as many narratologists have argued. Our ethos constructions are also defined by our framing of the text's genre and its most relevant communication level, as well as by our interpretive strategies.

These elements have been discussed extensively in previous chapters, so I would like to concentrate here on ethos topoi, which provide an interface between perceived textual clues and cultural norms and shared character repertoires (as analyzed by Amossy or Schneider). Zooming in on topoi signaling sincerity, I want to point out the extent to which such conventional tokens are tied to norms that change over time, a perspective that should be relevant in particular for narratological work on (un)reliability and on the authority granted to voices and modes of discourse in narrative.

An Old Debate

The tone and theme of Eggers's memoir, or of Hamsun's character's words, elicit a tension between sincerity and transparent communication on the one side and ideals of self-possession, self-masking, and indirect communication on the other. This tension regularly surfaces in the history of culture, under various guises. The complexity of this issue is well captured in Greenblatt's observation: "[W]hat distinguishes a 'natural' person from an 'artificial' person is that the former is considered to own his words and actions. . . . A great mask allows one to own as one's own face another mask" (Greenblatt, "Psychoanalysis and Renaissance Culture," quoted in Martin 1997, 1317).

In ancient rhetoric sincerity was a specific point of interest, though not under this exact label. Among the three means of persuasion distinguished by Aristotle and Cicero, *ethos* encompassed what we would nowadays subsume under sincerity, since sincerity contributes crucially to one's impression of a speaker's trustworthiness. But questions of sincerity also belong to the domain of *pathos*, as discursive and bodily tokens of emotion are taken to confirm the orator's true sentiment. Rhetoricians debated whether emotions needed to be truly experienced in order to be effectively expressed. For Cicero this was indeed the case, but he suggested that a speaker might inflame himself through speaking, just like an actor, so that his words were sincerely meant at the moment they were uttered (Wisse 1989, 195–98).[3]

In the Renaissance, as John Martin shows in a fascinating essay that I am going to quote extensively, two notions played a crucial role in the formation of an "increased sense of subjectivity and individualism": those of sincerity and prudence (Martin 1997, 1312). The latter was clearly important in a world dominated by the church, with its intrigues and hypocrisy. Self-fashioning included, among other virtues, "prudent accommodation," which recalls Aristotle's *phronesis*, as well as "honest dissimulation" and even strategically necessary deception (Martin 1997, 1314). Sincerity, a core value for various reform movements of the time, was better kept to the private realm, especially in political and religious matters.

Martin gives the example of the Sienese nobleman Bartolomeo Carli Piccolomini, who in his *Trattato della prudenza*, published in 1537–38, eloquently describes the skill of dissimulation required by the man who seeks inner freedom (among other reasons, in order to follow risky reformist inclinations): "[T]o project an impressive image of himself, training himself to be all things to all men, while at the same time preserving his own inner freedom and remaining detached from the world in spite of his dealings with it" (quoted in Martin 1997, 1324). For Machiavelli, who was probably one of Piccolomini's sources of inspiration, *prudence* could encompass outright insincerity and lying, which were indispensable social and political skills: "[O]ne must know how to disguise his nature well, and how to be a fine liar and hypocrite" (quoted in Martin 1997, 1324).

Under the influence of religious and ethical changes, from the fifteenth century on, predominant images of surface and exteriority were increasingly challenged by the imperative that one should express outwardly one's deepest inner self. An ethic of individualism emerged, with sincerity as a key notion. Tactical adulterations of sincerity with irony or feigning, such as Piccolomini's, became less evident. Direct expression of one's emotions gained a new legitimacy in what became, with Calvin and Luther, Protestant tradition (Martin 1997, 1330). Calvin's emblem, Martin recalls, was a handheld heart offered to his readers and to God, with the inscription reading *Prompte et sincere* (1327). The ideal, exemplified in the Psalms, was to "set open [one's] whole heart as it is"; conversely, "deceitful persons keep back a part of their meaning to themselves and cover it with the varnish of dissimulation, so that no certainty can be gathered from their talk. Therefore must our talk be sincere, that it may be the very image of an upright mind" (Calvin, *A Commentary on the Psalms*, 1571, quoted in Martin 1997, 1331).

Pursuing Martin's line, one might note that the French revolutionaries, in turn, adopted what were by that point "protestant" values, those of sincerity and transparency, with Rousseau acting as a famous intermediary. Prudence was associated with hypocrisy and dissimulation and connected with both the royal court and the church, each of which relied on the disciplined use of the body as a mask (striking illustrations are found in French eighteenth-century writers, such as Laclos, Crébillon, or Saint-Simon). Republicans valued instead the "unmediated expression of the heart above all other personal qualities. Transparency was the perfect fit between public and private; transparency is a body that tells no lies and keeps no secrets. It was the definition of virtue, and as such it was imagined to be critical to the future of the republic," as Lynn Hunt (1992, 70–96) observes.[4]

It is well known how, for their part, poets, writers, and philosophers of early German Romanticism cherished irony as a rhetorical figure and as an existential attitude, the artistic expression self-aware of its divided nature. The substitution of irony for prudence as sincerity's "Other" marks, I would surmise, the shift from a social-political or communal perspective to a private and individual one. The Romantics' caustic lucidity was shared by modern writers such as Flaubert and Baudelaire, in whose conception language and self-sincerity could only figure as painfully tied to (self-)irony.

The gist of this heritage, appropriated in different ways by modernism and postmodernism, has been well captured by Paul de Man's observation that "[t]he ironic language splits the subject into an empirical self that exists in a state of inauthenticity and a self that exists only in the form of a language that asserts the knowledge of this inauthenticity" (de Man 1983, 214). In this light, sincerity as an ideal belongs to a lost Edenic state or else, to the philistine's lack of lucidity. This pervasive kind of irony would be severely criticized as nihilistic by Hegel, as well as, more ambiguously, by Kierkegaard (1968).

For my purposes, the interest of Martin's and other cultural historians' material lies in the very concrete, embodied images of selves and ethos delineated here, which make wonderful material for an analysis à la George Lakoff and Mark Johnson, teasing out metaphors we live by: the body's inside and outside, the heart offered on an outstretched hand. Such imagery functions in a historically elaborated semiotics of the self. It is on the basis of such topoi that people read each other's bodies, minds, or hearts and offer theirs for scrutiny. The images of setting open one's heart for full transparency, or of protecting the inner self, that we find, for instance, in Dave Eggers's *AHWOSG*, might trace back to such historically defined notions, transmitted through religious, moral, and political traditions. Martin's research also vividly demonstrates how, in the analysis of norms and habits of communication, pulling one thread, here that of sincerity, brings into view the social fabric of a given period, with its codes for mind reading.

So when in 1999 Jedediah Purdy blamed postmodern irony for corroding social bonds and morals in American society; when, increasingly after 9/11, voices began to clamor for the need for a *new sincerity* and writers such as Dave Eggers, Matt Thorne, Nicholas Blincoe, and David Foster Wallace sought a way beyond irony, these debates and the positions they feature echoed, sometimes consciously, old topoi. Part of the new context in which these topoi are recycled is the invasion of television and the newest social media in our daily lives. These media, as argued, feed a desire for immediate emotional communication and offer their own models for self-fashioning. Writers have to compete with such visually and audio-based media, which affect their audiences' senses more directly than the written medium, which involves, more abstractly, conceptualization and requires more processing effort and time.

Written literary culture suffers, moreover, from the idea that it is more difficult, if not elitist. Such contextual factors could help explain why many writers nowadays cultivate a rhetoric of sincere and authentic communication, if not of the opportunity to bond with an author whose live, intimate presence is foregrounded, staged as attraction or enigma; and on the other hand, why metafictional playfulness and irony precisely target this widespread desire for communion with the author and for authenticity or attraction, as I will discuss further on, in connection with Eggers's *AHWOSG*.

This interlude on sincerity should also allow us to recognize historically evolved normative positions in current debates: that over postmodern irony, for instance, but also, within the scholarly field, the struggle waged between speech act theory and deconstruction over what constitutes the default in language and communication, a debate that concerns narratologists quite directly. Both John Austin (1962) and John Searle (1969), for instance, argue that sincerity belongs to utterances' felicity conditions, while for Habermas sincerity constitutes one part of the validity claims an utterance must meet for rational communication even to be possible.[5] Conversely, deconstructionists defend as the more sophisticated and lucid attitude a conception of language in which the dissemination and slippage of meaning are the default.[6] Though not simply discarded, sincerity is exposed as a fragile convention, a leap of faith, an ethical attitude toward communication, rather than a neutral description of actual language use (see also Miller 2001, esp. 32).[7]

Both positions in fact strategically essentialize one pole of language use, the one that best fits with their conception of selves, communication, and literature. Narratologists who tend to rely either on speech act theory and Habermasian discourse ethics, or instead on deconstructivist suspicion, would do well to acknowledge the normative basis on which they build their models of textual rhetoric.

This condensed discussion of sincerity as communication's default, along with the historical interlude, at least points to the importance of conjoined (meta)hermeneutic and pragmatic or rhetorical research on ethos norms, such as sincerity. This excursion is meant as a caveat against narratology's potentially normative bias (one way or the other) and a corrective to its rather exclusive focus on narrative *un*reliability.

Before demonstrating in a close reading of Eggers's *AHWOSG* the relevance of analyzing sincerity as a rhetorical effect, I would like to explore one of sincerity's "others," irony, which plays a similarly prominent role in how readers interpret assertions in narrative, and narrative as assertion. This time I will investigate the relevance that theories of irony, rather than a culture-historical perspective, might have for my approach. But my aim is in fact similar: to reflect on normative frames that underlie not just individual interpretations but also narratological approaches. Houellebecq's work, once again, will provide a kickoff example.

Irony and Ethos Attributions as an Exercise of Judgment

Let me start this section with a lengthy quotation from Houellebecq's novel *Atomised*.

> [T]he primary attractions for holidaymakers at the Cap d'Agde colony were sex and sunbathing. It was an archetype of a particular sociological concept. . . . That, at least, was how Bruno portrayed it in his article, "THE DUNES OF MARSEILLAN BEACH: TOWARDS AN AESTHETIC OF GOODWILL." . . . The article was rightly rejected by *Esprit*. . . .
>
> "[At Cap d'Agde, Bruno writes, "v]oyeurism is tacitly condoned: it is commonplace to see men on the beach stop to admire the female genitalia on show. . . . What we have here is a traditional, rather genial, seaside resort with the single distinction that sexual pleasure is recognized as an important commodity. It is tempting to suggest that this is a sexual 'social democracy,' especially as foreign visitors to the resort are principally German, Dutch and Scandinavian. . . . I intend to show that the dunes of the Marseillan beach are a defining example of the humanist proposition: striving to maximise individual pleasure without causing suffering to another." . . .
>
> At the end of the first week, Bruno stopped writing here. What remained to be said was more tender, more fragile and more uncertain. . . . [H]e said to Christiane, "I think I am happy." (259–65)

After many pages spelling out the sexual obsessions of Bruno, one of the two protagonists in the novel, the views expressed in the essay Bruno sends to *Esprit* (in real life, a leading French intellectual journal) are hardly striking on the level of the story world. My interest, which may be another reader's irritation, derives from the text's ironic shimmer, which draws me into a kind of cognitive gymnastics. Bruno's apparently single-voiced reflections, for me, teem with echoes of all kinds of sociolects: tourist brochures (the first sentence), a typically academic style ("an archetype of a particular sociological concept," "I intend to show that . . ."), conventional judgments served upside down ("What we have here is a traditional, rather genial, seaside resort," whereas one can almost hear the indignant outcries about the exhibitionism, free sex, and gang bangs that characterize this genial resort). His discourse is also inundated with diffuse illocutionary intentions beyond his own. So even such a brief textual fragment requires me to reconstruct a complex landscape of perspectives, intentions, and value positions in which my ethos attributions occur.

Whose ironizing intention, indeed, am I after in the Houellebecq quotation? Not Bruno's, as his assertions are fully congruent with his *prior ethos* and he seems to have the sincere enthusiasm of one who saw the light. Not Houellebecq's narrator's either, who or which is hardly one consistent, individualized voice.[8] The author's perspective, then, as I construct it in my own all-too-willing cooperation? Perhaps I am myself the chief ironist, as Booth suggested when he observed that irony is in the eye of the beholder? But why would I shift from empathizing with Bruno to another communicative level, a switch that rather drastically affects my reading experience? Is there an appropriate method for detecting or proving the irony I suspect, and should we expect that from narratology?[9]

Here are, to whet our appetite, seven theses that capture what constitutes, for me, irony's central relevance to the analysis of ethos in literary narrative:

Irony means trouble for any formal descriptive approach that assumes a reassuring indexical relation between speech and its utterer's ethos (one man, one voice). It feeds on the disturbing potential of language to mean something else or even the opposite of what it appears to express and to convey the views of another source besides those of the apparent speaker.

Irony comes in many kinds, generous or nasty (so with or without *eunoia*), courageous or cowardly (so with or without *arête*). Yet, as a person's habitual assertion mode, irony determines the mental model one would have of such a person, a model that then inflects, top-down, one's interpretation of that person's assertions.[10]

In literature, *pace* classical narratology, many are the ironies that send readers off to conjecture about the author's intentions and ethos, as well as about what values would be defended, while fiction's assertion conditions at the same time withdraw the author from their grasp.

Irony represents a state of affairs under an evaluative aspect. Its processing involves reasoning about value positions or evaluative processes, or metaevaluation (Booth 1974; Grice 1989, 53; Hutcheon 1994). The inferential and (meta)evaluative gymnastics it requires gives irony a prominent place among the metacognitive practices through which we socially test out and calibrate value positions (Kotthoff 2007, 381).[11]

Irony bonds and divides around such evaluative processes, and both ironist and interpreter act as relays in the distribution of values (see also Kaufer and Neuwirth 1982; Fish 1983).

Ironic communication is high-risk communication for both ironists and their interpreters, precisely because it exposes habits of mind reading and evaluative attitudes (Hamon 1996; Hutcheon 1994).

The capacities for detecting, practicing, and enjoying irony seem connected to those required for ambiguity. Both notions usually appear in twins in conceptions of art and literature. And although there is irony in other media, irony always seems to be relayed through language, as it is in language that we conceptualize cultural codes, worldviews, and evaluations.

While my seven theses capture what I have come to see as the point of irony, the following pages offer a more detailed exploration of theories and methods for irony analysis, which might be helpful for ethos more generally.

A Rhetoric of Irony

Ancient rhetoric classified verbal or rhetorical irony as an indirect way of blaming or praising, which makes it part of the distribution and reinforcement of values, as suggested in my fourth thesis. Irony was defined as saying, with a mocking intention, the opposite of what one means (irony by antiphrasis) or as saying something other than is expected, using euphemism, periphrasis, allusion, or hyperbole (Cicero 2001, 2.68, 3.53; Quintilianus 1921, 8.6.54–59, 9.2.44–51). So when Eggers, in his essay "Irony and its Malcontents" in *AHWOSG*, hyperbolically attacks all that the I-word subsumes, in impossibly small type, we may suspect his diatribe to be itself ironic and search for which or whose attitudes could be the target of blame or ironic praise. But not all hyperbole or euphemism is ironic, and readers may even construct Eggers's tone as ultimately sincere.

Indeed, for irony to be recognized, Cicero proposed, "[t]he disposition and the ethos of the orator must be in contradiction with the said" (Cicero 2001, 2.67.272). This implies, first, that we must identify an utterance's source(s). This is often unproblematic in the rhetorical situation Cicero had in mind, unless, as I will discuss below, a speaker is quoting another's words without marking his quoting. Identifying irony is more hazardous in written, indirect communication. Second, Cicero's remark implies that the interpreter must know, or intuit, the speaker's characteristic ethos, in order to make a reasonable guess about his or her being ironic in a particular utterance. This circularity cannot be avoided, as explained by Dilthey, with his description of the induction process, or by cognitive models of meaning making.

In the Houellebecq section, for instance, in order to sort out the tone of Bruno's utterances and to determine what other source(s) might endorse such a tone and the ethos it would express, I rely on my mental models and *prior ethos* for character, narrator, and author; I also use my knowledge about all kinds of character models and value standpoints and about how these in turn are evaluated in various cultural contexts.

Ancient rhetorical definitions of irony rightly called attention to the ironist's and audience's inferences about their reciprocal intentions, beliefs, and values. They also pointed out irony's role in the distribution of values. But clearly, their object was not *literary* irony. The latter stands central in Booth's landmark publication, *A Rhetoric of Irony* (1974). Booth proposed a four-step procedure for reconstructing irony in literary fiction:

(1) A reader rejects the surface meaning of an utterance, because she or he feels there is an incongruity "between the words and something else he knows" (10), especially between the beliefs she or he holds and those she or he thinks the author holds (73). This is where irony signals—incongruities or illogicalities, for instance— play their part.

(2) The reader then tries out alternatives, which come "flooding in" (11). These first two steps by themselves, however, cannot tell us that a statement is ironic; that requires

(3) The (re-)construction of the beliefs and intentions of the utterance's ultimate source—in the case of literature, the implied author (11).

(4) Finally, the reader constructs a meaning in harmony with those hypotheses (10–12).

This procedure describes the harmonious orchestration of stable verbal ironies. "The whole thing," Booth stipulates, "cannot work at all unless both parties to the exchange have confidence that they are moving together in identified patterns" (13). If one follows Booth, Houellebecq must have ironically intended Bruno's defense of the blessings of Cap d'Agde, as no one gifted with conventional good sense would consider the depicted exhibitionism and gang bangs as an example of mutual respect. These inference steps, however, are often vulnerable. Disturbing slippages of meaning occur, which Booth labels unstable ironies and discusses at length in his third chapter. This unstable irony is, I would say, the kind that pullulates in Houellebecq's works.

Let me note, in passing, that this commonality of norms also plays a central role in Fludernik's linguistic approach to irony, as when she writes, "It is our moral conventions as well as the stylistic conventions and the interpretive norms which one constructs for the text as a whole that determine the ironical reading" (Fludernik 1993, 351). Fludernik concedes that irony, dual voice, or free indirect discourse challenge the linguists', and her own, claims that one can catch subjectivity's tail in discourse itself. In such cases, deictic and evaluative markers are "no longer a reliable tool of interpretation," and readers must infer to whom the evoked perspective can be attributed (Fludernik 1993, 228). This same slipperiness holds, I argue, for all ethos attributions, which never are "purely linguistic" phenomena, as Booth, for his part, well knew.

Critics objected, of course, that there are no stable and objectively observable ironies, only interpretive communities that tend to read irony into an utterance, or not (Fish 1989, 194). They also found fault with Booth's confidence in the harmonious interpretive dance, uniting text (author) and reader. Yet what is often overlooked is not just that Booth fully acknowledged the complexity and precariousness of attributing ironic meanings to authors, even in cases of stable ironies, and the connection between irony and values, but also that his enterprise was not intended as a theory in the strong sense.[12] Booth's rhetoric of fiction has hermeneutics, not theory, as its counterpart and ally, ensuring that the instructions for world making and perspective are understood properly.

Booth's (1974, 84–85) insistence on the interpreter's responsibility to *argue* for his or her interpretation makes more sense if one considers culture as socially distributed cognition, as explained in chapter 1. There is a strong sense that Booth devoted a whole book to literary irony precisely because literature creates occasions for joining attention over such articulation and negotiation of values and worldviews.

Beyond Hermeneutics?

Compared to these (meta)hermeneutic or rhetorical models, cognitive and sociolinguistic linguistic theories of irony hold the promise of more rigorous conceptualizations. I will argue, however, that they also cannot avoid extensive interpretive conjecturing about subjects' value positions and ethos, about which they speak in terms of almost mechanical inferences, which makes their approach perhaps less self-reflective than Booth's.

Irony as Rule Violation

Linguists such as Grice can be considered to formalize Booth's idea of the commonality of norms presupposed by any successful ironic communication. In Grice's view such norms are in the first place communicational. Grice famously defined irony as an overt flouting of the maxim of quality ("be true"), the overtness of the flouting ensuring that the ironic utterance can be recuperated within the scope of the cooperative principle (Grice 1975, 41–58). Other linguists argued that irony can work through a breach of any of the maxims, which would include, besides quality, relevance ("be relevant"), quantity ("be informative"), and manner ("be unambiguous"; e.g., Attardo 2007, 140).[13]

A theory of irony based on the notion of rule violation, however, seems to work only for situations in which it is clear what being true entails (and similarly for the other maxims) and to whom the uttered words or implied thoughts can be attributed. Take this sentence from Voltaire's *Candide*, very popular among irony theorists: "When all was over and the rival kings were celebrating their victory with Te Deums in their respective camps." We can argue that this sentence must be ironic, as no authorial narrator could seriously intend to assert a contradictory proposition, which he would know cannot be true (Booth 1974, 10). In Stanley Fish's line, we might then object that we can imagine a recontextualization in which this sentence would be unproblematically seriously intended; for instance, one in which God shares the interests of all his faithful peoples, beyond the all-too-human contradiction principle. One could respond that an utterance is given meaning within a specific textual and historical-cultural context: in the case of *Candide*, it should be clear to all competent readers that Voltaire refers to a particular Christian conception of God and that the intratextual context strongly supports an ironic interpretation. There we are, drawn into arguing about contexts and value-laden worldviews, in a game of guessing ethos and relevance contexts, which indeed is what irony is about.

Moreover, one might object that Grice's maxims do not apply in all communication situations and discourse genres, nor in all times or places. For example, politeness may overrule the maxim of truth. Violation theory, as we might call it, also leaves open the problem that not all breaches of maxims signal irony and that potentially ironic utterances may perfectly respect all the maxims associated with the cooperative principle. Bruno's assertions in the quotation with which this chapter opens do make sense as cooperative communicational intentions. It is only if one switches to another communicative level, one in which the author's intentions become prominently relevant to the reader, that one perceives some maxim violation.

So while Grice's model usefully points out what infringements of communicative norms may function as an irony signal, it also brings us back to interpretation and imagining contexts. This is not to say that we are now lost in utter subjectivity but what counts is the argumentation of one's inferences, including the question of which is the most relevant narrative communication level.

Irony as Mention

Among the linguistic approaches to irony, Sperber and Wilson's echoic mention theory is of particular interest for literary studies. In irony, Sperber and Wilson propose, an utterance is in a sense set between quotation marks: it is mentioned rather than used, with the intention of expressing an attitude toward the implied views, usually a derogatory one (Sperber and Wilson 1981, 1995). Instead of having "the illocutionary force it would standardly have in a context," an utterance perceived as ironic is taken as pointing to itself; a speaker self-reflectively "express[es] a belief about [the] utterance, rather than by means of it" (Sperber and Wilson 1981, 302).

Mentioning thus involves for one and the same utterance more than one enunciation source, or rather, more than one value perspective. The echoed proposition, and the evaluations it implies, can be traced back to a precise source or target or, less personally, to a particular sociolect, or to the *doxa*, recognizable for those in the know. Irony can indeed also occur when we do not know for sure who is speaking or who is targeted: it suffices that we perceive an utterance as articulating or implying evaluations that are themselves displayed for evaluation. The victim position, then, stands open for anyone who would adhere to the expressed evaluation.

Critics have not failed to point out that mention theory is insufficiently precise. Not all mentions are ironic. And how to decide whether there is mention, and who would be responsible for it, if there are no indubitable signals of quotation or intention? Moreover, there is some circularity involved in the role played by one's knowledge of or hypotheses about the speaker's ethos, as demonstrated in a statement like the following: "[T]he relevance of an ironical utterance invariably depends, at least in part, on the information it conveys about the speaker's attitude to the opinion echoed" (Sperber and Wilson 1995, 239). An ironic utterance indeed conveys information about the speaker's attitude only if I have already classified it as ironic on the basis of what I perceive to be textual signals, or alternately, on the basis of my prior information or contextually situated hypotheses about a speaker's ethos, attitude, and values (Attardo 2007; remember also Cicero's remark that irony attribution implies knowledge of the speaker's disposition).

In other words, inferences about ironic meanings may be prompted if we have identified the mental profile of the utterance's source as an ironist, a jester, or *femme d'esprit*. This is where research on authorial postures, institutional framing, and the ethos of narrators or characters meets. It is because I already have a picture of Eggers as one who relishes pulling the reader's and his own leg that I tend to interpret his essay on irony as ironic, an ethos I am quick to infer from AHWOSG's title page or its extensive paratext. This circularity, mentioned by most irony theorists, is unavoidable, as it corresponds to how our meaning-making procedures work.[14]

Mention theory takes into account semiotic and rhetorical aspects of the way one discourse can embed or quote another voice or thought, with or without explicitly marking the quotation as such. In this respect, this theory seems remarkably suited to literature's fictionality conventions, which sever narrative discourse from its source and situational context, setting off readers' reconstructions of who may be speaking or thinking, and with what authority and scope. Unmarked mention, moreover, appears to be an apt designation for the kind of ironic shimmer many readers sense in the works of Flaubert, Houellebecq, Eggers, or the Dutch writer Arnon Grünberg. Such writers have a wonderful ear for socio- and idiolects and stereotypes and seem to weave these into their narrator's and character's discourse, not necessarily as part of their characterization but as targets for scrutiny in their own right. This kind of irony functions thanks to our cognitive capacity to memorize in typified forms discourses as perspectives on the world and to make whole social contexts resonate through metonymic activation. But, let me repeat it, we need to acknowledge more explicitly the interpretive work involved in detecting ironic mention.

Irony as Frame Switch

Like Sperber and Wilson's idea of mention, all irony theories imply in some sense a switch to another communication level, or a frame switch. This can be the switch to a world, in which a speaker suddenly holds different views from those his or her interlocutors may expect; or a switch to another, concrete or putative communication situation, in which someone would defend the expressed views; or, regarding literary narratives, a switch to another narrative communication level, as in Rabinowitz's distinction between narrative and authorial audience.

Thus, to read Bruno's utterances as ironically mentioned involves switching from a reading in which his story-world situation and his own communicative intentions are prevailing to one in which his ways of speaking and thinking are framed as being echoed by an author, whose intentions now become central. Such a shift has a strong impact on one's overall interpretation and evaluation and, clearly, on whose ethos would become priming for the reader.[15]

The idea of a frame switch has been explored in recent cognitive research on irony and humor. For instance, building on Arthur Koestler's idea that bisociation is a mechanism that underlies creative processes, Galinañes analyzes humor as a cognitive frame switch in which such a bisociation occurs, a description that might be applicable to irony as well. Bisociation, in Koestler's view, involves "the perceiving of the situation or an idea, L, in two self-consistent but habitually incompatible frames of reference, M1 and M2. The event, L, in which the two intersect, is made to vibrate simultaneously on two different wavelengths, as it were. While this unusual situation lasts, L is not merely linked to one associative context, but bisociated with two" (Koestler 1989, 35, quoted in Galinañes 2005, 81). The potential inappropriateness of a first understanding or framing of an utterance functions as a "script-switch trigger," which "involv[es] the receiver in an effort to resolve the incongruity" and a search for relevance (Galinañes 2005, 84; note the parallel with Booth's steps in irony detection).

If readers, for instance, perceive Bruno's views ("L") as too strikingly in opposition with the *doxa*, this may work as a frame-switch trigger, shifting the relevance of Bruno's views from M1, the story-world-level frame within which the character straightforwardly expresses his views, to an alternative framing, M2—and, I would add, perhaps M3 or M4. In this new framing the author, the tourist industry, or the intellectuals in *Esprit* become additional subjects whose value positions need to be assessed; readers have to figure out whose communicative intentions are most relevant, and what worldviews get invested with what evaluations.

Galinañes insists on the category uncertainty triggered by the simultaneous activation of multiple frames in humor and irony: a momentary uncertainty in the cases of humor and stable irony, more lasting in the case of what Booth called unstable irony. However, the notion of frame switching does not suffice to distinguish humor, irony, or ambiguity.[16] Elsewhere in this book I discussed generic hybridity and narratorial unreliability as phenomena similarly involving oscillations and shifts between frames. The interesting thing is that, in irony, the alternation pertains to the implicit or explicit evaluative dimension of propositions, which may extend to the evaluation path itself or to the kind of thinking for which the assertions may be held exemplary.[17] The frame switch includes the sources to which we attribute communicative intentions, hence the interpreters' reconstructions of the relevant discursive situations or contexts.

In the case of an ironic interpretation of Bruno's words, for instance, the author's and readers' contextual framing includes the ensemble of sociolects that we would have recognized as mentioned and displayed for evaluation, with their discursive situations and value-laden presuppositions. The frame switch also affects the interpretive and evaluative regimes considered appropriate. At story-world level Bruno's utterances can be interpreted psychologically and morally, as expressing his personal character and views; if we frame them as irony, their point becomes the metaevaluative exercise itself. Who, and what, exactly is targeted remains to be argued by the interpreter: Bruno's earnest tone in his defense of free sex? I tend to interpret, rather, the irony as aiming at the *doxa*, in line with my construction of Houellebecq's prior ethos.

A further eloquent example of the potential impacts of such ironic frame switching would be readers' conflicting interpretations of Houellebecq's provocative assertions about Islam in *Platform*, and the author's just as provocative public endorsements of these views. But I would like to submit another intriguing case, one in which political issues are at stake: Russian postmodern fiction by "imperialist writers" such as Aleksandr Prokhanov and Pavel Krusanov, whose works enjoy large audiences. They also raise the important question of whether their fictions are seriously meant propaganda, or rather examples of playful quotation or ironic critique of such propaganda. Answers to this question, in my view, can only be more or less normative in their reasoning, though narratologists can seek to reconstruct such pathways (again, not as an analysis with objective results but as a metahermeneutic argument). I must immediately add that I do not have access to these cases firsthand, as I do not read Russian. My point is not to offer another interpretation of these works but rather to discuss the ways in which other interpreters have dealt with ambiguities in these works and with the controversies in their reception.

Boris Noordenbos, from whom I borrow the following case, discusses among other recent Russian works the novel *Gospodin Geksogen* (Mister

Hexogen, 2002) by the journalist and writer Aleksandr Prokhanov. The novel's extravagant plot, in Noordenbos's summary, "reinterprets the tumultuous political events of 1999 as a series of bizarre . . . conspiracies surrounding the restoration of the Soviet empire. . . . [A] demonic underground serpent, which symbolizes Russia's sell-out, hypnotizes the political establishment in the Kremlin; Yeltsin himself is literally a walking corpse, kept 'alive' artificially for the sole purpose of defending the business interests of the fraudulent elite; Russia's most prominent liberal journalists are unmasked as robots, radio-controlled by the CIA" (Noordenbos 2011).

How to categorize such a work? Prokhanov had been known until then for fiction that programmatically "reflected the patriotic, anti-liberal, and often anti-Semitic ideas [also] expressed in his weekly newspaper *Zavtra*" (Noordenbos 2011). In my terms, these publishing activities provide material for a politically clear prior ethos and authorial posture. Indeed, critics often interpreted the anti-Western and authoritarian tone of books by Prokhanov as mirroring the renewed self-confidence of the Russian political establishment in the new millennium.

But in 2002 Prokhanov's new novel *Gospodin Geksogen* was released by the liberal and postmodern publishing house Ad Marginem, through which Sorokin's most scandalous novels also appeared, along with Russian translations of Derrida, Lyotard, and Baudrillard. The novel was awarded the Russian National Bestseller Prize. A category mistake?

Noordenbos notes that the mere fact that the novel was published by Ad Marginem encouraged constructions of Prokhanov as "a playful postmodernist" and of his work as "an entertaining 'deconstruction' of nationalist pulp writing . . . in the vein of Vladimir Sorokin's famous postmodern pastiches of naïve patriotic and Socialist Realist prose." Yet others interpreted the work's grotesque scenes against the foil of the author's prior ethos of "fanatic neo-Stalinist and anti-Semite." For some critics Prokhanov's prose evidently displays experimental, avant-garde qualities, while for others "the author's poor writing skills and unconventional imagery should not be mistaken for postmodern experimentation or deconstruction. What was pastiche for Sorokin was serious prose in the case of Prokhanov."

The parallel with Houellebecq's classification problem is striking, illustrating the general relevance of analyzing such framing acts. As Booth notes, irony is in the eye of the beholder, but clearly one's framing inflects what one sees. While for Noordenbos "it seems hard to maintain such distinctions based on the hypothetical intentions of the author," I would argue that precisely readers' constructions of authorial intention and ethos play a central role in such cases and that they are tied to categorizations, including one's framing of the work's genre and kind of writing as "postmodern."

In Noordenbos's view, Prokhanov's work erodes or blurs, even further than postmodern writing already did, the opposition "between skepticism and ideological commitment," and the "boundaries between the (nostalgic) reproduction and ironic deconstruction of Socialist Realist or Stalinist art." This may be the case for the author, which would in any case turn his presumed critical literary engagement into a rather messy affair. But the ambiguity need not be reproduced in the reception, as Noordenbos's own analysis shows. Rather, audiences are split between those who do interpret such works as ironic and those who don't (see Kaufer 1982 on irony's effect of dividing audiences), or between those who consider the irony to target the propaganda itself and those for whom it is the expectation of a critical positioning that should be ironized. The vehemence of audience responses, whether enthusiastic or deeply suspicious, points to the social, political, and ethical stakes of the framing.

In my view, the ways in which such interpretations follow conventional paths, with literary and political conceptions playing a decisive role, deserve further investigation. This also holds for the value positions attaching to these different framings, which may complement or rather challenge each other. What political interests does the "blurring" noticed by critics serve? In this case, Noordenbos suggests, it bonds at least one section of the intelligentsia with a mass audience by translating an avant-garde aesthetic and intellectual aura onto a nationalistic stance. As I see it, this move, however, draws attention to the "postmodern": is this label to be associated with a politically critical stance or with cynical laissez-faire? This might explain why some intellectuals felt such a strong urgency to denounce Prokhanov's writing as unacceptable in its blurring of categories.

If anything, this example suggests how the attribution of irony, or any other ethos, to a speaker or writer requires the reconstruction of a whole context in which the interplay between value perspectives is perceived. The example also suggests how fruitful a thorough analysis of such ethos categorizations might be, as it takes us deep into evaluation practices and "horizons."

Back to Narratology, and Further Considerations

Within narratology, several scholars have devoted specific attention to irony, often alongside unreliability or voice (especially Fludernik 1993). I will only rapidly discuss one such approach, namely Culler's understanding of irony as an interpretive strategy, which to some extent for me is quite congenial. Yet it also displays the rather typical injection of normative conceptions of literature into a narratology.

For Culler irony and parody together constitute one of five "naturalizations," that is, paths along which readers make textual incongruities "intelligible by relating [them] to various models for coherence" (Culler 1975, 152).[18] Parody and irony, he notes, both require the reader to keep in mind two conflicting orders (for instance, one in which Bruno seriously asserts views about Cap d'Agde, the other in which such views would be exposed for critical scrutiny). While parody unambiguously defines the relation between the two mental representations, freezing their oscillation (Culler 1975, 152), irony would prevent the cognitive instability from coming to "premature ending." In this respect, Culler argues, irony is intimately tied to fiction's pragmatic functioning.

In support of his argument Culler calls in Barthes's analysis of irony in Flaubert, who refuses "to halt the play of codes (or does so badly), with the result that . . . one never knows whether he [Flaubert] is responsible for what he writes (whether there is an individual subject behind his language); for the essence of writing (the meaning of the work which constitutes writing) is to prevent any reply to the question: Who is speaking?" (Barthes 1970, 146; quoted in Culler 1975, 158–59; his translation).

I fully endorse the idea that fiction, which I understand here as narrative art, "grant[s] the maximum scope to the play of formal features and semantic uncertainties" (Culler 1975, 160). But for me, what makes irony, or ambiguity, so characteristic for art experiences is the multiplication of frames that involve interpretations and evaluations of a state of affairs, which calls attention to these framings themselves (as also captured in Koestler's notion of bisociation, though I would not limit the mechanism to an oscillation between just two framings). What readers, and writers, do with such multiplicities—bringing them to a halt or keeping them open—is to my sense a matter of historically evolved normative conceptions of art and of personal disposition toward ambiguity.[19] Barthes's and Culler's essentializing of enunciative indeterminacy is, I would say, as normative as Booth's opposed preference for stable ironies. Strangely so, as Culler's own understanding of irony as just one among several interpretive strategies should precisely invite analysts to investigate the norms and conditions on the basis of which readers adopt one or the other of these strategies.

Irony and Readers' "Negative Capability"

In literary studies as well as in cognitive approaches, the assumption is widespread that one function of narrative art is to cultivate the faculty to deal with uncertainties and to adapt to the unexpected by exercizing our metacognitive capacity and mental flexibility. Irony par excellence fits such a program, if only because its semiotic complexity demands "endurance to ambiguity" and the readiness to "change [our] mental set" (Tsur 2006, 22). The pleasure irony provides may be hypothesized to stem from one's feeling of mental adequacy and agility, with an added tinge of satisfaction stemming from being on the right side of the social judgment line, or rather way beyond it, as in the case of Prokhanov—and perhaps also a hint of intellectual aggressivity (Zeki 2004; Galinañes 2005).

It is just one step from here to the hypothesis that by multiplying and problematizing interpretive frames, irony increases a work's aesthetic value (cf. Bortolussi and Dixon 2003; Gombrich 1960). The same can be argued for irony's interest from an ethical perspective, as it engages interpreters in reasoning about potential sources' values and ethos.

However, readers may have different thresholds when it comes to dealing with this multiplicity of values and perspectives. Affinity with ambiguity is a factor on which critics and critical styles differ, as Tsur suggested. There seem to be gradations in the duration and width of the "gating," that is, the openness to alternative interpretations of which critics are mentally capable, and also in their "negative capability," that is, their capacity to deal with uncertainties (Tsur 2006, 8). For some, ambiguity and irony, including those instances pertaining to ethos, form fundamental criteria for aesthetic value. Others instead seek "rapid closure" (Tsur 2006, 58), for which stereotypic and monolithic ethos profiles can be expected to be effective.[20]

Empirical proof that reading literary narrative exercises mental flexibility and metaevaluative capacities would provide important arguments for giving (back) to literary reading a more substantial role in education, if one considers these capacities as crucial for democracy (see Nussbaum's militant *Not for Profit*, 2010). I would expect the crux of such a mental and ethical exercising through literature to lie in how the reflexive dimension is organized, and so in the reception context and conditions, not just in a work's theme and form. Booth already drew attention to the importance of what he called the process of "co-duction," that is, the reasoning and comparing of one's own experience of a text with that of others (Booth 1988, 72–73, 375ff.). Ironic and ambiguous texts could be expected to form especially good material for such calibration and negotiation of meaning and value attributions: they require intensified mental activity, an examination of the text through multiple perspectives, a going-over again and again of one's response. This procedure can be expected to train one's capacity for questioning and crossing established frame borders and for creatively seeking out new frames. Collaboration with scholars skilled in designing empirical experiments is needed to turn these intuitive formulations into hypotheses that can be tested.

In what follows, Eggers's novel will serve for exploring how the framework just outlined affords heuristic strategies for engaging with issues of sincerity, irony, and ethos in particular literary narratives and how it allows reconstruction of some of the followed interpretive routes.

Sincerity and the Snake's Skin: Dave Eggers's *A Heartbreaking Work of Staggering Genius*

Dave Eggers's AHWOSG (2001), as mentioned, tells in more than four hundred pages how a twenty-one-year-old, living in mid-nineties San Francisco, loses in a short time both parents and takes upon himself the care of his younger brother. The grief, anxieties, survival strategies, and adventures of this orphan suddenly turned into a surrogate father are evoked in first-person narration, present tense, and direct address to the reader. The book displays a flourish of metafictional gimmickry but also much pathos and many protestations of sincerity. "Honestly," Eggers insists, there is "no irony whatsoever" in this book, only lots of "formal fun" (34). But Eggers would not be the first author to write ironically about rejecting irony.

Questions regarding the author's ethos assail the reader from the very moment he or she picks up Eggers's book. The theatrical front cover of my paperback edition, with its red curtain and technicolor sunset, from which the title and author's name emerge, makes me infer an author complicit with U.S. marketing strategies or, more probably, parodying these, like the book's hyperbolic, self-characterizing title. If I turn the book around, just like irony may turn evaluations upside down, the cover with its pastel picture of a young child blowing on a dandelion triggers opposite associations of innocence and vulnerability, or perhaps ironizes these as clichés. The nearly ninety pages of paratext make the authorial voice overwhelmingly present.

This authorial voice, which, to simplify, I will refer to as Eggers, moreover, self-consciously proclaims an ethos of sincerity, setting it off against postmodern irony. His discursive ethos, however, constantly calls for attention, with its hair-splitting self-scrutiny and self-centeredness, its pathos and hyperbolic use of hyperbole. The programmatic epigraph—"I am true of heart . . . You are true of heart"—sends me on sincerity's path, except for its curiously redundant formulation, a possible cue for irony.

After these and many other ludic threshold clues, the core life story opens soberingly with the poignant evocation of Dave's parents' death. If we bear in mind that Eggers's book is based on a true story, as the cover indicates, we may expect a referential or autobiographic reading frame to impose its rock-bottom ethos-cum-pathos effect of authentic suffering, the kind somewhat deceptively claimed by Frey. An author can allow himself much gimmickry before really putting at risk such a guarantee of authenticity.

Moreover, the author's colloquial tone in both paratext and actual narrative, as well as the frequent addresses to the reader, suggest a scenography of intimate and sincere communication between author or narrator and reader. The paratext's insistence on the book's fictional character, in the preface to the Picador edition, paradoxically reinforces the nonfictional framing, since fiction is emphatically defined here as stylization and generalization of real-life experience rather than as invention. Here is a writer, one would say, for whom there is or should be no fundamental separation between literature and life and for whom writing means communication, if not communion. But as in Angot's case, such effects of authenticity can be tricky.

Eggers's book was published in the midst of a debate about irony and postmodernism, which gives extra salience to the text's stance on ethos. In 1999 Jedediah Purdy eloquently described the devastating effects of the absence of sincerity on American society during the Clinton era.[21] Fellow writers such as David Foster Wallace, Matt Thorne, or Nicholas Blincoe distanced themselves as well from postmodern ("pomo") irony, yet with more ambiguity than can be found in Purdy's anti-irony pamphlet.[22]

I will use this case study to make explicit some steps in my own inference of "Dave's" or Eggers's ethos: what are the clues that I rely on, what frame switches do I perform, what do these mean for my overall interpretation of this book? Such inferences, I proposed in preceding chapters, are not merely subjective interpretive decisions. They at least in part correspond to conventional interpretive moves.

I will make my point through a close reading of three connected sections: first, the episode recounting young Dave's involvement in the satirical magazine *Might*, epitomizing the presumed ills of postmodern irony; then a crucial scene at the heart of the novel, Dave's interview with a casting agent for MTV's *Real World* program, which reads as a *mise en abyme* of the thematized issues of irony and sincerity in self-representation; and finally, the plea for trust and explicit rejection of irony in the paratextual essay "Irony and its Malcontents."

Mediated Immediacy

Narratologists would start by pointing out that narrative transmission involves three levels on which readers would create an image of "Dave": as (1) narrator Dave, (2) as young Dave, the protagonist whose story and voice are evoked, and (3) the author Dave, whose voice is foregrounded in the paratext and by the suggested, yet uncertain, nonfiction framing. To these figures should be added other manifestations of the author: as a biographical person, as a citizen, and so on. In actual reading experiences, readers may well forget about the mediation and conflate these various subject effects.

My mental model for the protagonist is formed by his actions and his ways of speaking and thinking, as recounted and conveyed through discourse. On the basis of young Dave's behavior, the ethos I would construct for him oscillates between, on the one hand, his caring and responsible behavior within the family, proved by his behavior all through the trying family situation, and on the other hand, his habitus in the *Might* episodes, which display postmodern irony at its most irresponsible. Note that my inferences about Dave's character at this stage are beholden to real-life frames, such as folk psychology and folk morality.

It is not so clear, however, to which Dave one should attribute discursive ethos effects such as might be inferred from the obsessive self-reflection, denegations of denegations, hyperbolic use of hyperbole, and all the "formal fun." Is this stylistic ethos characterizing older and wiser narrator Dave, or even author Dave? Does it mimetically convey, with possibly self-ironic dual voice effects, young Dave's way of thinking? As with Angot's work, one's decision about whose voice one reads, and how one constructs an ethos for it, is connected to how one frames the work's genre.

Might: *"Doing Something Sociologically Huge"*

Long sections in the novel depict the attempts of young Dave and a little bunch of comrades to launch the satirical magazine *Might*, which should mark its founders' distance from the philistines. The heavily emphasized contrast between young Dave's and his pals' words and their deeds for me oozes rhetorical irony. Narrator Dave especially castigates his younger self's ironic attitude and the solipsistic attention-craving of this bunch of purportedly critical intellectuals. The narrating voice sharply catches the sociolect and habitus of the journal's in-crowd, which interpose their ironic we've-seen-it-all-and-seen-through-it-all suspicion between themselves and the world—a world they've hardly even started exploring, as the text does not fail to point out. Like his friends, young Dave appears more obsessed by his own posturing than by any effective form of social action. The closest his little group gets to "do[ing] something sociologically huge" is shooting a clumsy photo series of their bunch of friends in the nude (247).

A montage of scenes rubs in narrating Dave's judgment. The text juxtaposes the coma of a dear friend, the real personal damage caused by a hoax mounted by Dave and his pals in their magazine, and their reaction to both events, which would appear rather inadequate (according to widely shared norms), caught up as they are in their symbolic battles and verbal bubbles. The text's rhetorical irony defines by antiphrasis the ironist's (older Dave's) own ethos, with values such as empathy, sincerity, and personal commitment. These values were also displayed in young Dave's responsible conduct as a family member. A gap is thus suggested between young Dave's professional ethos, with its corrupting habitus of self-centered irony, and his genuinely other-oriented private ethos. This antithetic structure, which runs through the whole book, would justify a reading of the work as bildungsroman, scripted to lead "from irony to commitment." But, as young Dave observes about his chameleonic in-group, "We can play it both ways, all ways" (245).

Authenticity, Sincerity, and the Snake's Skin

In comparison to the *Might* sections, ethos attribution is more complex in the MTV interview scene. Comprising more than fifty pages located in the center of the book, the scene draws attention to issues of ethos both explicitly and through its ambiguous assertion mode. On story-world level we have a competitive testing situation in which young Dave defends his selling points for the TV show, so ethos management is to be expected. The previous pages of the novel have made clear how badly he wants to be on the show. There is some ironically emphasized character contradiction here, as the text earlier mentioned how this young intellectual and his *Might* pals of course "see right through" the show's petit bourgeois cult of standardized individual uniqueness and uninhibited emotion.[23]

The section at first glance reads as a realistic scenic representation of a dialogue. Young Dave rambles on in apparently quoted near-monologic direct discourse, while the casting lady does little more than facilitate his outpour. Some elements, however, may strike readers as odd, although a mimetic-realist reading frame, for which Eggers cues us, can be very effective in narrativizing away breaches in verisimilitude. Precisely these disturbing elements may, however, work as frame-switch clues, which they do for me.

Take the section in which young Dave points out his assets to the casting staffer, Laura: "I can do last breaths, last words. . . . I can do it any way you want, too—I can do it funny, or maudlin, or just straight, uninflected—anything. . . . Can you not see what I represent? I am both a) martyred moralizer and b) amoral omnivore born out of the suburban vacuum + idleness + television + Catholicism + alcoholism + violence; I am a freak in secondhand velour" (236).[24] In a mimetic-realist framing, this section could be perceived as young Dave's actual words or unvoiced thoughts. In both cases, one might infer the smart-ass ethos of a critical intellectual, highly conscious of the prerequisites of such a TV show. This tone and the way in which Dave speaks about his "self" contrast with the ethos of sincerity and trust professed in the paratext, according to which one would not *do* but *be* oneself. Not only does Dave refer to himself as an actor who can adopt any role that would be desirable for the TV show's format, but the formulaic self-characterization is also strikingly written, with its use of graphic symbols such as *a)* or +. Metanarrative prolepses elsewhere in the same section similarly disturb the mimetic-realist framing (as in, "I'll do so later in this section" [214], a remark that playfully conflates experiencing *I* and writing *I*). Such defamiliarizing cues, if perceived, trigger a search for a more adequate framing. As soon as one adopts this other framing perspective, this entire direct discourse section appears as double- or multivoiced, as an unstable composite of perspectives. The section might be read now as narrator Dave's sympathetic rendering of his younger self's craving for attention and empathy; alternately, as his critical representation of young Dave's readiness to prostitute his dramatic life story; or also as the effectively synthetic evocation of Dave's and Laura's interaction, which Alan Palmer or Lisa Zunshine would describe in terms of reciprocal mind reading.[25] Note that these inferences all still belong to the same kind of mimetic-realist reading strategy, feeding on folk psychology.

Alternately, the whole interview scene may be understood more abstractly and its staging as only pseudo-realistic. This framing drastically changes the focus of one's ethos attribution and the point of the reading experience. From empathizing with the personal experience of young Dave or with narrator Dave looking back on his younger self, one's involvement shifts to a much less personal enterprise. The scene now echoes particular discourses and the practices they afford—in particular, the ways in which such reality shows mold individual authenticity to a particular format. (Phelan would speak here of a thematic as well as a synthetic reading of the character's discourse and thought.)[26]

At this point it is the author's communicative intention that becomes relevant (an author who is, clearly, my own construction). The narrator's or author's tone now does not so much signal self-irony, as it did in a mimetic framing. Ambiguities of voice now connote literary skills, reinforcing the authority posture of a self-conscious and expertly verbal author, sharply aware of cultural fashions and formats in their linguistic expression. The show of sincerity clues unfolds differently in this other communication context, and the clues come to seem discursive baits, with calculated pathos effects. The author's rhetorical and aesthetic mastery is demonstrated precisely by the extent to which one has been emotionally wrapped up in the life story one reads, an immersion effect the text now makes one scrutinize. Such a writing practice exemplifies a conception of literature as autonomous art rather than as emotional communication or even communion.

As in Angot's work, the play with alternate interpretive framings becomes particularly interesting when a programmatic conception of literature seems to get voiced. I would like to focus here on a number of core images pertaining to notions of selves and writing. I take these images to work as condensates of value-laden conceptions, which change as if viewed through a kaleidoscope depending on the communication level on which one makes them function.

One such core image can be read in Dave's repartee with Laura, who hints that he may have been too exhibitionistic about his private life. Young Dave retaliates: "These things, details, stories . . . are like the skin shed by snakes, who leave theirs for anyone to see. . . . I own none of it. It is everyone's. It is shareware. . . . I would kill or die to protect those who are part of it, but I do not claim exclusivity" (215–16). If I frame this reply as young Dave's contribution to the dialogue with the casting agent, I'd take the section's style and content to express his character. From his outcry I might infer that he is an impassioned and self-conscious communicator, intent on sharing ("I would kill or die"). Such an ethos is in congruence with narrator Dave as well as with the "author's" own exhortations to open and free communication, or with the extra-literary ethos one may construct from Eggers's own social deeds (see the last pages of this analysis).

At the heart of the quoted section there is an image that appears particularly intriguing in such a mimetic-realist framing: that of one's identity as a snake's skin. This image raises moral questions: Is identity a matter of surface and appearance, as easily dropped and renewed as a snake's skin? Should one not take responsibility for one's old skins? ("What does he care where it is, who sees it, this snake, and his skin?" Dave also asks.) Or does the image suggest, in Piccolomini's sense, a mask or shield protecting an inner self unscathed by exhibitionism? Endorsed insincerity is itself a sincerity topos, the author helpfully recalls in the preface: "[B]eing aware of and open about one's motives at least means one is not lying. . . . We all like full disclosure" (xxxi). Indeed, with its dissection of motivations, the phrasing of the entire section conventionally suggests an ethos of obsessive and ruthlessly honest self-scrutiny and full disclosure, unless the heavy insistence prompts us to perceive these topoi as ironically mentioned rather than used.

We may also frame this image of the snake's skin in a much less personal way, for instance, as an ironic reference to the simulacrum of authenticity achieved in tightly formatted genres such as the MTV show or autobiography. In any case, such uncertainty regarding the assertion's endorsement (who means this, and how seriously?) endangers the scene's clarity as a *mise en abyme* of autobiography, sorting out Eggers's memoir for aesthetic reading rather than immersive "consumption."

Following right on the snake image, the programmatic topos of the transfiguration of the commonplace is likely to work just as ambiguously. The section pertains to the value of individual experience, which understandably is a central topic in much self-writing. As it is staged in this section, the theme hovers between competing framings, to which correspond wholly different value regimes. "Have it [all this life experience of Dave's]. . . . [M]ake it useful. This is like making electricity from dirt; it is almost too good to be believed, that we can make beauty from this stuff" (215–16). To make electricity, or beauty, from dirt (from one's life as "this stuff") activates the topos of the transfiguration of the everyday (Baudelaire, as recalled, spoke about poetry as making gold from dirt). We encountered the topos in the work of François Bon, in which I take it to be seriously meant, bolstered by images of the writer invested with social responsibility. In the case of *AHWOSG*, as in Angot's case, it is not at all certain whether we should extend, through the logic of *mise en abyme*, the claim to Eggers's own writing.

The contrast between the enthusiastic embrace of mediatic sharing in this section and the *Might* crew's unmasking of the MTV show's distortive effects on people's authenticity could instill doubts about the author's actual endorsement of such a claim. The theme may well function on several planes simultaneously, with differences of tone and ethos resulting from how an interpreter would define the priming situation. One may construct this idea of transfiguration as young Dave's naïve ideal but also as his own, and his older self's, self-ironic dismissal of such grandiose aspirations. Such dismissals, however, can still work as a topos of true sentiment, for instance, by being interpreted as pudical rhetorical denegations.

When Dave, in that same section, further characterizes his experience as "everyone's" and as "shareware," such formulations could express the disinterestedness that befits the posture of the writer who suffers for the common good and narrates the common experience. This posture would correspond to the axiology of what Boltanski and Thévenot called the Inspired World, in which art would usually be classified.[27] The image of shareware, however, might also be classified as referring to the Commercial World, an interpretation sparked by remarks such as, "Reward me for my suffering—Pardon?—Have I given you enough? Reward me. Put me on television. . . . I deserve this. . . . I know how this works. I give you these things, and you give me a platform" (235). Or elsewhere, "Give me something. Quid pro quo."[28] Is this young Dave self-consciously marketing his ethos, asking a good price for his "authentic" life story? After all, authenticity is what the emotion industry feeds on and what constitutes autobiographers' or witnesses' both symbolic and very real capital. The notion of *reward* interestingly hovers between the economic and the moral or religious registers: patient suffering in this world makes one a good candidate to be rewarded in the hereafter, with in this case TV—and the reader, if one extends the scenography to the book itself—playing the role of God as just retributor. A more suspicious ethos construction for young Dave could even translate back onto the author of this pathos-ridden real-life inspired work. Is self-irony sufficient to ward off suspicion of commercial interest?

Last but not least, a suspicion of irony affects an even more programmatic metaphor, salient throughout the book, including its paratext: that of the "lattice," which I would like to discuss in some detail.

Young Dave invokes this image, among others, in the climactic last pages of the interview scene, as one of his motivations for wanting to be on the MTV show. I need to quote from these pages extensively:

I am bursting with the hopes of a generation, their hopes surge through me, threaten to burst my hardened heart! Can you not see this? . . . I am rootless, ripped from all foundations, an orphan raising an orphan. . . . I have nothing but my friends and what's left of my little family. I need community, I need feedback, I need love, connection, give-and-take—I will bleed if they love. . . . Oh please let me show this to the millions. Let me be the lattice, the center of the lattice. . . . Oh I want to be the heart pumping blood to everyone, blood is what I know, I feel so warm in blood.

    —and that will heal you?

    Yes! Yes! Yes! (236–37)

Taken as *use* (in Sperber and Wilson's sense), so as seriously endorsed, this section invites me to construct a story-world situation in which young Dave craves love and understanding. As he says earlier, being broadcast would "prove to all and to ourselves that we are real, that we like everyone else simply want our lives on tape, proven, feel that what we are doing only becomes real once it has been entered into the record" (246). If instead one takes the section as older and wiser Dave's mentioning of his own youthful self-centered megalomania, the increasing self-insight might become the section's *point*. In this reading as well, sincerity remains a leading value. This particular ethos is foregrounded precisely through the ironic staging of the duplicities of the self. The exaggeration could easily be "narrativized" as an instance of dual voice or self-irony (older and wiser narrator Dave ironizing young Dave's high-strung feelings).

In a less personalizing and less psychologizing framing, other signals light up, in particular the play with language. Consider, first, some potential mention effects. The anaphor ("what I need," "I am," and so on) may work as estranging. Rather than as Dave's emotional outcry, the repetition reminds me of a chorus of suffering individuals. This may still reinforce the emotional vein, generalizing Dave's unique experience. But the anaphor may also be perceived as ironic mention of the kind of things people in such emotional situations would conventionally, and perhaps somewhat dramatically, say. To decide on the text's tone and how that feeds into an ethos for character, narrator, or author is not without significance, since one's decision affects how seriously we should take this image of the lattice as literature's aim. Ultimately, our ethos attribution here determines what value—and programmatic value—Eggers's work may have for us.

Second, there is the incongruity of images exploited for their literalness. The blood metaphor, for instance, at first seems a regular dead metaphor—the pun is almost unavoidable. The image activates a familiar cognitive schema that regards society as an organism before toppling over into grotesque literalness: "blood is what I know, I feel so warm in blood."

A similar estranging literalization, finally, affects the image of the lattice itself:

–Why do you want to share your suffering?

–By sharing it I will dilute it. . . . This is where the lattice comes in. [follows almost a whole page with lyrical praise of the lattice, for instance:] I see us as one, as a vast matrix, an army, a whole, each one of us responsible to one another, because no one else is. . . . [A]nd if we can bring everyone to grab a part of another, like an arm at the socket, everyone holding another's arm at the socket, and if we can get everyone to, instead of ripping this arm from the socket, instead hold to it, tight, and thus strengthening—Then, um—Like a human ocean moving as one, the undulating, the wave-making—

–Ahem

–Or like a snowshoe

–A snowshoe

–You wear a snowshoe when the snow is deep and porous. The latticework within the snowshoe's oval distributes the wearer's weight over a wider area, in order to keep him or her from falling. (210–11)

For me, this is a truly hilarious section. The abstract notion of responsibility is concretized into something like holding on to each other, almost pulling arms from sockets. In a chain of substitutions running wild, the lattice morphs into a matrix, an army, the human ocean; and yes, there we are, doing the wave . . . The unexpected reference to snowshoes works as an anticlimax, as does the (pseudo-)earnest explanation of what they are meant for, literally and symbolically. One may take this as bad literature (the author cannot get his metaphors straight) or as really funny play with conventional expressions of emotion. One's overall framing acts indeed make all the difference.

The "Stupid Risks" of Direct Address

In his paratextual notes on specific sections of his book, the "author" comments on this interview scene in a manifesto-like little essay about "Irony and its Malcontents" (literally little, as it is partly rendered in unreadably small type). The scare quotes around *author* are required here as we cannot simply take the paratext as the real Eggers's voice.

The essay on irony features in the appendix of the book and refers to pages 235–37 of the novel, which are the last pages of the interview scene I just discussed, extending to the book "in general all over." In this somewhat pedantic (Eggers's own qualification) essay, the author distinguishes irony from humor and "formal fun," since neither of these latter terms implies that one does not mean what is said (33–34). To which one could add, just as pedantically, that there are many shades of not meaning what one says, especially within postmodern irony.

The essay displays the posture and authority of the *literary* writer who knows his classics, as the allusion to Swift's *A Modest Proposal* makes clear (the whole essay's scholarly tone may either bolster the authorial authority or be perceived as ironic quoting of authority topoi, which does not necessarily annul the authority effects). This scholarly ethos, in turn, is toned down by a (whose?) characteristic self-irony, and even more so by the section's colloquial and emotional tone, conveyed through conventional stylistic emotion indicators. Indeed, in even smaller type, with expressive capitals and italics, the author lays before the reader what looks like unfinished notes. Their unpolished quality suggests their authenticity and pathos: "YES BUT SELF-AWARENESS *IS* SINCERITY." This discursive pathos seems to warrant the professed ethos: *this* irony is nothing intellectual, it has roots in raw feeling!

While postmodern attitudinal irony is often associated with a solipsistic or elitist worldview, the book's formal fun would instead seek to effect bonding, putting forth a sincere offer of communion (the "lattice"). The authorial voice dismisses the association of "his" work with postmodernism, as would be typically made by "venally impatient and yet startlingly lazy cultural bystanders." The periphrasis nicely casts critics for whom "everything in the world falls into two categories: the Earnest and the Ironic. . . . Everything is either glib and shallow, or maudlin and boring" (34). The authorial voice hastens to—playfully, or ironically?—

present his own classifications, such as: "Irony, of course, is very much [not] good" (35). But, as mentioned, this would not be the first ironic attack on irony.

Meanwhile, like the interview scene on which it comments, the section moves toward a climactic, pathos-imbued conclusion, which I must again quote at some length:

> When *I* was done [writing *AHWOSG*], *I* was ashamed, because *I* had written what *I* saw as a much too revealing and maudlin thing, overflowing with blood and sentiment and a simple bare longing for people who are gone. The book was seen by *its author* as a stupid risk . . . a mistake which nevertheless . . . *he* would encourage everyone to make. . . . Because *your* life is worth documenting. . . . Because if *you* do it right and go straight towards them *you like me* will write to *them*, and will look straight into *their* fucking eyes, like a person sometimes can do with another person. . . . [E]ven so [if without knowing them, *you*] wrote a book that was really a letter to them, *a messy fucking letter* that *you* could barely keep a grip on, but a letter *you* meant, and a letter *you* sometimes wish *you* had not mailed, but a letter *you* are happy that made it from *you* to *them*. (35; italics mine)

The section apparently takes us into full-fledged sincere pathos, bending the potentially ironic mention effects into something like "laughing to keep from crying" (note my recourse to folk psychology frames). The "messy fucking letter," to which the author compares his writing, is addressed to an indiscriminate "you," a fine slot for the empathic reader.

As scenography (Maingueneau 2004), the letter format to which the book is compared aptly steers one's reading in the psychologizing, empathic direction, also activated by the autobiographic and intimist generic framing (compare, for instance, the far more distanced tone in Coetzee's autofictional and autobiographic writing). There is an evident contrast here to the artificially formatted MTV show on which this irony essay comments. In the MTV show spontaneity was unmasked as a carefully crafted effect. Instead, the letter format suggests the spontaneous outpour of emotion, one "that you could barely keep a grip on": a stereotypical conceptualization of "hot" overflowing sentiment as a natural force, crucially different from the trope of irony, which is associated with cool rational control. The stylistic ethos ties in with the overall anti-ironic and antiaesthetic stance. The colloquial register and the syntax, with its repetitions and crafted-clumsy phrasing, connote the intensity of the feeling and the authenticity attributed to first-impulse speech.

The topos of the risks incurred in sincerely laying bare one's self in writing, familiar in autobiographical as in engagé writing, seems to function in a contract of mutual trust and empathic identification.[29] An appeal is sent to the reader to reciprocate in that low-threshold emotional communication and to become just as naked and vulnerable as the author himself. The interchangeability of author and reader is also conveyed by the intriguing twofold shift in pronouns, which I underlined in the quotation: First "I" suddenly becomes "the author," which for me reads as a shift from a suggested interpersonal framing (*I*, Eggers, the real person, communicate directly with *you*, the personalized reader) to a professional one (the author comments on his writing). The shift would also include a move from an ethos of *eunoia* (I am close to you) to one of authorial authority. The next pronoun shift puts "you"—the reader?—in the role of potential agent, summoned to imitate the gesture of baring one's soul and becoming an author oneself. My little excursion on the historically evolved topoi of sincerity, earlier in this chapter, should enable us to recognize stereotypical sincerity clues—the direct look, the emotional lexicon: "[You] will look *straight into their fucking eyes*, like a person sometimes can do with another person."

The pathos-laden appeal to the reader seems to be grounded in a stereotypical "Dr. Phil" psychology: "[y]our life is worth documenting" as well; I'm okay, you're okay. Is this, then, a programmatic conception of living and self-writing, captured in the idea of the lattice? By *mise en abyme*, reinforced by the apparent autobiographic pact, the value and social legitimization of Eggers's own book would similarly reside in the example it affords for socially bonding self-expression. But once again, how convincing is this professed rhetoric of sincerity or this call for empathic conarration?

Extratextual Ethos Clues

While the irony essay, like the rest of the paratext, hardly disambiguates the assertion mode, in interviews Eggers seems more set on getting his ethos straight. To a critic's suggestion that he capitalized on his suffering, an interpretation anticipated in the MTV scene, Eggers retaliated that he invested the money he earned from AHWOSG in social projects. We are very far here from Houellebecq's and Angot's extension of their ambiguous stances to the public sphere. Critics also frequently mention how Eggers financially backed projects such as 826 Valencia, "a nonprofit organization dedicated to supporting students ages six to eighteen with their creative and expository writing skills" (says the organisation's website, https://826valencia.org/); Voice of Witness, a series of books based on authentic oral histories of victims of human rights crises; and the review *McSweeney's Quarterly* and the publishing house of the same name, which "makes available books and articles without commercial intermediaries." Real-life deeds "prove" the author's good character and goodwill.

While Eggers's social initiatives enroll literature for very practical social use, his literary work, for its part, seems to break down the conventional borders between the Civic, Domestic, and Inspired Worlds. The question then arises whether one of these Worlds ultimately swallows up the others. I would argue that the concordance between the ethos of sincerity professed in AHWOSG and the one of Eggers's real-life deeds is likely to foster a mimetic-psychologizing reading of Eggers's work. Many readers and critics alike have indeed felt justified to apply to his work a moral-psychological regime rather than an aesthetic one.[30]

The ethos of sincere commitment that one might attribute to Eggers seems confirmed in subsequent novels, such as *What Is the What: The Autobiography of Valentino Achak Deng* (2006) or *Zeitoun* (2009). Analyzing ethos cues in these works would require another essay. I only want to make a few observations on *What Is the What*, as it sheds, a posteriori, a light on the author's ethos in AHWOSG.

In this later novel we have a character-narrator, Deng, a Sudanese refugee, who is presented as the author of the text we read. If it is understood as authentic, the story exerts a double and powerful ethos: Deng's gruesome life story builds on the daunting authenticity topos of first-hand experience of the violence of war and being a refugee; In addition, Eggers, the author-spokesman, postures as truly committed, putting his art in service of suffering people. If we frame the work as fictional, the author's spokesman posture may still enlist strong ethos effects. Deng's story is then likely to function as a verisimilar synthesis of thousands of real-life cases. The author would still be considered to display genuine commitment, putting his writing skills and extensive documentation work in the service of an empathetic broadcasting of refugees' experiences. Deviations from verisimilitude do not always hamper the effect of authentic and sincere commitment, nor of an overall nonfiction global scene, as Maingueneau called it.[31] Indeed, by convention literary or fictional devices may enhance the rhetorical appeal of an overall factually intended text. But unlike his debut, and unlike Angot's writing, Eggers's later novel does not, to my mind, exploit hesitations about generic framing, missing out on the potential aesthetic and ethical effects of ambiguity.

Does this—admittedly sketchy—recourse to extratextual ethos clues and to the ethos that would result from his other works help pinpoint the author's assertion mode in AHWOSG? In my interpretation, in his first big novel Eggers reaches out of the ivory tower, seeking to mend the rift between words and being, between self and others, and to overcome the culture of suspicion associated with postmodern irony. But he does this, to my sense, in an effectively ambiguous way, as did David Foster Wallace or Christine Angot. The text presents sincerity, trust, and bonding as salient themes and stages them as attitudes the reader is made to desire. At the same time, we're kept aware of the complexities of writing-oneself-in-language and of contemporary culture's contradictory injunctions: *Thou shall exhibit and share with us thy most private inner self,* while *Thou shall mistrust any exhibition of sentiment.* The personalizing and empathic framing required of the reader becomes part of what is mentioned, exhibited for critical reflection. The same textual clues, plus their psychologizing interpretation by the reader according to all-too-familiar frames, become recontextualized as signifiers at this further level of interpretation. But the pathos appeal and the "pattern of desire" (Booth 1988: 201) are so strong that the metafictional framing does not, in my view, demolish the impact of the first-level reading. These computations and imputations, for me, result in an unstable authorial ethos that is at some point stabilized by Eggers's other works and real-life commitment.

Discussing the perception of the famous ambiguous rabbit/duck drawing, Gombrich observes in *Art and Illusion* that we can see each of the two figures distinctly. But "[w]hat is difficult—indeed impossible—is to see all these things at the same time. We are not aware of the ambiguity as such, but only of the various interpretations. It is through the act of 'switching' that we find out that different shapes can be projected into the same outline. We can train ourselves to switch more rapidly, indeed to oscillate between readings, but we cannot hold conflicting interpretations" (Gombrich 1960, 198).

While I have tried to capture similar frame-switching experiences, I wonder whether Gombrich rightly discards the possibility that we can hold conflicting interpretations simultaneously. Certain kinds of irony, as Linda Hutcheon (1988, 49) also suggests, open up conflicting interpretations, not in terms of exclusive alternatives *either/or-*, but rather as *either/and*. One can imagine that memory retains simultaneously contradictory emotions and thoughts, conflicting framings, each casting the other in a new perspective. Perhaps it is by their dynamic complexity, their built-in conflict, that such semiotic processes convey the opacity of real experience as a layered and time-engaging process.

An advantage, though, of Gombrich's notion of oscillation is that it accounts for the restlessness of the interpretation experience. Such instability of perspective does not necessarily result in "postmodern" relativism, since there is a strong sense that what is ultimately meant does matter, as well as *how* it is meant and endorsed, by whom, and from what position. The burden of making sense, however, lies with the reader.

To give two—provisional—last turns to the kaleidoscope: to eschew categorizing his or her ethos profile, hence the *point* of one's work, is for a writer a good way to establish literary interest and value. It allows authors to secure the legitimacy of the writing and reading acts in several Worlds simultaneously. Distancing himself from postmodern irony yet keeping irony center stage, Eggers trumped staunch pomo-ironists with their own weapon. This strategy arguably allowed him to carve out his niche in contemporary American literature, paving the way for more full-fledged sentiment. His later work, published by a now-celebrated author, could afford to be much less ambiguous. In American post-9/11 culture, moreover, sincere commitment has also become much more accepted as an attitude for a seriously "literary" writer. From both an ethical and an aesthetic perspective, though, I would myself defend the ambiguous work as the more interesting one. The more intense cognitive work it makes readers do increases the attention one brings to the themes and attitudes that are thematized and "performed" in the reading, in this case, sincerity and ironic disinvestment.

On Narrative, Ethos, and Ethics

The notion of ethos has been characterized by Ruth Amossy as a cross-roads at which different critical approaches meet. I hope this book has highlighted the fruitfulness of making narratology encounter some perspectives focused on the social construction and negotiations of meanings and values.

My own privileged image for readers' ethos attributions and for their engagement with narrative more generally is that of the kaleidoscope. The kaleidoscope stands for viewing from a certain angle, under a certain aspect, and for reframing a scene or a mental representation with the wonder of seeing configurations change before our own eyes.

Among the framing acts that interpreters may share, or in which they may differ, I highlighted those of genre and reading strategies. These reading strategies root in normative conceptions of literature, conceptions of selves—and also, for narratologists and other literary professionals, conceptions of what is required in terms of scholarly knowledge and relevance frames. I hope to have shown that narratologists' own prisms—some would call them biases—appear with particular clarity in their typologies and models for aspects of narrative that involve ethos characterizations.

My aim has also been to bring out the hermeneutic orientation that complements, sometimes tacitly, narratology's attention to textual devices, especially in the rhetorical perspective that is currently quite strong. Yet to expose narratology's normative biases or interpretive inclinations is not, in this book, part of a striving for *more scientificity*. Rather, I have argued that much is to be gained from this paradoxical metahermeneutic attempt: to catch interpreters' cognitive processes in the act, to reconstruct their pathways and their textual, extratextual, and even nondiscursive triggers—and to show that this holds for narratologists as well as, perhaps, for ordinary readers, though empirical research clearly is required to find out more about the latter.

This book itself also feeds on wishful thinking, values, and convictions, which may have been conspicuous all along, from my own discursive ethos among other clues. One core assumption is the idea that interpretation, as a social negotiation of meanings, exercises the reasoning we need to cultivate if we want to be creatures with more than episodic and mimetic modes of cognition (to refer to Donald's terms). Thorough verbal metacognition is not something that comes naturally: it requires mental and verbal training in situations of social interaction or through practices of intensified self-scrutiny.

Other such convictions are, first, the idea that theories of narrative fiction that elude the diversity of interpretive perspectives amputate themselves from a critical reflective dimension. Second, regarding narratives and narratology, I find appealing the idea that both the aesthetic and the ethical interests of narratives result from the multiplication of (conflicting or ambiguous) framings for issues with existential relevance. One can read *A Heartbreaking Work of Staggering Genius* as an autobiographic narrative, grippingly recounting a moving human experience; one can also read it as a narrative that frames such existential material in multiple ways, creating the kaleidoscope effect that puts readers' minds at work in other than empathic ways, eliciting reflection on the meaning-making paths themselves.

Third, as a heuristics for close reading, narratology works, I'd like to argue, as a semiotic training simply by drawing attention to the expressive and semantic potential of narrative form (which is the tacit or avowed goal of many textbooks on narratology, stylistics, or textual rhetoric). Close attention to narrative devices and aesthetic form, steered by some kind of systematic heuristics, can be argued to develop readers' arsenal of strategies for meaning making and subsequent interpretation. Methodical textual scrutiny can give us some distance, increasing a text's strangeness and hence the metacognitive effects of the reading experience. Far from representing a "merely" aesthetic kind of attention, such intensified attention to particulars of narrative and discursive form constitutes the first step of any careful ethical reading.

This elucidation of some convictions underlying this book brings me to an issue that I have left unaddressed so far: how does the proposed framework for analyzing ethos attributions relate to ethical narratology or criticism? To start with, it should provide extra arguments for the need to tease out narrative levels and perspectives, which is a prominent concern—and contribution—of rhetorical narratology. I hope to have demonstrated that interpreters' framing of a work's genre and priming communication situation determines whose ethos becomes relevant to reflect on (a character's, a narrator's, or an [implied or constructed] author's) and what ethical expectations and judgments might arise from there.

From a heuristic angle this book's contribution to ethical analysis lies, I think, in the attention it draws to sincerity, reliability, irony, authority, and so on, as ethos effects resulting from readers' reading habits and framing acts, the rhetorical potential of textual elements, and cultural stereotypes or topoi activated in readers' memory by textual clues.

But the main ethical interest of the proposed framework lies elsewhere, I believe. The proposed metahermeneutic perspective, as mentioned, invites interpreters—and not only professional ones—to explore diversity in interpretations. Why do readers react differently to a case such as Frey's? Such an investigation can be done in two distinct modes: a scholarly one, which seeks to objectivate cultural patterns in meaning and value attribution, or a more personal one (both directions have been discussed in relation to Gadamer and Ricoeur's hermeneutic orientation, in chapter 1). How does one react to Frey's, Littell's, or Roth's book, compared to other readers? To negotiate, in explicit debate, differences in ways of interpreting can make one aware of one's own "prejudices," as Gadamer would say. Such an awareness might make one embrace these prejudices all the more, or perhaps incite one to abandon them. It seems likely, however, that the exercise in any case increases one's self-awareness. This understanding of ethical inquiry goes beyond ethical-narratological approaches that seek to locate the interpreter's ethical experience in his or her rapport with the story world or in the mode of telling. The analyst's or reader's own ethical standards and pathways for interpretation and judgment are now explicitly included in the scrutiny. The relevance of such a practice should not be underestimated, especially in educational and personal or social development settings.

Here comes, indeed, another of my convictions: the idea that metahermeneutic practices such as those described can intensify processes of negotiations of values and meanings and can foster shared consciousness of the paths along which they are achieved. This reflexivity, however, is by no means self-evident and very much also depends on the conditions under which this exercise is performed. On an individual level, following Ricoeur (see the discussion in chapter 1), reflection on one's own—and others'—interpretation can be expected to stimulate one's capacity for perspective-taking and empathizing, and perhaps tolerance for otherness. These are the same attitudes that are often assumed to be core elements of the ethical experience elicited by fictional narrative. There is, however, more than a risk of circularity in this reasoning: do the conditions of the interpretive exchange—respect for difference, readiness to empathize with another standpoint or to accept that one cannot empathize but still wants to reason about differences, and so on—not themselves convey the values that the interpretive exercise is meant to foster? This is probably the case, but I would defend this circularity as a valuable recursivity that engrains a desired attitude on several levels simultaneously. There are no value-free interpretive exercises.

A stronger objection comes from the simple observation that violent controversies, such as the ones over Houellebecq's or Frye's ethos, do not exactly show any readiness among critics to empathize with each other's ethos constructions or to reflect on their own interpretive and evaluative pathways. Patricola's comments on Noguez's interpretation of Houellebecq's persona and work are indeed also a form of metahermeneutics, virulently defending its own way of seeing. The metaethical approach I propose requires another—more reflective—stance and another use of the interpretation of literary narratives, one that cultivates self-reflection and the readiness to weigh arguments, together with the value regimes in which they operate and a person's hermeneutic "horizon." The ethical relevance of narrative literature then moves from the values staged in a work, or demonstrated in its telling, to the debates we have over an artifact and over our divergent interpretations.

More empirical research on the validity of the assumptions voiced here is welcome and urgently needed. Indeed, even if only a part of such ideas would prove correct, we had better change something in our education systems and exploit more lucidly the reflection on values that debates about artworks afford, as Martha Nussbaum—and others—also keep arguing (see, e.g., Nussbaum 2010; Citton 2010; Jouve 2010).

Any investigation of the kind undertaken in this book brings to light other issues to be explored. Here are some paths that appear promising to me. The first is that of literature and the values it thematizes. The ways in which literary texts bring evaluative stances into circulation in language through style, tone, and so on remains a puzzling issue. The combination of ethos cues and expectations, as well as acts of framing, has rich potential, as I hope to have shown.

This investigation on thematized values needs to be extended, secondly, to research on the evaluation regimes and practices to which literature is exposed. Pragmatic or sociological approaches to literature have attended to the conditions in which literary works circulate and are invested with meaning and value. Boltanski and Thévenot's model, I proposed, interestingly points to the need to connect evaluations to what, following Goffman, I called acts of framing. Both investigations—of the values thematized in literary narratives and of evaluative regimes and their applications—should be pursued more systematically, especially in light of current changes in the mode of circulation and evaluation of artefacts. This kind of investigation definitely requires empirical research on actual readers' evaluative engagement with narratives.

A third, related, path that needs further exploration is culture-historical research on ethos topoi. Maingueneau and Johansen—the first from the perspective of discourse analysis, the second from that of a semiotics of culture—signal the importance for writers and their audiences of securing literature's legitimacy. Writers direct readers in how to construct their work as valuable and legitimate. This is what Eggers does, ambiguously, in his paratext, as does Bon's narrator when he justifies the act of writing by the need to counterbalance the erasure of whole sections of social life in the public media. Broad comparative research on contemporary "Defenses of Fiction" and their legitimizing strategies would yield insight on negotiations of the value of literature and their competing axiologies. Such research could tease out patterns and shifts in the legitimizing arguments and in the kinds of ethos that determine writers' authority and responsibility in a given culture.

Yet another path, connected to the previous ones, combines a cognitive perspective and cultural analysis. I ventured at several points in this book the hypothesis that Aristotle's triad of ethos, pathos, and logos, as the three main means of persuasion, might be mapped onto the different cognitive modes distinguished by Merlin Donald, from the most concrete modes of cognition, perception, and imagination to the most abstract ones, conceptualization and analysis (see also van Heusden 2011). Pathos, the appeal to emotions, seems quite evidently positioned toward perception, feeling, and is often perceived as direct and immersive in its effects. Logos appeals, in contrast, fall on the side of conceptualization and analysis, requiring a different form of processing, involving procedures for generalizing and reflecting. Ethos appeals, in turn, seem less clearly positioned, taking the form that seems most fitting in a given cultural situation and genre: the register of pathos seems appropriate in a context where emotions are likely to be accepted as the common ground: that of logos, when *common* sense is built through argumentation and an appeal to rationality. An investigation into the kind of ethos appeals that are actually privileged by writers, critics, and readers could shed more light on the kinds of cognitive registers that are addressed by a particular kind of literature, against the background of a given culture's preferences regarding cognitive modes.

As an example, I have proposed that in current forms of engagé writing pathos-oriented ethos clues supersede logos-oriented ones. While Sartre's mode of engagement privileged argumentation and intellectual debate, contemporary writers who take seriously their social responsibility instead display an ethos that taps into emotional identification and participation. It is also striking that many best-selling middlebrow literary works, which seem to activate what I continue to call a *mimetic* reading, simultaneously allow more abstract readings, in which habitual patterns of meaning making become themselves the object of mimesis and of reflection. On whatever level they are read, their reading may be expected to weld together particular interpretive communities and confirm specific ethos expectations regarding an author. Some readers and critics would agree in judging that of course it's a good thing that Eggers advocates and practices sincerity; another community of readers would instead appreciate his irony, which is perceptible and valuable for those in the know. However, the more abstract approach to texts requires additional reading competences, in particular the capacity for multiplying interpretive frames and for enjoying this multiplicity and the accompanying ambiguities. The issues at stake are important enough to deserve more than these impressionistic observations.

To conclude this book on a somewhat exhortative note: if human beings create their *world* and fine-tune their cognitions through the stories they live by and through "conversation," then we do well to cultivate not only our capacity for narrative world-making but also some other capacities: for interpretation as a negotiation of worldviews and value positions, as well as the faculty to critically gauge interpretive pathways themselves.

Notes

Why Ethos?

1. I am certainly not the only scholar or critic who felt compelled to figure out Houellebecq's ethos; see Baroni 2009; Meizoz 2007; or Willems 2005. My own first publication—in Dutch—on this subject dates back to 2000.
2. In the United States, this novel has been published with the title *The Elementary Particles*. Since I used the British edition, I will refer to *Atomised*.
3. Throughout this book, translations from the French or German are mine, unless indicated otherwise in the cited works or in the text.
4. For a more detailed analysis of ethos, see the excellent collection of essays edited by Baumlin and Baumlin (1994). This volume has a twenty-page bibliography of English-language scholarship on ethos, from 1960 onward. The pioneering work on ethos of Amossy and Maingueneau will be amply discussed in chapter 2. Interest in ethos in relation to narrative fiction is currently booming in French-language literary scholarship. See, e.g., Amossy and Adam 1999; Bokobza Kahan and Amossy 2009; Baroni 2009; Langevin 2011.
5. Eggs notes that Aristotle's writings express a sharp sense that man is "a political (→ ethos) animal (→ pathos) with the capacity to speak and think (→ logos)" (Eggs 1999, 47). This kind of observation, again, strongly suggests a filiation from contemporary cognitive research on the human capacity of mind and its embodiedness back to Aristotle.
6. Aristotle's notion of *phronesis* crucially connects rhetoric to ethics. For one of the many revivals of this notion, in relation to narrative literature, see studies by Nussbaum (1990), who defends the idea that (reading) fiction is a necessary complement to moral philosophy, or Gallagher (2004), who, from a quite different cognitive perspective, insists on the importance of *phronesis* itself, as well as on that of hermeneutic approaches, which, more than cognitive approaches, can do justice to this component of human experience and culture.
7. I will use masculine forms, as most aspects of classic rhetoric concerned social uses of speech that were a male prerogative.

8. My emphasis points, in anticipation, to my own assumption that when a literary work is experienced as controversial or ambiguous, readers—including professional interpreters—will tend to construct an authorial ethos.

9. See Aristotle's (2007) observations on various groups and their basic attitudes and norms, 1389a-b or 1390b, 149–51; 152–53. Ethos clues in turn set out for audiences particular interpretive and evaluative positions. It is tempting to suggest a connection here with positioning theory, in which "framing inferences about the stance one is being prompted to adopt toward particular positions represented in a narrative is a fundamental part of the process of reconstructing that narrative's story-world, no matter the medium in which it is presented" (Herman 2009, 63, 55).

10. For a discussion of Aristotle's emphasis on a rational ethos versus Cicero's emphasis on an ethos of sympathy, see Wisse 1989, esp. 32–34, 234.

11. Persuasion "should result from the speech, not from a previous opinion that the speaker is a certain kind of person" (Aristotle 2007, 1356a.38–39).

12. Binjamin Wilkomirski's *Bruchstücke: Aus einer Kindheit 1939–1948*, published by Jüdischer Verlag in 1995, was presented and hailed as an authentic memoir describing the author's experiences as a child survivor of the Holocaust (it was translated in English as *Fragments: Memories of a Wartime Childhood*). The author acted the full survivor part, giving interviews, providing details to Holocaust archives, and so on. He was exposed as a fraud in 1999 by the Swiss historian Stefan Maechler, who proved correct earlier accusations by the journalist Daniel Ganzfried. The case led to heated debates. See Maechler 2001 and, among other studies of the case, Suleiman 2006.

13. I do not mean that we should abandon this idea of literature's autonomy, but that it is better understood as an ideal, rooted in the freedom of expression, historically implemented in some countries by concrete institutional conditions and programmatic conceptions of literature—an ideal, moreover, which has remained contested and nuanced. See Dorleijn, Korthals Altes, and Grüttemeier 2007.

14. A good example is Felman and Laub's (1992) analysis of Camus's self-reflection on the (lack of) responsibility and authenticity of the writer, based on his wartime and postwar writings, literary and nonliterary.

15. See, on the Francophone side, in particular, Baroni 2009; Charles 2001; Couturier 1995; Edelman 2004; or Sapiro 2011, besides the works of Amossy, Heinich, Maingueneau, or Meizoz, to which I will refer extensively in the following chapters. In the English-language domain, Burke (1992, 1995) and Bennett (2005) offer thorough analyses of the academic debates around authorship; likewise, on the German-language side, see Heinen

2002 and the wide-ranging edited volumes Jannidis et al. 1999 and Detering 2002; see also the recently founded e-journal *Authorship*.

Part 1. Ethos, Narrative, Social Construction

1. For example, Hogan (2003, 30–31) distinguishes four levels of theorization and analysis of narrative from a cognitive perspective, ranging from "pure intentionalism" to neurophysiology. Meanwhile, he does not refer at all to correspondences with hermeneutic perspectives. Pettersson, for his part, keenly notes that hermeneutics' near absence in the *Routledge Encyclopedia of Narrative Theory* "tallies with the deep-seated view that narratological study does not make use of interpretation" (Pettersson 2009, 16). Ankersmit's (2005) entry on hermeneutics presents an excellent historical overview but hardly addresses hermeneutics' relation to narrative theory. Exceptions, unsurprisingly, are found especially in Germanic narrative theory; besides Pettersson, see, e.g., Jannidis 2004; Kindt and Müller 2006.
2. For thorough discussions of the connection between hermeneutics and cognitive sciences, see Gallagher 2004; Jackson 2000, 2003; or Keestra 2008.

1. Interpretation, Attributions, and Negotiation

1. Again, I do not mean to suggest that a full-fledged theory of culture (of narrative, and so on) emerges from the discussed disparate elements. My aim is only to point out that there are, unsurprisingly, concording observations across disciplines concerning the fundamental role of language, narrative, art, and interpretation for our understanding of culture as a human achievement. Scholars working on various positions along the disciplinary spectrum might feel challenged to explore how their disciplinary take on these issues can benefit from those of other disciplines, and in turn help sharpen these.
2. *Funktionslust* also seems involved in the pleasure we take in the arts, both in the "doing" and in being cooperative audiences, say, of a pianist's or dancer's virtuosity. In a more cerebral vein, Joyce's or Nabokov's intricate intertextuality elicits the joyful experience of one's mental agility, which sometimes may even supersede the quest for meaning as the *point* of the reading experience.
3. An alternative conceptualization of this two-level structure is Greimas's model of the sequences of action as represented in narrative. According to Greimas, action logically moves through four stages, which, however, need not all be actually represented or figure in (chrono)logical order. The two central—"pragmatic"—stages are the action-performance itself and, before

that, the acquisition of the competence for acting. The two other stages form around this pragmatic level of the action a "structure of intelligibility" in which, quite fundamentally, are defined the values and meanings that are at stake in the action program. These two stages are the "manipulation," in which the incentive, desire, or imperative to act are established, and the "sanction," in which meaning and value are assigned to the action. (Greimas and Courtés 1979; see also Korthals Altes 1992 for an elaboration of this model for the analysis of values as connected to the representation of action in narratives.)

4. This section owes a lot to my discussions with Barend van Heusden.

5. For good overviews of cognitive research on narrative theory, see, e.g., *The Work of Fiction: Cognition, Culture, and Complexity*, edited by Alan Richardson and Ellen Spolsky, 2004; the special issue of *Poetics Today*, 23.1, "Literature and the Cognitive Revolution," edited by Alan Richardson and Francis F. Steen; Herman 2003, 2007; Hogan 2003.

6. Goffman himself borrowed the notion from Gregory Bateson's *Steps to an Ecology of Mind* (1972), in which Bateson analyzes the importance of metacommunication in play, marking to all involved that one is playing.

7. Risking a sketchy bridge here to the vocabulary of rhetoric, one could argue that our mental model of specific people includes what ancient rhetoric called their prior ethos—the inferences about their character we make on the basis of previous behavior and language use—and subsumes this to more general character types.

8. Herman (2011, 18) speaks instead of the "exceptionality thesis," which lays the burden of proof for the distinction of fiction on the fictionalist's side; more on this in part 2.

9. This does not mean that empirical testing of the role of particular frames in actual readers' responses is impossible or irrelevant. However, such testing would not have proof value beyond demonstrating that this particular group of people responds in this particular mode. In principle, other interpretations remain possible, because historical-cultural contexts might differ, as Gadamer's hermeneutics acknowledged, or the literary competence of the readers involved may differ.

10. Anticipating later theories of discourse, from Bakhtin's to Foucault's, Schleiermacher observes that "each person represents one locus where a given language takes shape in a particular way, and his speech can be understood only in the context of the totality of the language" (1985, 75).

11. Schleiermacher (1985, 96) seems indeed to have a male interpreter in mind. A good hermeneutician, however, needs "feminine" divinatory capacities; comparative knowledge, instead, would be masculine.

12. I have worked on the German edition of Dilthey's work, in particular volume 7 of his *Gesammelte Schriften: Der Aufbau der Geschichtlichen Welt in den Geisteswissenschaften*, 1960 (orig. 1926). Similarly, I read Schleiermacher's work in the 1977 edition of *Hermeneutik und Kritik*, edited and introduced by Manfred Frank. This includes the so-called *Compendium* of 1819, which presents the draft of Schleiermacher's ideas on hermeneutics. For Dilthey as well as for Schleiermacher, the sections that are most relevant for my argument can be found in the excellent *Hermeneutics Reader* compiled by Kurt Müller-Vollmer (1985), so for both scholars, this is the edition I will refer to.

13. Another appealing phrasing of this idea reads, "Every square planted with trees, every room in which seats are arranged, is intelligible to us from our infancy, because human planning, arranging and valuing—common to all of us—have assigned a place to every square and every object in the room" (Dilthey 1985b, 155).

14. In the context of the arts and perception, Shklovsky's notion of "ostranenie" comes to mind, the idea that through defamiliarizing techniques, art interrupts automatic processing, giving back to us the sharpness of first experience (Shklovsky 1965; see also Van den Oever 2010).

15. By *horizon*, Gadamer means "the range of vision that includes everything that can be seen from a particular vantage point" (1991, 302).

16. The idea that humans develop their identity and grasp of the world in dialogic interaction and interpretive negotiation plays a key role in the works not just of Gadamer or Ricoeur but also of Taylor (1989), who, in an apt formulation, describes identity constructions as elaborated in "webs of interlocution."

17. See, for instance, within narrative studies, Bortolussi and Dixon (2003, 8), which characterizes hermeneutics as "a myriad of contradictory theories" that have left us "with much confusion and no consensus as to the nature of the text, the reader, and the reading experience." I will comment on this remark in chapter 4. For now let me just say that regarding such issues consensus also often seems more wishful thinking than an achieved state within cognitive narrative studies or empirical reader research themselves. But let's keep on striving.

18. On the painful "disrupted" or "improbable" dialogue between Derrida and Gadamer, see Michelfelder and Palmer 1989.

19. In his comparison of cognitive sciences and hermeneutics, Keestra (2008, 133) concludes, "Hermeneutics emphasizes particularly the intersubjective and interactive nature of understanding, which is difficult to investigate empirically. . . . Understanding is variously dependent on contexts (as hermeneutics shows) that our brain is capable of incorporating in its

functioning (as cognitive science shows; Gallagher 2004). This has led to hypotheses that also acknowledge the cognitive influences of cultural models . . . or that incorporate social and cultural aspects in theories of situated, embodied, or embedded perception and cognition. . . . Clearly, hermeneutic processes that include the figurations of mimesis play a role in these aforementioned processes that imply understanding and experience of many forms of divergence."

20. Thus Gallagher lucidly notes that "when philosophers of mind, psychologists, and neuroscientists [as well as narrative theorists, one might add] address what is usually referred to as *theory of mind*, they are (in most cases unknowingly) entering into the older hermeneutical debates about understanding and empathy" (2004, 9; his emphasis).

21. This is where Pettersson's and my ways part: though I fully share his critique of narratology's "textualism," I cannot share his defense of one particular hermeneutic, "contextual intention inference," as the most appropriate for narratology. While this hermeneutic, which revives and updates Schleiermacher's philological requirements, constitutes a respectable position, it is not the only one relevant for narratologists.

22. The recognition of the crucial capacity for pondering arguments is also at the heart of Toulmin's (2001) work on reasoning or Daniels's (2011) on deliberation and reflective equilibrium, in line with John Rawls and Nelson Goodman.

2. Ethos as a Social Construction

1. See Herman and Vervaeck 2011 for a kindred overview of French approaches.

2. The notion comes close to that of *persona* in Latin, "which refers to the theatre mask: etymologically, that through which one speaks (*per-sonare*), instituating in the same time a voice and its social locus of intelligibility," something like an "authority mask" (Meizoz 2009, citing Claude Calame, *Masques d'autorité: Fiction et pragmatique dans la poétique grecque antique* [2005]; translated by Peter M. Burk as *Masks of Authority: Fiction and Pragmatics in Ancient Greek Poetics* [2005]).

3. On historical practices and conceptions of authorship, see Bénichou 1973; Charles 2001; Sapiro 1999; or Viala 1985; see also Jannidis et al. 1999; and the essays collected in Detering 2002. This kind of historical-sociological research, mostly focused on Europe, devotes ample attention to various facets of literary authorship, notably the idea of the author's social mission.

4. Bourdieu does not always sharply distinguish between ethos, posture, and habitus. There is a sense that posture indicates the author's active adoption

of traits associated with a particular habitus, in a strategic move within a particular literary field. Habitus, instead, would refer to the internalized social determinations. I will not go into details of the debate about the determinism of Bourdieu's model, which is the issue that arises here. My own, heuristic-hermeneutic, use of his and Meizoz's model should be clear.

5. Amossy's and Maingueneau's approach stands in the French tradition of enunciation linguistics and of affective stylistics; see Patron 2009 for a good contextualization of this attention for enunciation. For a useful overview of various strands of discourse analysis, see the entries by Ruth Wodak on Foucault's notion of discourse analysis and Barbara Johnstone on the linguistic pragmatic orientation in the *Routledge Encyclopedia of Narrative Theory* (Herman, Jahn, and Ryan 2005).

6. Developed in the seventies by Claude Duchet et al., sociocritique aimed to refine Marxist theories of ideology and art as reflection, integrating the analysis of style, composition, and discourse, from Benveniste's work on subjectivity in discourse to Bakhtin's on polyphony and heteroglossia.

7. The notion of tone crops up in the writings of any scholar attentive to affective dimensions of style, from Bally's affective stylistics and Leo Spitzer's stylistic analysis to Maingueneau's (2004, 207) own considerations on voice, tone, and tonality as a discursive indicators of ethos or Molly Hite's (2010) fine work on tonal cues, which, however, does not, to my sense, sufficiently take into account readers' possibly divergent overall framing of the text, which I aim to emphasize in this book. Baudelle (2003) offers a timely recall of phenomenological traditions of reflection on tonality, from the notion of "Stimmung," dear to German Romantic philosophy, and Hölderlin's "Grundstimmung" (basic mood), to Northrop Frye's modal tonalities and the French phenomenologist Dufrenne's connection of stylistic tonality to an existential worldview.

8. There is some resonance here with Phelan and Martin's (1999) classification of kinds of unreliability along the axes of events and facts, of evaluation, and of knowledge and perception.

9. At stake here is the distinction between bodily ethos clues that are codified (e.g., culturally determined gestures and ways of looking that express sincerity and thus back up a moral ethos effect) and clues that would be biological, though this distinction is not at all clear-cut and requires empirical testing.

10. With his focus on embodiment, Maingueneau moves from a rhetorical or discourse analytical perspective to a more general psychological outlook, focusing on how readers "participat[e], through imagining a body-of-discourse . . . , in a global experience of the world" (Maingueneau 2004, 97–98). Ethos now comes to refer, more broadly, to the expression of, and

readers' engagement with, embodied experientiality of fictional or real minds, an exciting domain for ethos effects in particular but one for which a phenomenological approach seems more suited. In this book I will limit myself to potentially persuasive effects of ethos.

11. See my comments on fictionality as a frame in chapter 4 and on generic framings in chapter 6. On genre as "categories to make sense of the world," cf. Herman 2009 (81) and Wolf 2006, among many others.

12. Maingueneau notes that the whole issue of ethos demonstrates that a work's reception is much more than simple decoding and that something belonging to the order of sense experience occurs in the process of verbal communication (Maingueneau, "L'Ethos, de la rhétorique à l'analyse du discours," http://dominique.maingueneau.pagesperso-orange.fr/intro _company.html, accessed January 20, 2011). As mentioned, phenomeno-logical-cognitive work on perception in interaction may be expected to shed light on our ethos attributions.

13. Gisèle Sapiro (2003a, 2003b) and Benoît Denis (2000), among others, have opened up the notion of autonomy, arguing that within the autonomous pole, writers could very well adopt conceptions of literature that were built on the (apparently heteronomous) idea of the moral or social responsibil-ity of the writer. For example, Sartre's defense of writers' obligation to be politically engaged precisely drew its effectiveness from the autonomous position of the writer-intellectual, who did not have to conform to a party ideology or specific political pressures (Denis 2000).

14. On the trials in which Houellebecq has been engaged, see Isabelle Wil-lems's (2005) pioneering analysis, which offers an excellent demonstration of the usefulness of Boltanski and Thévenot's model.

15. More on literary engagement in chapter 6; see also Denis 2000,31; Heinich 1997, 2000; Boltanski and Thévenot 1991.

16. Not only does Houellebecq write poetry, fiction, and essays, he combines writing and photography, as in *Lanzarote* (2000), writes texts for art and photography books, performs his own poems in public, and makes films. One of these is the short film *La Rivière* (2001), a utopian erotic film de-picting a future world from which the last men and their aggressive com-petitiveness have disappeared, leaving only young, slender, near-naked girls, who engage in much slow-motion love making.

17. Noguez observes that Houellebecq became fond of playing with the media and of polemicizing only in his later career, moving from an authentic and resisting posture to a playful mastery over the media. The media them-selves, in fact, would have forced him to adopt these marked personas (No-guez 2003, 163, 159–62).

18. This sort of moralistic outlook on literature is not unique; Nussbaum's (1990) discussion of Beckett's and Proust's work displays a fairly similar argument, yet in a much more respectful tone.

3. Between Hermeneutics and Cognitive Science

1. Metanarratological reflection has been a popular exercise in the past fifteen years or so; see, among others, Prince 1995; Herman 1999; Nünning 2003; Kindt and Müller 2003; Meister, Kindt, and Schernus 2005; Heinen and Sommer 2009; Hühn et al. 2009; Patron 2011.
2. For a recent discussion, see Patron 2011; see also the distinction of description versus interpretation in narratology in Kindt and Müller 2003. For them, some narratological notions are descriptive, while others clearly involve interpretation. In my view, the range of interpretive moves is definitely wider than these theorists allow. From a metahermeneutic perspective, this doesn't pose a problem. It does mean, however, that narratology should include such a metahermeneutic (self)reflection and reconstruct the values and presuppositions that feed into narratological models.
3. See also Suleiman 1980; Stierle 1980; Barthes 1970; Rabinowitz 1998.
4. See, e.g., Fludernik 1996; Jahn 1997; Herman 2003, 2009; Bortolussi and Dixon 2003; Palmer 2004. Jens Eder rightfully observes that "there are many different kinds of cognitive theories available for narratologists. . . . [S]ome of these are empirical, others non-empirical, and they have a disparate range of essential basic concepts." They have in common their treatment of "communication and reception as active, constructive, rationally motivated, and cognitively guided processes of information processing that are anchored in human physicality and experience. . . . Only a small number of cognitive theories have so far attempted to model the entire communication process in detail" (Eder 2003, 282).
5. The observation that hermeneutics covers a whole range of theories is right. But a point is missed if one does not see this multiplicity itself as a phenomenon that deserves explanation and that may be legitimate. Precisely from a cognitive or anthropological angle, this lack of consensus could be fruitfully considered as expressing the necessary diversity of value perspectives (see chapter 1). This does not mean, however, that a metahermeneutic approach should not seek to understand structural processes underlying this diversity, which, I believe, is what Herman's CAPA model aims to do (see below), as does my own framework.
6. For instance, when analyzing the cognitive frames that a particular text activates in the reader (actually, in himself as a reader), Palmer (2004) moves from hypotheses about the general process of narrative meaning making

to analyses of concrete texts, in which he teases out *the* frames activated in the reading of a specific text, generalizing his own interpretation. See also, among others, Patron's (2011, esp. 9) pointed analysis of narratologists' "objective description" claims.

7. Nünning (2003) presents a much more detailed scale, on which he posits the many practices that consider themselves to belong to narratology. His scale, to my sense, is very ecumenical and does not always bring out sharply differences in argumentation and validation. Much closer in spirit to my own is Marie-Laure Ryan's (2010) mapping of the various tendencies within narratology, which unfortunately I read only when this book was nearly completed.

8. See Patron 2011 for a discussion of Kindt and Müller's own normative underpinnings.

4. Key Concepts Revised

1. See also Eder (2003, 282), with whom I couldn't agree more: "It is now no longer unproblematic to adopt a theory of communication which is purely production-orientated or assumes fixed textual meanings and denies the possibility of varying interpretations. . . . Communication, reception, and cognition have a place in the foundations of every narrative theory."

2. A broader pragmatic understanding of the way in which literary texts are "framed" and made to signify appears, for instance, in Genette's work on paratexts, *Seuils* (Thresholds; 1987).

3. I will not discuss here the heterogeneity that goes into the notions of "unnaturalness" and "mimesis" used in "unnatural narratology." See the debate staged in Herman et al. 2012. Herman formulates with clarity what is also my point:

> If mimesis is defined narrowly as imitation or reproduction, the very concept becomes untenable—since there can be no direct representation of the world, no bare encounter with reality, without mediating world-models. . . . [I]f mimesis is defined as part of a family of strategies for deploying world-models, then the concept cannot do the work my coauthors try to get it to do—for example, when they set mimesis up as a standard or touchstone against which "antimimetic" stories, or the "synthetic" and "thematic" dimensions of narrative, can be measured. But changing the grammar of the question—asking not about mimesis or its absence but about how story designs can be arranged along a scale corresponding to more or less critical and reflexive methods of worldmaking—opens up new avenues for narrative inquiry. (Herman 2012, 16)

4. The mechanism to which I draw attention with this notion of frame switch recalls the process described by Catherine Emmott in her contextual frame theory (Emmott 1997). See in particular her discussion of frame switches and frame recalls and their effects on readers' mental modeling of story world scenarios. My emphasis, however, is more decidedly on the interpretation-steering effects of clues for frame switching.

5. The embeddedness of voices, thoughts, and perspectives has received much attention in recent cognitive approaches to narrative fiction, which draw on Theory of Mind. Butte (2004), Palmer (2004), Schneider (2001), and Zunshine (2006, 2008) draw attention to reciprocal activities of mind reading and to the access to a fictional world provided by embedding perspectives. But I am not yet convinced that this really offers an improvement in methods for analyzing the effects of embeddedness in concrete texts. Too little attention goes to the role, in readers' hermeneutic calculus, of possibly competing textual clues, generic framings, and reading conventions.

6. On intentionality, action, and speech, see, e.g., Searle 1983; Dennett 1987. On literary interpretation, see Herman 2008; Iseminger 1992; Levinson 1996; Livingston 2005; and Lamarque 2009.

7. Arguably, even surrealist *écriture automatique* implied on the part of the writer the intention to let chance determine what was intended as a work of art and on the part of audiences that of considering the result with the same attention to the meaning potential as in purposefully made art.

8. This phrasing was coined by Neil Wilson (1959). See also Davidson 1984.; Dennett's "principle of humanity" (1987, 343); or Grice's "cooperation principle" (1989). All three seem to express a similar idea, that of shared assumptions about the kind of cooperative action participants engage in and the kind of rules that would apply in it.

9. See Alber et al. 2010. In fact, in everyday communication as well we often presume intentionality for apparently nonsensical elements in other people's behavior and stories, usually not from aesthetic interest but out of generosity, suspicion, or indifference, for instance.

10. See Mahajan (1993); the chapter "Reason-Actions Explanations" describes such reasoning.

11. An article in *Slate* exposed Houellebecq's extensive use of Wikipedia articles, at which point blogger and jurist Florent Gallaire put the whole novel online to further test copyright law—which in turn prompted Houellebecq's editor to take quick protective action and to settle with Wikipedia (actually, Wikimedia). The author had to mention in later editions the borrowings, which included, the author indicated with typical humor, sec-

tions on the housefly and on the city of Beauvais. It would be interesting to investigate more precisely how, over time, jurisprudence has dealt with ethos and intention attributions in order to establish the line between plagiarism and what Raymond Federman (1976) called "playgiarism," as the latter would fall under *exceptio artis*, but the former would not (Boltanski and Thévenot's [1991] value regimes are appropriate here).

12. On the connection between play, fiction, and art, see the discussion in chapter 1. The comparison of literary fiction to children's play also makes clear the fragility of the conventional line between play and "for real." If real physical or moral pain ensues from playing, conflicts often arise about how to categorize the offense as well as the intention and ethos of the perpetrator. From this categorization follows the kind of evaluation regime that is considered to apply (see my discussion of Boltanski and Thévenot in chapter 2).

13. There is a clear connection here to Goffman's (1974) notions of frame and frame borders.

14. On this idea of fiction as a shared convention, see Gorman 2005, 165; Walton 1990; and Lamarque and Olsen 1994.

15. Rabinowitz also formulated four "reading rules," which would belong to the common repertoire of authors and readers and "specify the grounds on which the intended reading should take place" (Rabinowitz 1998, 43). These reading rules comprise "rules of notice," "rules of signification," "rules of configuration," and "rules of coherence." I have not yet explored the relevance these rules might have for an approach to ethos attributions. The same holds for Kearns's "Ur-Conventions" that readers would count on in their literary reading (Kearns 1999). Current work from a cognitive-psychological perspective may be expected to specify such "rules," as well as my own assumptions about ethos attributions.

16. Schneider indeed proposes that "experienced readers and those who have received special training are able to activate schemata that help them describe the structural and linguistic construction principles of a text without much effort, and that they find it easier to make sense of apparently incoherent information" (Schneider 2001, 612).

5. Whose Ethos?

1. The role of emotions in the experience of literary narratives and, more generally, the capacity for empathy constitute an exciting domain within cognitive research. Findings in this field can be expected to have a direct bearing on the understanding of ethos attributions and their function in the literary experience and in fictional and aesthetic experiences more generally; see, e.g., Coplan 2004; Damasio 1994; Tan 2000. Susanne Keen

(2007) presents a good overview of research on readers' emotional involvement in narrative. Further empirical research should help find answers to such questions as whether and how clues for trustworthiness or authority, irony or unreliability affect the emotional engagement of readers; to what extent groups of readers differ in this respect; or what connections can be made between reading strategies, readers' moral and social norms, and their capacity to engage empathically with narratives perceived as morally transgressive, ambiguous, or ironic.

2. See also Bortolussi and Dixon 2003; Gerrig and Allbritton 1990; Herman 1999; Hernadi 2003; Jannidis 2004; Margolin 1986, 1990, 2010. Jannidis's 2004 monograph on character combines cognitive and pragmatic approaches, shedding light on "the cognitive dynamic and . . . the rule-governed character of the hermeneutic process. It . . . tries to stay clear from fundamental presuppositions, [hence] can claim intersubjective plausibility, even in a period of method pluralism" (10, 19). Jannidis, however, also postulates a model reader. In my view, either the model of such a reader should be based on the findings of empirical research or the reader should be specified as the scholar him- or herself or as a person who incarnates particular reading strategies that the scholar reconstructs on the basis of experience, reception research, etc. The last two perspectives, however, in my view are clearly hermeneutic and metahermeneutic, respectively.

3. Fludernik borrows the concept of "naturalization" from Culler (1975), which refers to the idea that readers try to "recuperate [strange or inexplicable elements in a narrative] by taking recourse to available interpretative patterns" (Fludernik 1996, 31–32). Fludernik considers narrativization as one particular way of naturalizing.

4. Discussing experimental writing, Fludernik interestingly remarks, "Experimental fiction can be read as intertextual play with language and with generic modes, and this—since it projects an intentional meta-narrative function—is a mimetic strategy just like any other. Such experimental texts are therefore not mimetic in terms of reproducing, if in a different medium, a prototypical version of narrative experience, but are mimetic in their structured anticipation of readers' attempts at reinterpreting them mimetically if only at a meta-meta-realist level of self-reflexive, explicitly antimimetic language games" (Fludernik 1996, 35). While the first sentence seems to enlarge the notion of mimesis (the iconic evocation of an "an intentional meta-narrative function"), the last part seems to take this back.

5. Ideas about the importance of estranging form date back at least to Russian Formalism and the waves of experimental writing, e.g., Calle-Gruber 1989; of course Robbe-Grillet's seminal *Pour un nouveau roman* (1963); or more

recently, Richardson 2006. With respect to what I call the continuity thesis, Richardson, in a similar spirit, speaks of "mimetic reductionism" (quoted in Alber et al. 2010, 115).

6. One example here is Lucien Goldman's (1955) notion of *homology*, according to which relations between characters stand for relations between the classes in society or for ideological possibilities.

7. In fact the whole generic frame, that of the novel, which would have us read for the experientiality of fictional minds or for the plot, was itself "revealed" as playfully deceptive, for whatever such revelations are worth. *Djinn* was purportedly written as a textbook for American students learning French, turning a grammatical exercise into fiction, a welcome narrative facelift for the teeth-grinding *passé simple* and *imparfait* distinction. Such a revelation gives yet another turn to the multifaceted play with the book's generic framing, eliciting metacognition on our framing acts, we could say with Merlin Donald.

8. This also seems to be Herman's CAPA approach (briefly introduced in my chapter 4), which aims to capture in what I tend to call a metahermeneutic way the complex "process that leads to the co-construction" of characters by reader and text, against the background of "a culture's or subculture's understandings of persons" (Herman et al. 2012, 127). The model proposes a heuristic protocol, with a list of questions such as: "For which elements of the WHAT dimension of the narrative world are questions about WHO, HOW, and WHY pertinent?," or "How does the text, in conjunction with broader understandings of persons, prompt interpreters to build a profile for the characters who inhabit these domains of action?" (128–29).

9. This more abstract interest seems to correspond with conceptions and practices of art that developed over course of the twentieth century, in which artistic mimesis tends toward representation of human cognition itself: still human experience, but another facet of it (see, e.g., Goodman 1978).

10. Beyond its typological aims, Genette's model of narrative levels arguably fostered among other scholars the awareness that the truth value of any information retrieved from the text needs to be assessed in light of the information source's own trustworthiness and perspicacity, which must first be determined in and of itself. See especially the work of Mieke Bal, who, from the (structuralist) start, paid attention to the rhetorical and ideological potential of the distribution of voice and focalization (Bal 1977).

11. The intense debate about the notion of voice is partly about the lack of clarity regarding this expressive dimension of the notion; see also Aczel 1998; and the special issue "Voice and Human Experience," *New Literary History*

32.3 (2001). In Korthals Altes 2006 I trace the expressivity component in various definitions of "voice" in connection to the notion of ethos.

12. Research on subjectivity in narrative discourse partly builds on stylistic and linguistic analysis of subjectivity in discourse, such as Bally's affective stylistics (*Traité de stylistique française*, 1963 [1909]); Benveniste's (1966) theory of discourse and enunciation; Kerbrat-Orecchioni (1980) and Fludernik (1993) on discursive subjectivity markers; Cohn (1978) on the verbal representation of consciousness; and Bakhtin (1981) on discourse as the vehicle of values. It continues up to rhetorical narratology's work on narrative and ideological or ethical points of view, such as Booth 1961; Lanser 1981; Suleiman 1983; Phelan 1996; and Rabatel 2009.

13. Cf. Bakhtin (1981) on the dialogic character of narrative discourse; Cohn (1978) on the consonance or dissonance of narrative voices; and Pascal (1977) on dual voice. In contrast, see Banfield's (1982) critique of the dual voice concept.

14. For research that draws on experimental psychology and seeks to account for readers' emotional involvement and empathy in narratives and (fictional) characters, an issue that classical narratology conspicuously failed to address, good work has been done by David Comer Kidd and Emanuele Castano, with their recent article in *Science*, "Reading Literary Fiction Improves Theory of Mind" (www.sciencemag.org, accessed October 9, 2013). See also Els Andringa, "Effects of 'Narrative Distance' on Readers' Emotional Involvement and Response," *Poetics* 23.6 (1996): 431–52; Willie Van Peer and Henk Pander Maat, "Perspectivation and Sympathy: Effects of Narrative Point of View," in *Empirical Approaches to Literature and Aesthetics*, ed. Roger J. Kreuz and Mary Sue MacNealy (Norwood NJ: Ablex, 1996), 143–56; H. Sklar, "Narrative Structuring of Sympathetic Response: Theoretical and Empirical Approaches to Toni Cade Bambara's 'The Hammer Man,'" *Poetics Today* 30.3 (2009): 561–607; and Marco Caracciolo, "Two Child Narrators: Defamiliarization, Empathy, and Reader-Response in Mark Haddon's *The Curious Incident* and Emma Donoghue's *Room*," *Semiotica* (forthcoming).

15. For a sociological understanding of the connection between social roles, implied norms, values, and the representation of action in narrative and of the heuristic role of sanctions as pointers to an often-tacit norm, see Hegenbarth-Rösgen 1982; Herman 2002, chap. 4. In Korthals Altes 1992, I aimed to integrate sociological, semiotic/actantial, and discursive frameworks into an approach that would account for the complex ways in which literary narrative are vehicles for values, norms, and social roles. This synthetic approach to narrative as a vehicle of values was further developed by Jouve 2001.

16. Schneider's distinction might trigger unwanted associations with characters being perceived as less or more sophisticated or verisimilar. Categorized characters are not necessarily less lifelike. In real life, as well, our perceptions of people range from stereotyping to complex understanding, depending on the communicative situation and genre in which we feel we're engaged. Nor does a lack of personalizing mean a lack of aesthetic or literary interest, as any reader familiar with medieval allegorical fiction would know.

17. An interesting case here would be Henry James, one of the writers Martha Nussbaum (1990) privileges in her demonstration of fiction's ethical value. Nussbaum extensively dwells on the importance for James's characters of proving "finely aware and richly responsible" (Nussbaum 1990). James's stylistic sophistication, in particular, is considered by Nussbaum to draw readers into the tiniest shades of his characters' mental—and ethical— movements. In my view, it may also foreground the author's aesthetic craftsmanship and, as such, even stand in the way of empathizing with character. But such a reaction, again, depends on one's aesthetic norms and kind of empathetic sensibility.

18. See Fludernik (1993) on Banfield's (1987) notion of "empty deictic centers." Fludernik repeatedly observes that the inference of subjectivity from a discourse's or voice's expressive features involves interpretation, rather than being a matter of linguistic description (422, e.g.).

19. Genette 1976; 1988, 766, 770; compare earlier formulations by Friedemann (*Die Rolle des Erzählers in der Epik*, 1910) and Stanzel (*Die typischen Erzählsituationen im Roman*, 1955).

20. As mentioned, speech act and communication theories assume as a default that in everyday life, utterances are indexically expressive of their utterer's character, intentions, and overall worldview and that the utterer is accountable for his or her assertions and the views they implicate, unless one is joking, daydreaming, or the like.

21. Margolin (2009, 361) acknowledges in a similar way that a narrator's manner of telling has "a decisive influence on our assessment of his credibility and ultimately on how much of what he claims about the narrated domain we are ready to accept." He also observes that what I would call the narrator's ethos cannot "be strictly defined in any systematic and exhaustive manner." "Equally incapable of formal definition and fail-safe determination yet every bit as important," Margolin adds, "is the narrator's attitude towards the told, as manifested in the way characters and events are represented." Yet "[t]he drawing of such inferences is not an exact science, for it depends on the specific inner-textual contexts as well as on the reader's

cultural context; even so, such inferencing plays an important role in any portrait of the narrator drawn by the reader."

22. See the discussion between Patron and Margolin (Margolin 2009), which analyzes issues discussed here (with, however, some regrettable harshness of tone on one side).

23. Jonathan Franzen's narrator in *Freedom* is as omniscient as Balzac's; while some readers will delight in the promise of true psychological insight and intellectual control over human affairs this entails, others may less easily accept this mode of narrative authentication and perceive it as also aesthetically retrograde.

24. Phelan and Martin (1999) usefully distinguish six types of unreliability, corresponding to the three functions narrators can have (to report, to evaluate, to interpret) and depending on whether narrators fall short or distort: (1) underreporting and misreporting, on the axis of facts and events (NB: the information about which there is unreliable reporting is in principle mentioned in, or inferable from, the text itself); (2) under-regarding and misregarding/misevaluating, on the axis of ethics and evaluation (the standard for this, for Phelan and Martin, is the implied author's norms; for Nünning (2005, 2008), the reader's own norms); and (3) under-reading and misreading, on the axis of knowledge and perception; again, the correct vision can, according to Phelan and Martin, be drawn from the text.

25. See, among many others, Olson 2003; Phelan 1996, 2005, 2007; Phelan and Martin 1999; Yacobi 1981, 2001; A. Nünning 1999, 2005, 2008; and D'Hoker and Martens 2008.

26. Nünning rightly allows for competing psychological theories instead of invoking the notion of folk psychology, which seems more (unduly) homogenizing.

27. These sections in Mitchell's novel, in which characters are described with much stylistic flourish, explain what I meant in the previous section when I discussed Schneider's idea about style as contributing to the foregrounding of character effects. Here, beyond characterizing effects, it is very much the author's display of virtuosity that gets foregrounded.

28. For instance, quite a few of the boatsmen from all over the world who are stranded in Decima are good for a life story in succulent slang. The novel thus offers excellent course material on microhistories, featuring all the currently politically correct topoi: diaspora, multicultural encounter, oppression, marginality, and so on.

29. Within narratology, Susan Lanser (1981) was one of the first to draw attention to the importance of author images in readers' interpretations of literary narratives, turning what she calls the extrafictional voice—the reader's

image of the author—into the overarching authority of a text. This proposition earned her stern reproof: the concept of extrafictional voice would be vague; her work would thus venture beyond the borders of fictional communication, against narratological *doxa*. Her work on the ways in which women writers secured authority for their writing and set out cues for interpretive and evaluative pathways shows, however, the productivity of her approach for understanding meaning-making processes (Lanser 1992; see note 37). See also Heinen 2002, which calls for systematic research on author images for readers' interpretations, as this has rich potential from a culture-historical perspective. While Heinen's approach is in many respects congenial to my own, I do not follow her idea that the author's textual manifestation is amenable to objective description while readers' author constructions, as interpretations, are not. In my view, as argued, there is no noninterpretive access to the author as inferred from the text; both this implied or inferred author and readers' author images are interpretive (re)constructions, a reader's or an analyst's.

30. On this authorial image and posturing in social media, see, for instance, Serfaty 2004; and Viires and Sarapik 2010.

31. It is tempting to draw a parallel with Pine and Gilmore's (1999) analysis of the "experience economy." In their view, the ethics of capitalism is being replaced by the cultivation of sensation and direct emotion, all cognitive distance abolished. Correspondingly, contemporary society develops new strategies to sell products by stressing their experiential potential: to sell, in this sense, means to organize experiences. (Concrete) experience supersedes (more abstract) reflection.

32. One may hypothesize that, given the importance of emotions and lived experience in current Western culture, the self-fashioning of writers (and their fashioning for marketing aims) is intended to translate pathos effects into an ethos of authenticity. This, too, is an area where empirical research can be fruitfully combined with metahermeneutical work.

33. As mentioned in the introduction, many recent studies on authorship distinguish various functions for the author, starting with Foucault's seminal 1969 article (see also, e.g., Detering 2002; Jannidis 1999; Jannidis et al 1999).

34. See also Kim (2008, 254), which suggests that readers' aesthetic conceptions, and their ideas about the social, political, or ethical function of fiction, affect what Kim aptly calls their *desire* for "attached" reading. For instance, an audience may have a "desire for a voice to represent an entire group"; social norms, such as liberalism or attitudes toward minorities, can have a great influence on whether or not we identify narrators or characters with their author.

35. More research is needed on different kinds of ethos appeal in different genres, their connection to the argumentation paths underlying the attribution of value to literary works, and the different ways in which the relevance of literary works is *generalized*: as an exemplum, for instance, and so pertaining by homology to real-life experience, or rather as invention. Between factual and verisimilar literature there is a sliding scale; ethos clues for both, however, may not be so different.

36. A pinch of suspicion regarding the authorial ethos and intentions suffices to make authors or artists who seem to give full disclosure about their "true" personalities just as ungraspable as utmost secrecy does. See also Baroni's thoughtful comments on writers' ethos management and their playful multiplication of authorial images, in a culture in which readers are made to cultivate their hunger for the real person (Baroni 2009, 162–63).

37. An important exception is, again, Susan Lanser, who in *Fictions of Authority* (1992) analyzes the complex ethos management and posturing undertaken by women writers in eighteenth- to twentieth-century England, France, and the United States. As newcomers to what was the male province of serious literature, these authors needed to gain admission to the "restricted" section (Bourdieu) of the literary field; hence they needed to invent, socially validate, and carefully manage what could be called an authorial posture, ensuring their ethos and authority as women writers. Lanser's work is exemplary for its historical documentation, which specifies the context against which patterns of rhetorical validation and legitimization for this "subaltern's" writing and posturing emerge. Here also lies an important difference between her work and the kind of rhetorical analysis proposed by Phelan. The latter instead constructs the authorial ethos in its existential and ethical dimensions, setting the author in the role of moral vis-à-vis, which to some extent eschews historical and sociological contexts.

38. Rich work is being done at the moment, as mentioned, in French-language research, inspired by the long tradition in literary sociology and sociocritical work on style and narrative; see chapter 2.

39. "[T]he implied author is not—and by definition cannot be—a specific textual entity. . . . If the implied author exists 'in' a text, it exists as inferred and imagined; the implied author is a reading effect" (Lanser 2001, 154). See also Kindt and Müller's (2006) extensive study.

40. Even the advantage claimed for the concept of implied author—that at least it impedes a hasty amalgamation of the views of the author as a person and those conveyed in his or her work—corresponds to a reading convention. This is a reading convention that I would myself defend; from a metahermeneutic perspective, however, this convention calls for closer scrutiny,

as there are many shades in how the relation is constructed between a writer and his or her work in terms of adhesion to conveyed views and responsibility.

6. Generic Framing, Authorial Ethos

1. For a more thorough overview of literary engagement in France, see, among others, Denis 2000; Sapiro 1999, 2003a, 2011; and Gefen 2005.

2. Just to mention the main publications preceding *Daewoo*: six novels, one essay on Rabelais, and two unlabeled texts, all published by Minuit between 1982 and 1998; six "récits" (shorter stories) and a play published by Verdier between 1992 and 2002; and, since 2000, *Daewoo*, a manual for writing workshops, a well-received biography of the Rolling Stones, and a book on Led Zeppelin, published by Fayard. On top of all that, Bon has published, with various confidential artistic editors, essays on the playwright Koltès, on art (Hopper), and on photography.

3. The parallels to Eggers's and other writers' and artists' public activities are striking. However, while Eggers aims to empower the "voiceless" by stimulating them to write their life stories, Bon insists on the aesthetic, autonomous dimension of their writing exercises: "The writing workshop has an ethic, and for the group leader, it implies a responsibility: to teach the autonomous use of literature" (Bon and Congiu 2003).

4. The book, which received the Prix Wepler, was meant as a complement to the play the author first wrote at the request of and in collaboration with the director of the Théâtre de la Manufacture in Nancy. The play was a success at the Avignon festival and received both the Molière award for the best play in the region and the Prix de la Critique in 2005.

5. I do not make distinctions here between documentary and engagé writing, although these come in various guises, with different conventions regarding referentiality and authorial implication and accountability. But to keep track of these distinctions would require more space than I want to take up here.

6. Bon's attention to the concrete living conditions that determine people's perception and language brings his work close to ethnographic and sociological investigations of the social construction of reality, as well as to Bourdieu's analysis of habitus (see chapter 2).

7. A similar concern for anchoring an author's or artist's authority in his or her subjective, contextually located perspective rather than in impersonal reason (logos) is found in the works and self-presentation of many contemporary documentary writers and artists. See, e.g., Rouillé 2005 on this theme in documentary photography.

8. On Bon's style, see, in particular, Baetens 1996.

9. Sapiro (2003b: 449) interestingly points out the topos of the professionalism of the writer, defined by his dedication to truth, which grounds the deontology of this profession.

10. Bon borrowed the motto for his book from Rabelais, the sixteenth-century French writer about whose work he also wrote a study, *La Folie Rabelais: L'Invention du Pantagruel* (1990).

11. There is an evident parallel with the practice of various contemporary filmmakers and producers who offer to their viewers, alongside their films, some form of civic activity, like signing petitions or participating in campaigns (see, for instance, the activities of Participant Productions, www .participantmedia.com).

12. The notion of broadcasting, which would qualify Bon's writing, is borrowed from Suzanne Keen's (2007) analysis of empathy-raising strategies: the narrator presents himself as spokesman for the workers, addressing a possibly broad audience.

13. Another eloquent example is the programmatic evocation of the writing impulse, connected to the concrete confrontation with the factory buildings, explored by the narrator in search of the traces of the activities of the factory's workers: where one could expect the social drama to be the trigger for writing, the narrator instead observes, "Ultimately, one calls a book a novel, because one has walked, one morning, in this hall where everything, frame, ground and lines, had once again become pure geometry" (13).

14. Angot's literary work comprises, between 1990 and 2011, some seventeen works of fiction (many of which include strong autobiographic elements), along with short stories, plays, film scenarios, videos, and so on. With her characteristic, simultaneously mannered and apparently authentic style of writing and being, Angot had the dubious honor of being pastiched and turned into a fictional character herself.

15. Lejeune famously defined autobiography as a "retrospective prose narrative produced by a real person concerning his own existence, which focuses on his individual life, in particular on the development of his personality" (Lejeune, 1975, 14). This definition has been subjected to critique since, and Lejeune himself has moved on to include autobiographic writing that challenges generic boundaries; arguably, though, the idea of sincerity remains central in all of these.

16. But see my discussion in chapter 7 on the normativity of such assumptions about the default of language use.

17. Think of Maingueneau's observations on literature as *paratopy* (see chapter 2), requiring strong ethos clues authorizing a writer's right to claim readers' time investment; autobiography combines this requirement for relevance

with the need to compensate for infringing the communicational norm, which does not appreciate endless self-expression.

18. Angot's live performances, in which she reads her own work, tend to make a strong impression of authenticity on audiences (Dubois 2011).

19. Bécassine was the heroine of one of the first graphic novels in France, which met with huge success: the young peasant girl, naïve and golden-hearted, fresh from her native Bretagne, lost in the big town. Although Bécassine might have been credited for her lucid appraisal of the customs of bourgeois life, and for her intrepidity, her name became a synonym for a naïve, slightly obtuse girl.

20. *Sujet Angot* refers to the author's name in an aptly polysemic way: The title may carry connotations of clinical or scientific distance, as *sujet* may refer to "a living being about whom one makes observations," as in an official report (*Dictionnaire Larousse du Français contemporain*). *Sujet* may also carry derogatory connotations, as in "mauvais sujet" (a bad person). In order to distinguish the actual author from the textually evoked Christine, I use the first name to indicate the latter, and Angot for the author. The name Claude will be used to refer to the book's narrator, Christine's ex; the few occasions in which I refer to Angot's real ex should be clear from the context.

21. For further discussion, see Korthals Altes 2005. Gill Rye (2004, 118) offers a congenial analysis of Angot's "grammar of uncertainty," her "oscillation between 'feint' and 'seriousness,'" and the difficulty, for readers, of "know[ing] whether we are reading about 'Christine Angot' the author or about the literary persona 'c. a.,'" and how seriously one should take this writing.

22. Kristeva defines abjection as "the recognition of the lack at the heart of all being, meaning, language, desire. . . . The signifier of [this lack] being literature" (Kristeva 1980, 12–13). The patient who lives in abjection aspires to a "renaissance that s/he would achieve through a language use [*parole*] retrieved as his/her own" (62).

23. This injunction could be taken as a reply to the fragment, in *Les Autres*, in which "Angot" cites Claude's parents' reproach that she made him lose his dignity by exhibiting in public all the intimate stuff love is made of ("notre fils a perdu tout sens moral"; 62). Claude, in *Sujet Angot*, himself admits his desire to wallow in this exhibitionism.

7. Sincerity and Other Ironies

1. Interestingly, Eggers's text differs in the British and U.S. versions of the Vintage paperback editions. The U.S. version (Vintage paperback 2001) has the typographically foregrounded line "PEOPLE, PLEASE: TRUST THE MOTIVES

AND HEARTS OF YOUR MAKERS OF THINGS." This line casts, still indirectly, though, the writer—"maker of things"—as the one to be trusted.

2. Commenting on the "rhetoric of sincerity," Joan Livingston-Webber (2009) analyzes linguistic/stylistic devices such as dialect, orality, and first-impulse speech markers. Students, she writes, tend to receive these devices as authentic and sincere, whereas "trained academics tend to find this kind of authenticity marker suspect and seem to prefer irony (especially about the self) as a marker of sincerity or authenticity."

3. This casuistry has had a long career. In Diderot's famous 1773 work on acting, the relevance of which extended to the social stage, it was labeled the "comedian's paradox."

4. Meizoz (2007, 2010), as we saw, analyzes Rousseau's self-fashioning as fitting and configurating this ethos, while paying less attention, however, to Rousseau's duplicities as a person who knew by experience the tensions between ideal transparency and muddy practice, tensions that have been masterfully disentangled by Starobinski 1988.

5. Habermas's three validity claims include (a) what the speaker says is true, (b) the speech act is right with respect to the existing normative context, and (c) the manifest intention of the speaker is meant as it is expressed, which amounts to "truthfulness or sincerity for the manifestation of subjective experiences" (Habermas 1996, 126).

6. See Derrida's 1988 polemics with Searle, nastily renamed "SARL," a debate recounted with glee in Miller 2001 (if I may interpret their discursive ethos).

7. This position is not incompatible with Habermas's, who proposes an "ethics of discourse." Awareness that "stability and absence of ambiguity are rather the exception in the communicative practice of everyday life" does not, he argues, diminish the importance of sincerity as a leading ideal, one that is indispensable for democracy (Habermas 1984, 100).

8. The narrating voice adopts, in my view, discontinuous profiles: that of a traditional, omniscient authorial narrator, who fathoms human nature; a scientifically informed voice, which presents characters from the distantly analytic perspective of sociology, ethology, or psychology; and a biased, ontologically distanced (collective) first-person perspective, that of the clones issued from the human race, for whom human emotions and conducts are wholly unfamiliar. These are ever so many prisms through which the human experience of the two brothers, Bruno and Michel, is reconstructed, their sheer number calling attention to the prisms themselves.

9. Conventionally, a distinction is made between verbal or rhetorical irony, dramatic irony, and situational irony; between targets of irony (self, oth-

ers); and between irony as a global attitude and worldview or as a historically defined attitude (Socratic or Romantic irony or postmodern irony). For this book's purposes verbal and rhetorical irony and irony as an attitude are most relevant, as they contribute to—and are detected on the basis of—a speaker's perceived ethos. See Hutcheon's (1994) excellent study; for a historical approach, see, among others, Behler 1990; Hamon 1996; Mücke 1969; Wilde 1981; for the social functions of irony, Colston and Gibbs 2007, 297–407; Hutcheon 1994, 47; Kaufer and Neuwirth 1982."

10. In research on irony, as with studies of sincerity, attention tends to slide from the local level (irony as a local rhetorical strategy) to synthesizing ethos attributions, to a speaker's global character and attitude, inferred from a habitual ironic assertion mode, but also to an ethos taken to be characteristic for a collective (Romantic irony, modernist or postmodern irony).

11. In a similar line of thought, Curcó observes that irony is characterized by the high "degree of the meta-representation involved in handling communicative acts" (Curcó 2007, 288–89).

12. "The wonder of it is not that it should go awry as often as it does, but that it should ever succeed" (Booth 1974, 13–14).

13. Similarly, Searle (1979, 113) describes irony as an inappropriate utterance that, "while maintaining relevance, explicitly or implicitly violates the conditions for contextual appropriateness . . . in terms of the knowledge by the participants of the opinions and belief systems of the speakers." This approach would be safer than mention detection (Attardo 2007, n24; on mention theory, see below). Yet in my view it requires just as much the analyst's argued defense of the context in which inferences are made and a particular relevance is assumed.

14. The linguist Attardo, for his part, presents as a "chain of inferences" the ironist's and that audience's reciprocal anticipations of intentions and value positions. The image of a chain suggests a highly determined concatenation, amenable to description. Sperber and Wilson at least open the door for readers' constructions of relevance, which I take as almost a recognition of the process's hermeneutic nature. One problem with linguistic theories of irony is that they are mostly based on artificial or extremely familiar examples for which a situational context can be neatly specified, or filled in blindly. In real-life cases, or in literary ones, weak implicatures tend to be the norm and readers' decisions about irony go far beyond "automatically triggered inferencing processes" (Galiñanes 2005, 83).

15. The idea that any utterance, any literary work, can be contextualized by the interpreter as not just used but mentioned tends to be contested by schol-

ars who seek to contain language's slippage-potential (by tying utterances to retrievable authorial intentions or to norms or maxims ruling over language use). To adopt the position that intention and ethos attributions are contextual, in my view, need not open the door to any wild interpretation; rather, it constrains the interpreter to making explicit the adopted contextual frames and to arguing for their relevance.

16. Frame switching is what irony would share with ambiguity. Gombrich interestingly describes ambiguity in arts as perceptive oscillation, often taken as a symptom of the aesthetic, though it is definitely not exclusive to art. Ambiguity, Gombrich suggests, is connected to Wittgenstein's idea of "aspect seeing": "Ambiguity—rabbit or duck?—is clearly the key to the whole problem of image reading" (Gombrich 2002, 198).

17. An interesting case consists of ambiguities regarding the generic classification of artworks, hence regarding the value regimes that should be applied. Critics are sometimes very anxious about such ambiguities, especially in the case of works that they perceive as kitsch but whose kitschiness might be intended as ironic. When does our charity principle become critical blindness or self-fulfilling prophecy? See David Cohen's discussion of such anxieties and his justification of his own ethos constructions for two contemporary artists whose works and personas he experienced as ambiguous, John Currin and Elizabeth Peyton (Cohen 2002).

18. These strategies include, besides irony and parody, a text's reference to what counts as real; cultural stereotypes (not always easily distinguishable from the previous); genre conventions; and other literary conventions (Culler 1975, 152–60).

19. Readers—and critics—are very able to construct an authorial ethos that would "halt the play of codes," as we saw for Houellebecq (chapter 2), since their reading strategies codetermine whose voices, which communicative level, and which kinds of ethos clues and regimes appear relevant.

20. Tsur's distinction seems to apply also to public cultural norms and, a fortiori, to political positions on ambiguity and irony, often little favored by authorities. As the case of Prokhanov illustrates, the cultivation of ambiguity or irony in art does not function in a vacuum but engages in complex negotiations with ethical or political framings of artworks in the broader sociocultural and political context.

21. For similar diagnoses, see Brooks and Toth 2007; Burn 2008; Dalton-Brown 2006; Lopez and Potter 2001; McLaughlin 2004; Mileur 1998; Rorty 1989; Timmer 2010.

22. David Foster Wallace's work, in particular, wrestles, like Eggers's, with postmodern irony, the spread of which in mass culture (namely television) he

discusses in "*E Unibus Pluram*: Television and U.S. Fiction," in *A Supposedly Fun Thing I'll Never Do Again* (1997).

23. Dave and his intellectual pals are actually fascinated both by the reality effect and by its distortion: "Maybe this is indeed us. Watching the show is like listening to one's voice on tape: it's real of course, but . . . once [your words are] sent through this machine and are given back to you, they're high-pitched, nasal, horrifying. Are our lives that?" (167–68). One of them, seeking admission, sends a letter to the MTV producers with arguments that read as a parody of the standard participant's motivation and as an ironic echo of Dave's self-conscious reflections in the interview scene.

24. Heinich would say that Dave capitalizes on both singularity and commonality, both on being unique and on being average; see chapter 2.

25. Narrator Dave would iconically, and perhaps ironically, render how young Dave anticipates Laura's perspective on himself, seeing himself through her taxation and vocabulary ("second-hand velour").

26. In chapter 5 I discussed Phelan's distinction of the three levels on which characters could function: mimetic, thematic, and synthetic, which for him add up. In my perspective these three dimensions are fruitfully considered as recursive framings, which can deeply change the way readers construct the communication situation and their interpretation and evaluation of the work at stake.

27. This interpretation sheds another light not just on Dave's lack of shame but also on that of all those real people who are so eager to exhibit their most intimate selves. Perhaps individuality and privacy are indeed overrated; perhaps such emo-programs, and literary autobiography as well, usefully contribute to the social co-construction of reality through narrative.

28. We may also frame these utterances as narrator Dave's synthetic portrayal of his younger self, which lucidly recognizes young Dave's narcissistic sense of having been unduly wronged by the death of his parents. This somewhat negative ethos would be compensated by narrator Dave's self-indictment, resulting in a perspectivized ethos for Dave the author, whose autobiographic writing we imagine ourselves to be reading. Alternately, we may frame the phrase as only pseudoautobiographical, extending its scope thematically, as Phelan would say, beyond the personal case to a generational attitude that "we are owed."

29. See Rousseau's *Confessions* (1782; Rousseau 2000) or Leiris's description of literature, in particular self-writing, as bullfighting, in his preface to his autobiographic work *L'Âge d'homme* (1939).

30. Just one exemplary quote from the reception of Eggers's work and persona: "A heartwarming work of literary altruism: author Dave Eggers cultivates

new generation of writers in the Mission. . . . Dave Eggers, one of the brightest writing stars in the literary firmament, could be enjoying the high life offered an author of his growing stature"; instead, he invests "his time and considerable fortune to help less privileged young people learn the craft that has fueled his career" (Ganahl 2002).

31. There are interesting parallels here with the authenticity effects in Bon's novel *Daewoo*, discussed in chapter 6.

Works Cited

Abrams, Meyer Howard. 1953. *The Mirror and the Lamp: Romantic Theory and the Critical Tradition*. New York: Oxford University Press.

Aczel, Richard. 1998. "Hearing Voices in Narrative Texts." *New Literary History* 29.3: 467–500.

Alber, Jan, Stefan Iversen, Henrik Skov Nielsen, and Brian Richardson. 2010. "Unnatural Narratives, Unnatural Narratology: Beyond Mimetic Models." *Narrative* 18.2: 113–37.

Alber, Jan, Henrik Skov Nielsen, Brian Richardson, and Stefan Iversen, comps. and eds. 2011. *Dictionary of Unnatural Narratology*. Revised March 7. http://projects.au.dk/narrativeresearchlab/unnatural/undictionary/. Accessed February 2011.

Amossy, Ruth. 1991. *Les Idées reçues: Sémiologie du stéréotype*. Paris: Nathan.

——. 1999. "L'Ethos à la croisée des disciplines: Pragmatique, rhétorique, sociologie des champs." In *Images de soi dans le discours*, edited by Ruth Amossy and Jean-Michel Adam, 127–54. Lausanne: Delachaux et Niestlé.

——. 2001. "Ethos at the Crossroads of Disciplines: Rhetoric, Pragmatics, Sociology." *Poetics Today* 22.1: 1–23.

Amossy, Ruth, and Jean-Michel Adam. 1999. *Images de soi dans le discours: La Construction de l'ethos*. Lausanne: Delachaux et Niestlé.

Amossy, Ruth, and Anne Herschberg-Pierrot. 1997. *Stéréotypes et clichés: Langue, discours, société*. Paris: Nathan.

Amossy, Ruth, and Dominique Maingueneau. 2009. "Autour des 'scénographies auctoriales': Entretien avec José-Luis Diaz, auteur de *L'Ecrivain imaginaire* (2007)." *Argumentation et Analyse du Discours* 3. http://aad.revues.org/678. Accessed November 18, 2010,

Andringa, Els. 2004. "The Interface between Fiction and Life: Patterns of Identification in Reading Autobiographies." *Poetics Today* 25.2: 205–40.

Andringa, Els, and Margrit Schreier, eds. 2003. "How Literature Enters Life." Special issue, *Poetics Today* 252.

Angenot, Marc. 1982. *La Parole pamphlétaire: Contribution à la typologie des discours modernes*. Paris: Payot.

Angot, Christine. 1997. *Les Autres*. Paris: Fayard.

———. 1998. *Sujet Angot*. Paris: Fayard.

———. 1997. Interview by Thierry Guichard. *Le Matricule des Anges* 21 (November–December). http://www.lelibraire.com/din/tit.php?Id=3892. Accessed December 10, 2010.

Ankersmit, Frank. 2005. "Hermeneutics." In *Routledge Encyclopedia of Narrative Theory*, edited by David Herman, Manfred Jahn, and Marie-Laure Ryan. London: Routledge. 211–12.

Aristotle. 2007. *On Rhetoric: A Theory of Civic Discourse*. Trans. George A. Kennedy. 2nd rev. ed. New York: Oxford University Press.

Attardo, Salvatore. 2007. "Irony as Relevant Inappropriateness." In *Irony in Language and Thought: A Cognitive Science Reader*, edited by Raymond W. Gibbs and Herbert L. Colston, 135–70. New York: Taylor and Francis.

Austin, John L. 1962. *How to Do Things with Words*. Ed. James Urmson. Cambridge MA: Harvard University Press.

Baetens, Jan. 1996. "Mot: travail, adjectif: Bon (Notes sur le style de *Temps machine*)." *Esperienze Letterarie* 21.1: 27–36.

Bakhtin, Mikhaïl. 1981. *The Dialogic Imagination: Four Essays*. Trans. Michael Holquist and Caryl Emerson. Ed. Michael Holquist. Austin: University of Texas Press.

Bakken, Arild Michel. 2011. "Textual Self-Branding: The Rhetorical Ethos in Mallarmé's Divagations." *Authorship* 1.1 (Fall). http://www.authorship.ugent.be.

Bal, Maria G. 1977. *Narratologie: Essais sur la signification narrative dans quatre romans modernes*. Paris: Klincksieck.

Banfield, Ann. 1982. *Unspeakable Sentence: Narration and Representation in the Language of Fiction*. London: Routledge and Kegan Paul.

———. 1987. "Describing the Unobserved: Events Grouped around an Empty Centre." In *The Linguistics of Writing: Arguments between Language and Literature*, edited by N. Fapp et al., 265–85. Manchester: Manchester University Press.

Baroni, Raphaël. 2009. *L'Oeuvre du temps: Poétique de la discordance narrative*. Paris: Seuil.

Barthes, Roland. 1970. *S/Z*. Paris: Seuil.

———. 1973. *Le Plaisir du texte*. Paris: Seuil.

———. 1984. "La Mort de l'auteur." In *Le Bruissement de la langue*, 61–68. Paris: Seuil. First published 1968.

Bataille, Georges. 1957. *La Littérature et le mal*. Paris: Gallimard.

Baudelle, Yves. 2003. "Sur les tonalités littéraires: Contribution à une poétique phénoménologique." *Littérature* 132: 85–99.

Baumlin, James, and Tita Baumlin, eds. 1994. *Ethos: New Essays in Rhetorical and Critical Theory*. Dallas: Southern Methodist University Press.

Beckett, Samuel. 1990. *Not I*. In *The Complete Dramatic Works*, 373–84. London: Faber and Faber. First published 1972.

Behler, Ernst. 1990. *Irony and the Discourse of Modernity*. Seattle: University of Washington Press.

Bénichou, Paul. 1973. *Le Sacre de l'écrivain, 1750–1830: Essai sur l'avènement d'un pouvoir spirituel laïque dans la France moderne*. Paris: José Corti.

Bennett, Andrew. 2005. *The Author*. New York: Routledge.

Benveniste, Émile. 1966. *Problèmes de linguistique générale*. Vol. 1. Paris: Gallimard.

Berger, Peter Ludwig, and Thomas Luckmann. 1991. *The Social Construction of Reality: A Treatise in the Sociology of Knowledge*. Harmondsworth: Penguin Books. First published 1966.

Bokobza Kahan, Michèle, and Ruth Amossy, eds. 2009. "Ethos discursif et image d'auteur." Special issue, *Argumentation et Analyse du Discours* 3. http://aad.revues.org/656. Accessed October 15, 2010.

Boltanski, Luc, and Laurent Thévenot. 1991. *De la justification: Les Économies de la grandeur*. Paris: Gallimard.

Bon, François. 1982. *Sortie d'usine*. Paris: Minuit.

———. 1998. *Impatience*. Paris: Minuit.

———. 2004. *Daewoo*. Paris: Fayard.

Bon, François, and Sylvain Bourmeau. 2004. "Finalement, on appelle roman un livre parce que . . ." *Inrockuptibles*, August 25. http://www.tierslivre.net/livres/DW/inrocks.html. Accessed October 2, 2006.

Bon, François, and Christian Congiu. 2003. [Untitled interview]. www.tierslivre.net/arch/itw_nouvelles.html. Accessed September 20, 2008.

Bon, François, and Jean Claude Lebrun. 2004. "Parler pour?" July. http://www.tierslivre.net/livres/DW/Lebrun.pdf. Accessed October 2, 2006.

Bon, François, and Benoît Lecoq. 2002. "Une Recherche d'intensité." *Contrepoints*, April 2. http://remue.net/bulletin/TB020402.html. Accessed June 18, 2004.

Bon, François, and Jean-Christophe Millois. 1995. "En marge." *Prétexte*. www.tierslivre.net/arch/itw_Pretexte98.html. Accessed October 2, 2006.

Booth, Wayne. 1961. *The Rhetoric of Fiction*. Chicago: University of Chicago Press.

———. 1974. *A Rhetoric of Irony*. Chicago: University of Chicago Press.

———. 1988. *The Company We Keep: An Ethics of Fiction*. Berkeley: University of California Press.

Bortolussi, Marisa, and Peter Dixon. 2003. *Psychonarratology: Foundations for the Empirical Study of Literary Response*. Cambridge: Cambridge University Press.

Bourdieu, Pierre. 1980. *Le Sens pratique*. Paris: Minuit.

———. 1984. *Distinction: A Social Critique of the Judgement of Taste*. Trans. Richard Nice. London: Routledge and Kegan Paul. First published 1979.

———. 1991. *Language and Symbolic Power*. Trans. Gino Raymond and Matthew Adamson. Ed. John B. Thompson. Cambridge MA: Harvard University Press. First published 1982.

———. 1993a. *The Field of Cultural Production: Essays on Art and Literature*. Ed. Randal Johnson. Cambridge: Polity Press.

———. 1993b. *Sociology in Question*. Trans. Richard Nice. London: Sage. First published 1984.

———. 1996. *The Rules of Art: Genesis and Structure of the Literary Field*. Trans. Susan Emanuel. Cambridge: Polity Press. First published 1992.

Boyd, Brian. 2009. *On the Origin of Stories: Evolution, Cognition, and Fiction*. Cambridge MA: Harvard University Press.

Brooks, Neil, and John Toth, eds. 2007. *The Mourning After: Attending the Wake of Postmodernism*. Amsterdam: Rodopi.

Bruner, Jerome. 1990. *Acts of Meaning*. Cambridge MA: Harvard University Press.

Buber, Martin. 1923. *Ich und Du*. Leipzig: Insel-Verlag.

Bühler, Axel. 1999. "Die Vielfalt des Interpretierens." *Analyse und Kritik* 21.1: 117–37.

Bühler, Karl. 1965. *Die Krise der Psychologie*. Stuttgart: Gustav Fischer Verlag.

Burke, Sean. 1992. *The Death and Return of the Author: Criticism and Subjectivity in Barthes, Foucault, and Derrida*. Edinburgh: Edinburgh University Press.

———, ed. 1995. *Authorship from Plato to the Postmodern: A Reader*. Edinburgh: Edinburgh University Press.

Burn, Stephen. 2008. "The End of Postmodernism: American Fiction at the Millennium." In *American Fiction of the 1990s: Reflections of History and Culture*, edited by J. Prosser, 220–34. Abingdon: Routledge.

Butte, George. 2004. *I Know What You Know That I Know: Narrating Subjects from "Moll Flanders" to "Marnie."* Columbus: Ohio State University Press.

Calle-Gruber, Mireille. 1989. *L'Effet-Fiction: De L'Illusion romanesque*. Paris: A.G. Nizet.

Carey, John. 2005. *What Good Are the Arts?* London: Faber and Faber.

Caracciolo, Marco. 2014. "Interpretation for the Bodies: Bridging the Gap." *Style* 48 (in press).

Carroll, Noël. 1998. "Art, Narrative and Moral Understanding." in *Aesthetics and Ethics: Essays at the Intersection*, edited by Jerrold Levinson, 126–60. Cambridge: Cambridge University Press.

Carruthers, Peter. 1996. "Simulation and Self-Knowledge: A Defence of Theory-Theory." In *Theories of Theories of Mind*, edited by Peter Carruthers and Peter K. Smith, 22–68. Cambridge: Cambridge University Press.

Charles, Christophe. 2001. *Les Intellectuels en Europe au XIXème siècle: Essai d'histoire comparée*. Paris: Seuil. First published 1996.

Chatman, Seymour. 1978. *Story and Discourse: Narrative Structure in Fiction and Film*. Ithaca NY: Cornell University Press.

Christmann, Ursula, and Margit Schreier. 2003. "Kognitionspsychologie der Textverarbeitung und Konsequenzen für die Bedeutungskonstitution literarischer Texte." In *Regeln der Bedeutung: Zur Theorie der Bedeutung literarischen Texte*, edited by Fotis Jannidis et al., 246–85. Berlin: de Gruyter.

Cicero, Marcus Tullius. 2001. *On the Ideal Orator (De Oratore)*. Ed. James M. May and Jacob Wisse. New York: Oxford University Press.

Citton, Yves. 2010. *L'Avenir des humanités: Économie de la connaissance ou cultures de l'interprétation?* Paris: La Découverte.

Cixous, Hélène, Madeleine Gagnon, and Annie Leclerc. 1977. *La Venue à l'écriture*. Paris: Union Générale d'Éditions.

Claessens, Eefje. 2009. "The Author's Footprints in the Garden of Fiction: Readers' Generation of Author Inferences in Literary Reading." Ph.D. diss., Vrije Universiteit Amsterdam, 2009.

Cohen, David. 2002. "Ambiguity and Intention." *Interdisciplines: Art and Cognition*. (November). http://www.interdisciplines.org/medias/confs/archives/archive_1.pdf. Accessed September 20, 2009.

Cohn, Dorrit. 1978. *Transparent Minds: Narrative Modes for Presenting Consciousness in Fiction*. Princeton NJ: Princeton University Press.

———. 1999. *The Distinction of Fiction*. Baltimore: Johns Hopkins University Press.

Colston, Herbert L., and Raymond W. Gibbs. 2007. *Irony in Language and Thought: A Cognitive Science Reader*. New York: Lawrence Erlbaum.

Compagnon, Antoine. 1998. *Le Démon de la théorie: Littérature et sens commun*. Paris: Seuil.

Coplan, Amy. 2004. "Empathic Engagement with Narrative Fictions." *Journal of Aesthetics and Art Criticism* 62.2: 141–52.

Coste, Didier, and John Pier. 2011. "Narrative Levels." In *The Living Handbook of Narratology*, edited by Peter Hühn, John Pier, Wolf Schmid, and Jörg Schönert. August 4. www.lhn.uni-hamburg.de/article/narrative-levels. Accessed November 20, 2011.

Couturier, Maurice. 1995. *La Figure de l'auteur*. Paris: Seuil.

Culler, Jonathan. 1975. *Structuralist Poetics: Structuralism, Linguistics and the Study of Literature*. London: Routledge and Kegan Paul.

———. 1980. "Prolegomena to a Theory of Reading." In *The Reader in the Text: Essays on Audience and Interpretation*, edited by Susan Suleiman and Inge Karalus Crosman, 46–66. Princeton NJ: Princeton University Press.

Curcó, Carmen. 2007. "Irony: Negation, Echo, and Metarepresentation." In *Irony in Language and Thought: A Cognitive Science Reader*, edited by Raymond W. Gibbs and Herbert L. Colston, 269–93. New York: Taylor and Francis.

Curtius, Ernst Robert. 1979. *European Literature and the Latin Middle Ages*. Trans. Willard R. Trask. London: Routledge and Kegan Paul. Originally published in German, 1948.

Dällenbach, Lucien. 1977. *Le Récit spéculaire: Contribution à l'étude de la mise en abyme*. Paris: Seuil.

Dalton-Brown, Sally. 2006. "The Dialectics of Emptiness: Douglas Coupland's and Viktor Pelevin's Tales of Generation X and P." *Forum for Modern Language Studies* 42.3: 239–48.

Damasio, Antonio R. 1994. *Descartes' Error: Emotion, Reason, and the Human Brain*. New York: Putnam.

Daniels, Norman. 2011. "Reflective Equilibrium." In *The Stanford Encyclopedia of Philosophy*, edited by Edward N. Zalta. Spring 2011 ed. Revised January 12, 2011. http://plato.stanford.edu/archives/spr2011/entries/reflective -equilibrium. Accessed January 13, 2012.

Danto, Arthur. 1981. *The Transfiguration of the Commonplace: A Philosophy of Art*. Cambridge MA: Harvard University Press.

Davidson, Donald. 1984. *Inquiries into Truth and Interpretation*. Oxford: Clarendon Press.

Deacon, Terrence. 2006. "The Aesthetic Faculty." In *The Artful Mind: Cognitive Science and the Riddle of Human Creativity*, edited by Mark Turner, 20–56. New York: Oxford University Press.

de Man, Paul. 1983. *Blindness and Insight: Essays in the Rhetoric of Contemporary Criticism*. 2nd rev. ed. London: Methuen First published 1971.

Denis, Benoît. 2000. *Littérature et engagement: De Pascal à Sartre*. Paris: Seuil.

Dennett, Daniel C. 1987. *The Intentional Stance*. Cambridge MA: MIT Press.

Derrida, Jacques. 1988. *Limited Inc*. Trans. Samuel Weber and Jefrey Mehlman. Evanston IL: Northwestern University Press.

———. 1992. "The Law of Genre." In *Acts of Literature*, translated by Derek Attridge, 223–52. New York: Routledge. First published 1980.

Detering, Heinrich, ed. 2002. *Autorschaft: Positionen und Revisionen*. Stuttgart: Metzler Verlag.

D'Hoker, Elke, and Martens, Gunther, eds. 2008. *Narrative Unreliability in the Twentieth-Century First-Person Novel*. Berlin: Walter de Gruyter.

Diaz, José Luis. 2007. *L'Écrivain imaginaire: Scénographies auctoriales à l'époque romantique*. Paris: Champion.

Diderot, Denis. 2000. *Paradoxe sur le comédien*. Paris: Flammarion. First published 1773.

Dilthey, Wilhelm. 1985a. "Awareness, Reality: Time. From 'Draft for a Critique of Historical Reason.'" In *The Hermeneutics Reader: Texts of the German Tradition from the Enlightenment to the Present*, edited by Kurt Müller-Vollmer, 149–52. New York: Continuum. Published in German in *Der Aufbau der Geschichtlichen Welt in den Geisteswissenschaften, Gesammelte Schriften*, 2nd ed., vol. 7, edited by B. Groethuysen (Göttingen: Vandenhoeck und Ruprecht, 1960); first published 1926.

———. 1985b. "The Understanding of Other Persons and Their Life-Expressions." In *The Hermeneutics Reader: Texts of the German Tradition from the Enlightenment to the Present*, edited by Kurt Müller-Vollmer, 152–64. New York: Continuum.

Doležel, Lubomír. 1980. "Truth and Authenticity in Narrative." *Poetics Today* 1.3: 7–25.

———. 1988. "Mimesis and Possible Worlds." *Poetics Today* 9.3: 475–96.

———. 2010. *Possible Worlds of Fiction and History: The Postmodern Stage*. Baltimore: Johns Hopkins University Press.

Donald, Merlin. 1991. *Origins of the Modern Mind: Three Stages in the Evolution of Culture and Cognition*. Cambridge MA: Harvard University Press.

———. 2006. "Art and the Cognitive Revolution." In *The Artful Mind: Cognitive Science and the Riddle of Human Creativity*, edited by Mark Turner, 3–20. New York: Oxford University Press.

Dorleijn, Gillis J., Liesbeth Korthals Altes, and Ralf Grüttemeier, eds. 2007. *The Autonomy of Literature at the Fins de Siècles (1900 and 2000): A Critical Assessment*. Leuven: Peeters.

Drouin, Jean-Luc. 2000. "Christine Angot (re)fait sa rentrée." *Le Monde*, September 15.

Dubois, Jacques. 1992. "L'Institution du texte." In *La Politique du texte: Enjeux sociocritiques*, edited by Jacques Neefs and Marie-Claire Ropars, 125–44. Lille: Presses Universitaires de Lille.

———. 2011. "Christine Angot: L'Enjeu du hors-jeu." *Contextes* 9 http://contextes.revues.org/index4789.html. Accessed December 10, 2011.

Ducrot, Oswald. 1984. *Le Dire et le dit*. Paris: Minuit.

Dupuis, Jérôme. 2008. "Angot est un roman-photo." *L'Express*, August 21. http://www.lexpress.fr/informations/angot-est-un-roman-photo_724574.html. Accessed October 2011.

Easterlin, Nancy. 2012. *A Biocultural Approach to Literary Theory and Interpretation*. Baltimore: Johns Hopkins University Press.

Eco, Umberto. 1990. *The Limits of Interpretation*. Bloomington: Indiana University Press.

Edelman, Bernard. 2004. *Le Sacre de l'auteur*. Paris: Seuil.

Eder, Jens. 2003. "Narratology and Cognitive Reception Theories." In *What Is Narratology? Questions and Answers Regarding the Status of a Theory*, edited by Tom Kindt and Hans-Harald Müller, 277–301. Berlin: Walter de Gruyter, 2003.

———. 2008. *Die Figur im Film: Grundlagen der Figurenanalyse*. Marburg, Germany: Schüren.

Eggers, Dave. 2001. *A Heartbreaking Work of Staggering Genius*. New York: Vintage Books.

———. 2006. *What Is the What: The Autobiography of Valentino Achak Deng: A Novel*. San Francisco: McSweeney's.

Eggs, Ekkehard. 1999. "Ethos Aristotelicien, conviction et pragmatique moderne." In *Images de soi dans le discours: La construction de l'ethos*, edited by Ruth Amossy and Jean-Michel Adam, 31–59. Lausanne: Delachaux et Niestlé.

Emmott, Catherine. 1997. *Narrative Comprehension: A Discourse Perspective*. Oxford: Clarendon Press.

Eskin, Michael. 2007. "Narratology Made User-Friendly: Rhetoric, Ethics, Storytelling." *Poetics Today* 28.4: 795–805.

Federman, Raymond. 1976. "Imagination as Playgiarism [An Unfinished Paper . . .]." *New Literary History* 7.3: 563–78.

Felman, Shoshana, and Dori Laub. 1992. *Testimony: Crises of Witnessing in Literature, Psychoanalysis, and History*. London: Routledge.

Fetterley, Judith. 1978. *The Resisting Reader: A Feminist Approach to American Fiction*. Bloomington: Indiana University Press.

Fish, Stanley. 1980. *Is There a Text in This Class?: The Authority of Interpretive Communities*. Cambridge MA: Harvard University Press.

———. 1983. "Short People Got No Reason to Live: Reading Irony." *Daedalus* 112.1: 175–91.

Fludernik, Monika. 1993. *The Fictions of Language and the Languages of Fiction: The Linguistic Representation of Speech and Consciousness*. London: Routledge.

———. 1996. *Towards a "Natural" Narratology*. London: Routledge.

Foucault, Michel. 1969. "Qu'est-ce qu'un auteur?" *Bulletin de la Société Française de Philosophie* 63.3: 73–104.

Frey, James. 2003. *A Million Little Pieces*. New York: Random House.

Gadamer, Hans-Georg. 1977. *Philosophical Hermeneutics*. Trans. David E. Linge. Berkeley: University of California Press.

———. 1991. *Truth and Method*. 2nd revised ed. Trans. Joel Weinsheimer and Donald G. Marshall. New York: Crossroad.

Galinañes, Cristina Larkin. 2000. "Relevance Theory, Humour and the Narrative Structure of Humorous Novels." *Revista Alicantina de Estudios Ingleses* 13: 95–106.

———. 2005. "Funny Fiction; or, Jokes and Their Relation to the Humorous Novel." *Poetics Today* 26.1: 79–111.

Gallagher, H. L., and C. D. Frith. 2003. "Functional Imaging of 'Theory of Mind.'" *Trends in Cognitive Sciences* 7: 77–83.

Gallagher, Shaun. 2004. "Hermeneutics and the Cognitive Sciences." *Journal of Consciousness Studies* 11.10–11: 162–74.

Gallagher, Shaun, and Dan Zahavi. 2008. *The Phenomenological Mind: An Introduction to Philosophy of Mind and Cognitive Science*. London: Routledge.

Gallese, Vittorio, and Alvin Goldman. 1998. "Mirror Neurons and the Simulation Theory of Mind-Reading." *Trends in Cognitive Sciences* 2.12: 493–501.

Ganahl, Jane. 2002. "A Heartwarming Work of Literary Altruism: Author Dave Eggers Cultivates New Generation of Writers in the Mission." *San Francisco Chronicle*, August 2. http://www.sfgate.com/cgi-bin/article.cgi?f=/c/a/2002/08/02/MN49346.DTL&ao=all. Accessed February 2011.

Gasparini, Philippe. 2008. *Autofiction: Une aventure du langage*. Paris: Seuil.

Gefen, Alexandre. 2005. "Responsabilités de la forme: Voies et détours de l'engagement littéraire contemporain." In *L'Engagement littéraire*, edited by Emmanuel Bouju, 75–85. Rennes: Presses Universitaires de Rennes.

Genette, Gérard. 1976. *Figures*. Paris: Seuil. First published 1966.

———. 1987. *Seuils*. Paris: Seuil. (*Paratexts: Thresholds of Interpretation*. Trans. Jane E. Lewin. Cambridge: Cambridge University Press, 1997).

———. 1988. *Narrative Discourse Revisited*. Trans. Jane E. Lewin. Ithaca NY: Cornell University Press. First published 1983.

———. 1993. *Fiction and Diction*. Trans. by Catherine Porter. Ithaca NY: Cornell University Press. First published in French 1991.

Gerrig, Richard J., and David W. Allbritton. 1990. "The Construction of Literary Character: A View from Cognitive Psychology." *Style* 24: 380–91.

Gibson, Andrew. 1996. *Towards a Postmodern Theory of Narratology.* Edinburgh: Edinburgh University Press.

——. 1999. *Postmodernity, Ethics, and the Novel: From Leavis to Levinas.* London: Routledge.

Goffman, Erving. 1974. *Frame Analysis: An Essay on the Organization of Experience.* New York: Harper and Row.

Goldman, Lucien. 1955. *Le Dieu caché: Etude sur la vision tragique dans les Pensées de Pascal et dans le théâtre de Racine.* Paris: Gallimard.

Gombrich, Ernst H. 2002. *Art and Illusion: A Study in the Psychology of Pictorial Representation.* New York: Phaison. First published 1960.

Goodman, Nelson. 1978. *Ways of Worldmaking.* Hassocks: Harvester Press.

Gordon, Robert M. 1996. "'Radical' Simulationism." In *Theories of Theories of Mind*, edited by Peter Carruthers and Peter K. Smith, 11–21. Cambridge: Cambridge University Press.

Gorman, David. 2005. "Fiction, Theories of." In *Routledge Encyclopedia of Narrative Theory*, edited by David Herman, Manfred Jahn, and Marie-Laure Ryan, 163–67. London: Routledge.

Greenblatt, Stephen. 1988. *Shakespearean Negotiations: The Circulation of Social Energy in Renaissance England.* Berkeley: University of California Press.

——. 1995. "Culture." In *Cultural Terms in Literary Study*, edited by Frank Lentricchia and Thomas McLaughlin, 225–32. Chicago: University of Chicago Press. First published 1990.

Greimas, Algirdas Julien. 1966. *Sémantique structurale: Recherche de méthode.* Paris: Larousse.

Greimas, Algirdas Julien, and Joseph Courtés. 1979. *Semiotique: Dictionnaire raisonné de la théorie du langage.* Paris: Classiques Hachette.

Grice, Herbert Paul. 1975. "Logic and Conversation." In *Syntax and Semantics*, vol. 3, *Speech Acts*, edited by P. Cole and J. Morgan, 41–58. New York: Academic Press.

——. 1978. "Further Notes on Logic and Conversation." In *Syntax and Semantics*, vol. 9, *Pragmatics*, edited by P. Cole, 113–27. New York: Academic Press.

——. 1989. *Studies in the Way of Words.* Cambridge MA: Harvard University Press.

Grünzweig, Walter, and Andreas Solbach, eds. 1999. *Grenzüberschreitungen: Narratologie im Kontext / Transcending Boundaries: Narratology in Context.* Tübingen: Narr.

Habermas, Jürgen. 1984. *The Theory of Communicative Action.* Volume 1, *Reason and the Rationalization of Society.* London: Heinemann.

——. 1990. *Moral Consciousness and Communicative Action.* Trans. Christian

Lenhardt and Shierry Weber Nicholsen. Cambridge: Polity Press. First
published 1983.

——. 1996. *Between Facts and Norms: Contributions to a Discourse Theory of
Law and Democracy.* Trans. William Rehg. Cambridge: Polity Press.

Halsall, Albert. 1988. *L'Art de convaincre: Le Récit pragmatique, rhétorique,
idéologie, propagande.* Toronto: Paratexte.

Hamburger, Käte. 1968. *Die Logik Der Dichtung.* 2nd ed. Stuttgart: Klett. First
published 1957.

Hamon, Philippe. 1983. *Le Personnel du roman: Le Système des personnages
dans* Les Rougon-Macquart d'Emile Zola. Genève: Droz.

——. 1996. *L'Ironie littéraire: Essai sur les formes de l'écriture oblique.* Paris:
Hachette Supérieur.

Hamsun, Knut. 1971. *Mysteries.* Trans. Gerry Bothmer. New York: Farrar, Straus
and Giroux. First published in Danish in 1892.

Harpham, Geoffrey Galt. 2005. "Beneath and Beyond the 'Crisis in the
Humanities.'" *New Literary History* 36.1: 21–36.

Hegenbarth-Rösgen, Annelie. 1982. *Soziale Normen und Rollen im Roman:
Dargestellt am Beispiel der 'Éducation des filles' bei Zola, den Brüdern
Goncourt, Daudet, Huysmans und Prévost.* München: Fink.

Heinen, Sandra. 2002. "Das Bild des Autors: Überlegungen zum Begriff
des 'Implizen Autors' und seines Potentials zur kulturwissenschaftlichen
Beschreibung von inszenierter Autorschaft." *Sprachkunst* 33.2: 329–45.

——. 2009. "The Role of Narratology in Narrative Research across the
Disciplines." In *Narratology in the Age of Cross-Disciplinary Narrative
Research,* edited by Sandra Heinen and Roy Sommer, 193–211. Berlin: Walter
de Gruyter.

Heinen, Sandra, and Roy Sommer, eds. 2009. *Narratology in the Age of Cross-
Disciplinary Narrative Research.* Berlin: Walter de Gruyter.

Heinich, Nathalie. 1997. "Entre oeuvre et personne: L'Amour de l'art en régime
de singularité." *Communications* 64: 153–71.

——. 2000. *Etre écrivain: Création et identité.* Paris: La Découverte.

Herman, David, ed. 1999. *Narratologies: New Perspectives on Narrative Analysis.*
Columbus: Ohio State University Press.

——. 2002. *Story Logic: Problems and Possibilities of Narrative.* Lincoln:
University of Nebraska Press.

——. 2003. *Narrative Theory and the Cognitive Sciences.* Stanford CA: CSLI.

——. 2007. "Storytelling and the Sciences of Mind: Cognitive Narratology,
Discursive Psychology, and Narratives in Face-to-Face Interaction."
Narrative 15. 3: 306–34.

———. 2008. "Narrative Theory and the Intentional Stance." *Partial Answers: Journal of Literature and the History of Ideas* 6. 2: 233–60.

———. 2009. *Basic Elements of Narrative*. Chichester: Wiley-Blackwell.

———, ed. 2011. *The Emergence of Mind: Representations of Consciousness in Narrative Discourse in English*. Lincoln: University of Nebraska Press.

Herman, David, Manfred Jahn, and Marie-Laure Ryan, eds. 2005. *Routledge Encyclopedia of Narrative Theory*. London: Routledge.

Herman, David, James Phelan, Peter J. Rabinowitz, Brian Richardson, and Robyn Warhol. 2012. *Narrative Theory: Core Concepts and Critical Debates*. Columbus: Ohio State University Press, 2012.

Herman, Luc, and Bart Vervaeck. 2009. "Narrative Interest as Cultural Negotiation." *Narrative* 17.1: 111–29.

———. 2011. "The Implied Author: A Secular Excommunication." *Style* 45.1: 11–28.

Hermerén, Göran. 1983. "Interpretation: Types and Criteria." *Grazer philosophische Studien* 19: 131–61.

———. 1991. *Art, Reason, and Tradition: On the Role of Rationality in Interpretation and Explanation of Works of Art*. Stockholm: Almqvist and Wiksell.

Hernadi, Paul. 2003. "Why Is Literature: A Coevolutionary Perspective on Imaginative Worldmaking." *Poetics Today* 23.1: 21–42.

Heydebrand, Renate von, and Simone Winko. 1996. *Einführung in die Wertung von Literatur: Systematik—Geschichte—Legitimation*. Paderborn: Schöningh.

Hirsch, David H. 1991. *The Deconstruction of Literature: Criticism after Auschwitz*. Hanover NH: University Press of New England for Brown University Press.

Hirsch, Eric D. 1967. *Validity in Interpretation*. New Haven CT: Yale University Press.

Hite, Molly. 2010. "Tonal Cues and Uncertain Values: Affect and Ethics in *Mrs. Dalloway*." *Narrative* 18.3: 249–75.

Hogan, Patrick Colm. 2003. *Cognitive Science, Literature, and the Arts: A Guide for Humanists*. London: Routledge.

Houellebecq, Michel. 1991a. *H. P. Lovecraft: Contre le monde, contre la vie*. Paris: Le Rocher.

———. 1991b. *Rester vivant: Méthode*. Paris: La Différence.

———. 1994. *Extension du domaine de la lutte*. Paris: Nadeau.

———. 1998a. *Interventions*. Paris: Flammarion.

———. 1998b. *Les Particules élémentaires*. Paris: Flammarion. Published in English, translated by Frank Wynne, as *Atomised* (London: Heinemann 2000) and as *The Elementary Particles* (New York: Knopf, 2000).

———. 2000. *Lanzarote*. Paris: Flammarion.

———. 2001. *Plateforme*. Paris: Flammarion.

———. 2005. *La Possibilité d'une île*. Paris: Fayard.

———. 2010. *La Carte et le territoire*. Paris: Flammarion Published in English as *The Map and the Territory*, trans. Gavin Bowd (New York: Knopf, 2012).

Hühn, Peter, John Pier, and Wolf Schmid, and Jörg Schönert, eds. 2009. *The Living Handbook of Narratology*. http://www.lhn.uni-hamburg.de.

Hunt, Lynn. 1992. *The Family Romance of the French Revolution*. Berkeley: University of California Press.

Hutcheon, Linda. 1988. *A Poetics of Postmodernism: History, Theory, Fiction*. New York: Routledge.

———. 1994. *Irony's Edge: The Theory and Politics of Irony*. London: Routledge.

Iseminger, Gary. 1992. *Intention and Interpretation*. Philadelphia: Temple University Press.

———. 1996. "Actual Intentionalism vs. Hypothetical Intentionalism." *JAAC* 54.4: 319–26.

Iser, Wolfgang. 1974. *The Implied Reader: Patterns of Communications in Prose Fiction from Bunyan to Beckett*. Baltimore: Johns Hopkins University Press.

———. 1978. *The Act of Reading: A Theory of Aesthetic Response*. London: Routledge and Kegan Paul. First published 1976.

Iversen, Stefan. 2011. "States of Exception: Decoupling, Metarepresentation, and Strange Voices in Narrative Fiction." In *Strange Voices in Narrative Fiction*, edited by Per Krogh Hansen, Stefan Iversen, Henrik Nielsen, and Rolf Reitan, 127–46. Berlin: Walter de Gruyter, 2011.

Jackson, Tony. 2000. "Questioning Interdisciplinarity: Cognitive Science, Evolutionary Psychology, and Literary Criticism." *Poetics Today* 21.2: 319–48.

———. 2003. "Literary Interpretation and Cognitive Literary Studies." *Poetics Today* 24.2: 191–206.

Jahn, Manfred. 1997. "Frames, Preferences, and the Reading of Third-Person Narratives: Towards a Cognitive Narratology." *Poetics Today* 18.4: 441–68.

———. 2001. "Commentary: The Cognitive Status of Textual Voice." *New Literary History* 32: 695–97.

Jannidis, Fotis. 1999. "Der Nützliche Autor: Möglichkeiten eines Begriffs zwischen Text und historischem Kontext." In *Rückkehr Des Autors: Zur Erneuerung eines umstrittenen Begriffs*, edited by Fotis Jannidis et al., 353–89. Tübingen: Niemeyer.

———. 2002. "Zwischen Autor und Erzähler." In *Autorschaft: Positionen und Revisionen*, edited by Heinrich Detering, 540–56. Stuttgart: Metzler.

———. 2003. *Regeln der Bedeutung: Zur Theorie der Bedeutung literarischer Texte*. Berlin: Walter de Gruyter.

——. 2004. *Figur und Person: Beitrag zu einer historischen Narratologie.* Berlin: Walter de Gruyter.

——. 2012. "Character." In *The Living Handbook of Narratology*, edited by Peter Hühn, John Pier, Wolf Schmid, and Jörg Schönert. December 6. http://www.lhn.uni-hamburg.de/article/character. Accessed November 13, 2012.

Jannidis, Fotis, et al., eds. 1999. *Rückkehr Des Autors: Zur Erneuerung eines umstrittenen Begriffs.* Tübingen: Niemeyer.

Janssen, Suzanne. 1997. "Reviewing as Social Practice: Institutional Constraints on Critics' Attention for Contemporary Fiction." *Poetics* 24.5: 275–97.

Johansen, Jørgen Dines. 2002. *Literary Discourse: A Semiotic-Pragmatic Approach to Literature.* Toronto: University of Toronto Press.

——. 2007. "A Semiotic Definition of Literary Discourse." *Semiotica* 165: 107–32.

Johnson, Barbara. 1980. *The Critical Difference: Essays in the Contemporary Rhetoric of Reading.* Baltimore: Johns Hopkins University Press.

Johnson, Mark. 1993. *Moral Imagination: Implications of Cognitive Science for Ethics.* Chicago: University of Chicago Press.

Johnson-Laird, Philip. 1983. *Mental Models: Towards a Cognitive Science of Language, Inference, and Consciousness.* Cambridge: Cambridge University Press.

Jouve, Vincent. 2001. *Poétique des valeurs.* Paris: Presses universitaires françaises.

——. 2010. *Pourquoi étudier la literature?* Paris: Armand Colin.

Kaufer, David, and Christine Neuwirth. 1982. "Foregrounding Norms and Ironic Communication." *Quarterly Journal of Speech* 68.1: 28–36.

Kearns, Michael. 1999. *Rhetorical Narratology.* Lincoln: University of Nebraska Press.

Keen, Suzanne. 2007. *Empathy and the Novel.* New York: Oxford University Press.

——. 2011. "Empathetic Hardy: Bounded, Ambassadorial, and Broadcast Strategies of Narrative Empathy." *Poetics Today* 32.2: 349–89.

Keestra, Machiel. 2008. "The Diverging Force of Imitation: Integrating Cognitive Science and Hermeneutics." *Review of General Psychology* 12.2: 127–36.

Kerbrat-Orecchioni, Catherine. 1980. *L'Énonciation de la subjectivité dans le langage.* Paris: Librairie Armand Colin.

Kibédi Varga, Aron. 1989. *Discours, Récit, Image.* Liège: Mardaga.

Kierkegaard, Søren. 1968. *The Concept of Irony: With Constant Reference to Socrates.* Trans. with an introduction and notes by Lee M. Capel. Bloomington: Indiana University Press. First published 1841.

Kim, J. Sue. 2008. "Narrator, Author, Reader: Equivocation in Theresa Hak Kyung Cha's *Dictee*." *Narrative* 16.2: 163–77.

Kindt, Tom, and Tilmann Köppe, eds. 2008. *Moderne Interpretationstheorien: Ein Reader*. Göttingen: Vandenhoeck & Ruprecht.

Kindt, Tom, and Hans-Harald Müller, eds. 2003. *What Is Narratology? Questions and Answers Regarding the Status of a Theory*. Berlin: Walter de Gruyter.

———. 2006. *The Implied Author: Concept and Controversy*. Trans. Alastair Matthews. Berlin: Walter de Gruyter.

Kinneavy, James, and Susan Warshauer. 1994. "From Aristotle to Madison Avenue: Ethos and the Ethics of Argument." In *Ethos: New Essays in Rhetorical and Critical Theory*, edited by James Baumlin and Tita Baumlin, 171–90. Dallas: Southern Methodist University Press.

Koestler, Arthur. 1989. *The Act of Creation*. Harmondsworth: Penguin. First published 1964.

Korthals Altes, Liesbeth. 1992. *Le Salut par la fiction? Sens, valeurs et narrativité dans le Roi des aulnes de Michel Tournier*. Amsterdam: Rodopi.

———. 2005. "Ironie, ethos textuel et cadre de lecture: Le Cas de *Sujet Angot*." In *L'Expérience de lecture*, edited by V. Jouve, 85–100. Paris: L'Improviste.

———. 2006. "Voice, Irony and Ethos: The Paradoxical Elusiveness of Michel Houellebecq's Polemic Writing in *Les Particules élémentaires*." In *Stimme(n) im Text: Narratologische Positionsbestimmungen*, edited by Andreas Blödorn, Daniela Langer, and Michael Scheffel, 165–93. Berlin: Walter de Gruyter.

———. 2007. "Aesthetic and Social Engagement in Contemporary French Literature: The Case of François Bon's *Daewoo*." In *The Autonomy of Literature at the Fins de Siècles (1900 and 2000): A Critical Assessment*, edited by Gillis J. Dorleijn, Liesbeth Korthals Altes, and Ralf Grüttemeier, 261–84. Leuven: Peeters.

———. 2008. "Sincerity, Reliability and Other Ironies—Notes on Dave Eggers' *A Heartbreaking Work of Staggering Genius*." In *Narrative Unreliability in the Twentieth-Century First-Person Novel*, edited by Elke D'Hoker and Gunther Martens, 107–28. Berlin: Walter de Gruyter.

———. 2010. "Slippery Author Figures, Ethos, and Value Regimes: Houellebecq, a Case." In *Authorship Revised: Conceptions of Authorship around 1900 and 2000*, edited by Gillis J. Dorleijn, Ralf Grüttemeier, and Liesbeth Korthals Altes, 95–117. Leuven: Peeters.

———. 2013. "Narratology, Ethical Turns, Circularities, and a Meta-Ethical Way Out." In *Narrative Ethics*, edited by Jakob Lothe and Jeremy Hawthorn, 25–40. Amsterdam: Rodopi.

Kotthoff, Helga. 2007. "Responding to Irony in Different Contexts: On Cognition in Conversation." In *Irony in Language and Thought: A Cognitive*

Science Reader, edited by Raymond W. Gibbs and Herbert L. Colston, 381–407. New York: Taylor and Francis.

Kristeva, Julia. 1980. *Pouvoirs de l'horreur: Essai sur l'abjection*. Paris: Seuil.

Lamarque, Peter. 2009. *The Philosophy of Literature*. Malden MA: Blackwell.

Lamarque, Peter, and Stein Haugom Olsen. 1994. *Truth, Fiction, and Literature: A Philosophical Perspective*. Oxford: Clarendon Press.

Langevin, Francis. 2011. "La Posture exotique du narrateur-personnage: Inconfort et non-fiabilité dans quelques romans contemporains." In *La Transmission narrative: Modalités du pacte romanesque contemporain*, edited by Andrée Mercier and Frances Fortier, 207–33. Québec: Nota Bene.

Lanser, Susan S. 1981. *The Narrative Act: Point of View in Prose Fiction*. Princeton NJ: Princeton University Press.

———. 1992. *Fictions of Authority: Women Writers and Narrative Voice*. Ithaca NY: Cornell University Press.

———. 2001. "(Im)plying the Author." *Narrative* 9.2: 153–60.

———. 2005. "The 'I' of the Beholder: Equivocal Attachments and the Limits of Structuralist Narratology." In *A Companion to Narrative Theory*, edited by James Phelan and Peter J. Rabinowitz, 206–19. Malden MA: Blackwell.

Lasch, Christopher. 1979. *The Culture of Narcissism: American Life in an Age of Diminishing Expectations*. New York: Warner Books. First published 1978.

Lejeune, Philippe. 1971. *L'Autobiographie en France*. Paris: Armand Colin.

———. 1975. *Le Pacte autobiographique*. Paris: Seuil.

———. 1980. *Je est un autre: L'Autobiographie de la littérature aux médias*. Paris: Seuil.

Levinas, Emmanuel. 1980. *Otherwise than Being; or, Beyond Essence*. Trans. Alphonso Lingis. The Hague: Martinus Nijhoff. First published 1974.

Levinson, Jerrold. 1996. "Intention and Interpretation in Literature." In *The Pleasures of Aesthetics: Philosophical Essays*, 175–213. Ithaca NY: Cornell University Press.

Livingston, Paisley. 2005. *Art and Intention: A Philosophical Study*. Oxford: Clarendon Press.

Livingston-Webber, Joan. 2009. "Rhetoric of Sincerity." Post to American Dialect Society e-mail list ADS-L. January. http://www.americandialect.org /americandialectarchives/aprxx94015.html. Accessed May 2, 2011.

Lopez, Jose, and Garry Potter, eds. 2001. *After Postmodernism: An Introduction to Critical Realism*. London: Athlone Press.

Lotman, Yuri. 1977. *The Structure of the Artistic Text*. Trans. from Russian by Gail Lenhoff and Ronald Vroon. Ann Arbor: University of Michigan Press.

Lyotard, Jean-François, and Jean-Loup Thébaud. 1985. *Just Gaming*. Trans.

Wladyslaw Godzich and Brian Massumi. Minneapolis: University of Minnesota Press.

Maechler, Stefan. 2001. *The Wilkomirski Affair: A Study in Biographical Truth.* Trans. from German by John E. Woods. New York: Schocken Books.

Mahajan, Gurpreet. 1993. *Explanation and Understanding in the Human Sciences.* Delhi: Oxford University Press.

Maingueneau, Dominique. 1996. "Ethos et argumentation philosophique: Le Cas du *Discours de la méthode.*" In *Descartes et l'argumentation philosophique*, edited by Frédéric Cossutta, 85–110. Paris, PUF.

———. 1999. "Ethos, scénographie, incorporation." In *Images de soi dans le discours*, edited by Ruth Amossy and Jean-Michel Adam, 75–100. Lausanne: Delachaux et Niestlé.

———. 2004. *Le Discours littéraire: Paratopie et scène d'énonciation.* Paris: Armand Colin.

———. 2008. "Stylistique, analyse du discours littéraire." *Collection des Congrès Mondial de Linguistique Française* 136: 1501–5. http://dx.doi.org/10.1051/cmlf08328.

———. 2010. "Literature and Discourse Analysis." *Acta Linguistica Hafniensia* 42.1: 147–58.

Maingueneau, Dominique, and John P. O'Regan. 2006. "Is Discourse Analysis Critical? and This Risky Order of Discourse." *Critical Discourse Studies* 3.2: 229–35.

Margolin, Uri. 1990. "The What, the How, and the When of Being a Character in Literary Narrative. *Style* 24.3: 453–69.

———. 1986. "The Doer and the Deed: Action as a Basis for Characterization in Narrative." *Poetics Today* 7.2: 205–25.

———. 2009. "Narrator." In *The Living Handbook of Narratology*, edited by Peter Hühn, John Pier, Wolf Schmid, and Jörg Schönert Hamburg: Hamburg University Press. http://www.lhn.uni-hamburg.de/article/narrator. Accessed December 10, 2012.

———. 2010. "From Predicates to People Like Us. Kinds of Readerly Engagement with Literary Characters." In *Characters in Fictional Worlds: Understanding Imaginary Beings in Literature, Film, and Other Media*, edited by Jens Eder, Fotis Jannidis, and Ralf Schneider, 400–415. Revisionen: Grundbegriffe der Literaturtheorie, 3. Berlin: Walter de Gruyter.

Martin, John. 1997. "Inventing Sincerity, Refashioning Prudence: The Discovery of the Individual in Renaissance Europe." *American Historical Review* 102.5: 1309–42.

Marx, William. 2005. *L'Adieu à la littérature: Histoire d'une dévalorisation, XVIIIe–XXe siècle.* Paris: Minuit.

McLaughlin, Robert L. 2004. "Post-postmodern Discontent: Contemporary Fiction and the Social World." *Symplokē* 12.1 2: 53 68.

Meister, Jan Christoph. 2011. "Narratology." In *The Living Handbook of Narratology*, edited by Peter Hühn, John Pier, Wolf Schmid, and Jörg Schönert. 26 August. http://www.lhn.uni-hamburg.de/article/narratology. Last accessed November 8, 2013.

Meister, Jan Christoph, T. Kindt, and W. Schernus. 2005. *Narratology beyond Literary Criticism. Mediality, Disciplinarity*. Berlin: De Gruyter.

Meizoz, Jérôme. 2004. *L'Œil sociologique et la littérature: Essai*. Genève: Slatkine.

———. 2007. *Postures littéraires: Mises en scène modernes de l'auteur: Essai*. Genève: Slatkine.

———. 2008. "Posture et biographie: *Semmelweis* de L.-F. Céline." *Contextes* 3. http://contextes.revues.org/2633. Accessed August 20, 2012.

———. 2009. "Ce que l'on fait dire au silence: Posture, *ethos*, image d'auteur." *Argumentation et Analyse du Discours* 3. http://aad.revues.org/667. Accessed August 20, 2012.

———. 2010. "Modern Posterities of Posture." In *Authorship Revisited: Conceptions of Authorship around 1900 and 2000*, edited by G. J. Dorleijn, R. Grüttemeier, and E. J. Korthals Altes, 81–93. Leuven: Peeters.

Michelfelder, Diane, and Richard Palmer, eds. 1989. *Dialogue and Deconstruction: The Gadamer-Derrida Encounter*. Albany: State University of New York Press.

Miller, Joseph Hillis. 1987. *The Ethics of Reading: Kant, de Man, Eliot, Trollope, James, and Benjamin*. New York: Columbia University Press.

———. 2001. *Speech Acts in Literature*. Stanford CA: Stanford University Press.

Millet, Catherine. 1997. "Qu'est-ce que l'art contemporain?" *Art Press* 222: 19–24.

———. 2001. *La Vie sexuelle de Catherine M.* Paris: Seuil.

Mileur, Jean-Pierre. 1998. "Revisionism, Irony and the Mask of Sentiment." *New Literary History* 29.2: 197–233.

Minsky, Marvin. 1977. "Frame-System Theory." In *Thinking: Readings in Cognitive Science*, edited by Philip Johnson-Laird and Peter Wason, 355–76. Cambridge: Cambridge University Press.

Mitchell, David. 2010. *The Thousand Autumns of Jacob de Zoet*. London: Random House.

Montfrans-van Oers, Manet van. 2010. "'Faire face à l'effacement': Voix du réel et voix du théâtre dans *Daewoo*." In *Francois Bon: Éclats de réalité*, edited by Dominique Viart and Jean-Bernard Vray, 185–99. Saint-Etienne: Publications de l'université de Saint-Etienne.

Morrissette, Bruce. 1975. *The Novels of Robbe-Grillet*. Ithaca NY: Cornell University Press. First published 1963.

Mücke, Douglas C. 1969. *The Compass of Irony*. New York: Barnes and Noble.

Musil, Robert. 1978. *Der Mann ohne Eigenschaften*. Reinbeck: Rowohlt. First published 1930–32.

Nagel, Thomas. 1984. "What Is It Like to Be a Bat?" *Philosophical Review* 83.4: 435–50.

Nielsen, Henrik Skov. 2004. "The Impersonal Voice in First-Person Narrative Fiction." *Narrative* 12.2: 133–50.

———. 2011. "Theory and Interpretation, Narration and Communication, Authors and Narrators—James Frey's *A Million Little Pieces* as a Test Case." In *Théorie, analyse, interprétation des récits / Theory, Analysis, Interpretation of Narratives*, edited by Sylvie Patron, 73–94. Bern: Peter Lang.

Noguez, Dominique. 2003. *Houellebecq, en fait*. Paris: Fayard.

Noordenbos, Boris. 2011. "Ironic Imperialism: How Russian Patriots Are Reclaiming Postmodernism." *Studies in East European Thought* 63. 2: 147–58.

Nünning, Ansgar. 1997. "Deconstructing and Reconstructing the Implied Author: The Resurrection of an Anthropomorphized Passepartout or the Obituary of a Critical Phenomenon?" *Anglistik: Organ des Verbandes Deutscher Anglisten* 8: 95–116.

———. 1999. "Unreliable, Compared to What? Towards a Cognitive Theory of *Unreliable Narration*: Prolegomena and Hypotheses." In *Grenzüberschreitungen: Narratologie im Kontext / Transcending Boundaries: Narratology in Context*, edited by Walter Grünzweig and Andreas Solbach, 53–73. Tübingen: Narr.

———. 2003. "Narratology or Narratologies? Taking Stock of Recent Developments, Critique and Modest Proposals for Future Usages of the Term." In *What Is Narratology? Questions and Answers Regarding the Status of a Theory*, edited by Tom Kindt and Hans-Harald Müller, 239–75. Berlin: Walter de Gruyter.

———. 2005. "Reconceptualizing Unreliable Narration: Synthesizing Cognitive and Rhetorical Approaches." In *A Companion to Narrative Theory*, edited by J. Phelan and P. J. Rabinowitz, 89–107. Oxford: Blackwell.

———. 2008. "Reconceptualizing the Theory, History, and Generic Scope of Unreliable Narration: Towards a Synthesis of Cognitive and Rhetorical Approaches." In *Narrative Unreliability in the Twentieth-Century First-Person Novel*, edited by Elke D'Hoker and Gunther Martens, 29–76. Berlin: Walter de Gruyter.

Nünning, Vera. 1998. "Unreliable narration und die historische Variabilität von Werten und Normen: *The Vicar of Wakefield* als Testfall für eine kulturgeschichtliche Erzählforschung." In *Unreliable Narration: Studien zur Theorie und Praxis unglaubwürdigen Erzählens in der englischsprachigen Erzählliteratur*, edited by A. Nünning, 257–85. Trier: Wissenschaftlicher Verlag Trier.

Nussbaum, Martha. 1990. *Love's Knowledge: Essays on Philosophy and Literature*. New York: Oxford University Press.

———. 2010. *Not for Profit: Why Democracy Needs the Humanities*. Princeton NJ: Princeton University Press.

Olsen, Stein Haugom. 1987. "Text and Meaning." In *The End of Literary Theory*, 42–52. Cambridge: Cambridge University Press First published 1982.

Olson, Greta. 2003. "Reconsidering Unreliability: Fallible and Untrustworthy Narrators." *Narrative* 11.1: 93–109.

Palmer, Alan. 2004. *Fictional Minds*. Lincoln: University of Nebraska Press.

Pascal, Roy. 1977. *The Dual Voice: Free Indirect Speech and Its Functioning in the Nineteenth-Century European Novel*. Manchester: Manchester University Press.

Patricola, Jean-François. 2005. *Michel Houellebecq, ou, La provocation permanente*. Paris: Écriture.

Patron, Sylvie. 2009. *Le Narrateur: Introduction à la théorie narrative*. Paris: Armand Colin.

———, ed. 2011. *Théorie, analyse, interprétation des récits / Theory, Analysis, Interpretation of Narratives*. Bern: Peter Lang.

Pavel, Thomas G. 1986. *Fictional Worlds*. Cambridge MA.: Harvard University Press.

Pettersson, Bo. 2009. "Narratology and Hermeneutics: Forging the Missing Link." In *Narratology in the Age of Cross-Disciplinary Narrative Research*, edited by Sandra Heinen and Roy Sommer, 11–34. Berlin: Walter de Gruyter.

Phelan, James. 1989. *Reading People, Reading Plots: Character, Progressions, and the Interpretation of Narrative*. Chicago: University of Chicago Press.

———. 1996. *Narrative as Rhetoric: Technique, Audiences, Ethics, Ideology*. Columbus: Ohio State University Press.

———. 2005. *Living to Tell about It: A Rhetoric and Ethics of Character Narration*. Ithaca NY: Cornell University Press.

———. 2007. *Experiencing Fiction: Judgments, Progressions, and the Rhetorical Theory of Narrative*. Columbus: Ohio State University Press.

Phelan, James, and Mary Patricia Martin. 1999. "The Lessons of 'Weymouth': Homodiegesis, Unreliability, Ethics, and *The Remains of the Day*." In *Narratologies: New Perspectives on Narrative Analysis*, edited by David Herman, 88–109. Columbus: Ohio State University Press.

Pine, Joseph B., and James H. Gilmore. 1999. *The Experience Economy: Work Is Theatre and Every Business a Stage*. Boston: Harvard Business School Press.

Pratt, Mary Louise. 1977. *Toward a Speech Act Theory of Literary Discourse*. Bloomington: Indiana University Press.

Premack, David, and Guy Woodruff. 1978. "Does the Chimpanzee Have a Theory of Mind?" *Behavioral and Brain Sciences* 1.4: 515–26.

Prince, Gerald. 1995. "Narratology." In *The Cambridge History of Literary Criticism*, vol. 8, edited by Raman Selden, 110–30. Cambridge: Cambridge University Press.

Prokhanov, Aleksandr. 2002. *Gospodin Geksogen* [Mister Hexogen]. Moscow: Ad Marginem.

Purdy, Jedediah. 1999. *For Common Things: Irony, Trust, and Commitment in America Today*. New York: Knopf.

Quintilianus, Marcus Fabius. 1921. *The Institutio Oratoria of Quintilian*. Vol. 3. Ed. H. E. Butler. Loeb Classical Library. London: William Heineman. http://www.archive.org/stream/institutioorator03quinuoft/institutioorator03 quinuoft_djvu.txt. Accessed April 2010.

Rabatel, Alain. 2009. *Homo narrans: Pour une analyse énonciative et interactionnelle du récit*. Limoges: Lambert-Lucas.

Rabinowitz, Peter J. 1998. *Before Reading: Narrative Conventions and the Politics of Interpretation*. Columbus: Ohio State University Press.

Ramachandran, Vilayanur S., and William Hirstein. 1999. "The Science of Art. A Neurological Theory of Aesthetic Experience." *Journal of Consciousness Studies* 6.6–7: 15–51.

Rancière, Jacques. 2010. *Dissensus: On Politics and Aesthetics*. Edited and translated by Steven Concoran. London: Continuum.

Ravenscroft, Ian. 2010. "Folk Psychology as a Theory." In *Stanford Encyclopedia of Philosophy*, edited by Edward N. Zalta. http://plato.stanford.edu/entries /folkpsych-theory/. Accessed October 2, 2011.

Ricardou, Jean. 1972. *Nouveau roman: Hier, aujourd'hui*. Paris: Union Générale d'Éditions.

Richardson, Alan, and Ellen Spolsky, eds. 2004. *The Work of Fiction: Cognition, Culture, and Complexity*. Aldershot: Ashgate.

Richardson, Brian. 2006. *Unnatural Voices: Extreme Narration in Modern and Contemporary Fiction*. Columbus: Ohio State University Press.

——, ed. 2011. "Implied Author: Back from the Grave or Simply Dead Again." Special issue, *Style*, 45.1.

Ricoeur, Paul. 1981. "What Is a Text? Explanation and Understanding." In *Hermeneutics and the Human Sciences: Essays on Language, Action and Interpretation*, edited and translated by John B. Thompson, 145–64. Cambridge: Cambridge University Press.

———. 1984–88. *Time and Narrative*. Vols. 1–3. Trans. Kathleen McLaughlin and David Pellauer. Chicago: University of Chicago Press. First published 1983, 1984, 1985.

———. 1990. *Soi-Même comme un autre*. Paris: Seuil.

———. 1991a. "Life: A Story in Search of a Narrator." In *A Ricoeur Reader*, edited by Mario Valdes, 425–37. Toronto: University of Toronto Press.

———. 1991b. "Mimesis and Representation." In *A Ricoeur Reader*, edited by Mario Valdes, 137–155. Toronto: University of Toronto Press.

Riggan, William. 1981. *Pícaros, Madmen, Naifs, and Clowns: The Unreliable First-Person Narrator*. Norman: University of Oklahoma Press.

Rigney, Ann. 1998. "What's in a Name? Fictie, ervaring en autoriteit." *TvL: Tijdschrift voor literatuurwetenschap* 3.2: 136–46.

Rimmon-Kenan, Shlomith. 1983. *Narrative Fiction: Contemporary Poetics*. London: Methuen.

Robbe-Grillet, Alain. 1963. *Pour un nouveau roman*. Paris: Minuit.

———. 1981. *Djinn: Un Trou rouge entre les pavés disjoints*. Paris: Minuit.

Rorty, Richard. 1989. *Contingency, Irony, and Solidarity*. Cambridge: Cambridge University Press.

Rosch, Eleanor. 1977. "Classification of Real-World Objects: Origins and Representations in Cognition." In *Thinking: Readings in Cognitive Science*, edited by P. N. Johnson-Laird and P. C. Wason, 212–22. Cambridge: Cambridge University Press.

Roth, Philip. 2000. *The Human Stain*. London: Cape.

Rouillé, André. 2005. *La Photographie: Entre document et art contemporain*. Paris: Gallimard.

Rousseau, Jean-Jacques. 2000. *Confessions*. Trans. Angela Scholar. New York: Oxford University Press. First published 1782–89.

Rousseau, Nita. 1998. "Emoi, émoi et moi . . . Dominique Muller et Christine Angot." *Le Nouvel Observateur*, September 3–9, 61.

Ryan, Marie-Laure. 1991. *Possible Worlds, Artificial Intelligence, and Narrative Theory*. Bloomington: Indiana University Press.

———. 2001. *Narrative as Virtual Reality: Immersion and Interactivity in Literature and Electronic Media*. Baltimore: Johns Hopkins University Press.

———. 2004. *Narrative across Media: The Languages of Storytelling*. Lincoln: University of Nebraska Press.

———. 2010. "Narratology and Cognitive Science: A Problematic Relation." *Style* 44.4: 469–95.

Rye, Gill. 2004. "'Il faut que le lecteur soit dans le doute': Christine Angot's Literature of Uncertainty." In "Hybrid Voices, Hybrid Texts: Women's Writing at the Turn of the Millennium," ed. Gill Rye. Special issue, *Dalhousie French Studies* 68: 117–26.

Sapiro, Gisèle. 1999. *La Guerre des écrivains, 1940–1953*. Paris: Fayard.

———. 2003a. "Forms of Politicization in the French Literary Field." *Theory and Society* 32.5: 633–52.

———. 2003b. "The Literary Field between the State and the Market." *Poetics* 31.5: 441–64.

———. 2011. *La Responsabilité de l'écrivain: Littérature, droit et morale en France, XIX–XXIème siècle*. Paris: Seuil.

Sarraute, Nathalie. 1967. *Tropisms*. New York: Braziller, 1967. First published 1939; repr., trans. Maria Jolas, (New York: Riverrun Press, 1986).

Savigneau, Josyane. 1998. "Littérature et bien-pensance." Horizons Analyses. *Le Monde*, November 11, 1.

Schaeffer, Jean-Marie. 1999. *Pourquoi la fiction?* Paris: Seuil. Published in English as *Why Fiction?*, trans. Dorrit Cohn (Lincoln: University of Nebraska Press, 2010).

———. 2002. "De L'Imagination à La Fiction." *Vox Poetica*, December 10. http://www.vox-poetica.org/t/articles/schaeffer.html. Accessed January 10, 2009.

———. 2010. "Pourquoi la fiction? Interview by Alexandre Prstojevic." *Vox Poetica*, December 15. http://www.vox-poetica.org/entretiens/intSchaeffer.html.

Schank, Roger, and Robert Abelson. 1977. *Scripts, Plans, Goals and Understanding: An Inquiry into Human Knowledge Structures*. Hillsdale NJ: Erlbaum.

Schleiermacher, Friedrich. 1977. *Hermeneutik und Kritik: Mit einem Anhang sprachphilosophischer Texte Schleiermachers*. Ed. Manfred Frank. Frankfurt am Main: Suhrkamp. First published 1838.

———. 1978. "The Hermeneutics: Outline of the 1819 Lectures." *New Literary History* 10.1: 1–16.

———. 1985. "Foundations: General Theory and Art of Interpretation." In *The Hermeneutics Reader: Texts of the German Tradition from the Enlightenment to the Present*, edited by Kurt Müller-Vollmer, 72–96. New York: Continuum.

Schmidt, Siegfried J. 1991. *Grundriß der empirischen Literaturwissenschaft*. Braunschweig: Vieweg. First published 1980.

Schneider, Ralf. 2001. "Toward a Cognitive Theory of Literary Character: The Dynamics of Mental-Model Construction." *Style* 35.4: 607–39.

Searle, John. 1969. *Speech Acts: An Essay in the Philosophy of Language*. Cambridge: Cambridge University Press.

———. 1979. *Expression and Meaning: Studies in the Theory of Speech Acts.* Cambridge: Cambridge University Press.

———. 1983. *Intentionality: An Essay in the Philosophy of Mind.* Cambridge: Cambridge University Press.

Sénécal, Didier. 2001. "Entretien avec Michel Houellebecq." *Lire.* http://www .lexpress.fr/culture/livre/michel-houellebecq_804761.html. Accessed October 20, 2003.

Serfaty, Viviane. 2004. "Online Diaries: Towards a Structural Approach." *Journal of American Studies* 38.3: 457–72.

Shaw, Harry E. 2005. "Why Won't Our Terms Stay Put? The Narrative Communication Diagram Scrutinized and Historicized." In *A Companion to Narrative Theory*, edited by James Phelan and Peter J. Rabinowitz, 299–311. Malden MA: Blackwell.

Shklovsky, Viktor. 1965. "Art as Technique." In *Russian Formalist Criticism: Four Essays*, edited by Lee T. Lemon and Marion J. Reiss, 3–24. Lincoln: University of Nebraska Press. First published 1917.

Smoking Gun, The. 2006. "A Million Little Lies: Exposing James Frey's Fiction Addiction." January 4. http://www.thesmokinggun.com/documents/celebrity /million-little-lies. Accessed July 20, 2011.

Sperber, Dan, and Deirdre Wilson. 1981. "Irony and the Use-Mention Distinction." In *Radical Pragmatics*, edited by Peter Cole, 295–318. New York: Academic Press.

———. 1995. *Relevance: Communication and Cognition.* 2nd ed. Oxford: Blackwell. First published 1986.

Spoerhase, Carlos. 2007. *Autorschaft und Interpretation: Methodische Grundlagen einer philologischen Hermeneutik.* Berlin: Walter de Gruyter.

Starobinski, Jean. 1988. *Jean-Jacques Rousseau: Transparency and Obstruction.* Trans. Arthur Goldhammer. Chicago: University of Chicago Press. First published 1971.

Stein, Gertrude. 1966. *The Autobiography of Alice B. Toklas.* London: Penguin Books. First published 1933.

Stierle, Karlheinz. 1980. "The Reading of Fictional Texts." In *The Reader in the Text: Essays on Audience and Interpretation*, edited by Susan Suleiman and Inge Crosman, 83–105. Princeton NJ: Princeton University Press.

Strawson, Galen. 2004. "Against Narrativity." *Ratio* 17: 428–52.

Suleiman, Susan. 1980. "Introduction: Varieties of Audience-Oriented Criticism." In *The Reader in the Text: Essays on Audience and Interpretation*, edited by Susan Suleiman and Inge Crosman, 3–45. Princeton NJ: Princeton University Press.

———. 1983. *Authoritarian Fictions: The Ideological Novel as a Literary Genre.* New York: Columbia University Press.

———. 2006. *Crises of Memory and the Second World War.* Cambridge MA: Harvard University Press.

Suleiman, Susan, and Inge Crosman, eds. 1980. *The Reader in the Text: Essays on Audience and Interpretation.* Princeton NJ: Princeton University Press.

Tan, Ed. 2000. "Emotion, Art and the Humanities." In *Handbook of Emotions,* edited by Michael Lewis and Jeannette Haviland-Jones, 116–36. 2nd ed. New York: Guilford Press.

Taylor, Charles. 1989. *Sources of the Self: The Making of the Modern Identity.* Cambridge MA: Harvard University Press.

Tillotson, K. 1959. *The Tale and the Teller.* London: Rupert Hart-Davis.

Timmer, Nicoline. 2010. *Do You Feel It Too? The Post-postmodern Syndrome in American Fiction at the Turn of the Millennium.* Amsterdam: Rodopi.

Todorov, Tzvetan. 1969. *Grammaire du Décaméron.* The Hague: Mouton.

———. 2007. *La Littérature en péril.* Paris: Flammarion.

Tordjman, Gilles. 1998. "Houellebecq, héraut de la fin du monde." *L'Événement du jeudi,* August 27, 50.

Toulmin, Steven. 2001. *Return to Reason.* Cambridge MA: Harvard University Press.

Trilling, Lionel. 1972. *Sincerity and Authenticity.* Cambridge MA: Harvard University Press.

Tsur, Reuven. 2006. *"Kubla Khan": Poetic Structure, Hypnotic Quality and Cognitive Style: A Study in Mental, Vocal, and Critical Performance.* Amsterdam: Benjamins.

Turner, Mark, ed. 2006. *The Artful Mind: Cognitive Science and the Riddle of Human Creativity.* New York: Oxford University Press.

Uspensky, Boris. 1973. *A Poetics of Composition: The Structure of the Artistic Text and Typology of a Compositional Form.* Trans. Valentina Zavarin and Susan Wittig. Berkeley: University of California Press.

Van den Oever, Annie, ed. 2010. *Ostrannenie: On "Strangeness" and the Moving Image: The History, Reception, and Relevance of a Concept.* Amsterdam: Amsterdam University Press.

van Heusden, Barend. 2007. "Semiosis, Art, and Literature." *Semiotica* 165.1–4: 133–48.

———. 2011. "Semiotic Cognition and the Logic of Culture." In *Distributed Language,* edited by Stephen J. Cowley, 117–33. Amsterdam: Benjamins Publishing Company.

van Rees, Kees, and Gillis Dorleijn. 1993. *De Impact van Literatuuropvattingen in het Literaire Veld: Aandachtsgebied Literatuuropvattingen van de Stichting Literatuurwetenschap.* The Hague: Stichting Literatuurwetenschap.

Viala, Alain. 1985. *Naissance de l'écrivain: Sociologie de la littérature à l'âge classique.* Paris: Minuit.

———. 1993. "Éléments de sociopoétique." In *Approches de la réception: Sémiostylistique et sociopoétique de Le Clézio*, edited by Georges Molinié and Alain Viala, 139–220. Paris: Presses Universitaires de France.

———. 2006. "The Theory of the Literary Field and the Situation of the First Modernity." *Paragraph* 29.1: 80–93.

Viires, Piret, and Virve Sarapik. 2010. "Solitude in Cyberspace." In *Transforming Culture in the Digital Age*, edited by Agnes Aljas et al., 351–55. Papers presented at the conference in Tartu, April 14–16. Tartu: Estonia National Museum, Estonian Literary Museum, and University of Tartu. http://kirmus.academia.edu/PiretViires/Papers/1001269/Solitude_In_Cyberspace. Accessed September 13, 2012.

Voloshinov, Victor. 1981. "Le Discours dans la vie et dans la poésie." In *Mikhaïl Bakhtine, le principe dialogique: Suivi des écrits du cercle de Bakhtine*, edited and translated by Tzvetan Todorov, 181–216. Paris: Seuil.

Waal, Frans de. 2007. "The 'Russian Doll' Model of Empathy and Imitation." In *On Being Moved: From Mirror Neurons to Empathy*, edited by Stein Bråten, 49–69. Amsterdam: Benjamins.

Walsh, Richard. 2007. *The Rhetoric of Fictionality: Narrative Theory and the Idea of Fiction.* Columbus: Ohio State University Press.

Walton, Kendall L. 1990. *Mimesis as Make-Believe: On the Foundations of the Representational Arts.* Cambridge MA.: Harvard University Press.

Wilde, Alan. 1981. *Horizons of Assent: Modernism, Postmodernism and the Ironic Imagination.* Baltimore: Johns Hopkins University Press.

Wilkomirski, Binjamin. 1996. *Fragments: Memories of a Wartime Childhood.* Trans. from German by Carol Brown Janeway. New York: Schocken Books. Reprinted in Maechler 2001, 375–496.

Willems, Isabelle. 2005. "Michel Houellebecq au milieu du monde: Ce qu'un roman fait à la société." BA thesis, University of Liege. www.houellebecq.info/revuefile/48_socio.pdf. Accessed June 20, 2009.

Williams, Bernard. 2002. *Truth and Truthfulness: An Essay in Genealogy.* Princeton NJ: Princeton University Press.

Wilson, Neil. 1959. *The Concept of Language.* Toronto: University of Toronto Press.

Wimsatt, William, and Monroe Beardsley. 1946. "The Intentional Fallacy." *Sewanee Review* 54.3: 468–88.

Winko, Simone. 1999. "Einführung: Autor und Intention." In *Rückkehr Des Autors: Zur Erneuerung eines umstrittenen Begriffs*, edited by Fotis Jannidis et al., 353–89. Tübingen: Niemeyer, 39–46.

———. 2002. "Autor-Funktionen: Zur argumentativen Verwendung von Autorkonzepten in der gegenwärtigen literaturwissenschaftlichen Interpretationspraxis." In *Autorschaft: Positionen und Revisionen*, edited by Heinrich Detering, 334–54. Stuttgart: Metzler.

Wisse, Jakob. 1989. *Ethos and Pathos from Aristotle to Cicero*. Amsterdam: Hakkert.

Wolf, Werner. 2006. "Introduction: Frames, Framings and Framing Borders in Literature and Other Media." In *Framing Borders in Literature and Other Media*, by Werner Wolf and Walter Bernhart, 1–40. Amsterdam: Rodopi.

Yacobi, Tamar. 1981. "Fictional Reliability as a Communicative Problem." *Poetics Today* 2.2: 113–26.

———. 2001. "Package-Deals in Fictional Narrative: The Case of the Narrator's (Un)Reliability." *Narrative* 9.2: 223–29.

Zeki, Semir. 2004. "The Neurology of Ambiguity." *Consciousness and Cognition* 13.1: 173–96.

Zerweck, Bruno. 2001. "Historicizing Unreliable Narration: Unreliability and Cultural Discourse in Narrative Fiction." *Style* 35.1: 151–78.

Zipfel, Frank. 2001. *Fiktion, Fiktivität, Fiktionalität: Analysen zur Fiktion in der Literatur und zum Fiktionsbegriff in der Literaturwissenschaft*. Berlin: Erich Schmidt.

Zunshine, Lisa. 2006. *Why We Read Fiction: Theory of Mind and the Novel*. Columbus: Ohio State University Press.

———. 2008. "Theory of Mind and Fictions of Embodied Transparency." *Narrative* 16.1: 65–92.

Index

abjection, 278n22

Abrams, Meyer Howard, 58–59

abstract author. *See* implied author

action sequences, 259n3

actual intentionalism, 108

aestheticism: antiaesthetic style, 200;
authorial posturing and, 54, 165;
autonomy of, 2, 73; *Daewoo* case
study, 187–91; ethos attributions
and, 111–12; narratology and, 250;
reading strategies, 121

alethic (truth) ethos grounds, 63

all-narrator assumption, 145

ambiguity: frame switches and, 246–
47, 281n16; framing clues and,
111; in French discourse analysis,
72–73; in generic hybrids, 161–62;
reader thresholds for, 230–31; value
regimes and, 281n17. *See also* irony

Amis, Martin, 161

Amossy, Ruth, 60–65, 249

ancient rhetoric: ethos topoi, 62–63;
irony in, 218–19; means of persuasion, 2–5; notion of *phronesis*,
257n6; sincerity in, 211–12

Angot, Christine: authorial persona
of, 165, 191, 278n18; authorial posturing of, 194–95; ethos effects in
works, 66–68; framing ambiguities, 70, 75–76, 196–99; works of,
277n14; writing the self, 199–204

Ankersmit, Frank, 259n1

anonymity criterion, 160

antiaesthetic style, 200

anti-intentionalism, 107

arete (virtue), 3, 217. *See also* sincerity

argumentation, 4, 61, 99, 254

Aristotle: ethos topoi, 63; means of
persuasion, 2–5, 61, 212, 253, 257n5;
notion of *phronesis*, 48, 257n6

art: *funktionslust* in, 259n2; in metacognition, 25–26, 28, 30–31; mimesis in, 270n9; ostranenie notion
and, 261n13; play and, 22–23; writing transformed into, 201–2

Art and Illusion (Gombrich), 246–47

Atomised (Houellebecq): authorial
posturing in, 53; ethos riddles in,
7–8; irony in, 216–18; overview of,
1–2; reality presented in, 114; value
(de)construction of, 77–85

attached reading, 160–61, 191, 274n34

Attardo, Salvatore, 280n14

attributions. *See* ethos attributions

Attridge, Derek, 45

Austin, John, 215

authenticity: in authorial posturing,
274n32; in autofiction, 193; in *Daewoo* case study, 186–87; in *A Heartbreaking Work* case study, 239, 242,
244; markers of, 279n2; models of,
147–48; of narratorial voices, 153;

authenticity (*cont.*)
    sincerity and, 214; in *Sujet Angot*
    case study, 194–95, 198, 200; in
    What Is the What, 245–46
authorial audience, 134, 196, 198–99
authorial ethos: of Angot, 191, 194–
    95; of Bon, 178–87, 190–91; cir-
    cularity in, 7–8; construction of,
    156–60, 281n19; debates on, 12–15;
    of Eggers, 232–34, 237–39, 244–46,
    247; in French discourse analysis,
    61–65, 72; of Houellebecq, 77, 79–
    85; relevancy of, 160–64; of Roth,
    127
authorial posturing: ambiguity and,
    103; of Angot, 194–95; authenticity
    in, 274n32; of Bon, 178–87; con-
    struction of, 59–60, 156–59, 277n11;
    of Eggers, 242, 244; gender stereo-
    types in, 275n37; generic framing
    and, 34, 69–70; habitus and, 262n4;
    of Houellebecq, 77, 79–85; inten-
    tionality of, 275n36; irony and,
    223–24; *persona* (authority mask),
    262n2; of Prokhanov, 227; sociohis-
    torical perspectives, 53–58
authority: in ancient rhetoric, 4–5; of
    authors, 10, 27; *Daewoo* case study,
    183–84, 186–87; ethos topoi and,
    62–64; *A Heartbreaking Work* case
    study, 242; of narrators, 105–6, 147–
    48; sociohistorical perspectives
    on, 52
authors: accountability of, 118–19; au-
    tonomy of, 264n13; in communica-
    tion processes, 101–3; conceptions
    of literature and, 58–60; facets of
    authorship, 156–59; persona of, 10,
    165, 273n29; relation to narrators,

145–47, 160–61, 182–83, 186; (un)
    reliability of, 152–55; social mis-
    sions of, 9
autobiographical writing, 196–97,
    277n15, 277n17
autobiographic pact, 192
Autobiography of Alice B. Toklas
    (Stein), 196
autofiction, 191–94
autonomy in literature, 58–59, 165,
    167–68, 258n13, 264n13
Les Autres (Angot), 201–2, 203

Bakhtin, Mikhaïl, 13
Balzac, Honoré de, 65
Banfield, Ann, 145
Barthes, Roland, 14, 108, 129, 229–30
Bataille, Georges, 8
Bateson, Gregory, 260n6
Baudelaire, Charles, 213, 238
Beardsley, Monroe, 107, 108
Bécassine (literary character), 278n19
Beckett, Samuel, 103, 109, 141–42, 160
Beck-Nielsen, Claus, 111
Bennett, Andrew, 123
Berger, Peter Ludwig, 23–24
Berlusconi, Silvio, 64
Les Bienveillantes (Littell), 60
binary authentication model, 147
biological theory of narrative, 22–23
bisociation, 225
Blair, Tony, 65
Blanchot, Maurice, 13
bodily ethos signals, 63, 207–10
Boltanski, Luc, 74–77. *See also* worlds
    (value regimes)
Bon, François: aestheticism in writ-
    ing, 187–91; authorial posturing of,
    180–87; social activism, 238, 276n3;

views on writing, 176–80, 253; works by, 276n2

Booth, Wayne: co-duction process, 231; on irony, 217, 219–21; rhetorical-hermeneutic approach, 13, 148–51, 166–67

Bortolussi, Marisa, 144–45, 261n17

Bouillon de Culture (TV talk show), 191

Bourdieu, Pierre, 52–53, 55, 57, 73, 76, 262n4

Boyd, Brian, 22–23, 28, 47

branding in authorial posture, 10, 156

Bruchstücke (Wilkomirski), 258n10

Bruno (literary character), 1, 216–17, 219, 220, 224, 225–26

Bühler, Karl, 23

Butte, George, 267n5

Calvin, John, 213

Candide (Voltaire), 221–22

CAPA model, 94–95, 270n8

La Carte et le territoire (Houellebecq), 111–12

character ethos: analysis of, 134–43; attribution of, 128–34; in *A Heartbreaking Work,* 233–34, 235–41; in *Human Stain,* 124–27; irony and, 223–24; James's building of, 272n17

characters: categorization of, 62, 272n16; co-construction of, 270n8; functions of, 121, 131–33; relations between, 270n6; and sincerity topoi, 208–11

charity principle, 108, 281n17

Chatman, Seymour, 164

Cicero, Marcus Tullius, 5, 212, 219

Citton, Yves, 16

classical rhetoric. *See* ancient rhetoric

classical structuralist narratology, 91–92

classification. *See* framing

Claude (literary character), 66–68, 70, 75–76, 196–99, 199–204, 278n23

clues: ethos, viii, 110, 142, 149, 164, 179, 237; extratextual, 244–47; physical, 28, 63, 64–65, 207–10, 263n9

co-duction process, 231

cognition, Donald's modes of, 25–26, 253–54

cognitive approaches: on character analysis, 128, 136–37; to communication, 265n4; on irony and humor, 225–26; to meaning making, 31–37, 94–95, 265n6; narrators in, 144–47; reliability in, 148–51

cognitive frame theory, 150–51

cognitive sciences and hermeneutics, 15–16, 47–50, 261n19

Cohn, Dorrit, 117, 158

Coleman (literary character), 124–26, 131–33, 136, 138

communality of thought, 39, 43, 44

communication, 100–104, 215, 266n1, 267n9

communication contracts, 101, 115, 118, 161

communication levels, 222, 224–25

communication theory, 272n20

community regime, 59

comparative-historical interpretive method, 38

Comte, Auguste, 83

conceptions of literature: authorship and, 58–60; ethos riddles and, 8; gatekeepers of, 156–57; in *A Heartbreaking Work,* 237; implied authors and, 166, 168; intentionality and, 108, 190–91; notion of autonomy, 264n13; reading strategies and, 163–64

Eskin, Michael, 98

ethical approaches: character analysis in, 128, 135–36; communication processes in, 102; metahermeneutics and, xiii, 250–52

ethical (morality) ethos grounds, 63

ethics: authorial posturing and, 165; ethos and, 14; in experience economy, 274n31; in literature, 10–11, 215, 272n17; rhetoric connection, 257n6

ethos: in ancient rhetoric, 3–5, 212, 257n5; as an umbrella term, xiv; cognitive modes and, 253–54; construction of, 54–55, 72–73; distinction of, 262n4; French discourse analysis of, 60–65; language as communication means, 28; in narrative theory and criticism, 11–16; uncertainties in, 6–11, 131, 208–11

ethos attributions: characters and, 128–34; circularity in, 7–8; fictionality and, 112–19; in *A Heartbreaking Work*, 234, 235, 240–41; intention and, 107–12; irony and, 216–18, 219–21; narrative levels and, 104–7; narratological frameworks for, 134–43; narratology's relevance to, 250–51; reading strategy and, 121–22; reconstruction in, 228–29; relevance of, x; stereotypes in, 61–62. *See also* authorial ethos; narratorial ethos

ethos clues and topoi: in authorial posturing, 9–10, 59–60, 110; in case studies, 79–85, 179, 181–87; in discourse analysis, 62–64; extratextual, 244–47; as framing keys, 34, 258n9; further investigations in, 253; physical, 214, 263n9

eunoia (goodwill), 4

evaluation, 7–8, 192–93, 218, 229–30, 253. *See also* interpretation

exceptionality thesis, 260n8

experience economy, 274n31

Experiencing Fiction (Phelan), 92

experientiality, 40–41, 131, 141–43, 155

experimental writing, 140–41, 269n4

expressive conception of literature, 58–59

extradiegetic narrators, 104, 197

extrafictional voice, 274n29

Faunia (literary character), 124–26, 136, 138–39

Federman, Raymond, 268n11

feminist narratology, 14, 92, 96, 102

fiction. *See* literature; narratives

fictional characters. *See* characters

field model (Bourdieu's), 52–53, 55, 57, 76, 262n4

Fish, Stanley, 93, 121, 222

Fludernik, Monika: on commonality of norms, 220; on experientiality, 71, 125–26, 129, 141; on experimental writing, 269n4; on inferences of subjectivity, 272n18; on naturalization, 269n3

Forster, Edward M., 138

Foucault, Michel, 14, 157

frame switches: in *Daewoo* case study, 180–81; in *Djinn* case study, 134; in *A Heartbreaking Work* case study, 235–37; in *Human Stain* case study, 126; interpretation and, 247, 267n4; irony and, 224–29, 281n16; metalepses as, 106; narrator unreliability and, 151; in *Not I* case study, 142–43; in *Sujet Angot* case study, 199;

frame switches (*cont.*)

in *Thousand Autumns* case study, 153–55; triggers, 34, 116–17, 157, 196

framing: authorial posture and ethos in, 158–59, 162; benefits of, 250–52; character analysis in, 134–43; circularity in, 7–8; cognitive theories of, 32–34, 36–37; conflicts and uncertainties in, 75–77, 118; ethos attributions in, viii–ix; fictionality and, 112–19; generic scenes and, 69–73; in *Heartbreaking Work* case study, 232, 234, 235–41, 243, 246; irony and, 223–24, 225–29, 230–31; as a kaleidoscope, 249; in narrative art, 229–30; narratorial (un)reliability and, 149–50, 151; value attributions in, 74–76

Franzen, Jonathan, 273n23

Freedom (Franzen), 273n23

French discourse analysis, 68–73

Frey, James: authorial posturing of, 92, 158; controversies surrounding, vii, 89; generic framing of works, 59, 93, 110–11, 115

Funktionslust, 23, 131, 259n2

Gadamer, Hans-Georg, 44–45, 261n15

Galinañes, Cristina Larkin, 225

Gallagher, Shaun, 48–49, 257n6, 262n20

Gallaire, Florent, 267n11

Ganzfried, Daniel, 258n12

gender stereotypes, 275n37

generic contracts, 162–63

generic framing, 69–73, 152–55, 161–63, 180–87, 196–99, 270n7. *See also* framing

generic hybrids, 117–19, 153–55, 161–62, 191–94

generic scenes, 69–70, 110–11

Genette, Gérard, 102, 104–5, 135–36, 143–45, 167, 192, 270n10

Gilgamesh epic, 24–25, 109–10

Gilmore, James, 10, 274n31

global intentionality, 108–9

global scenes, 69–70, 110–11, 161

Goffman, Erving, 33–34, 45, 109, 151, 260n6

Goldman, Lucien, 270n6

Gombrich, Ernst H., 246–47, 281n16

Les Gommes (Robbe-Grillet), 130

Goodman, Nelson, 165

Gorman, David, 112

Gospodin Geksogen (Prokhanov), 226–28

grammatical (historical) interpretation, 38

Grass, Günther, 10

Greenblatt, Stephen, 22, 29–30, 211

Greimas, Algirdas Julien, 259n3

Grice, Herbert, 193, 221–22

Habermas, Jürgen, 215, 279n5

habitus, 56–57, 63–64, 203, 262n4

Hamsun, Knut, 208

A Heartbreaking Work of Staggering Genius (Eggers): authorial ethos in, 62, 231–33, 244–47; character construction in, 233–34, 282n23–25; ethos riddles in, 8; framing in, 235–41, 282n27–28; irony in, 218–19, 234–35, 242–44; setting, 231, 233; sincerity topoi in, 205–6, 207; trust topoi in, 278n1

Heinich, Nathalie, 59–60, 73, 75

Herman, David: CAPA model, 94–95, 270n8; exceptionality thesis, 260n8; on mimesis, 266n3; narrative's role,

24; on narrators, 146–47, 155; on negotiation, 30

hermeneutic circle, 38

hermeneutics: cognitive sciences and, 47–50, 259n1, 261n19; historical models, 37–47; multiplicity of, 265n5; in narratology, 96–99, 261n17; *phronesis* in, 257n6; scope of, 19, 37

heterodiegetic narrators, 104–5, 145–47, 153

Heusden, Barend van. *See* van Heusden, Barend

Hite, Molly, 142

Hogan, Patrick Colm, 259n1

homodiegetic narrators, 104–5, 145–47

homology, 270n6

horizons, Gadamer's notion of, 44–45, 261n15

Houellebecq, en fait (Noguez), 77, 79–82

Houellebecq, Michel: authorial intention of, 111–12; authorial posturing of, 52–53, 54, 56, 165, 252, 264n17; controversies surrounding, vii, 1–2, 57–58, 74, 226; Noguez on, 77, 79–82; Patricola on, 77, 82–85; plagiarism in works, 267n11; works of, 264n16. See also *Atomised* (Houellebecq)

The Human Stain (Roth), 124–27, 138–39

humor, 225

Hunt, Lynn, 213

Hutcheon, Linda, 247

hybrid works, 117–19, 153–55, 161–62, 191–94

hypothetical author. *See* implied author

hypothetical intentionalism, 108

identity constructions, 15, 261n16

imitation cognitive stage, 26

implied author, 101, 148–49, 159, 166–69, 275n39–40

The Implied Author (Kindt and Müller), 96

implied reader, 120

inductive process, 41–42

inference process, 32, 34–37, 41–42, 44, 219, 220, 272n18

inferred author. *See* implied author

intentionality, 107–12, 267n9, 275n36, 281n15

interpretation: ambiguity and, 246–47; authorial images and, 273n29; in autofiction, 192–93; circularity in, 7–8; ethos attributions in, viii–ix; historical-cultural models of, 12–13, 29–31, 37–50, 91–95, 121; identity constructions and, 261n16; implied authors and, 166, 167–68; inference and, 36, 272n18; irony and, 220–21, 222, 226–29, 230–31; metacognition in, x; in narrative art, 229–30; narratology's relevance to, 250–52; relevance of, 16, 19, 28–29; role of, 95–99. See also framing

interpretive communities (Fish's notion of), 93, 121

intradiegetic narrators, 104

intuition, 42–44

irony: characteristics, 279n9, 280n11; conflicting interpretations and, 247; context and, 280n13, 280n14; cultural-historical development of, 213–15; deconstruction of, 218–21; ethos attribution and, 216–18; framing and, xii, 224–29, 281n16;

irony (cont.)

in A Heartbreaking Work, 231–33, 234–35, 238, 239, 242–43; mention theory and, 222–24; narratological approaches, 229–30; negative capability, 230–31; as rule violation, 221–22. See also sincerity

"Irony and its Malcontents" (Heartbreaking Work essay), 242–44

Iser, Wolfgang, 121

La Jalousie (Robbe-Grillet), 130

James, Henry, 272n17

Jannidis, Fotis, 269n2

Johansen, Jørgen Dines, 28, 253

Johnson, Barbara, 14

Kearns, Michael, 108, 268n15

Keen, Suzanne, 277n12

Keestra, Machiel, 29, 261n19

Kierkegaard, Søren, 214

Kim, J. Sue, 274n34

The Kindly Ones (Littell), 60

Kindt, Tom, 166–67

Koestler, Arthur, 225

Kristeva, Julia, 278n22

Krusanov, Pavel, 226

Lacan, Jacques, 13

language, 23–24, 26, 27–28, 39, 215, 260n10

Lanser, Susan S., 101, 160–61, 273n29, 275n37

"Law of Genre, The" (Derrida), 175

Lejeune, Philippe, 161, 192, 196, 277n15

life-expressions (Dilthey), 40–41

linguistic approaches, 221–22, 222–24, 280n14

literary narratives. See narratives

literary value. See values

literature: approaches to uncertainty, 230–31; autonomy of, 11, 258n13; bodily signs in, 208; debates in, 8–11; defined, 192; fiction functionality, 46–47, 112–19, 274n34; fiction's ethical value, 252, 272n17; functions of, 130–31, 266n1; relevance of, 15–16, 130, 176; role in reality construction, 24; value attribution in, 73–77. See also conceptions of literature; narratives

Littell, Jonathan, 60, 161

Livingston-Webber, Joan, 279n2

Living to Tell about it (Phelan), 98

locuteur-L, 68–69

locuteur-lambda, 68–69

logos (rational), 3–5, 142, 253–54, 257n5

Luckmann, Thomas, 23–24

ludic pretense, 23, 113–14

Luther, Martin, 213

Machiavelli, Niccolò, 213

Maechler, Stefan, 258n12

Maingueneau, Dominique: character of the speaker, 68; levels of understanding, 69–70, 110; on literature, 71–73, 190, 253, 277n17; notion of ethos, 60–65, 263n10

Mallarmé, Stéphane, 13, 103

Mann, Thomas, 158

The Map and the Territory (Houellebecq), 111–12

Margolin, Uri, 135, 272n21

marketing strategies, 10, 156

Martha (literary character), 210

Martin, John, 212–13, 214

Martin, Mary Patricia, 207, 273n24

Martine S. (literary character), 188

meaning making processes: analysis of, 260n3; authorial images in, 274n29; in cognitive approaches, 31–37, 94–95, 265n6; irony and, 219–21, 231; metahermeneutics and, 251–52. *See also* interpretation

Meizoz, Jérôme, 53–55, 56–57, 65, 279n4

mental models: authorial postures and, 55–56; character analysis and, 137–38; in cognitive approaches, 32–33, 36–37, 62; in *Heartbreaking Work,* 233–34; irony and, 217; in *Mysteries* case study, 210, 211; prior ethos in, 260n7; in structuralism, 136

mention theory, 222–24, 240, 280n15

metacognition, x, 22, 25–27, 28, 30–31

metacommunication in play, 260n6

metahermeneutic approaches: benefits of, 249, 251–52; CAPA model, 95; implied author concept and, 167; in narratology, 96, 98–99, 265n2; relevance of, ix, xiii, 37; sincerity determination in, 211 Michel (literary character), 1

Michel Houellebecq; ou, La provocation permanente (Patricola), 77, 82–85

Millet, Catherine, 162

A Million Little Pieces (Frey), vii, 89, 93, 110–11, 115, 163

mimesis: in art, 270n9; definitions of, 132, 266n3; in literature, 130, 132, 269n4; in Ricoeur's model, 46; Schaeffer's notion of, 113–14

mimetic character effect, 131–33

mimetic conception of literature, 58–59

mimetic imitation stage (Donald), 26

mimetic impulse, 129–30

mimetic-psychological reading frame, 129–34, 245

mimetic-realist reading strategy, 121, 235–36

mind, theory of, 35–37, 262n20

mind reading, 34–37, 62, 267n5

Mitchell, David, 152–55, 273n27

Morrissette, Bruce, 129–30

Müller, Hans-Harald, 166–67

Musil, Robert, 114

Myśliwski, Wiesław, 160

Mysteries (Hamsun), 208–11

mythic stage, 26

Nagel, Johan (literary character), 208–11

narrative audience, 134, 196, 198

narrative levels, 104–7, 270n10

narratives: action sequences in, 259n3; as communication, 100–104; ethos in, 5–6; further investigations in, 253; interpretation of, 28–31; irony in, 219–21; role in metacognition, 25–27; role in reality construction, 24–25. *See also* literature

narratological hermeneutic practices, 97

narratology: controversial concepts in, 12–16, 100; hybridity in, 91–99, 266n7; intention and, 107–12; interpretation in, 50; irony in, 229–30; metahermeneutics in, 265n2; relevance of, 249–52

narratorial ethos, 143–47; circularity in, 7–8; in *Daewoo* case study, 182–87; in *Heartbreaking Work* case study, 233–34, 235, 237–39; in *Human Stain* case study, 124–27; inferencing and, 272n21; irony and, 223–24; in *Sujet Angot* case study, 197–98 narrators: authenticity and reliability of, 152–55, 273n23, 273n24; embedded voices, 104-7, as method, 155; posturing of, 147–51, 279n8; relation to authors, 160–61, 182–83, 186. *See also* narratorial ethos

naturalization, 269n3

negative capability, 230–31

negotiation of values, 29–31

Nielsen, Henrik Skov, 115

Noguez, Dominique, 53, 77–82, 85, 252, 264n17

nonbinary authentication model, 147

noncommunication concept of literature, 103

nonfiction classification, 116

non-narrativity criterion, 160

Noordenbos, Boris, 226–28

norms: commonality of, 220–22; ethos, 162–63; in hermeneutics, 97; subjective nature of, 193; of the work, 148–49, 150. *See also* values

Not I (Beckett), 141–43

Nünning, Ansgar, 148–51, 167, 266n7

Nussbaum, Martha, 252, 257n6, 272n17

Olsen, Stein Haugom, 109

On Rhetoric (Aristotle), 2–5

ostensive-inferential communication, 101

ostranenie notion, 261n13

Palmer, Alan, 36, 129, 236, 265n6, 267n5

paratext, 53, 106, 116–17, 232–33

paratopy, 71, 277n17

parody, 202, 229, 282n23

pathos (emotional), 3–5, 212, 253–54, 257n5

Patricola, Jean-François, 77–78, 82–85, 252

Peirce, Charles Sanders, 10, 27

Perec, Georges, 178

Le Père Goriot (Balzac), 65

Perpendiculaire (magazine), 2

persona (authority mask), 262n2

personalized characters, 138

person-centered reading approach, 60, 163–64

persuasion, Aristotle's means of, 2–5, 211–12, 253–54

Pettersson, Bo, 259n1, 262n21

Phelan, James: on character analysis, 121, 128, 131–33, 236; on the implied author, 167; on *A Million Little Pieces,* 93; rhetorical approach of, 92, 97–98; on unreliability, 151, 207, 273n24

phronesis (practical wisdom), 3, 48–49, 212, 257n6

physical ethos clues, 28, 63, 64–65, 207–10, 263n9

Piccolomini, Bartolomeo Carli, 212

Pier, John, 106

Pine, Joseph, 10, 274n31

Pinget, Robert, 160

Pivot, Bernard, 191

Platform (Houellebecq), 226

play: art as form of, 22–23; literary fiction comparison, 268n12; metacommunication in, 260n6

poetry, theories of, 58–59

positioning theory, 258n9

postclassical narratology, ix, 92, 164

posterior ethos, 6, 118, 245

postmodernism, 214, 227–28, 233, 242

poststructuralist approaches, 13–14, 47–48, 92–93

science, 13, 15–16, 19, 47–48, 94
scripts, 39, 43, 55–56, 62
Searle, John, 113, 143, 215, 280n13
self-awareness, 40, 45–47, 214, 251–52
self-writing, 192–94, 199–204, 237, 246
semanticist theory of fictionality, 112
shared ludic pretense, 113–14
Shaw, Harry, 166
Shklovsky, Viktor, 261n13
similarities criterion, 160
sincerity: in ancient rhetoric, 3–4; in
    autofiction, 193; cultural-historical
    development in, 206–8, 211–16; ge-
    neric framing and, xii; in *A Heart-
    breaking Work,* 231–33, 237, 238,
    240, 244–46; in *Mysteries,* 208–11;
    relevance of, 279n7, 280n10. *See
    also* authenticity
singularity, 59, 75, 160
social activism, 9, 176–78, 188–91, 277n11
sociocritique, 263n6
sociopolitical (power) grounds, 63, 64
Sortie d'usine (Bon), 177
speaker's ethos. *See* authorial ethos
speech act theory, 215, 272n20
Sperber, Dan, 100–101, 116, 222–24,
    280n14
Spoerhase, Carlos, 111
stable irony, 220–21, 225
standards. *See* norms
Stein, Gertrude, 196
Steps to an Ecology of Mind (Bateson),
    260n6
stereotypes, 61–62, 137–38, 195, 275n37
Strawson, Galen, 46
structuralism, 91–92, 107, 120, 135–36,
    143–46
style, 135–36, 138–39, 200, 202–3, 273n27
subjectivity, 140–43, 147–48

Sujet Angot (Angot): ethos effects
    in, 66–68; generic framing in, 70,
    196–99; title connotations, 278n20;
    value attribution in, 75–76; as writ-
    ing the self, 199–204
Suleiman, Susan, 93
Sylvia (literary character), 188
synthetic function, 132–33, 236

Taylor, Charles, 261n16
textual clues, 116–17, 149
thematic character effect, 131–33
theoretical (cognitive) stage, 26
theory of mind, 35–37, 262n20
therapeutic function of writing, 200–
    201
Thévenot, Laurent, 74–77. *See also*
    Worlds (value regimes)
Thomas, Michel, 158
Thousand Autumns of Jacob de Zoet
    (Mitchell), 152–55, 273n27
Tillotson, K., 155
Time and Narrative (Ricoeur), 45
tones, 7, 61, 139, 142, 240
Towards a "Natural" Narratology
    (Fludernik), 129
transfiguration of the commonplace
    topos, 201–2, 238–39
Trattato della prudenza (Piccolo-
    mini), 212
"triangle" communication process,
    102, 107
Tropisms (Sarraute), 21
trustworthiness: in *Daewoo,* 185–86;
    in *A Heartbreaking Work,* 236,
    278n1; sincerity's contribution to,
    212; universality of, viii
truth, 63, 116–17, 147, 270n10, 279n5
Tsur, Reuven, 230, 281n20

unadopted ethos effects, 140–43
understanding processes, 41, 44–45, 261n19. *See also* interpretation; meaning making processes
uniqueness, 202–3. *See also* authorial posturing
unnatural narratives, 103
unreliability, 147, 148–51, 154–55, 273n24
unstable irony, 220, 225
Ur-Conventions, 108, 268n15
Uspensky, Boris, 25

value regimes: ambiguities and, 163, 281n17; Angot case study, 195; authorial posturing and, 165–66; in autofiction, 192–93; Boltanski and Thévenot's model, 74–77; *Daewoo* case study, 183–84; in *A Heartbreaking Work*, 238; Houellebecq case study, 79–85; irony in, 218
values: assignment of, 52–53, 73–76, 156–57, 260n3; further investigations in, 253; hermeneutics and, 43–44; Houellebecq case study, 77, 79–85; irony and, 218–19, 225–29, 230–31; metahermeneutics and, 251–52; negotiations of, 29–31; transfer of, 188–89
van Heusden, Barend, 26–27
van Rees, Kees, 58
Vantroys, Carole, 197
Vauquer, Madame (literary character), 65
Vervaeck, Bart, 30
Viala, Alain, 53, 55
La Vie sexuelle de Catherine M. (Millet), 162
voice: analysis of, 135–36; authentication of, 153; debates over, 270n11; establishment of, 68–69; ethos attributions and, 105–7; extrafictional voice, 274n29
Voloshinov, Victor, 25
Voltaire, 65, 221–22
Vox Poetica (Internet forum), 113

Walraff, Günther, 10–11
Walsh, Richard, 116–18, 145–46
What Is the What (Eggers), 245–46
Wilde, Oscar, 165
Wilkomirski, Binjamin, 258n12
Wilson, Deirdre, 45, 100–101, 116, 222–24, 280n14
Wimsatt, William, 107–8
Winfrey, Oprah, vii
Winko, Simone, 15
Wolf, Christa, 10
Wolf, Werner, 33, 34
work-centered reading strategy, 60, 163–64
worlds (value regimes): Angot case study, 195; authorial posturing and, 165–66; in autofiction, 192–93; Boltanski and Thévenot's model, 74–77; *Daewoo* case study, 183–84; generic frauds and, 163; Houellebecq case study, 79–85
worldviews. *See* values
writer. *See* authors
writing: impulses, 277n13; self-writing, 192–94, 246; therapeutic function of, 200–201; transforming experience into art, 201–2

Yacobi, Tamar, 148, 150

Zuckerman, Nathan (literary character), 125–27, 132, 136, 138–39
Zunshine, Lisa, 35, 236, 267n5

To order or obtain more information on these or other University of Nebraska Press titles, visit nebraskapress.unl.edu.